UNIPART

MOTORISTS' ATLAS

**Produced and published for UNIPART by
The Automobile Association, Fanum House, Basingstoke, Hampshire.**

ROUTE PLANNING MAPS

Isle of Man

I R I S H   S E A

KEY

Motorways

Primary Routes

A Roads

o   Primary Towns

AA   24hour Breakdown & Information Service

E N G L I S

MILEAGE CHART

Distances are given to the nearest mile and are measured along the normal AA recommended route.

Map locations (Great Britain): Inverness, Aberdeen, Fort William, Perth, Glasgow, Edinburgh, Stranraer, Newcastle, Carlisle, Middlesbrough, Kendal, York, Hull, Preston, Leeds, Liverpool, Manchester, Holyhead, Sheffield, Lincoln, Stoke on Trent, Nottingham, Shrewsbury, Birmingham, Norwich, Aberystwyth, Northampton, Cambridge, Hereford, Carmarthen, Gloucester, Oxford, Colchester, Cardiff, Bristol, LONDON, Guildford, Maidstone, Dover, Barnstaple, Salisbury, Southampton, Brighton, Taunton, Dorchester, Exeter, Plymouth, Penzance.

To \ From	Distances to preceding cities (miles)
Aberdeen	—
Aberystwyth	463
Barnstaple	594 212
Birmingham	423 119 176
Brighton	594 261 200 177
Bristol	504 121 98 86 151
Cambridge	468 218 251 101 119 154
Cardiff	524 110 135 106 184 44 187
Carlisle	230 234 364 197 368 275 256 296
Carmarthen	512 48 200 134 249 109 234 66 282
Colchester	517 261 280 165 113 183 48 216 303 282
Dorchester	579 198 91 161 120 62 178 120 350 186 186
Dover	619 308 272 202 78 201 128 233 393 299 113 199
Edinburgh	127 334 464 296 467 374 342 395 98 383 390 449 493
Exeter	576 193 40 157 172 78 231 116 347 182 235 54 246 448
Fort William	171 445 575 405 577 484 465 503 211 494 560 513 598 135 555
Glasgow	143 330 461 292 462 371 351 394 95 379 399 446 488 45 442 105
Gloucester	469 109 126 52 151 35 118 58 240 112 161 111 191 339 107 450 336
Guildford	549 174 217 125 44 107 94 140 322 206 99 99 97 422 149 531 416 101
Hereford	455 85 144 55 179 53 141 56 226 85 189 130 222 325 125 436 323 31 129
Holyhead	452 106 307 155 326 217 251 211 225 155 315 292 351 327 290 432 321 182 273 157
Hull	363 229 321 146 266 234 160 254 150 276 207 288 285 236 307 363 245 196 242 200 218
Inverness	106 493 623 451 624 532 502 533 259 542 552 561 647 160 603 66 172 498 579 485 479 400
Kendal	279 191 318 149 322 229 218 248 50 240 266 305 344 149 301 260 147 195 277 183 179 128 308
Leeds	333 178 305 135 253 216 147 236 122 227 194 291 278 206 287 331 215 181 221 169 165 59 368 71
Lincoln	393 197 257 94 195 165 87 206 180 231 135 228 213 271 239 390 276 133 166 154 200 78 427 143 70
Liverpool	354 114 269 101 271 182 196 202 126 163 258 254 297 225 253 333 221 144 228 115 106 126 381 80 74 128
Maidstone	582 269 230 167 50 158 89 192 356 258 78 154 42 456 204 564 450 152 55 183 315 246 611 309 239 177 257
Manchester	346 134 257 87 258 168 155 190 118 183 203 242 283 218 239 326 214 133 213 121 125 97 373 72 44 88 36 247
Middlesbrough	274 246 358 182 312 271 200 288 93 295 248 324 335 146 341 304 186 232 280 236 236 88 309 87 64 122 146 295 115
Newcastle	236 275 386 214 342 302 231 320 58 324 273 354 367 109 370 244 150 261 312 264 265 125 270 94 96 152 173 331 144 38
Northampton	470 173 202 54 125 115 50 135 243 177 94 143 149 344 182 452 341 76 93 92 204 152 500 197 132 83 149 113 135 190 222
Norwich	498 279 312 163 167 216 62 251 284 293 59 237 170 370 293 493 379 180 151 202 312 314 529 246 175 105 234 131 184 230 259 112
Nottingham	399 160 236 59 188 146 84 164 187 192 130 205 212 273 217 397 281 111 153 115 176 88 432 160 72 37 104 178 72 132 162 66 123
Oxford	489 155 170 64 113 74 80 106 261 157 117 103 139 362 151 471 357 48 60 79 212 192 518 216 170 125 167 98 153 231 260 41 142 104
Penzance	694 313 111 277 292 199 352 236 465 301 353 173 366 565 120 675 562 226 267 245 407 422 722 419 406 281 370 324 358 458 488 303 411 337 271
Perth	83 380 510 339 512 419 384 440 146 429 433 495 534 44 491 105 60 386 467 371 367 284 117 196 252 310 269 499 261 192 154 388 413 317 406 611
Plymouth	617 236 67 200 217 121 275 158 388 224 276 96 290 488 43 598 484 149 191 168 330 344 651 343 329 358 292 248 281 381 410 226 337 260 194 80 534
Preston	315 149 278 107 280 187 197 206 86 198 267 269 302 185 258 296 183 158 235 141 136 119 344 43 68 123 30 267 33 102 131 155 226 120 174 378 232 302
Salisbury	540 173 116 114 83 52 137 96 311 161 146 40 161 409 91 520 406 74 60 102 253 248 568 265 229 188 214 117 202 284 313 103 196 164 63 211 456 134 223
Sheffield	373 167 259 83 223 169 122 188 161 215 167 241 250 247 242 372 256 135 195 138 160 68 407 119 34 45 78 212 38 106 136 105 150 45 143 360 295 283 79 201
Shrewsbury	403 75 202 50 223 111 143 108 174 125 210 183 245 273 183 383 271 77 167 52 105 169 431 131 117 122 64 210 68 186 214 98 203 85 106 302 319 225 89 147 93
Southampton	561 197 140 130 63 75 132 118 335 186 140 55 145 433 107 541 429 95 49 126 277 258 589 286 237 192 242 105 231 293 324 108 191 171 67 227 477 152 244 23 203 168
Stoke	381 111 218 45 217 130 141 148 149 161 208 203 241 252 200 359 248 93 171 88 124 121 406 105 91 88 57 205 43 164 191 93 171 51 110 320 294 242 63 164 52 36 185
Stranraer	239 346 475 305 478 385 365 404 111 395 413 461 500 126 457 192 93 351 432 337 333 285 260 161 232 291 234 465 227 204 164 353 393 297 371 576 155 499 197 421 272 285 442 263
Taunton	544 162 50 127 150 48 198 85 315 151 230 43 221 413 32 525 411 76 124 95 257 271 573 270 256 208 219 181 208 308 336 153 262 187 121 152 482 75 230 67 210 152 91 172 426
York	326 204 315 138 270 226 157 245 113 253 202 282 293 199 297 326 208 190 237 193 194 38 362 89 24 76 101 253 72 52 88 147 185 87 185 417 246 338 80 243 62 145 252 119 227 265
LONDON	535 211 215 118 53 120 60 153 307 218 64 125 78 405 172 516 402 104 30 135 267 206 564 261 194 141 211 37 199 252 280 67 115 128 56 290 452 212 219 82 167 162 78 165 417 167 209

SIGN LANGUAGE

Understanding road signs- and their link with the map

MOTORWAYS On the map - All Motorways are blue, Motorway signposts have white lettering on a blue background. Advance Direction signs approaching an interchange generally include the junction number in a black box. On the map the junction number appears in white on a blue circle.

Brighton
Crawley

Gatwick
A 23

9

PRIMARY ROUTES On the map - all the Primary Routes are green. The sign posts on Primary roads are also green, with white lettering and yellow numbers. Apart from the Motorways, Primary Routes are the most important traffic routes in both urban and rural areas. They form a network of throughroutes connecting 'Primary Towns', which are generally places of traffic importance. Usually Primary routes are along A roads.

Brighton A 23

Haywards Heath
Billingshurst
A 272
Lewes
(A 275)
Worthing
(A 24)

A ROADS All A roads are shown in red on the map, unless part of the primary network when they are green. (as above) The signposts along these roads have black lettering on a white background. At a junction with a Primary Route the Primary Road number appears yellow in a green box.

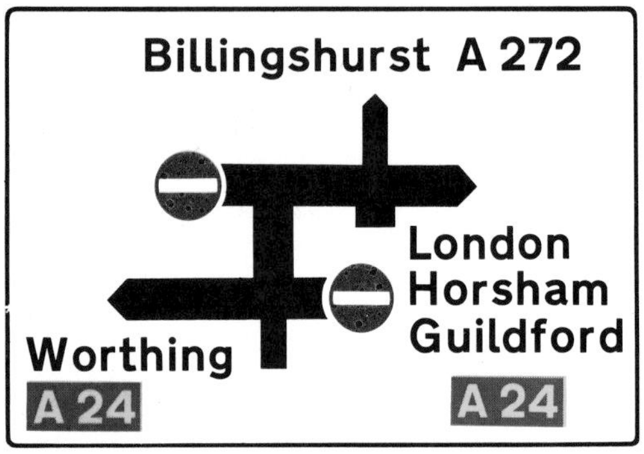

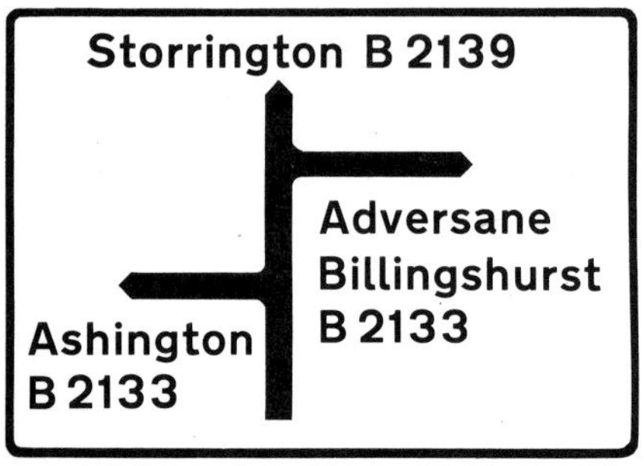

Billingshurst A 272

London
Horsham
Guildford
A 24

Worthing
A 24

Storrington B 2139

Adversane
Billingshurst
B 2133

Ashington
B 2133

B ROADS On the map - all B roads not in the Primary network are signified by the colour yellow. The signs on B roads are black lettering on a white background, the same as for A roads.

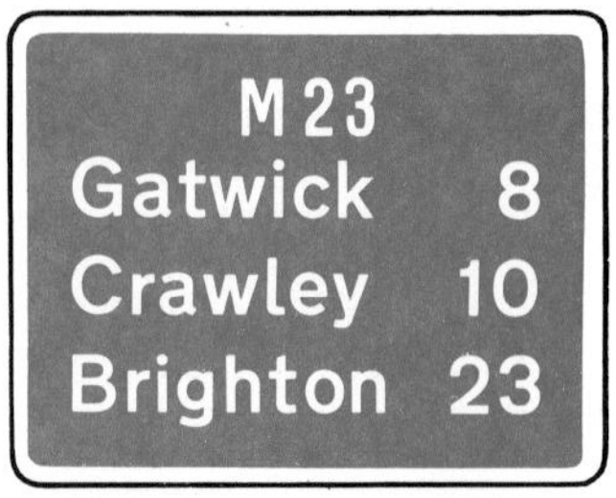

M 23
Gatwick 8
Crawley 10
Brighton 23

CONFIRMATORY SIGNS
These often appear after important road junctions and confirm that drivers have taken their intended route. The colour of confirmatory signs differs according to the road classification, eg blue for Motor ways, green for Primary Routes, and white for A and B roads.

UNCLASSIFIED ROADS On the map - all unclassified roads are white. New signposts along unclassified roads are usually of the Local Direction type. These have black lettering on a white background with a blue border. Local Direction signs may also appear in addition to Primary and non-Primary signs and indicate the route to local districts and amenities.

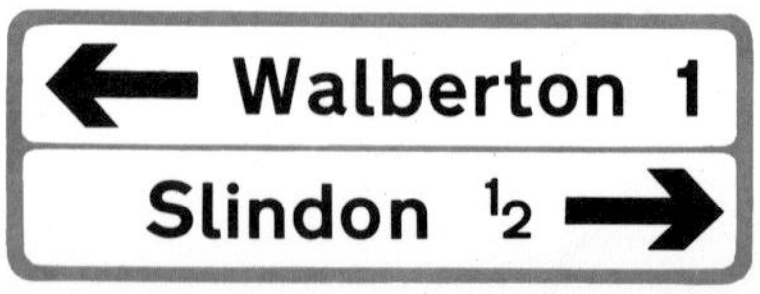

← Walberton 1
Slindon ½ →

GRASP THE GRID

Indexing System & The National Grid.

To locate a place in the atlas, first check the index at the back of the book, eg:

Weyhill (Hants)	10 SU 3146
Weymouth (Dorset)	8 SY 6778
Whaddon (Bucks)	18 SP 8034

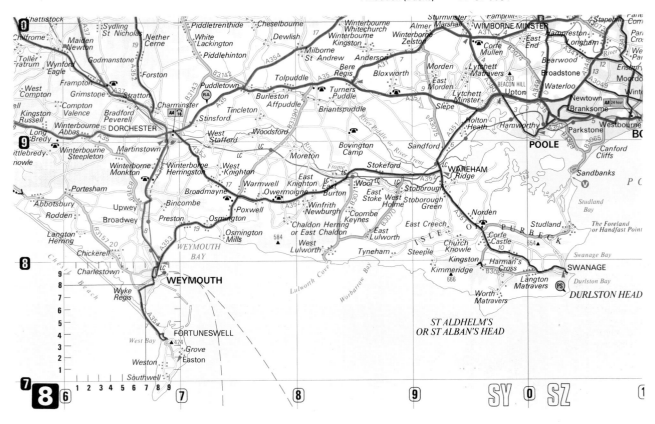

Using Weymouth as our example - this is the reference given in the index - 8 SY 6778

8 This is the number of the page on which Weymouth lies.

SY These first two letters show the major relevant area in which Weymouth is situated. They relate to an area labelled SY which is bound by heavy lines numbered in all cases O. (It can be seen that Poole lies in the next area labelled SZ).

67 The first set of numbers refer to the thin blue grid lines labelled along the bottom of the page. The 6 relates to the line of that number while the 7 is an estimated 7/10ths of the division between the 6 and 7.

78 The second set of figures refer to the numbers on the side of the page, the 7 relates to the line of that number, whereas the 8 is approximately 8/10ths of the division between 7 and 8.

If a line is drawn, from 67 vertically and from 78 horizontally, Weymouth should lie where the two intersect. Further examples of references given in the index, to the following appropriate towns may be checked against their locations in the map sample above:

Dorchester	8 SY 6990
Poole	8 SZ 0190
Swanage	8 SZ 0278
Wareham	8 SY 9287
Wool	8 SY 8486

It may be noted that, in every instance, it is the first set of figures after the area letters that applies to the number along the bottom of the grid. Therefore the second set will relate to the figures up the side of the page.

The National Grid

The National Grid provides a reference system common to maps of all scales. The country is divided into major grid squares (100kmsq), which are outlined on the map by heavy blue lines and each is designated two letters (eg SY) as its reference code. Each of these squares is then sub-divided into 100 10km sq, thus forming a finer grid which is numbered from 1 to 9, west to east, and south to north within each of the major lettered squares.

Thus each location can be referred to by first, two letters; showing the 100km square in which it lies, then a set of figures representing co-ordinates within the forementioned square, which gives precise location.

LEGEND

AUTOSTRADA	AUTOBAHN		MOTORWAY	AUTOROUTE
N. di autostrade	Autobahnnummer	M3	Motorway number	Numéro d'autoroute
Nodo stradale con e senza numeri	Anschlusstellen mit und ohne Nummern	5	Junctions with and without numbers	Echangeurs avec et sans numéros
Nodo stradale con entràte ed uscite limitate	Anschlusstellen mit beschränkten Auf-oder Abfahrten	7	Junctions with limited entries or exits	Echangeurs aux entrées ou sorties restreintes
Area di servizio	Tankstelle mit Raststätte	S	Service area	Aire de service
Autostrada e Snodo i costruzione	Im Bau befindliche Autobahn und Anschlusstelle		Motorway & Junction under construction	Autoroute et Echangeur en construction
STRADE	**STRASSEN**		**ROADS**	**ROUTES**
Rotta primaria	Hauptverbindungsstrasse	A9	Primary route	Route primaire
Altre strade A	Andere A Strasse	A129	Other A roads	Autres routes A
Strade Classe B	Strasse der Klasse B	B2137	B Roads	Routes catégorie B
Non-classificate	Nicht klassifizierte Strasse		Unclassified	Non classifiée
Corsia a due piste	Strasse mit getrennten Fahrbahnen	A7	Dual Carriageway	Double chaussée
In construzione	Im Bau befindliche Strasse		Under construction	En construction
Scozia : strade strette con aree di passaggio Scotland	Schottland: enge Strasse mit Uberholstellen		Scotland: narrow roads with passing places.	L'Écosse: Route étroite avec lieu de déplacement
SERVIZI AA DI SOCCORSO E DI INFORMAZIONI	**AA-PANNEN-UND INFORMATIONSDIENST**		**AA BREAKDOWN & INFORMATION SERVICES**	**SERVICES AA DEPANNAGE ET DE RENSEIGNEMENT**
Centro di servizio (24 ore ☎)	Dienststelle (24 Stunden ☎)	AA 24 hour	Service centre (24 hours ☎)	Station-service (24 heures ☎)
Centro di servizio (ore di lavoro normali)	Dienststelle (übliche Bürostunden)	AA	Service centre (normal office hours)	Station service (heures d'ouverture normales)
Centro di servizio autostrada	Autobahndienststelle	AA info	Motorway Information Centre	Centre-service d'autoroute
Centro di servizio strada	Strassendienststelle	AA 13	Road service centre	Centre-service de route
Centro di servizio porto	Hafendienststelle	AA	Port service centre	Centre-service de port
Telefoni AA & RAC	AA und RAC Telefonzellen	☎	AA & RAC telephones	Téléphones AA & RAC
Telefoni PTT in aree isolate	Öffentliche Telefonzellen in abgelegenen Gebieten (PO)	☎	PO telephones in isolated areas	Téléphones PTT dans endroits isolés
Area di pic-nic Area di riposo	Picknickplatz Rastzplatz	PS RA	Picnic site Rest area	Terrain de Pique-nique Aire de Repos
Punti di vista AA	AA-Aussichtspunkt	Bembridge Viewpoint	AA viewpoint	Points de vue AA
Inclinazione (la freccia indica in pendio)	Steigung (Pfeile weisen bergab)	←	Steep gradient (arrows point downhill)	Côte (la flèche est dirigée vers le bas)
Pedaggio Strada	Gebührenpflichtige Strasse	Toll	Road toll	Péage de route
Passaggio a livello	Bahnübergang	LC	Level crossing	Passage à niveau
Traghetto veicoli (Gran Bretagna)	Autofähre (Grossbritannien)	V	Vehicle ferry (Gt Britain)	Bac pour véhicules (Grande-Bretagne)
Traghetto veicoli (continentale)	Autofähre (Kontinent)	CALAIS V	Vehicle ferry (continental)	Bac pour véhicules (Continental)
Aeroporto	Flughafen	✈	Airport	Aéroport
Area urbana Villaggio	Stadtgebiet Dorf		Urban area Village	Zone urbaine Village
Confine nazionale	Nationale Grenze		National boundary	Frontière nationale
Confine di contea	Grafschaftsgrenze		County boundary	Frontière provinciale
Distanza in mille fra simboli	Entfernung zwischen Zeichen in Meilen	2	Distance in miles between symbols	Distance en milles entre symboles
A.S.M. in piedi	Ortshöhe nach Füssen	2525	Spot height in feet	Altitude en pieds anglais
Fiume e lago	Fluss und See		River and lake	Rivière et lac
Numeri di pagine di seguito	Hinweiszahlen für Anschlusskarten	13	Overlaps and numbers of continuing pages	Chiffres de guide pour cartes voisines

Scale   5 miles to 1 inch   1: 316,800

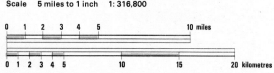

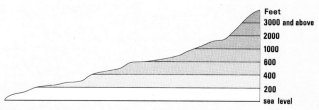

VIII

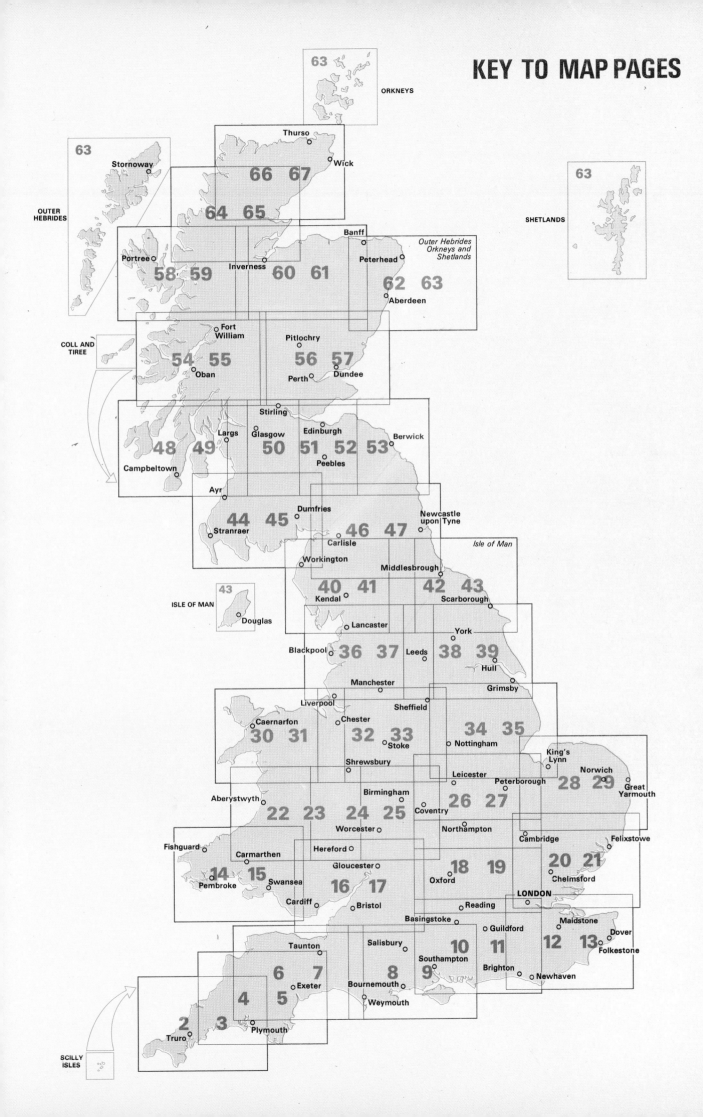

KEY TO MAP PAGES

ORKNEYS 63

63 Stornoway

OUTER HEBRIDES

SHETLANDS 63

Thurso
Wick

66 67

64 65

Banff

Outer Hebrides Orkneys and Shetlands

Portree 58 59 Inverness 60 61 Peterhead
62 63
Aberdeen

COLL AND TIREE

Fort William 54 55 Pitlochry 56 57
Oban Perth Dundee

Stirling

Largs Glasgow Edinburgh Berwick
48 49 50 51 52 53
Campbeltown Peebles
Ayr

Dumfries Newcastle upon Tyne
44 45 46 47
Stranraer Carlisle *Isle of Man*
Workington Middlesbrough
40 41 42 43
Kendal Scarborough

43

ISLE OF MAN
Douglas

Lancaster York
Blackpool 36 37 Leeds 38 39
Manchester Hull
Liverpool Grimsby
Sheffield
Caernarfon Chester
30 31 32 33 34 35
Stoke Nottingham
Shrewsbury King's Lynn
Leicester Norwich
Aberystwyth Birmingham Peterborough 28 29
22 23 24 25 Coventry 26 27 Great Yarmouth
Worcester Northampton
Cambridge Felixstowe
Fishguard Carmarthen Hereford 20 21
14 15 Gloucester 18 19 Chelmsford
Pembroke Swansea 16 17 Oxford **LONDON**
Cardiff Bristol Reading
Basingstoke Maidstone
Guildford Dover
Taunton Salisbury 10 11 12 13 Folkestone
6 7 8 Southampton Brighton
Exeter Bournemouth 9 Newhaven
4 5 Weymouth
2 3 Plymouth
Truro

SCILLY ISLES

9

4

ISLES OF SCILLY

2

BRYHER
▲138 St MARTIN'S
▲134 New Grimsby
▲129 Higher Town
Pool
TRESCO

SAMSON
▲166
ST MARY'S
SCILLY ISLES (ST MARY'S)
Hugh Town
Old Town
Scilly Isles-Penzance
V

Middle Town
ST AGNES

8

1
SV

1

7

SV

SV SW

SV 0 8 9 0 SW

6

New Polzeath
Padstow Bay
Polzeath
Trebetherick
Port Quin Bay
Port Quin
Rumps Point
Pentire Point

TREVOSE HEAD
Gunver Head
Crugmeer Rock
▲243 Trevone
St Merryn
B3276
Padstow
Trevans
St Issey
Constantine Bay
Treyarnon
Shop
Little Petherick
Penrose
A389
Tredinnick B

Park Head
St Ervan
Downhill
Rumford
A39

Berryl's Point
Trenance
B3274

Watergate Bay
St Mawgan
Talskiddy

Tregurrian
St Columb Major
Tregonetha
Belowda

Towan Head
Fistral Bay
Newquay Bay
Pentire
St Columb Minor
Colan
Trebudannon
A30

Kelsey Head
West Pentire
NEWQUAY
Mountjoy
Trevarren
Ruthvoes
LC

Holywell Bay
Crantock
Kestle Mill
A392
St Columb Road
Indian Queens

Holywell
Cubert
Carines
St Enoder
Fraddon
St De

Ligger or Perran Bay
Mount
▲490
Newlyn East
Retew
Treviscoe

Perranporth
Rejerrah
Rose
Summercourt
Brighton
B3279

Bolingey
Goonhavern
Mitchell
St Stephen
A30

Trevellas
Perranzabuloe
Carland Cross
Combe
Tre

St Agnes Head
Zelah
New Mills
Grampound Road
Stickle

St Agnes
▲629
Mithian
Callestick
Ladock
Sticker
1

Goonbell
St Allen
Trispen
A390
Grampoun

Porthtowan
Mount Hawke
Goonbell
Shortlanesend
St Erme
Probus
B3287 St Ew

5
Navax Point
Porthtowan
Mawla
Blackwater
Kenwyn
TRURO
Tresillian
Creed
Po

Portreath
Scorrier
St Day
AA 24 hour
Merther
Tregony

Illogan
REDRUTH
Chacewater
A390
St Clement
Trewarthenick

St Ives Bay
Kehelland
Carn Brea
Baldhu
Kea
Malpas
Ruan Lanihorne
Portholland

Gwithian
Roseworthy
A30
CAMBORNE
Twelveheads
Bissoe
St Michael Penkevil
Lamorran
Po

4
Gurnard's Head
Zennor
Halsetown
Connor Downs
Lanner
Carharrack
Carnon Downs
Old Kea
Carne

ST IVES
Carbis Bay
Phillack
Barripper
Troon
Gwennap
Penpol
Trelissick
Veryan
Gervans Bay

Porthmeor
Towednack
Crippleseaase
Lelant
Gwinear
Carnhell Green
Four Lanes
Perranarworthal
Devoran
Feock
Trewithian
Portscatho

Morvah
Georgia
Canonstown
Hayle
Praze-an-Beeble
Stithians
Ponsanooth
Carclew
Mylor
St Just
Nare Head

Pendeen
▲14
B28
PENZANCE
St Erth
Leedstown
B3280
Longdowns
Mabe
Bridge
PENRYN
Flushing
St Mawes
Bohortha
Greeb Point

Trewellard
Boskednan
New Mill
Ludgvan
St Erth Praze
Crowan
Rame
Burnthouse
Penjerrick
FALMOUTH
Zone Point

Botallack
Great Bosullow
Madron
Gulval
Relubbus
Townshend
Nancegollan
Porkellis
Treverva
Budock Water
Falmouth Bay

3
ST JUST
Carnyorth
Newbridge
Chyandour
Marazion
Goldsithney
Godolphin Cross
Wendron
Seworgan
Constantine
Port Navas
Rosemullion Head

Kelynack
Bosavern
Heamoor
St Hilary
Perranuthnoe
Ashton
Sithney
A394
Mawnan Smith
Mawnan

Sancreed
Tredavoe
PENZANCE
Praa Sands
Germoe
Breage
HELSTON
Gweek
St Anthony

Brane
Drift
Newlyn
Cudden Point
Rinsey
▲635
Porthleven
Helford
Manaccan
Nare Point

Escalls
Kerris
Paul
Mousehole
Trewavas Head
▲13
Garras
St Martin's Green
Mawgan
Tregidden
Porthallow

Sennen Cove
St Buryan
MOUNT'S BAY
Newtown
Porthoustock
Manacle Point

LAND'S END
Sennen
B3315
Lamorna
Berepper
B3293
Traboe
St Keverne

Porthcurno
Treen
Cribba Head
Cury
▲369

St Levan
Gwennap Head
V
Potdhu Point
Mullion
Gwenter
Coverack

2
Penzance-Scilly Isles
Mullion Cove
Porth Mellin
Black Head

Predannack Wollas
A3083
Ruan Minor
Cadgwith

Vellan Head
Lizard
Landewednack
Hot Point

4 5 6 7 8 9 S

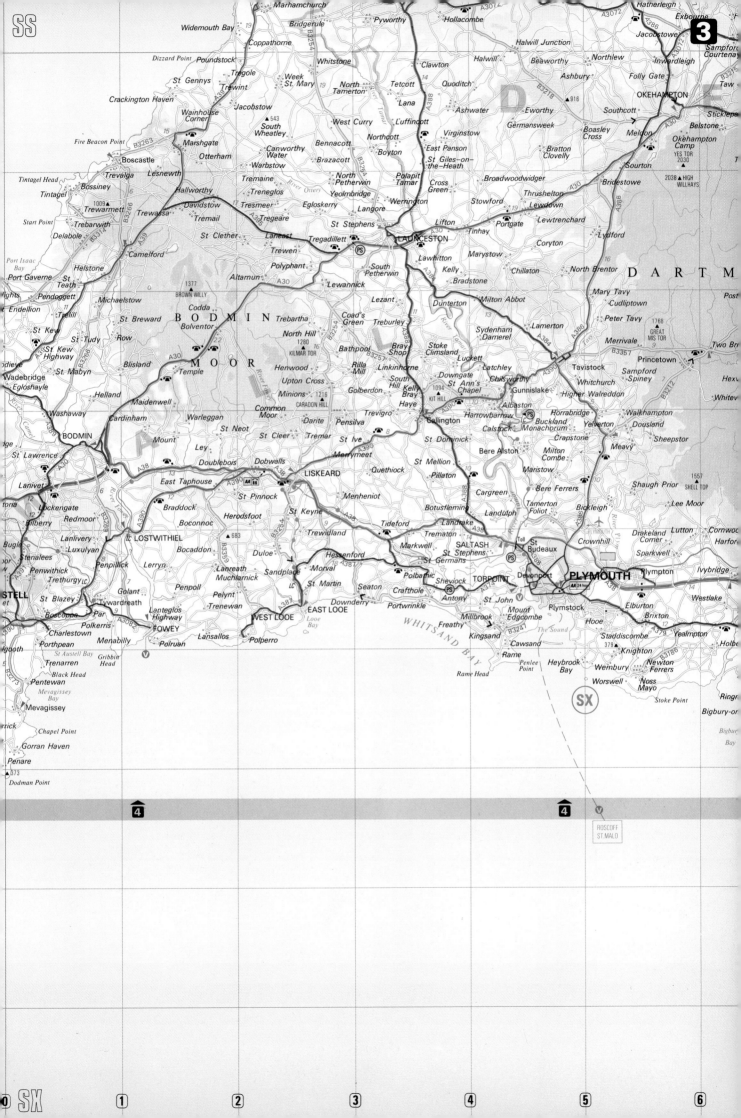

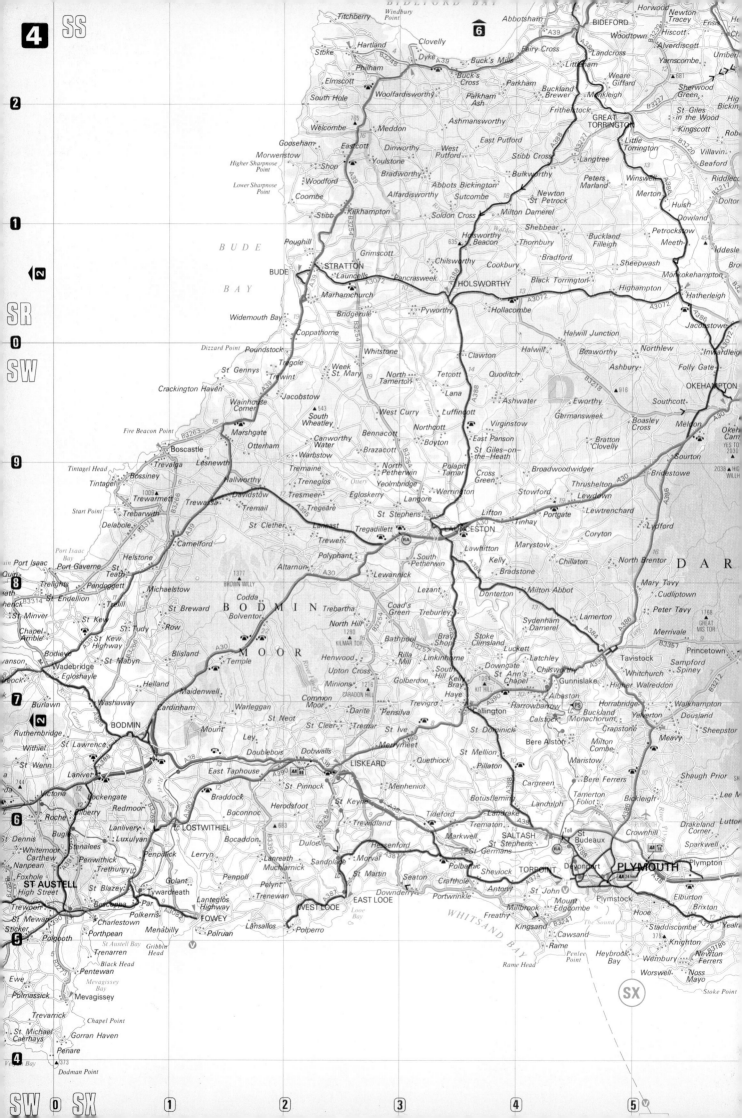

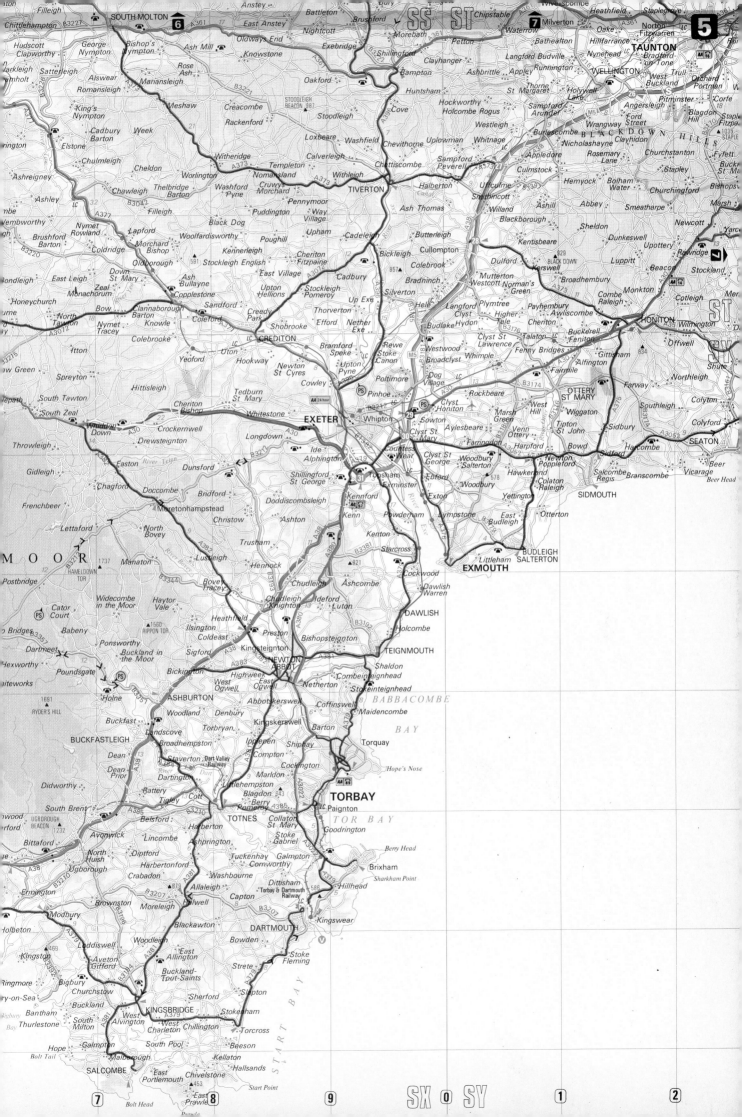

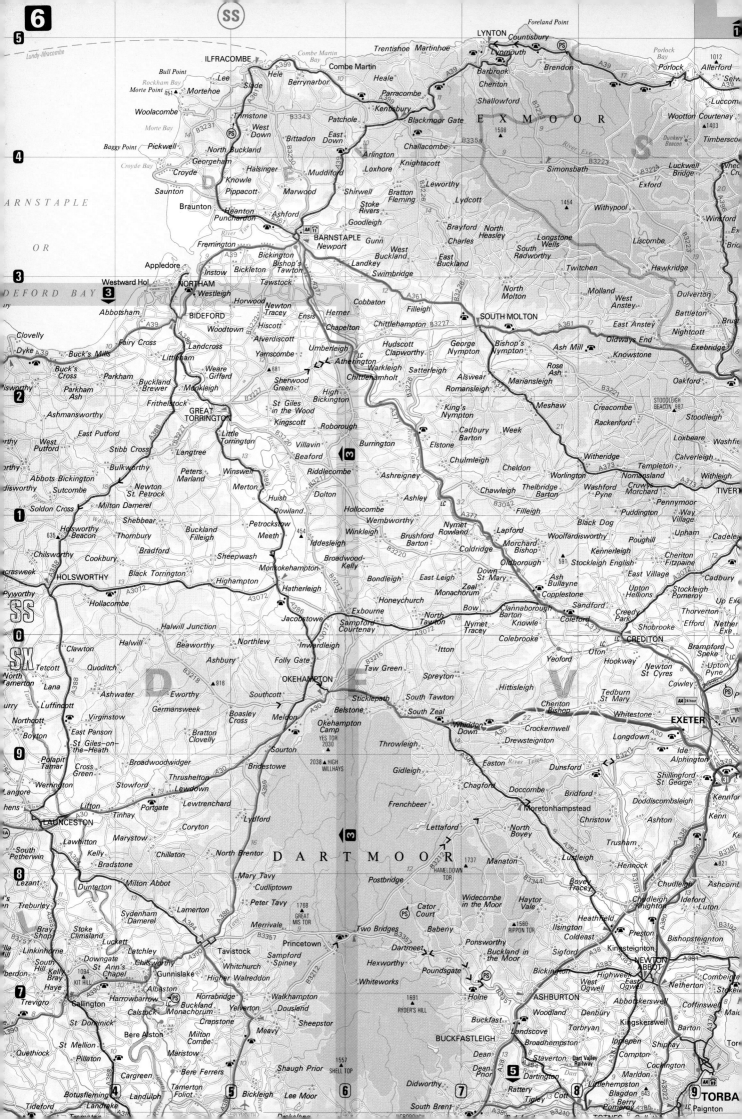

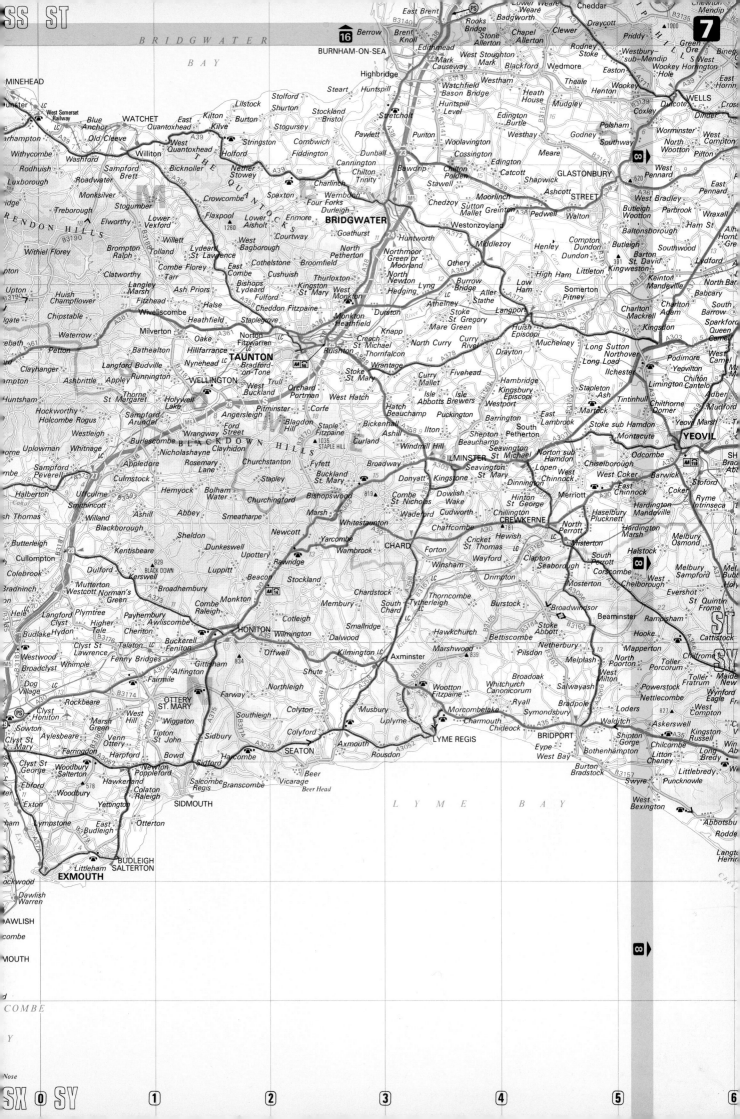

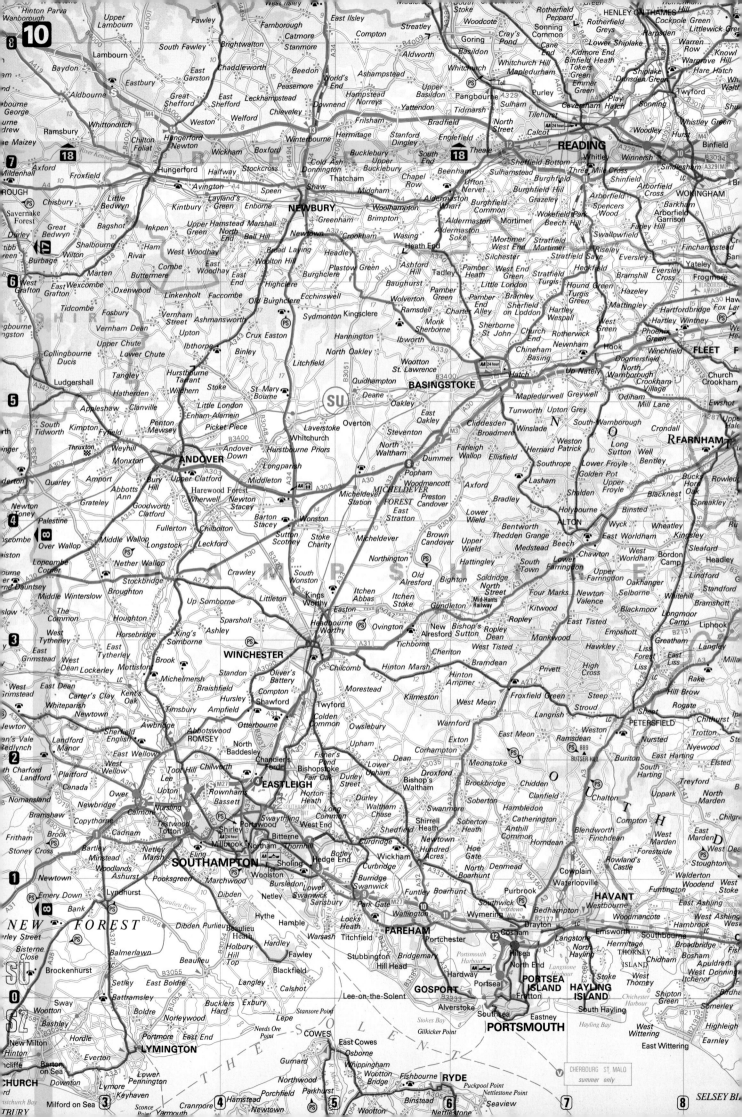

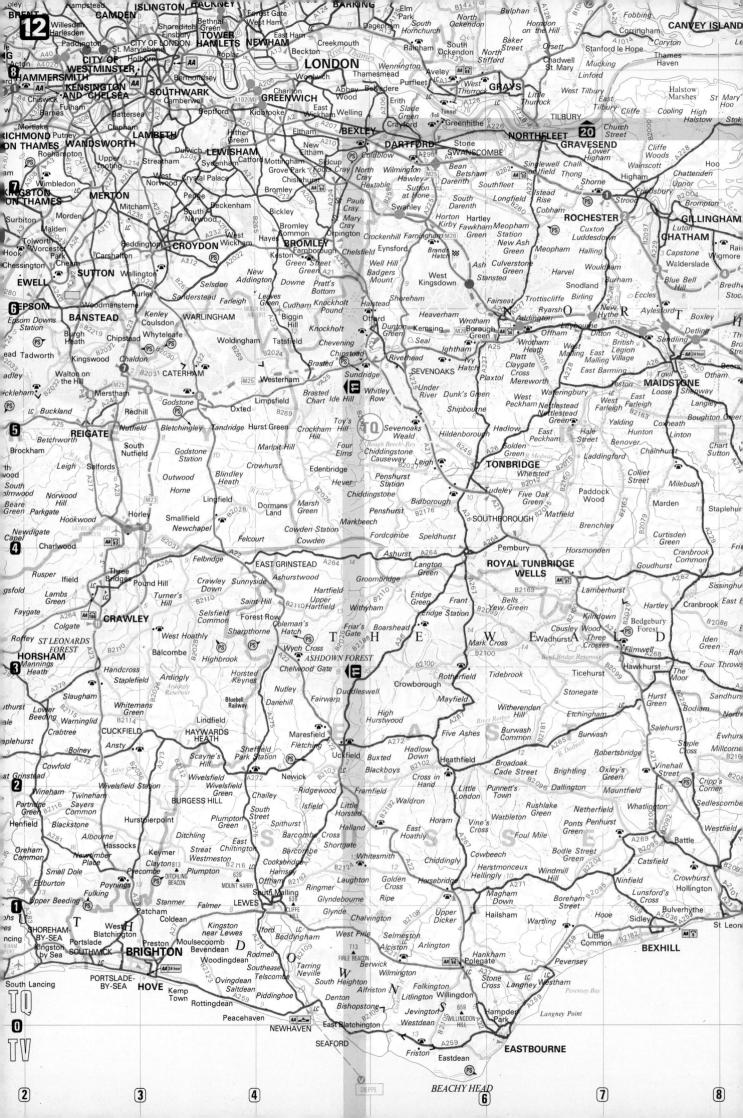

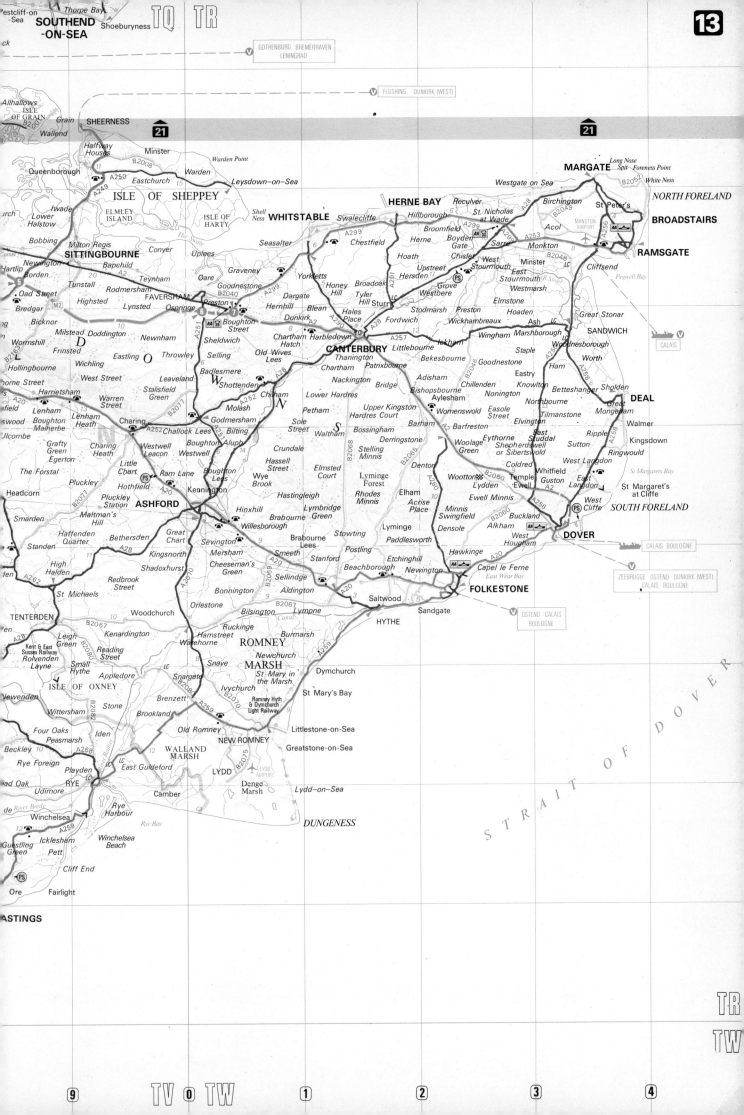

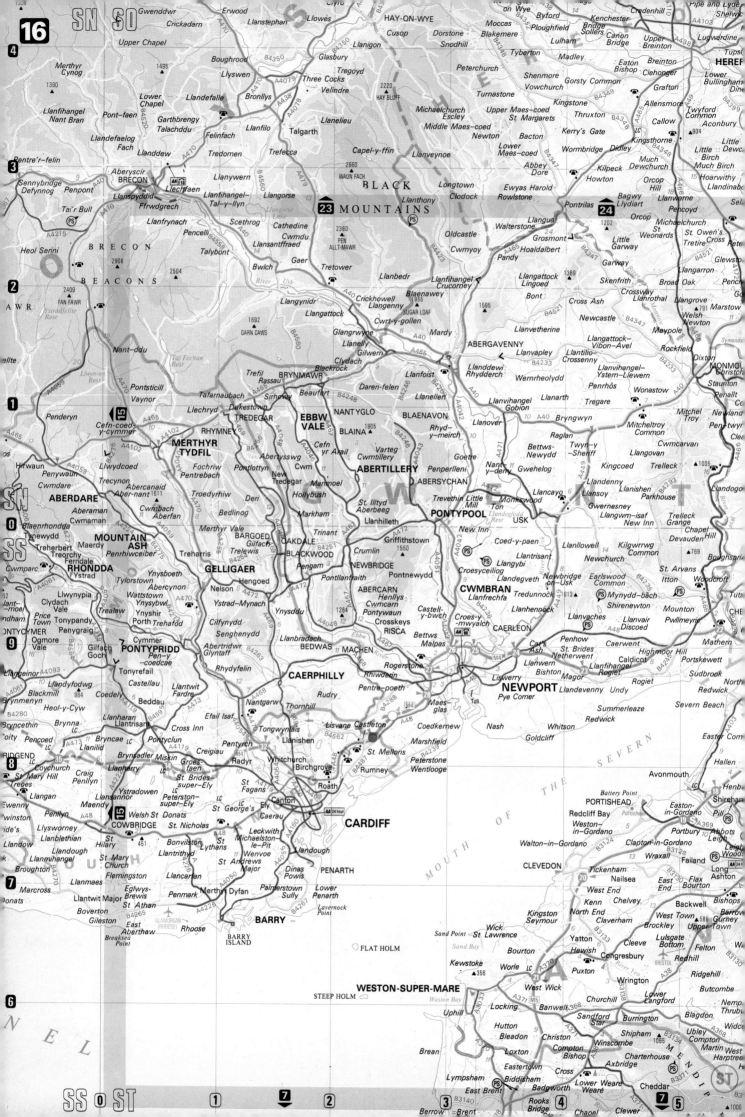

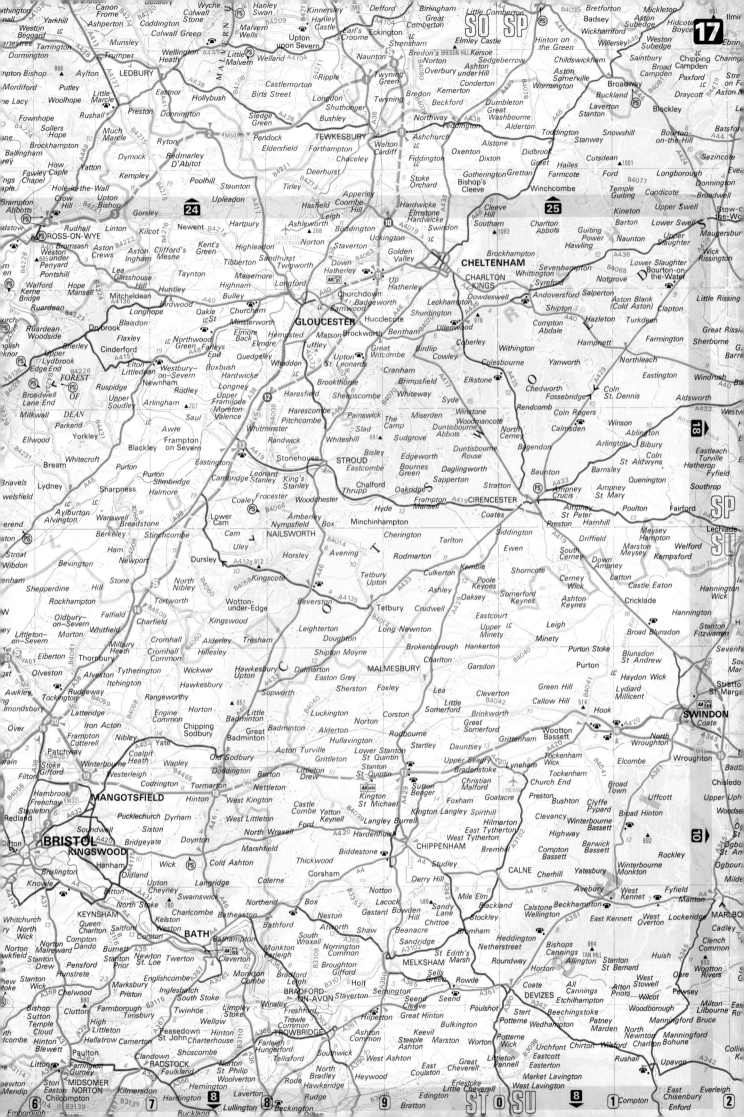

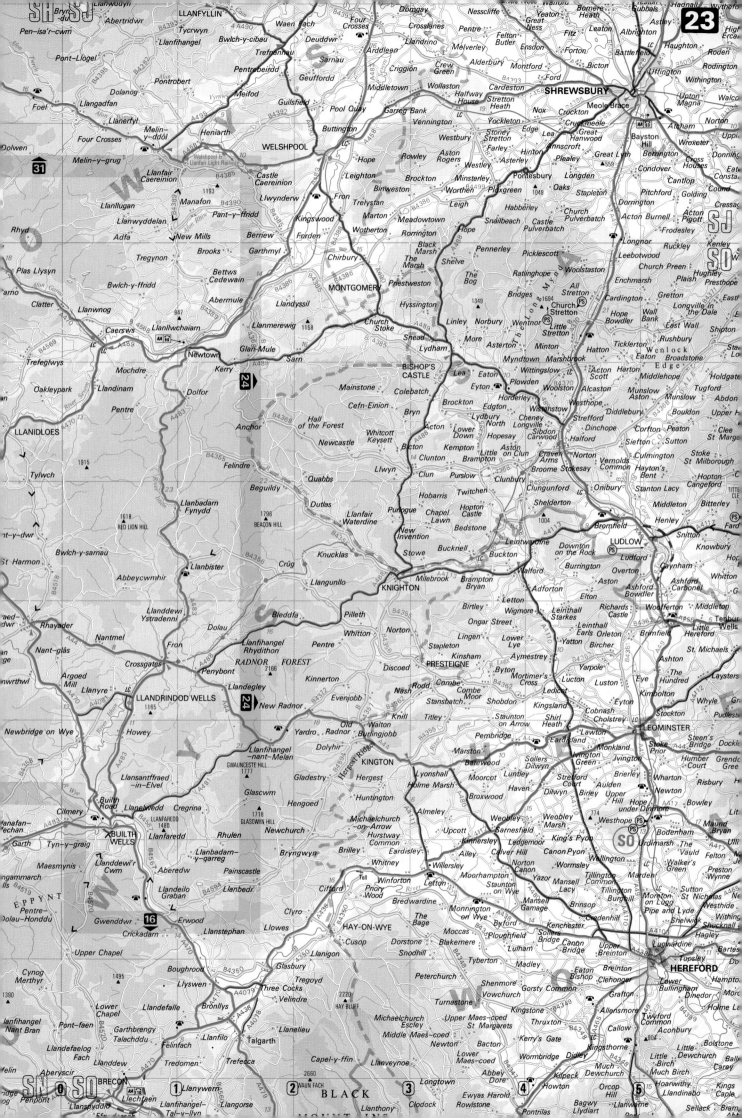

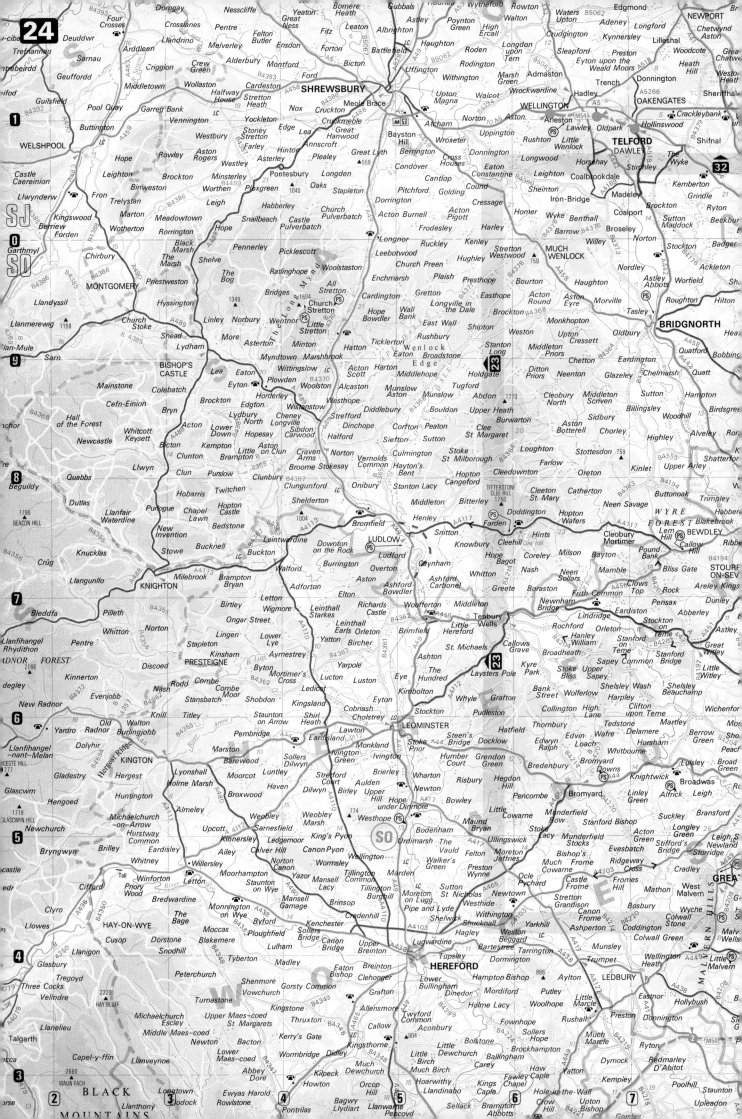

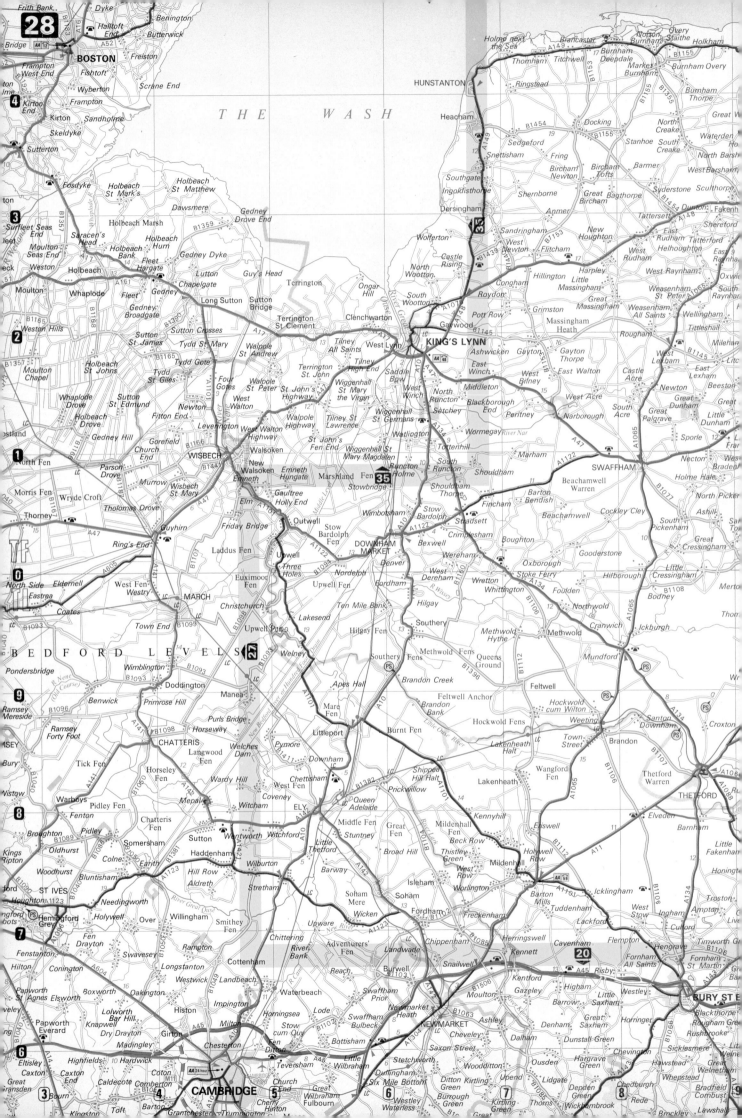

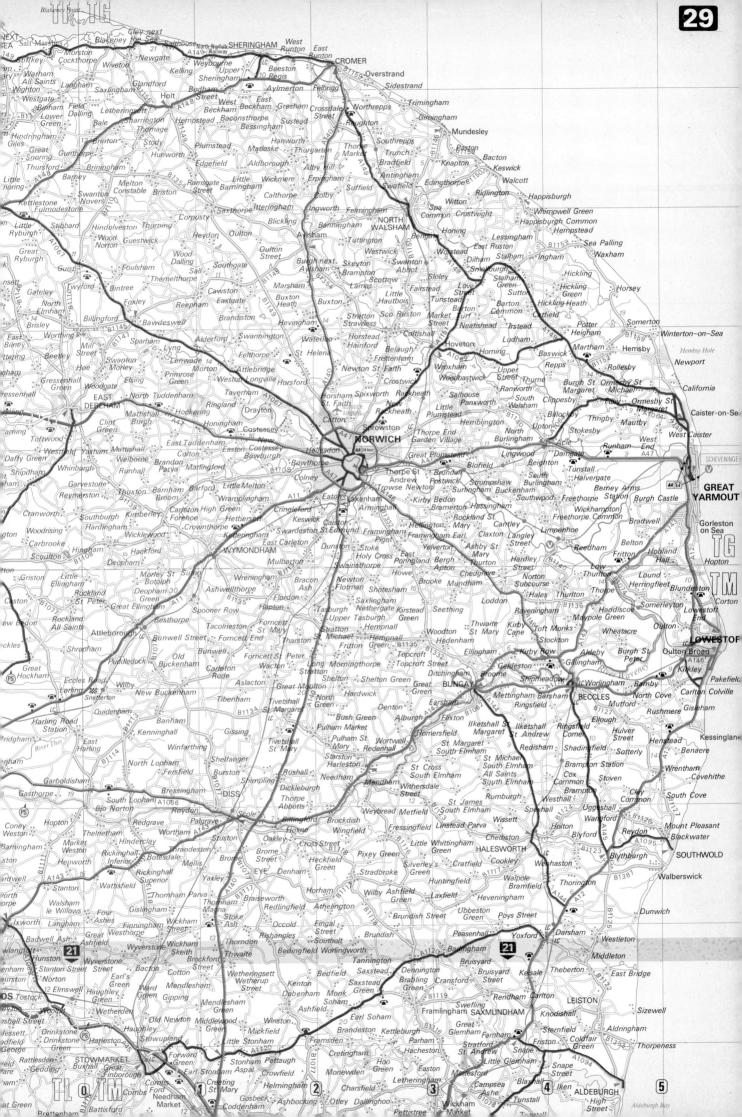

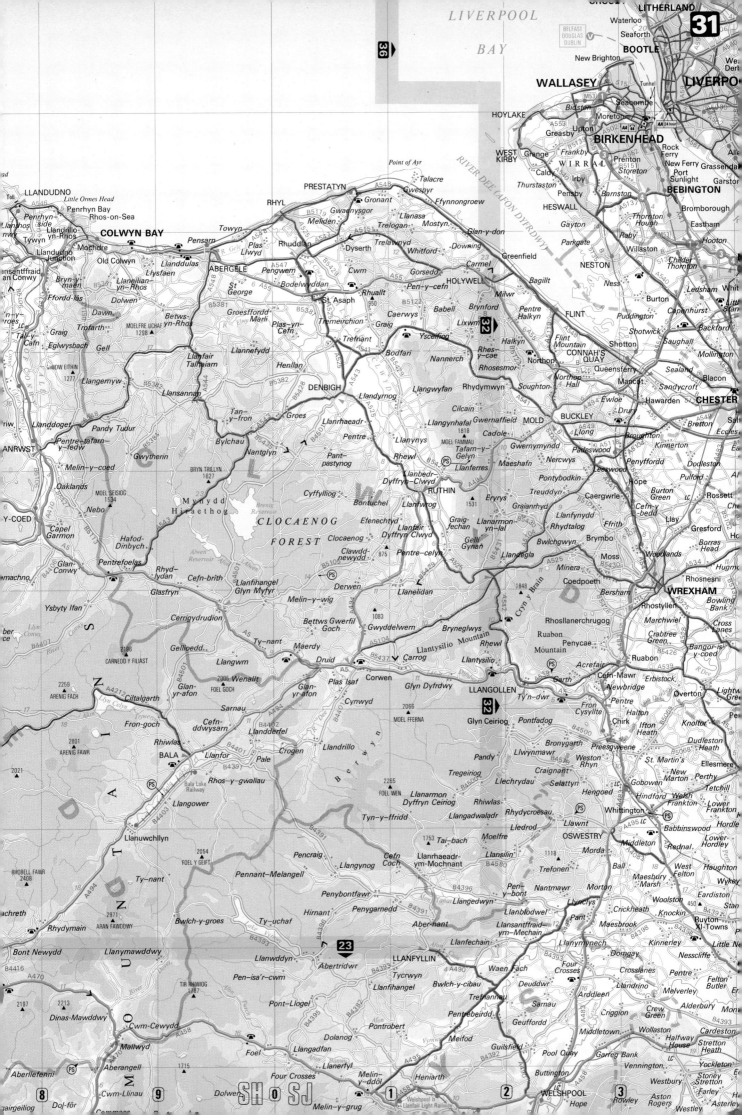

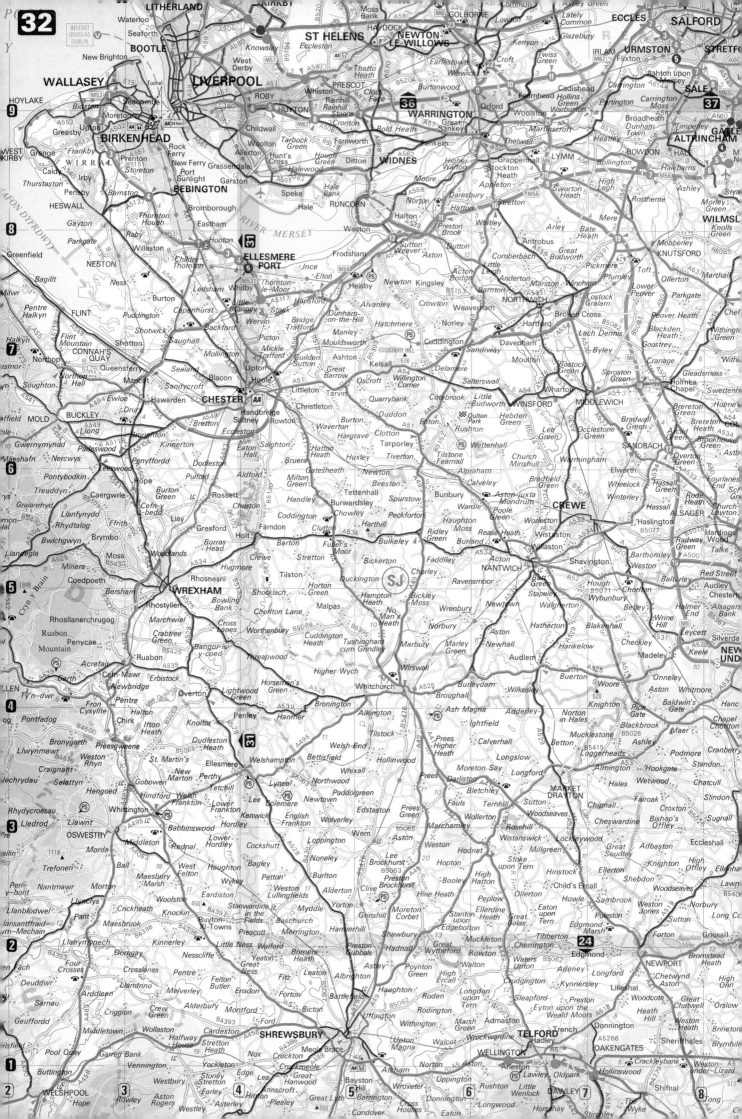

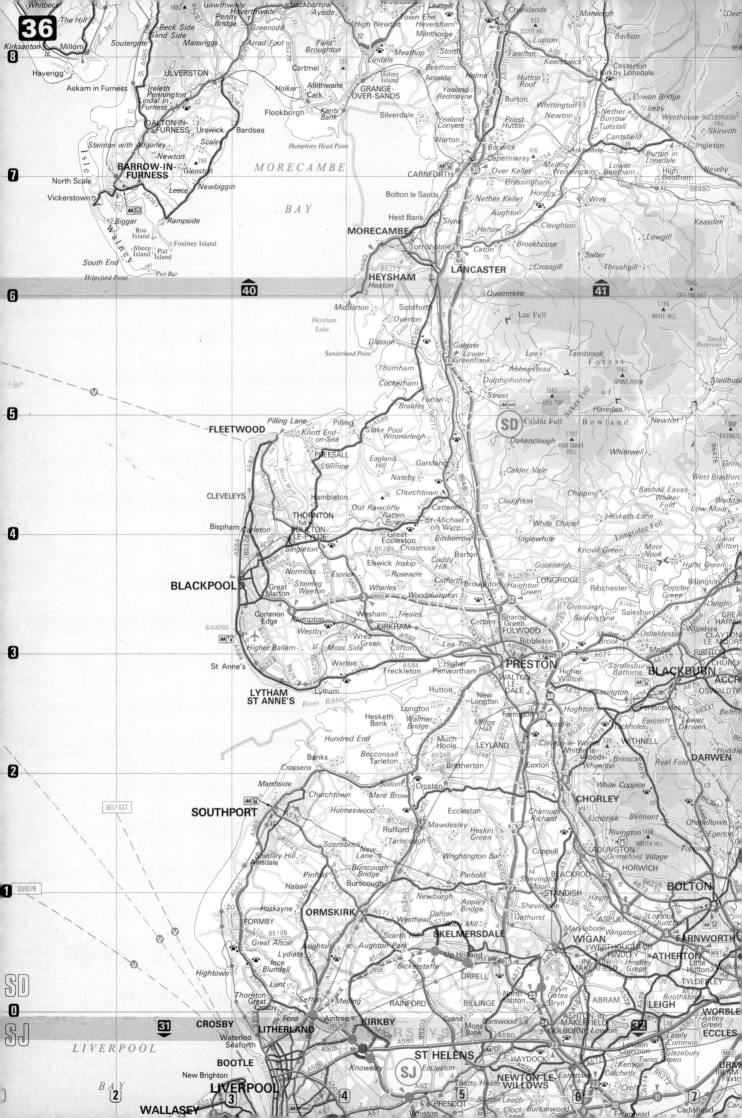

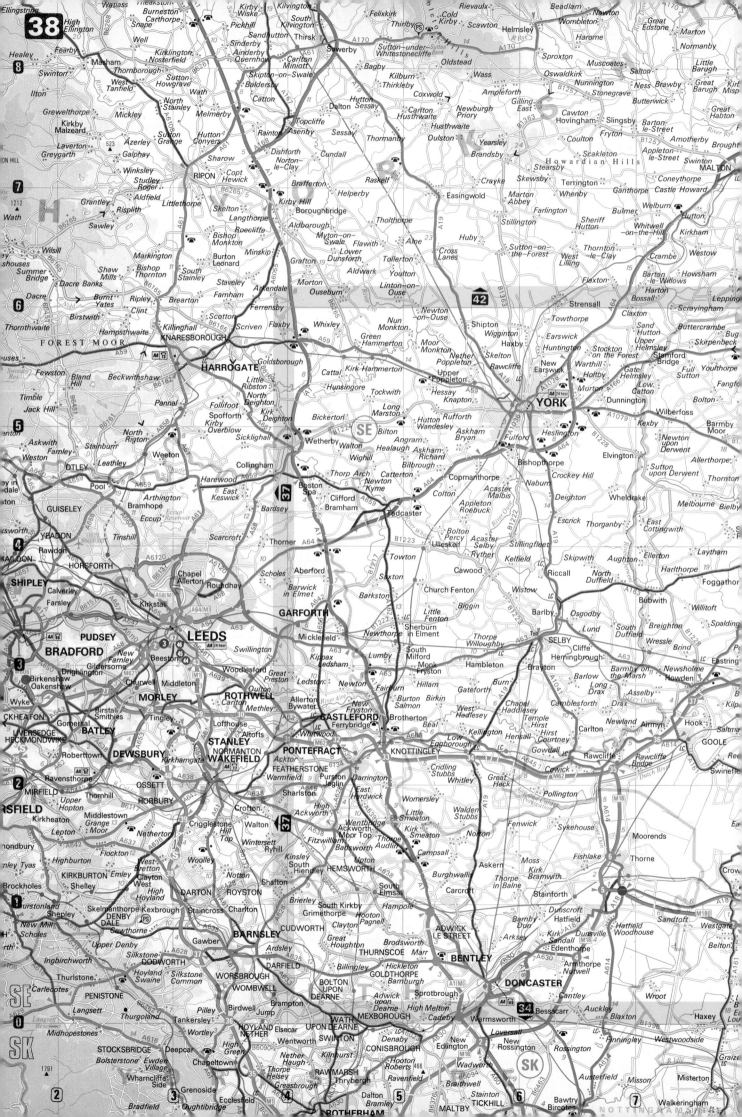

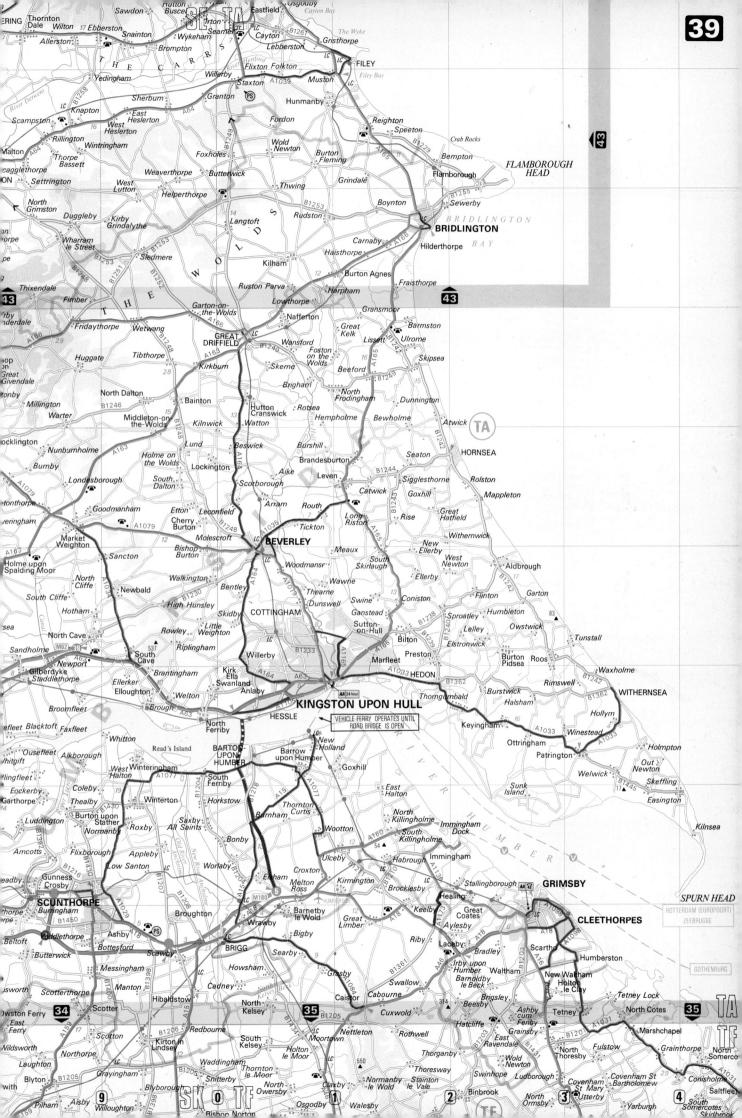

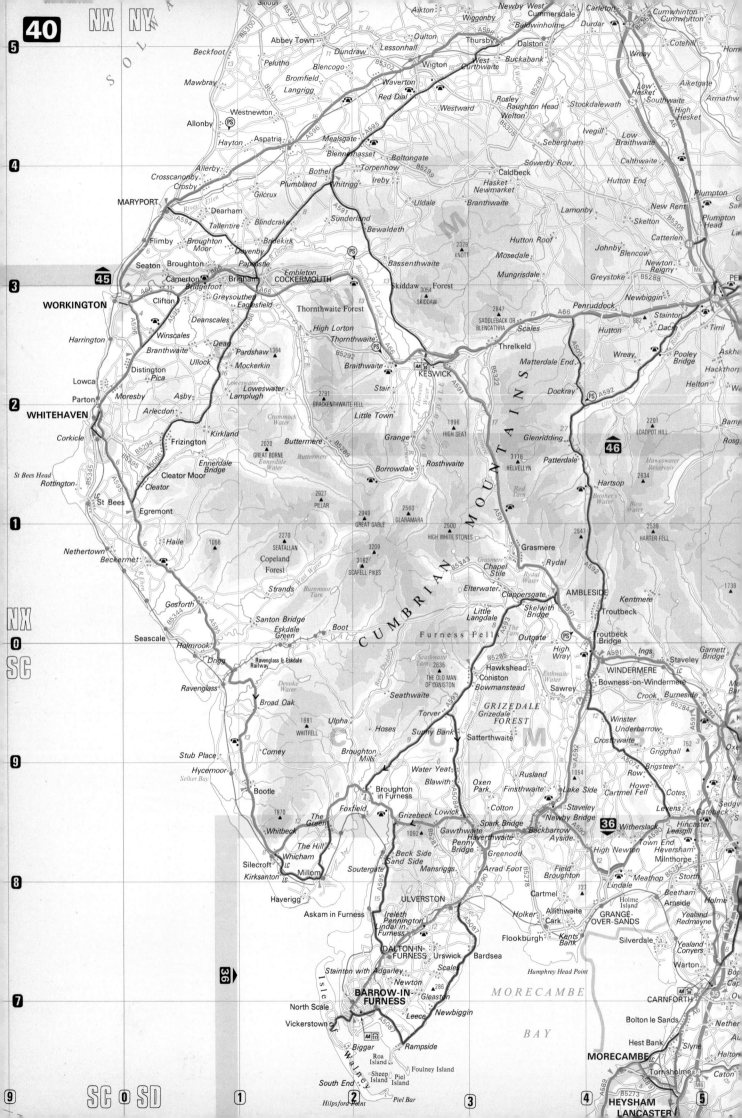

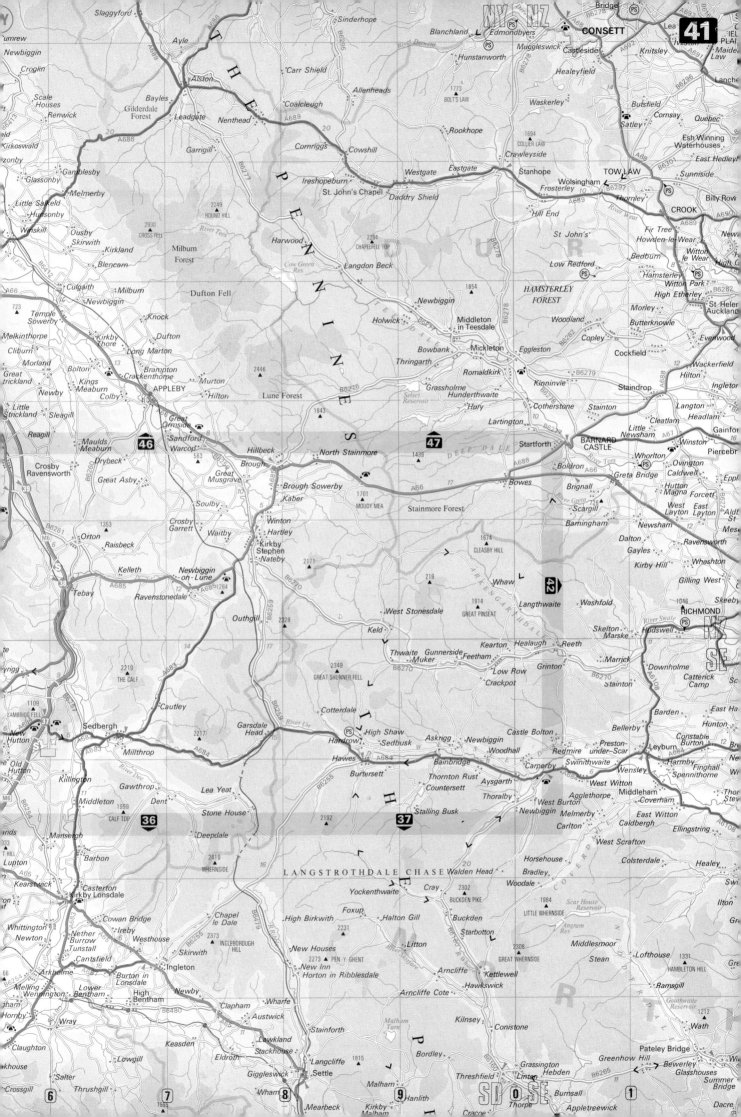

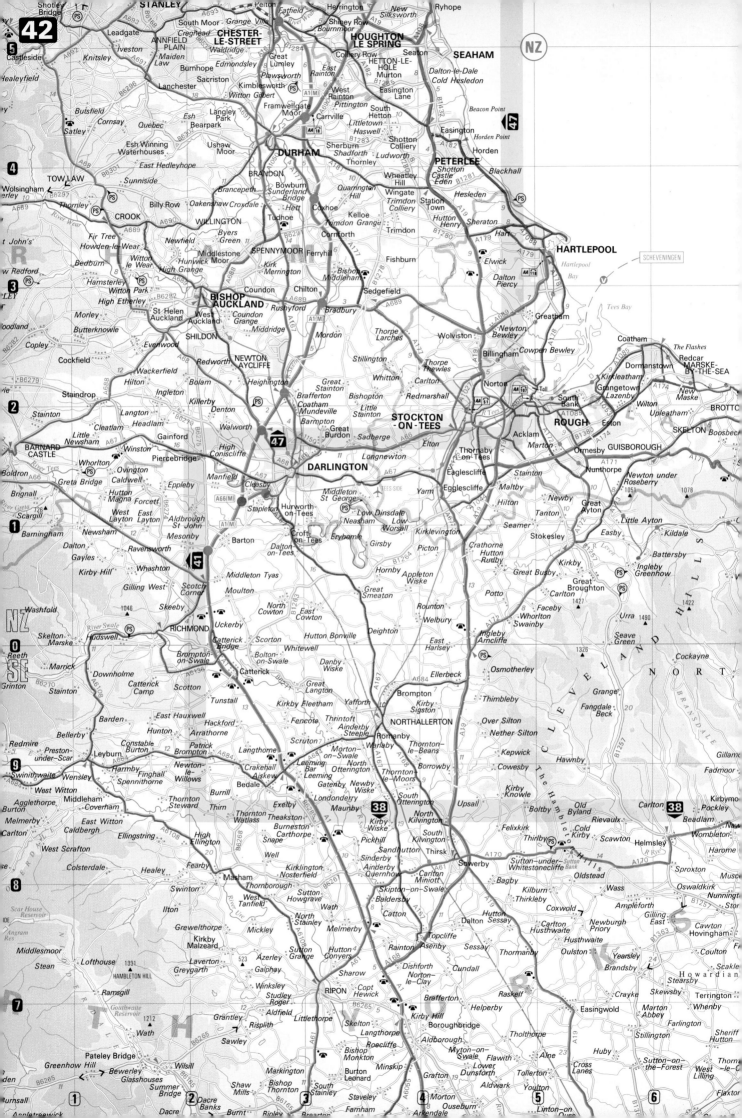

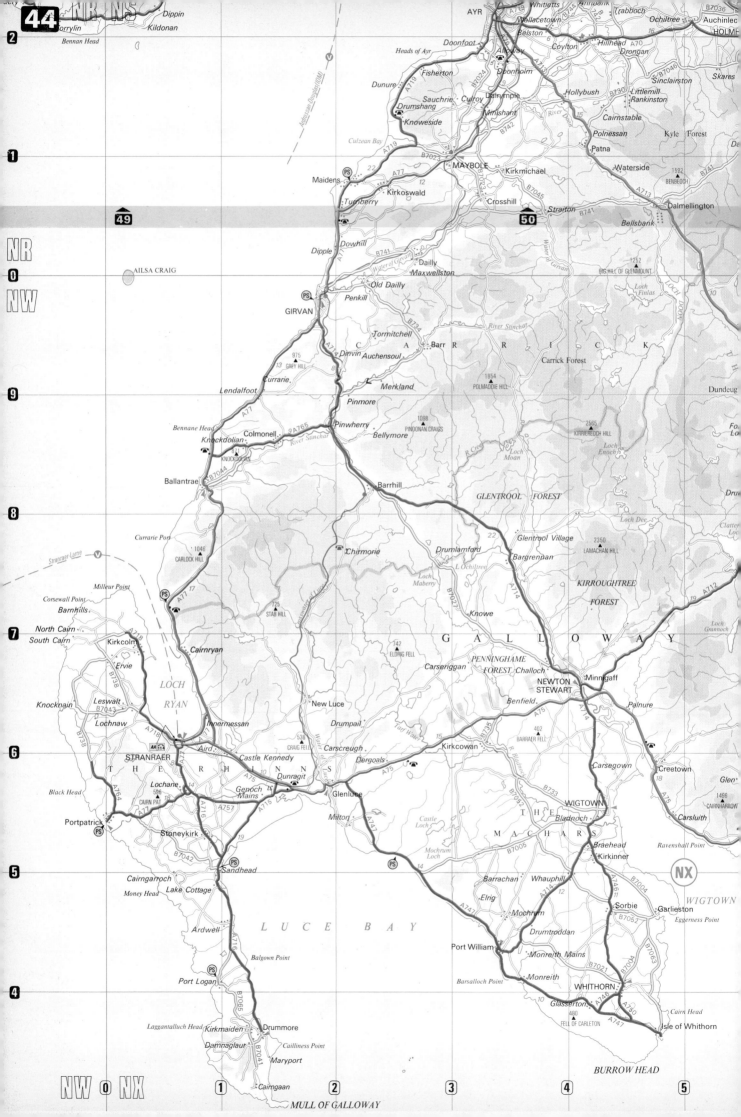

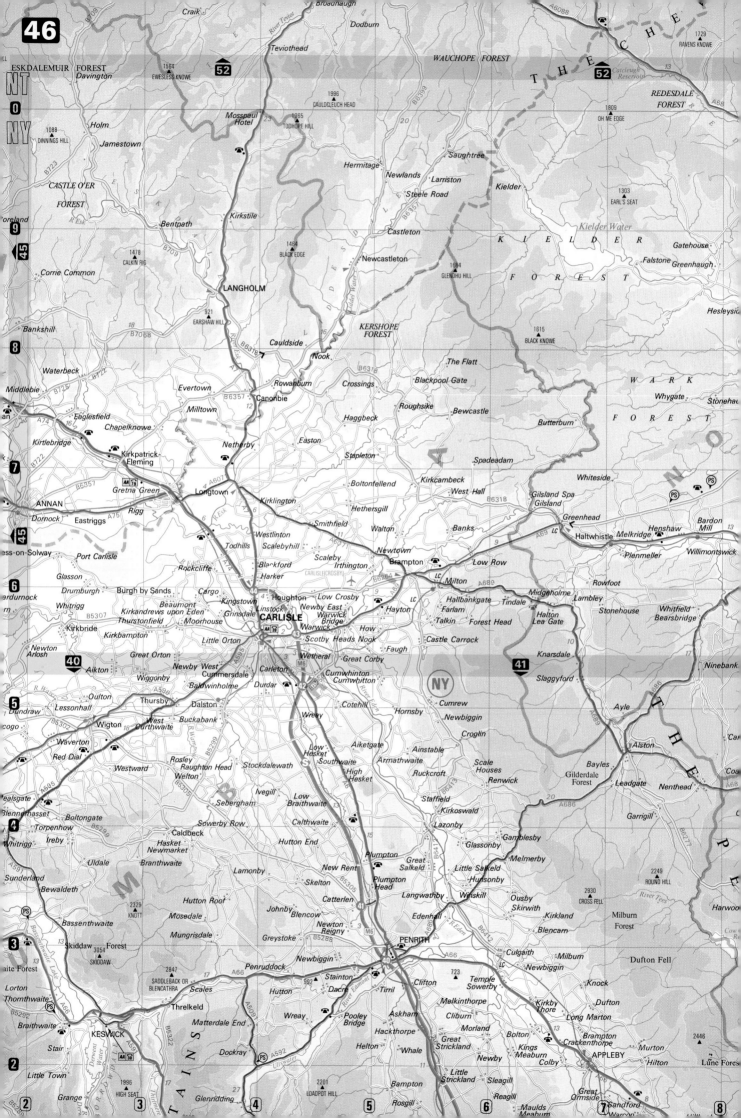

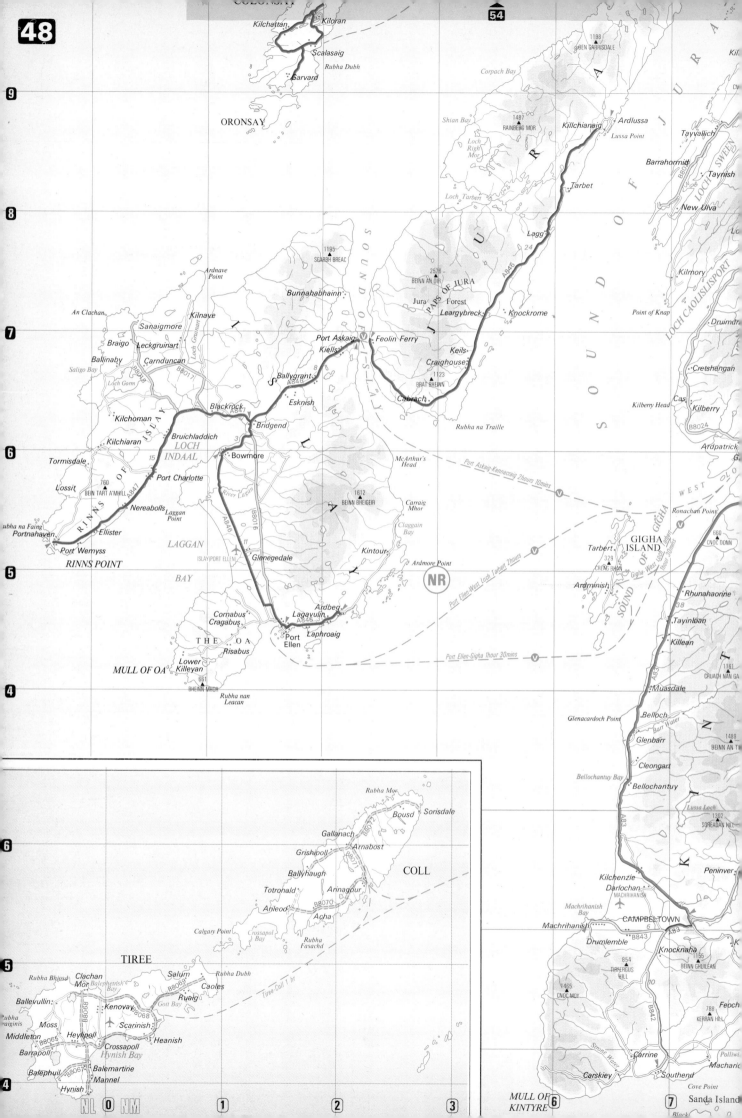

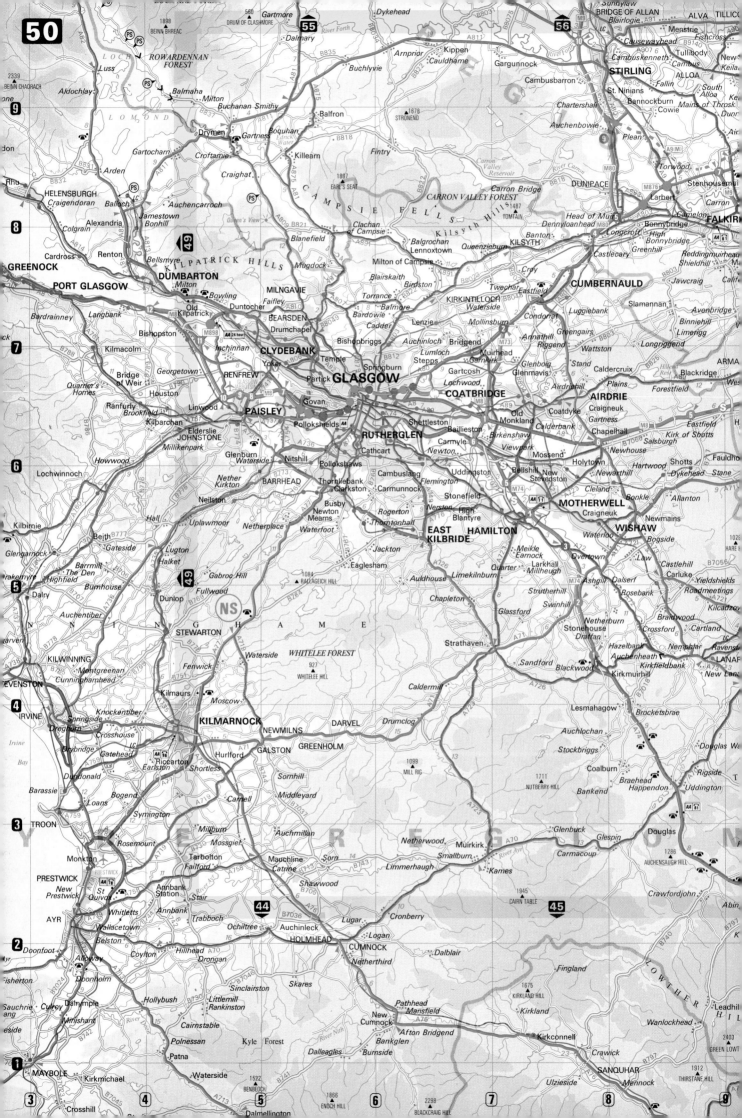

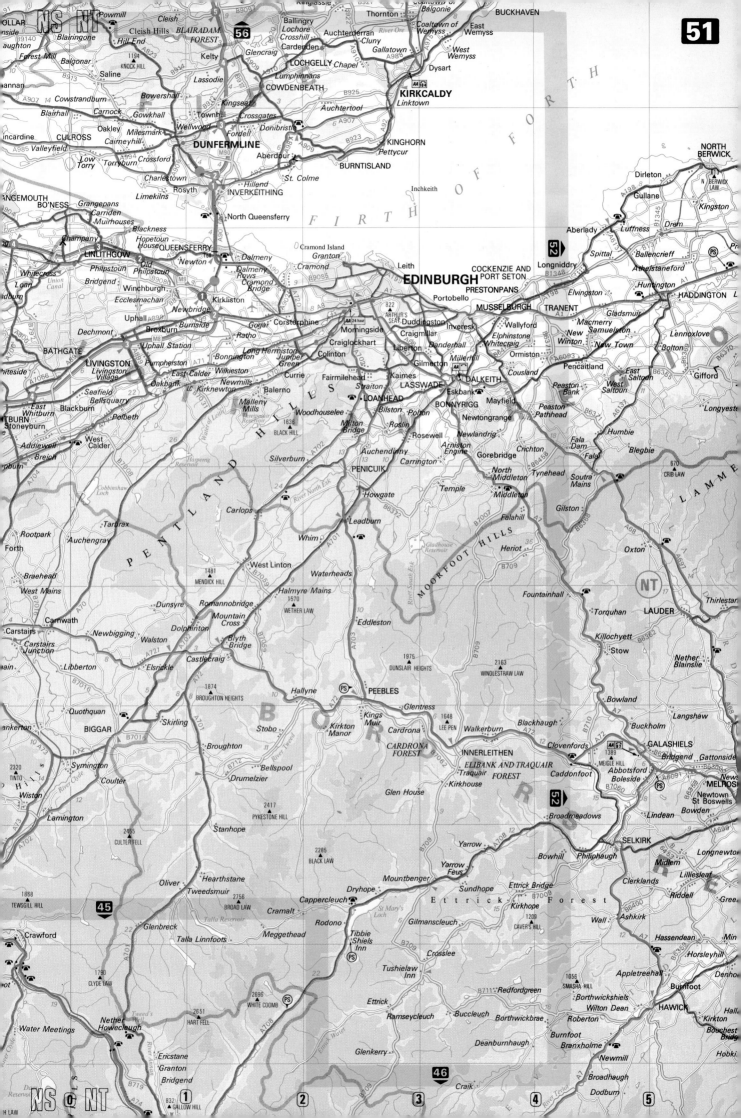

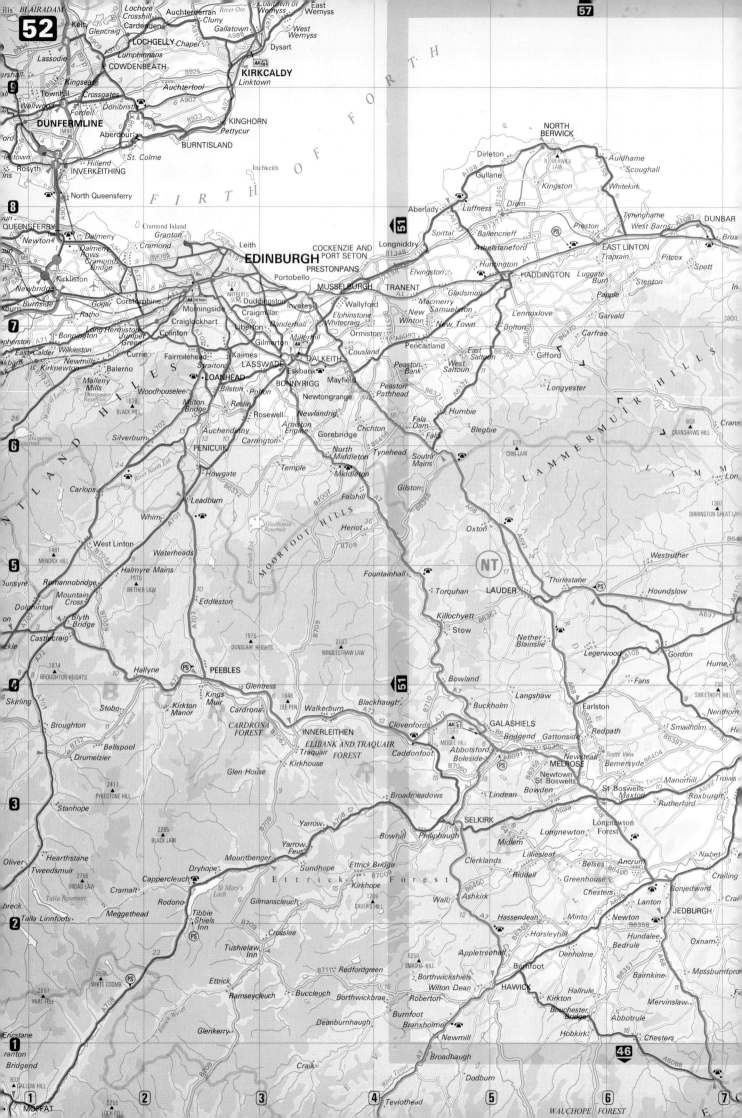

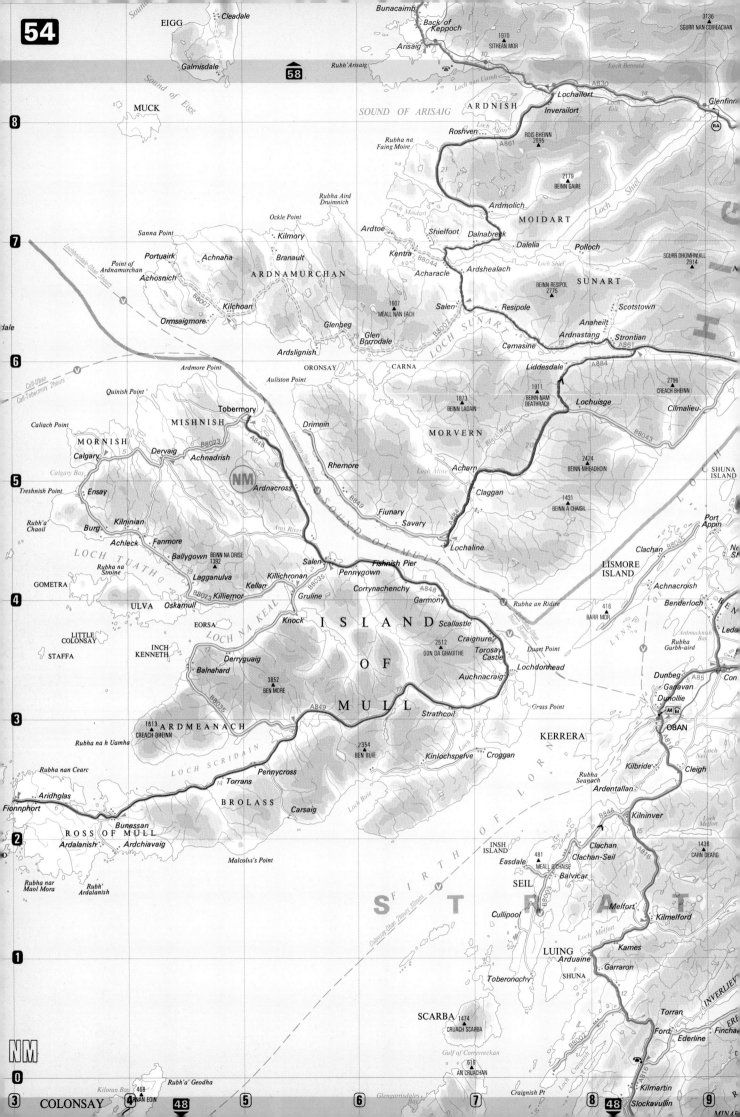

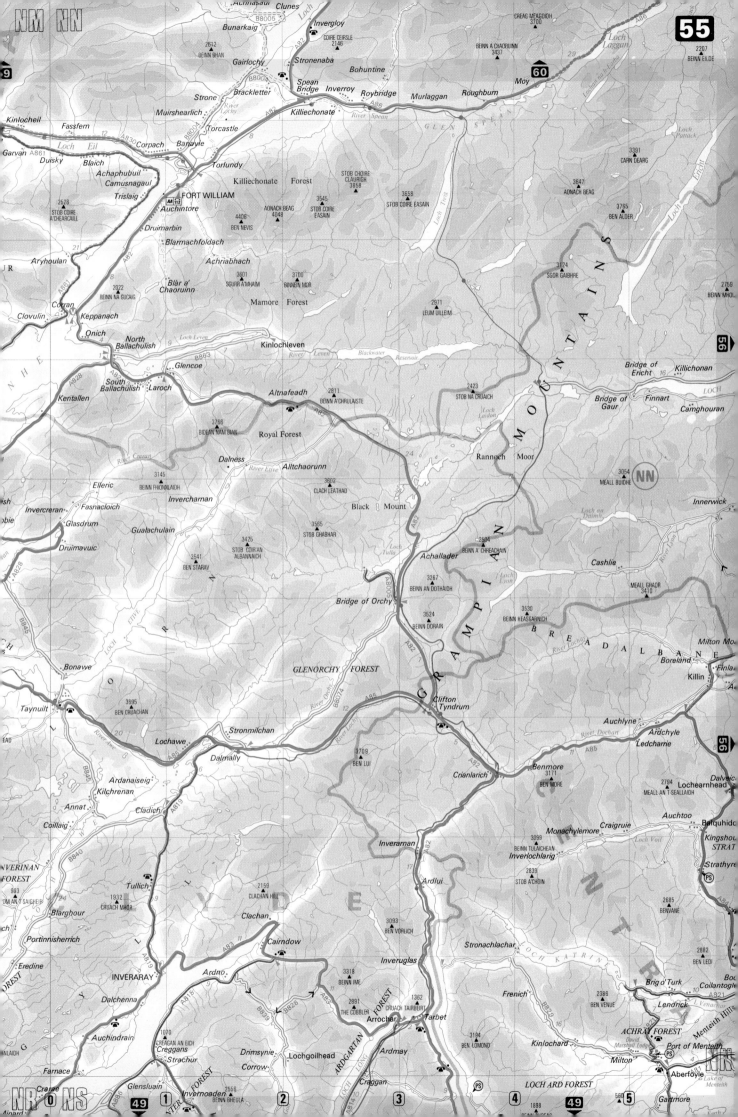

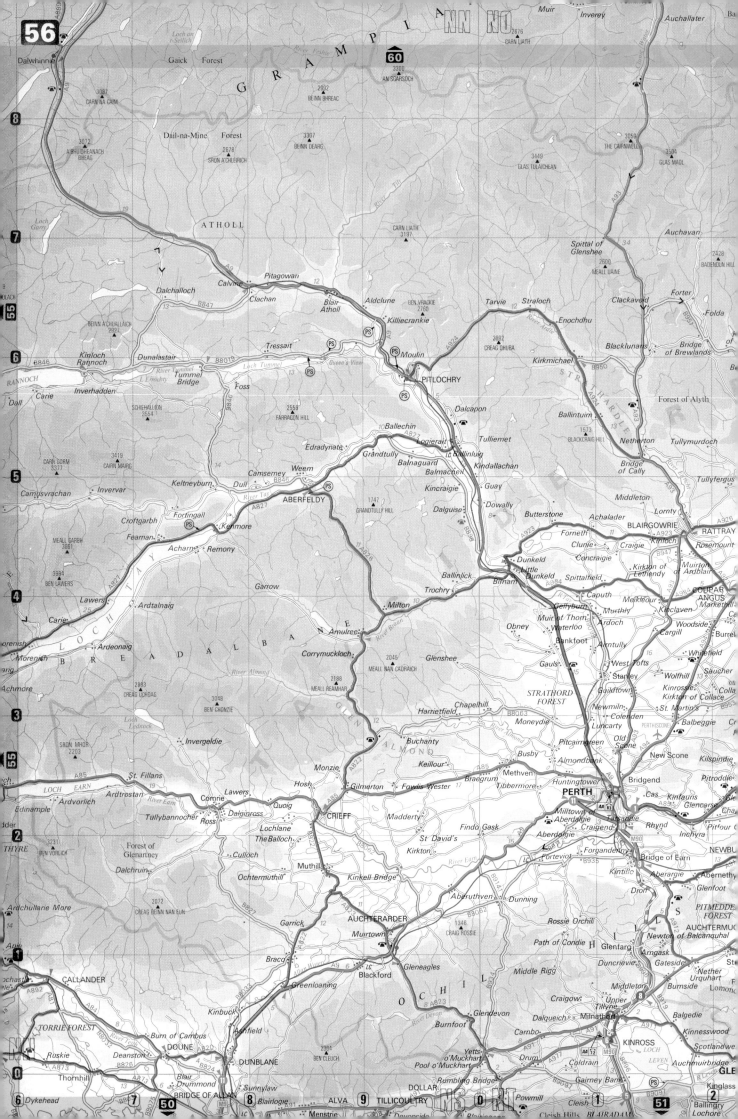

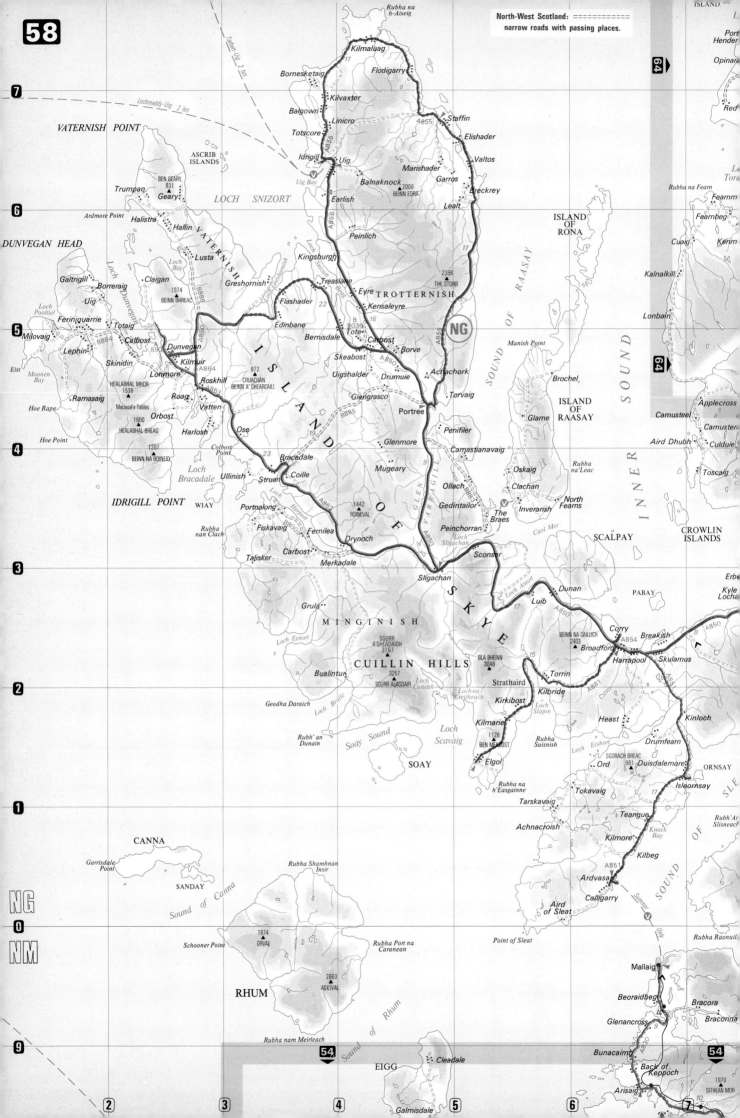

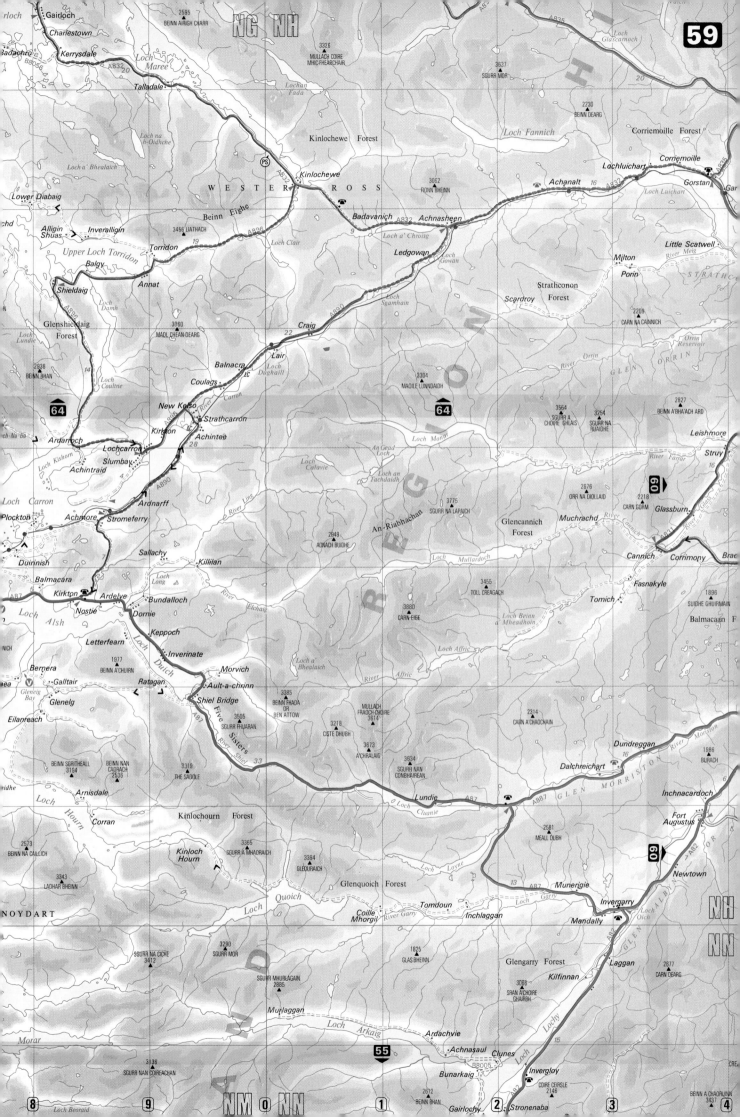

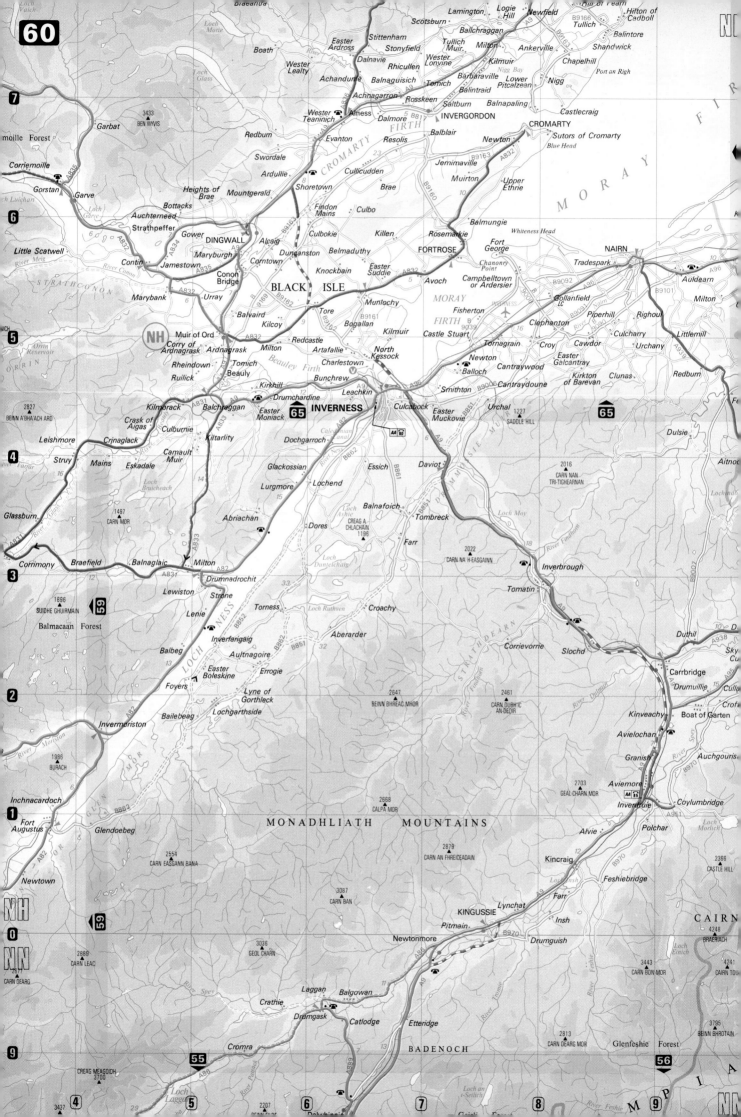

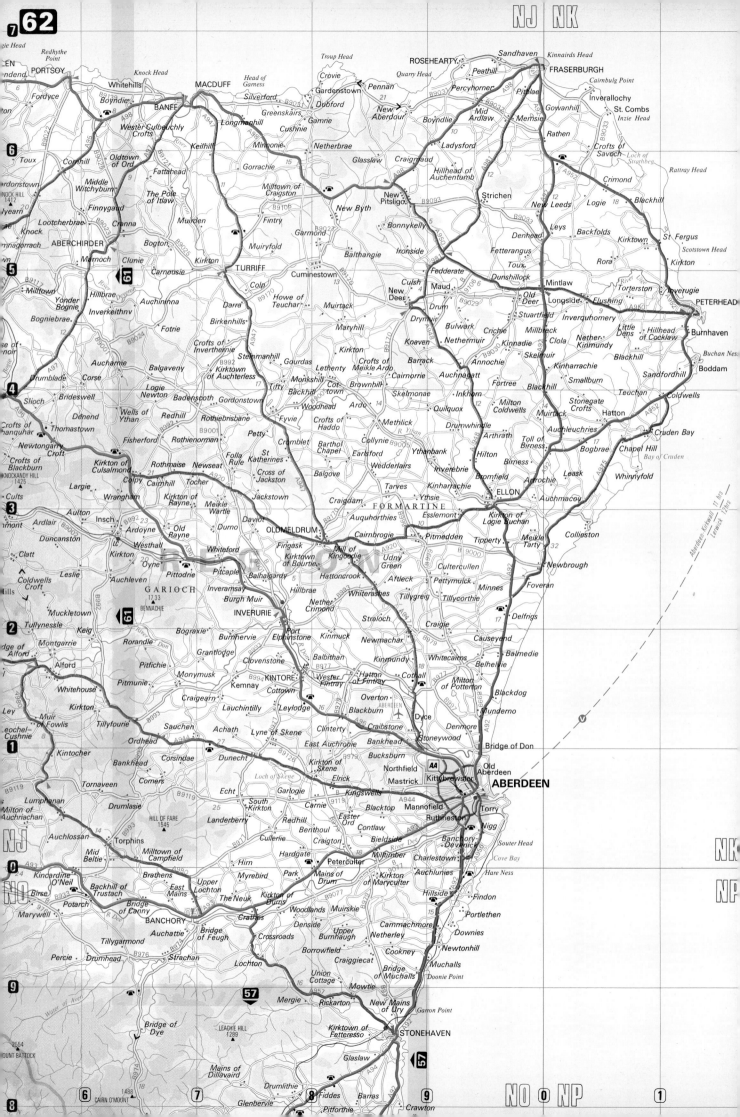

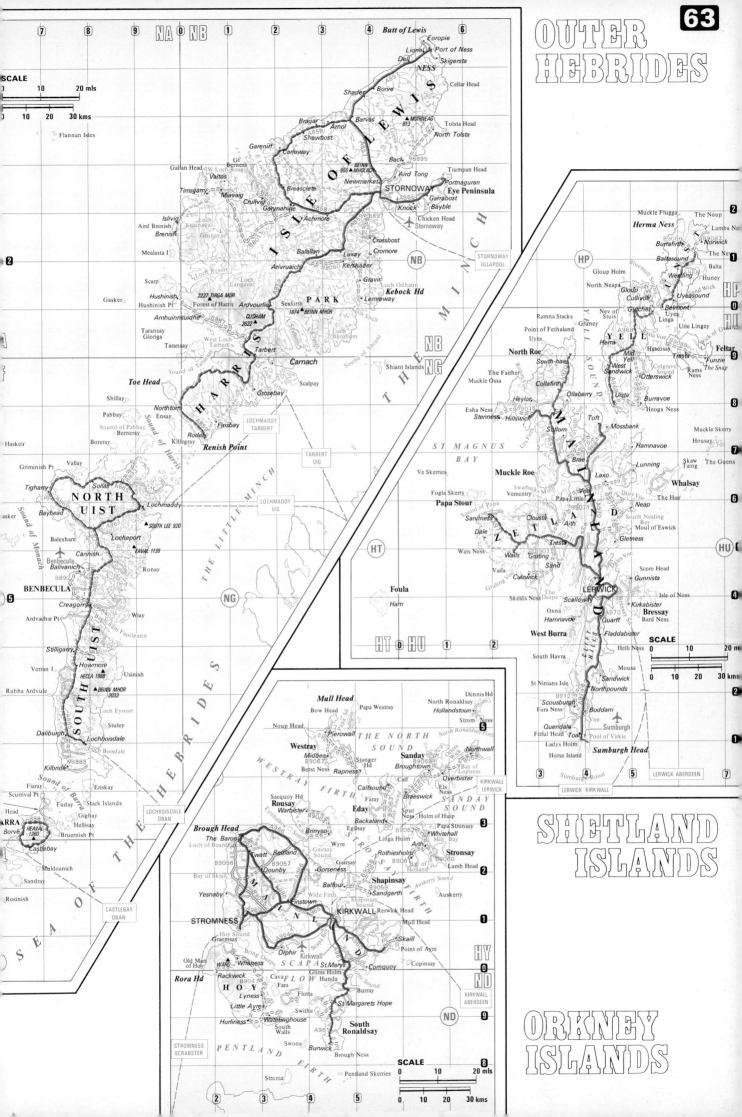

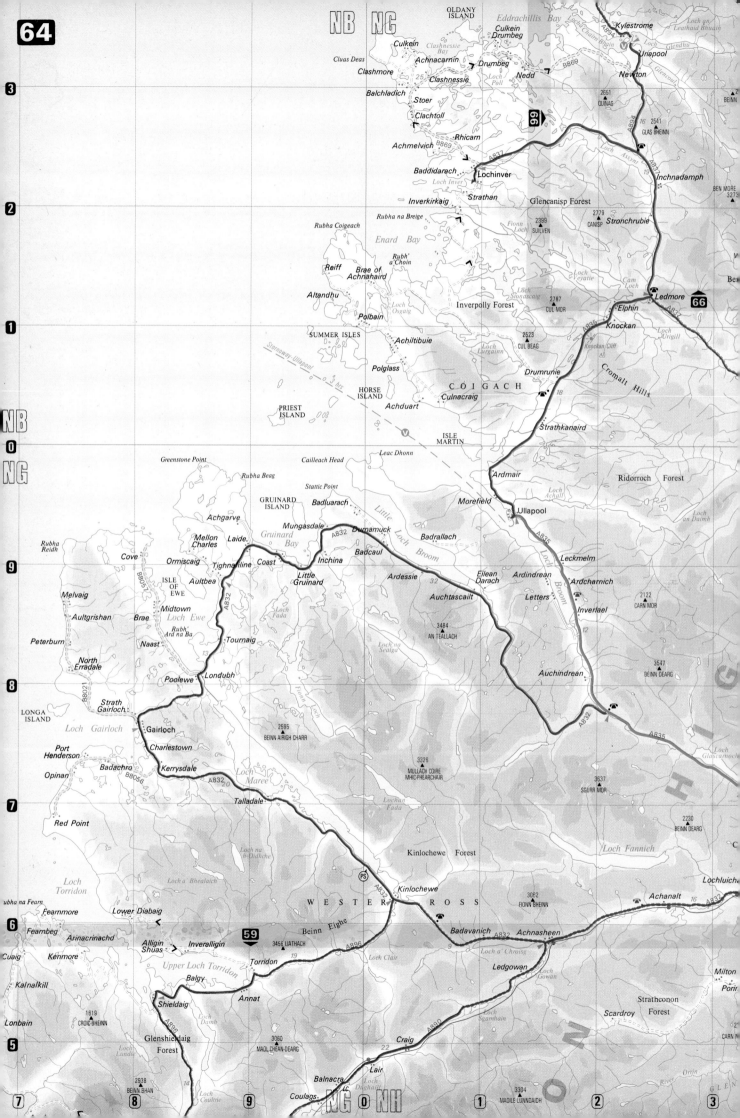

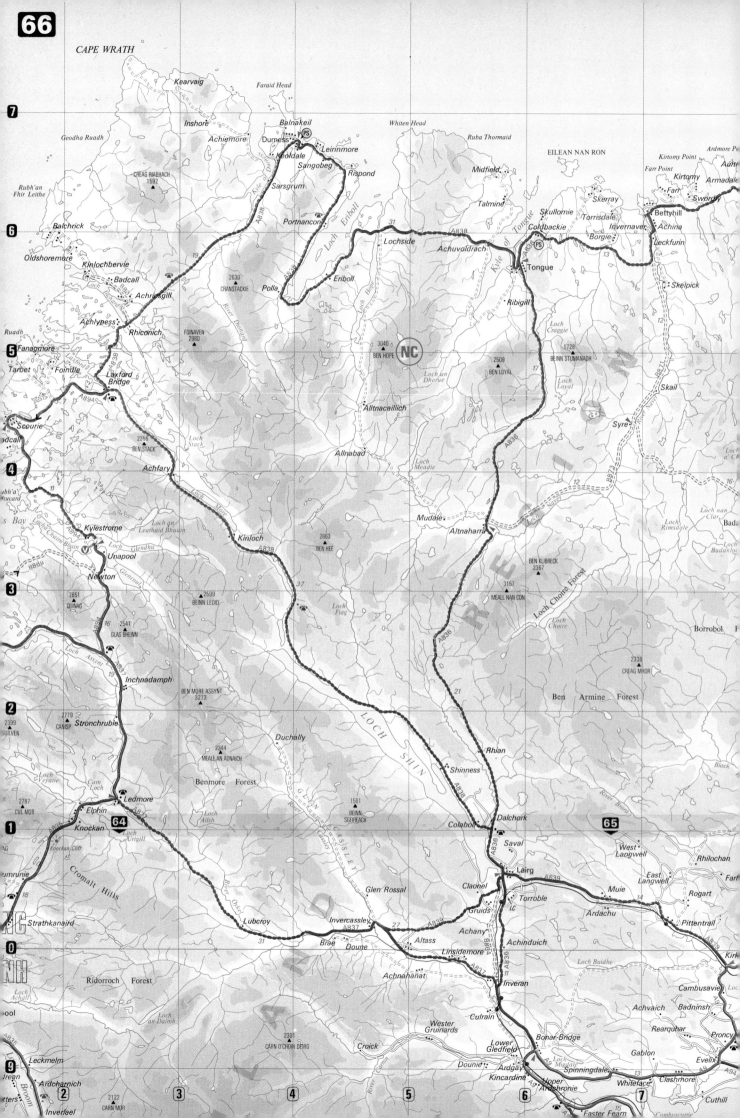

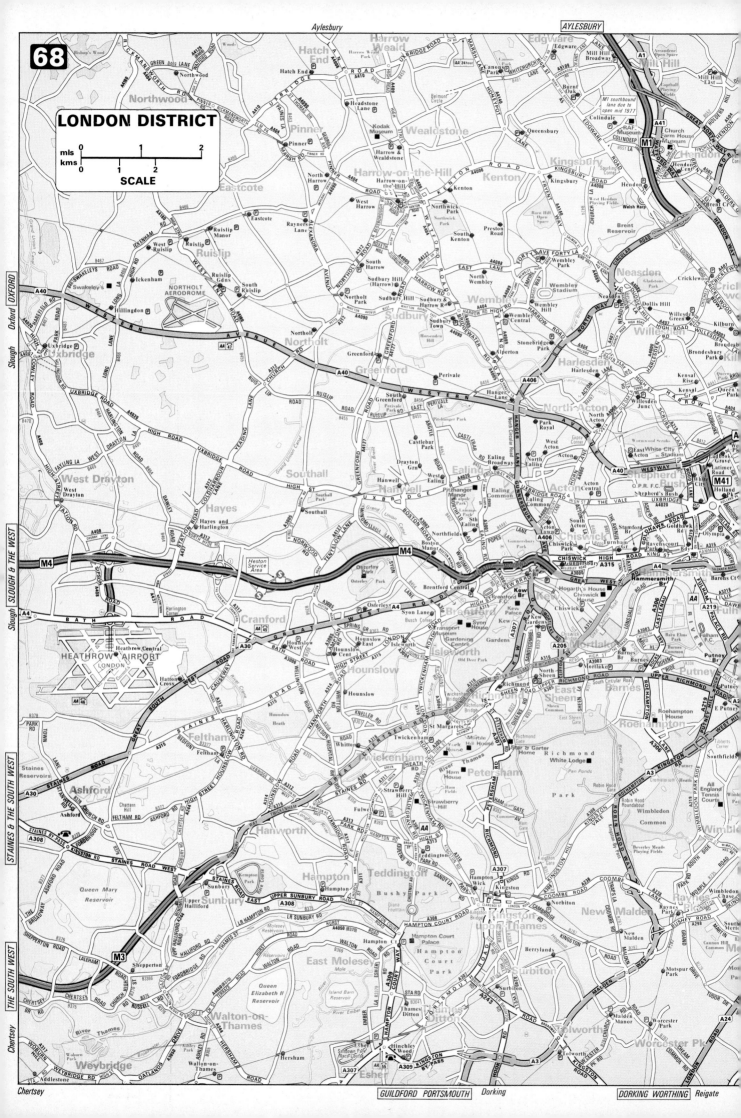

INNER LONDON

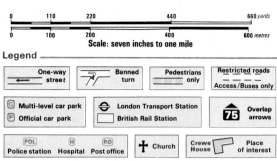

Legend

One-way street
Banned turn
Pedestrians only
Restricted roads — Access/Buses only

G Multi-level car park
P Official car park
London Transport Station
British Rail Station
75 Overlap arrows

POL Police station
H Hospital
P.O Post office
✝ Church
Crewe House — Place of interest

The one—way streets and banned turns shown on this map are in operation at time of going to press. Some of these are experimental and liable to change. Only the more important banned turns are shown, some of which operate between 7am and 7pm only, and these are sign—posted accordingly. No waiting or unilateral waiting restrictions apply to many streets. All such restrictions are indicated by official signs.

Key to Pages

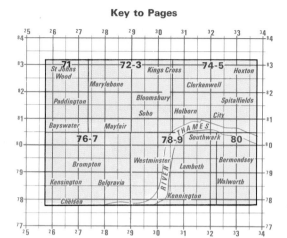

	St Johns Wood	Marylebone	Kings Cross	Clerkenwell	Hoxton
71		72-3		74-5	
	Paddington	Bloomsbury	Holborn	Spitalfields	
		Soho		City	
	Bayswater	Mayfair			
		76-7	78-9	Southwark	80
	Brompton	Westminster	Lambeth	Bermondsey	
	Kensington	Belgravia		Walworth	
	Chelsea		Kennington		

THEATRELAND

| 0 | 110 | 220 yards |
| 0 | 100 | 200 metres |

Scale

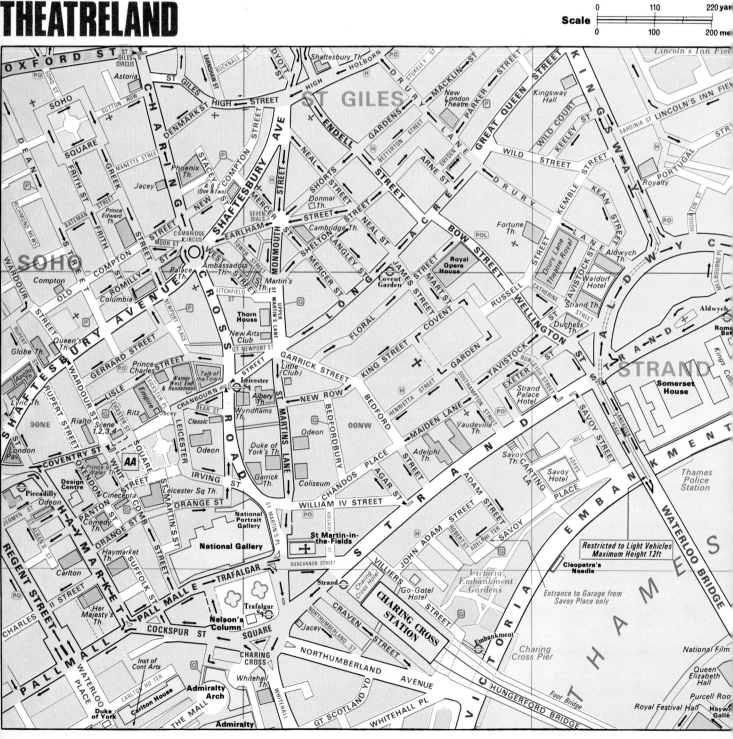

KEY TO TOWN PLANS

Figures in red denote page numbers

Recommended route	
Other roads	
Restricted roads (Access only/Buses only)	
Traffic roundabout	
Official car park free (Open air)	P
Multi-storey car park	G
Parking available on payment (Open air)	P
Parking Zone	
One-way street	←
Pedestrians only	
Convenience	C
Convenience with facilities for the disabled	C &
Tourist Information Centre	i

Inverness
97

Aberdeen
82

Dundee
92

Perth
108

Glasgow
95

Edinburgh
93

Ayr
83

Stranraer
111

Newcastle
upon Tyne
106

Carlisle
89

Sunderland
115

Stockton-on-Tees
114

Middlesbrough
102

Kendal
99

Scarborough
111

York
119

Blackpool
85

Bradford
83

Leeds
99

Hull
98

Liverpool
101

Manchester
103

Grimsby
96

Sheffield
112

Lincoln
99

Holyhead
97

Chester
89

Stoke-on-Trent
& Hanley
114

Derby
91

Nottingham
107

Norwich
105

Great Yarmouth
94

Aberystwyth
82

Leicester
100

Wolverhampton
119

Birmingham
84

Coventry
90

Northampton
105

Cambridge
88

Ipswich
98

Stratford-upon-Avon
115

Luton
100

Harwich &
Parkeston
96

Gloucester
90

Oxford
107

Chelmsford
89

Swansea
116

Southend-on-Sea
112

Cardiff
88

Swindon
116

Reading
110

District 68-69
Central 71-80

LONDON

Margate
102

Bristol
86

Bath
83

Guildford
96

Medway Towns
104
Chatham
Gillingham
Rochester

Ramsgate
110

Maidstone
100

Barnstaple
82

Taunton
117

Salisbury
111

Winchester
117

Folkestone
94

Dover
91

Southampton
113

Chichester
90

Brighton
85

Hastings
97

Exeter
92

Bournemouth
87

Poole
87

Portsmouth
109

Weymouth
115

Torquay
Paignton
Brixham

Torbay
118

Plymouth
108

Penzance
108

SCALE

mls 0   30   60

kms 0   50   100

ABERDEEN

This ancient Royal Burgh is an important centre of commerce and education, and has the largest fishing port in Scotland. Its unofficial title 'The Granite City' was earned by the extensive and generally pleasing use of local stone in its construction, but it could equally well be called the 'Floral City'. The outstanding skill of the city's gardeners and park keepers is evident in almost every street. Aberdeen's situation makes it an ideal touring base.

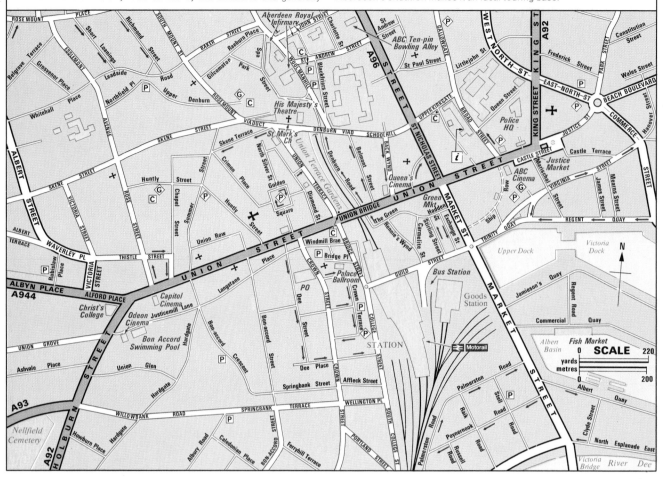

ABERYSTWYTH

Holiday resort and the seat of several government departments, this venerable Welsh town was founded *circa* 1277 and is a centre for Cambrian art and culture.

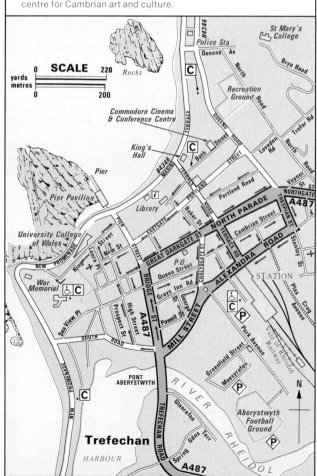

BARNSTAPLE

Possibly the oldest borough in England, this wool town has been the administrative centre of North Devon since Saxon times. It is pleasingly sited between the rivers Taw and Yeo.

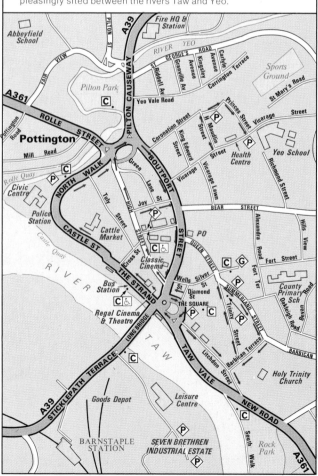

83

AYR

Excellent beaches and an attractive old-town layout are the main features of this popular Ayr Bay resort. Its situation in the heart of the 'Burns Country' makes it the ideal base from which devotees of the poet's work can make pilgrimages to his favourite places. The town's importance as a fishing centre is underlined by the activity of its busy fishing harbour, while its function as a holiday centre is complemented by the golf courses of nearby Prestwick and Troon.

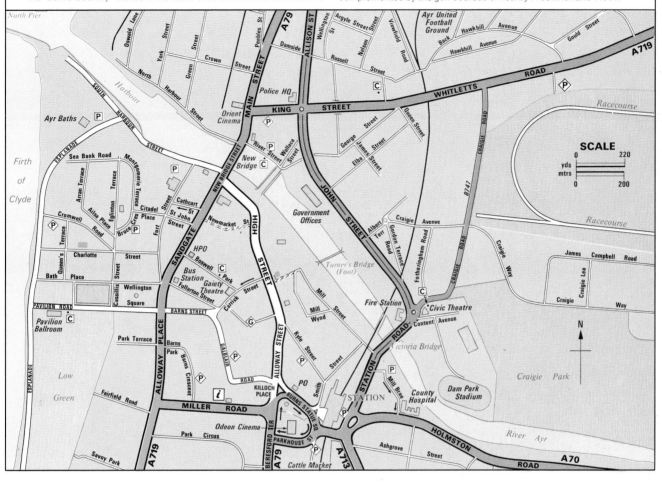

BATH

The high popularity of this town in Regency times has left it with a superb legacy of some of the finest period architecture in Britain. Its spa waters are said to be curative.

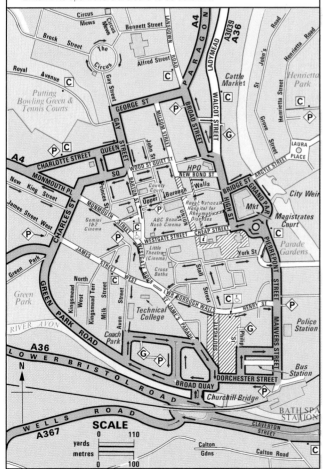

BRADFORD

In 1920 the parish church of this old wool and worsted centre was made a cathedral, and in 1966 the Bradford Institute of Technology was raised to university status.

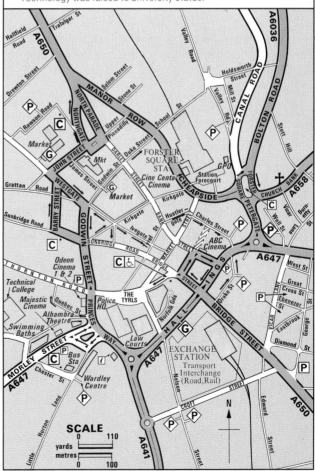

BIRMINGHAM

Much of this city's industrial success has grown out of its proximity to the rich mineral deposits of central England. As an early manufacturing community it boasted a large population of smiths, who settled because of the availability of coal. Later developments included gun making and brass founding. Today the city is second only to London in size, and operates a vast diversity of industries ranging from car manufacture to jewellery making.

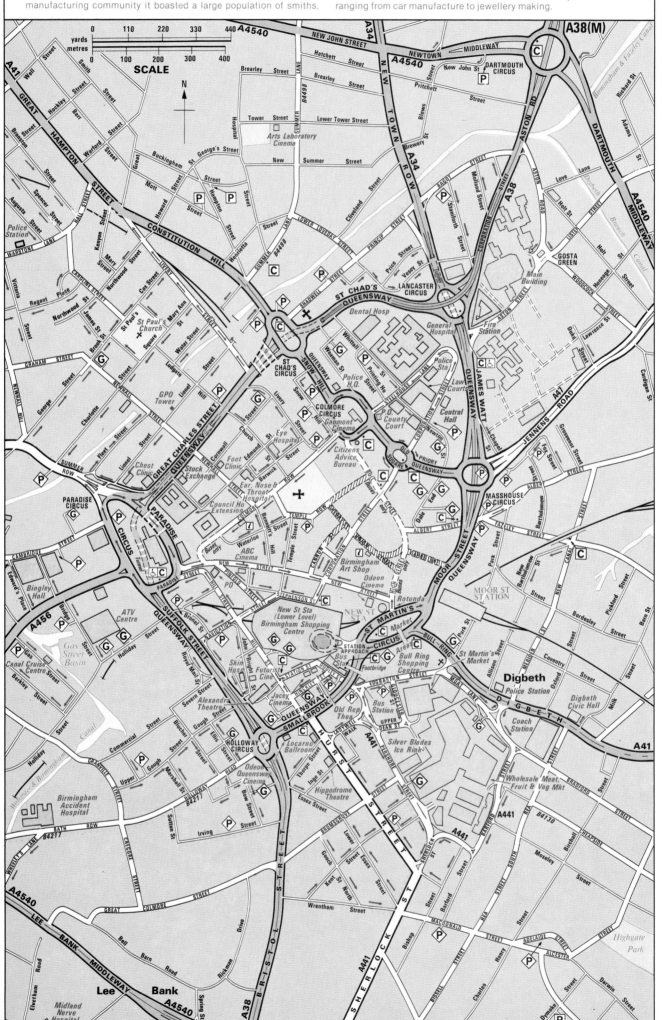

BLACKPOOL

Generations of Lancastrians, and indeed many other north-countrymen, have had a special affection for this famous holiday resort. Its development into a recreation centre began during the mid 18th-century vogue for 'bracing climates', and nowadays the town's resident population is swelled by several million visitors every summer. Good beaches offer safe bathing, and the famous Golden Mile is packed with a bewildering variety of funfair distractions.

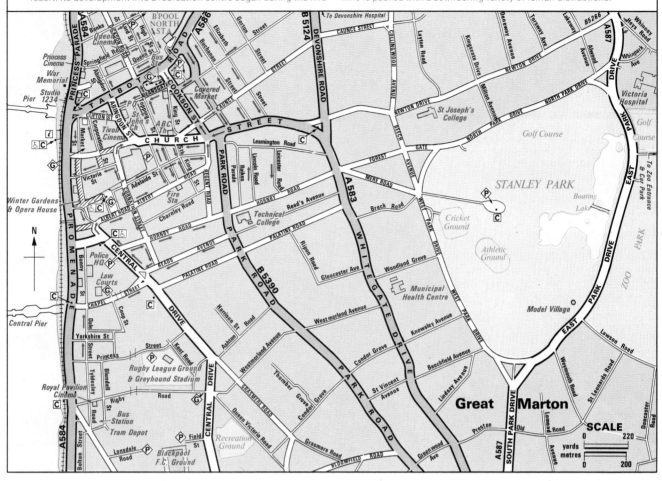

BRIGHTON

In Victorian times the pebble beach at Brighton, overlooked by terraces of trim Regency hotels, was very popular with enthusiasts of the current stone-collecting trend. Nowadays the resort is noted for its fashionable shops and leisure facilities, and is developing as an important conference and exhibition centre. The picturesque Lanes are eccentric little alleys that pre-date much of the town and are crowded with fascinating shops.

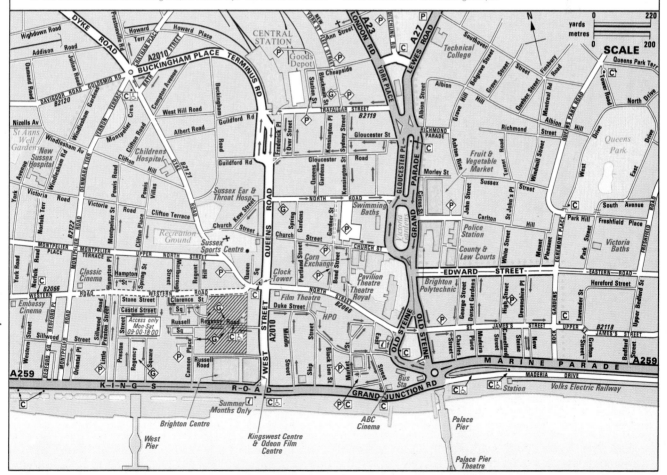

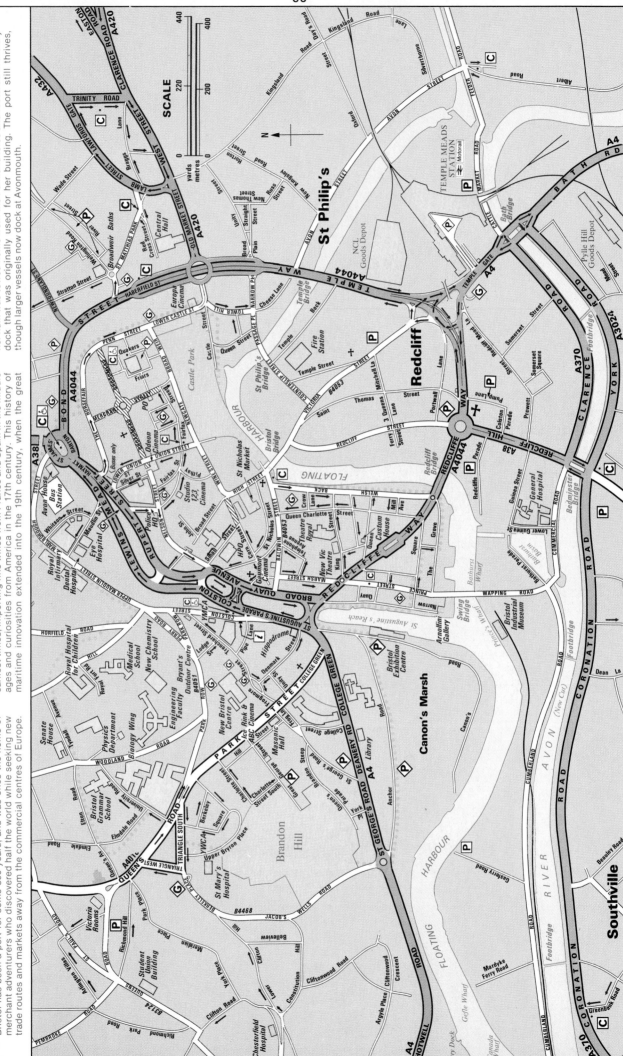

BRISTOL

Bristol has been a port for some 800 years, and was once the home of merchant adventurers who discovered half the world while seeking new trade routes and markets away from the commercial centres of Europe.

Merchant vessels from the port have plyed the oceans of the world since earliest times, importing fine wines from France and Spain in the middle ages and curiosities from America in the 17th century. This history of maritime innovation extended into the 19th century, when the great engineer Brunel designed his famous iron ship *SS Great Britain*. In 1970 her hulk was towed home from the Falkland Isles and restored in the dry dock that was originally used for her building. The port still thrives, though larger vessels now dock at Avonmouth.

BOURNEMOUTH & POOLE

Urban development has linked the genteel resort and retirement town of Bournemouth with neighbouring Poole, a busy port with developing industrial interests, but the two remain essentially different in character.

On either side of Bournemouth are high sandstone cliffs split by deep chines offering wooded paths to the beach. Poole harbour is a haven for craft of all sizes and has numerous creeks bordered by countryside and saltflats rich in many species of wildlife.

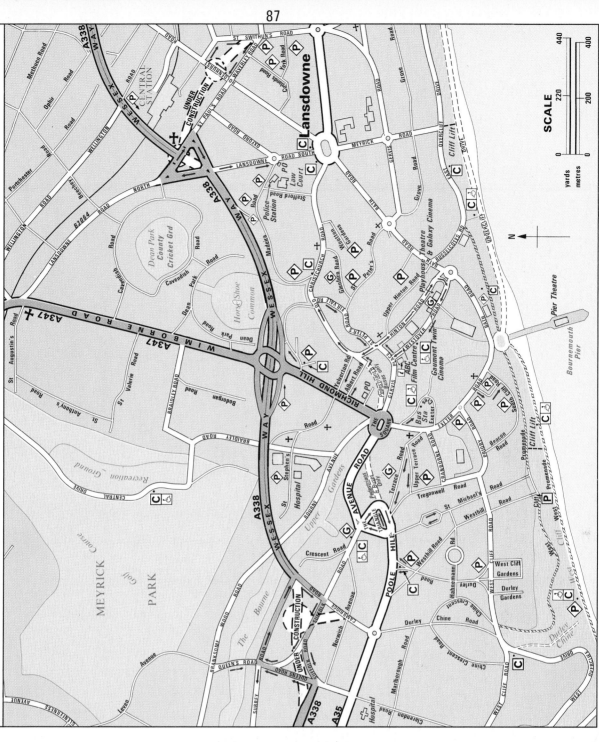

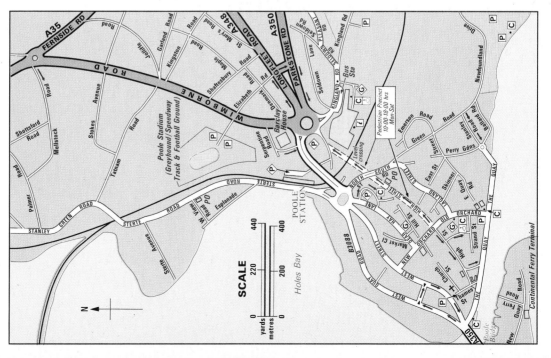

CAMBRIDGE

Settlements have existed on the strategic Cambridge site since prehistoric times. Various invaders, including Romans, Danes and Normans, recognised the importance of the ford that enabled the Cam to be crossed at this point, and of the river itself as a highway into the Fens. The origins of Cambridge University are hidden in church politics of the early 13th century, but the first foundation is thought to have resulted from a migration of scholars from Oxford.

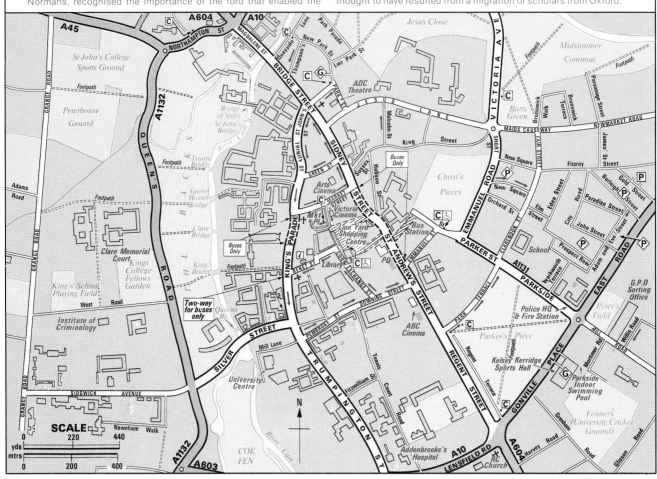

CARDIFF

The history of this large industrial seaport can be traced back at least as far as Roman times, and is thought to extend much farther. In 1955 Queen Elizabeth II created it the capital of Wales, and as befits such status the town is the home of many national institutions. Cardiff's industry does not intrude on the town centre, which presents a pleasing collection of quaint arcades and streets dominated by a fine castle standing in extensively wooded grounds.

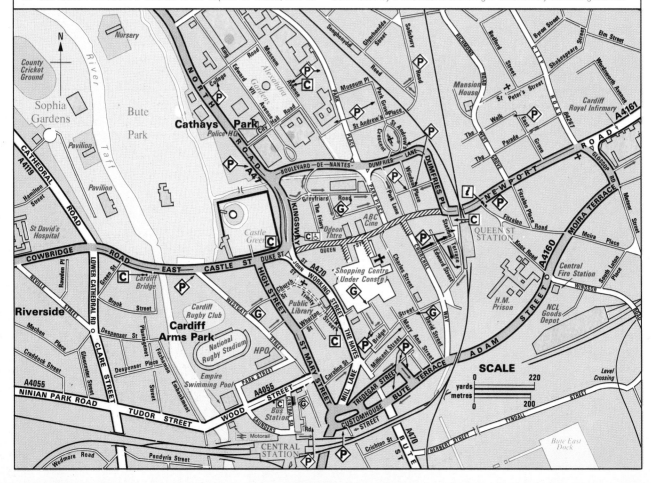

CARLISLE

This town owes its importance to Roman recognition of its strategic value in the fight against Scotland. It is an excellent base from which to tour the Border Country.

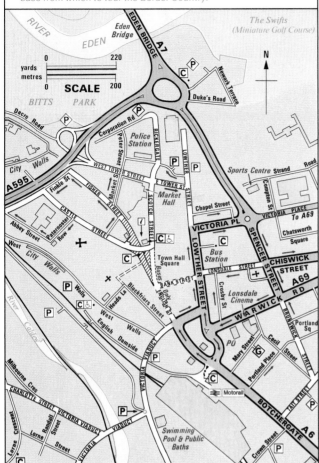

CHELMSFORD

The rivers Chelmer and Can split this farming and industrial centre into three sectors. Bridges that link the areas combine with old buildings to form an attractive townscape.

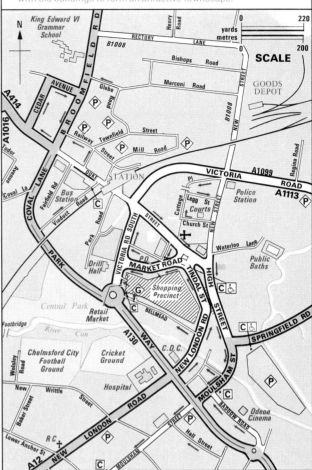

CHESTER

Ancient town walls, numerous timbered buildings and a basic road pattern that was originally laid down by the Romans help to preserve the distinctly medieval appearance of this town. Up until the 15th century Chester was a seaport, but severe silting in the River Dee forced traffic to the coastal village of Liverpool. At one point the town walls overlook the Roodee racecourse, where the Chester Cup has been run every year since 1540.

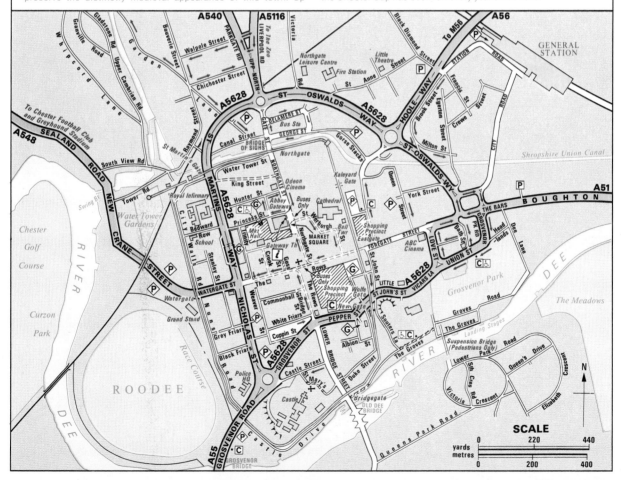

CHICHESTER

Well situated between the end of the South Downs and the wooded creeks of Chichester Harbour, this town has many fine buildings and is a good touring centre for West Sussex.

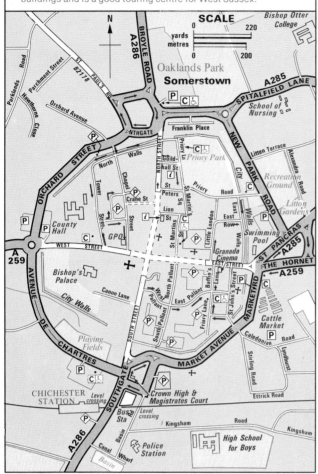

GLOUCESTER

A 19th-century canal that links Gloucester with the Bristol Channel virtually makes the city a seaport. Industrial developments do not overpower the town's good features.

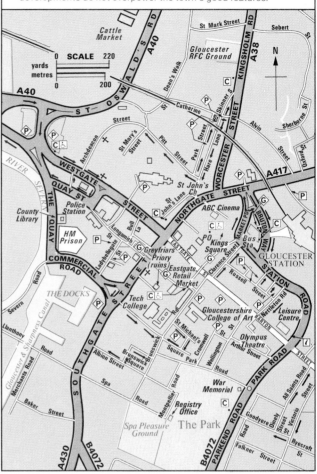

COVENTRY

Apalling war damage sustained in bombing raids aimed at munitions factories during the last war gave Coventry the chance to redevelop its centre almost from scratch. The new cathedral, joined to the ruined old building, is a symbol of the regeneration that has once more made the city a place of industrial and commercial significance. Engineering works here produce a variety of commodities used in the massive automobile industry.

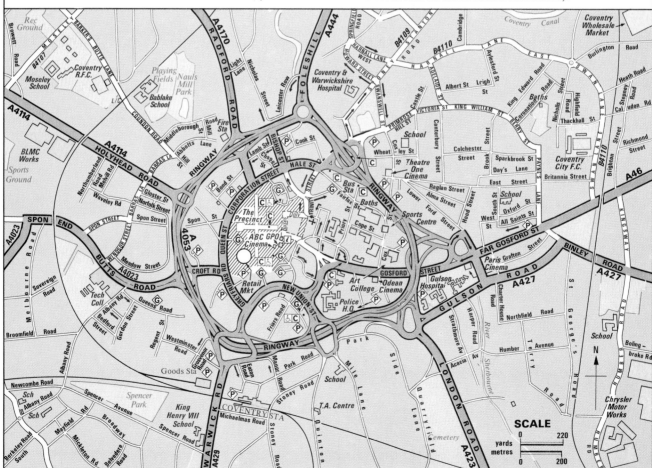

DERBY

During the 18th century Derby's evolution to industrial wealth was begun by the establishment of silk mills. Later years saw the building of large locomotive and coach works by the Midland Railway, the deserved rise to fame of Crown Derby porcelain, and the expansion of factories owned by the Rolls Royce Company. A statue raised to engineer Sir Henry Royce can be seen in the Arboretum Park. North east of Derby is the beautiful Peak District National Park.

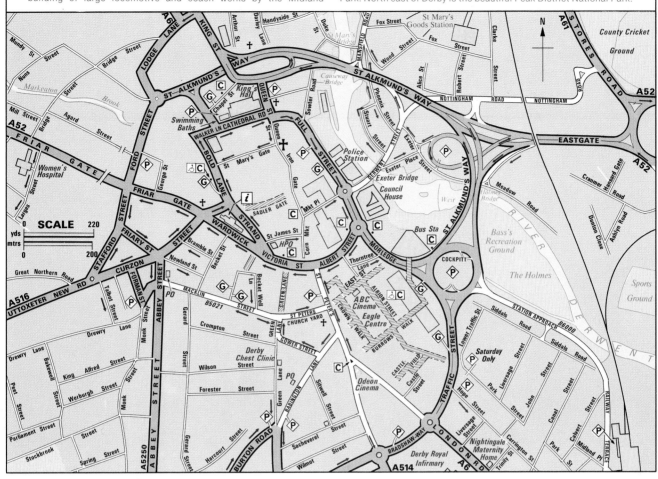

DOVER

This famous cross-Channel port lies along a narrow cleft between towering chalk cliffs that mark the end of the North Downs. The marks of war are all around the town and surrounding countryside, but most of these were made by the defenders and include gun mounts, camps, pill boxes, and the like. The cliffs on the east side of the town afford superb views of channel shipping and the hovercraft terminal; inland are the battlemented towers of Dover Castle.

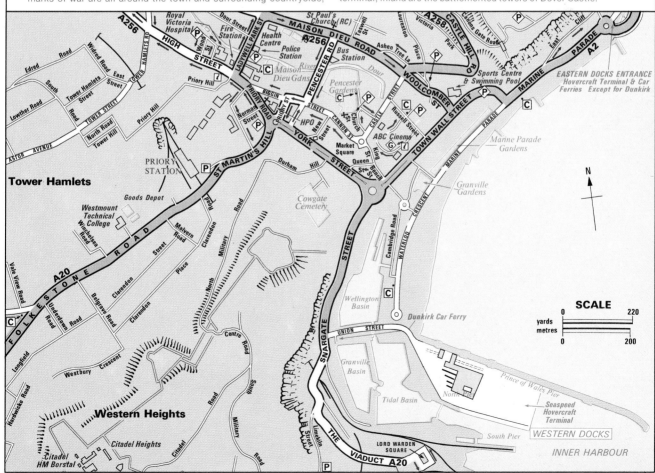

DUNDEE

A Royal Burgh since 1190 and Scotland's fourth largest city, Dundee stands on the Firth of Tay and has a dock area that covers more than 35 acres. Early industry included whaling and the production of jute material, while nearby Carse of Gowrie supplied fruit for a local preserve making concern. Mrs Keiller started making her famous marmalade in 1797. Modern Dundee, extensively redeveloped and expanded since World War II, operates considerable light industry.

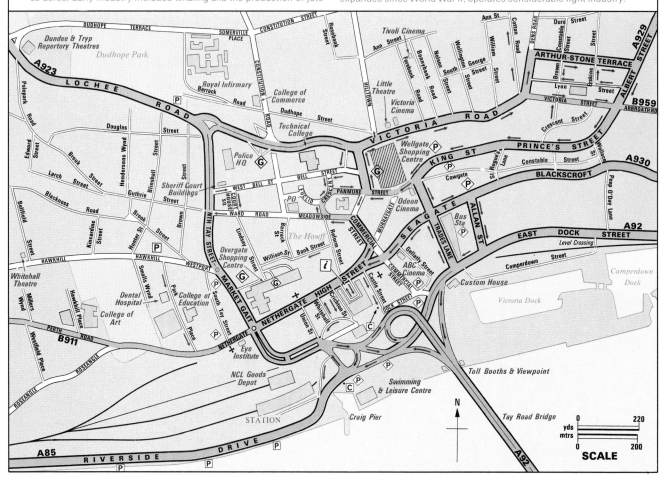

EXETER

It could almost be said that Exeter is two cities. High above the Exe on the north side of the valley are colourful modern shopping developments and spacious piazzas, while in the valley bottom older houses and commercial buildings cluster in hilly streets leading to the river. The Exe itself has a splendid old wharf which includes stores and workshops cut out of the red riverside sandstone. Various new waterside developments exist.

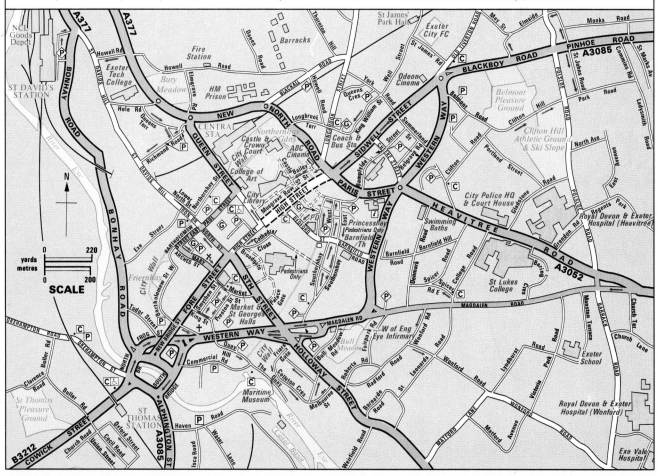

EDINBURGH

Rightly famous for its many beautiful parks and public open spaces, this city succeeded Perth as the capital of Scotland in the 15th century and has retained that status in one form or another ever since. The medieval part of the town developed along a windy ridge between the castle and Holyrood Abbey, an unusual location for the period, and later expansion extended coastwards to encompass the port of Leith. Leith's rise to prosperity and the building of New Town took place in the late 18th century. At the same time Nor' Loch was drained and bridged, leaving a chasm which still shows the division between the Old and New towns. Edinburgh later blossomed as one of Europe's cultural centres, and today the city is a world-famous centre of education, arts, and the law.

SCALE

440 ___ 400

yds 0 ___ 200 ___ 400
mtrs 0

N

FOLKESTONE

Cross-Channel steamers operate from this popular holiday resort. The town shows considerable post-war rebuilding, but the older area near the harbour is still picturesque and preserves many old structures. Local fishing boats bring their catches into the harbour for sale at the Fish Market. Attractive countryside around Folkestone includes The Leas, a grassy clifftop promenade connected to good beaches by wooded walks. The Warren nature reserve lies east.

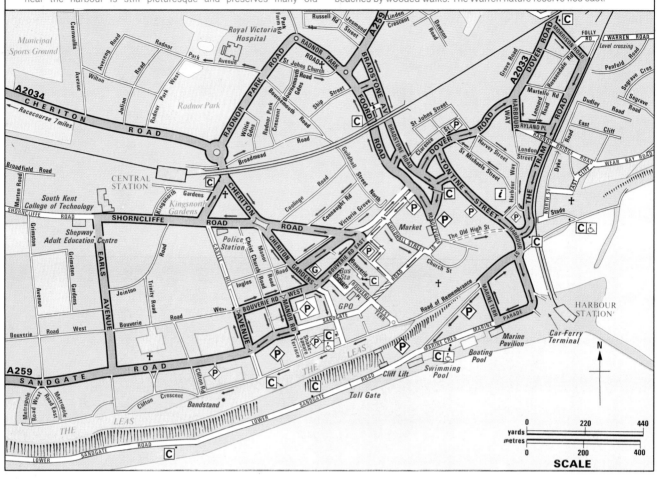

GREAT YARMOUTH

North sea oil has kept this a busy port since the decline of the herring fleet. Great Yarmouth is also a fine holiday resort offering sandy beaches along a 5 - mile seafront. Two piers offer a variety of entertainments, and the beach is backed by swimming pools, bowling greens and similar amusements interspersed with ornamental gardens. The peninsula on which the town stands was formed by the gradual silting of a giant three river estuary.

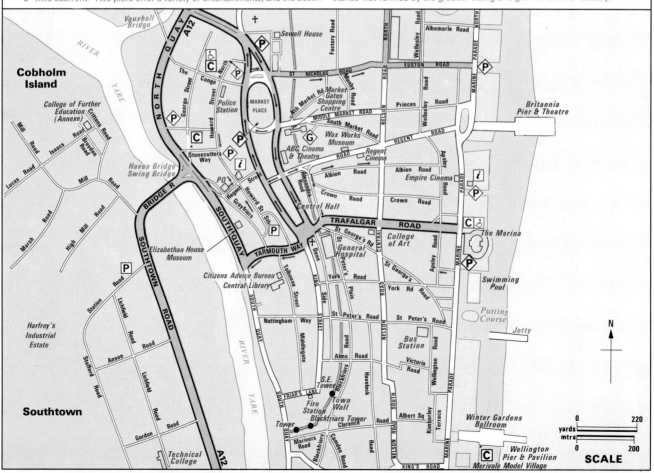

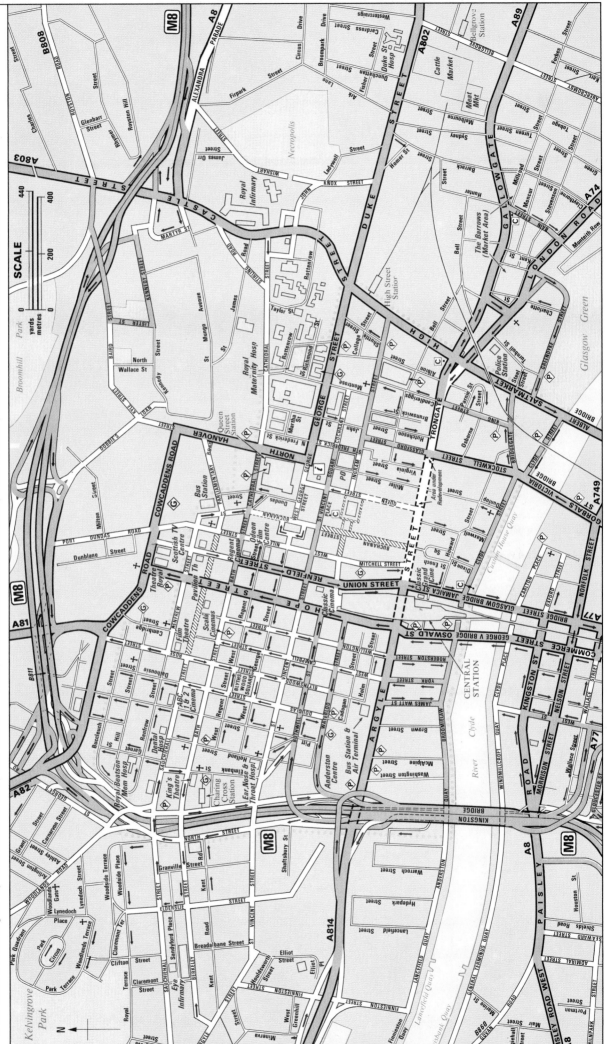

GLASGOW

After the Industrial Revolution Glasgow grew with astonishing speed to become one of the major centres of shipbuilding and heavy engineering in the world. It is the largest city in Scotland, but its upward rush to wealth left scars on itself and the small hamlets and villages that were quickly absorbed by its expanding boundaries. Not the least of these scars were the infamous slums that are being cleared to make room for clean, modern estates and sensible road systems. In recent years there has been a marked run down of the city's more traditional enterprises, and a notable increase in the number of light industries that have moved into the area to fill the gap. The city is fortunate in having many attractive and well-designed parks.

GRIMSBY

This is Britain's national fishing centre. Its fish market is one of the largest in the world and adjoins freezing and curing facilities for treating the catch as soon as it is unloaded.

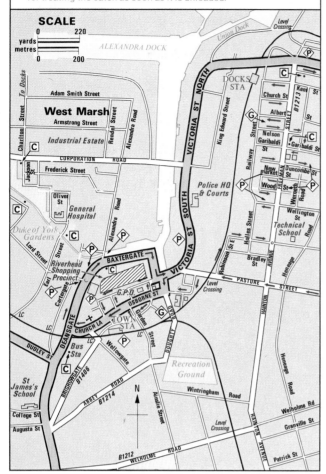

GUILDFORD

Several interesting old buildings have survived the recent modernization of this River Wey Town, including a medieval guildhall and 16th-century grammar school. Stag Hill is topped by Sir Edward Maufe's 20th-century cathedral.

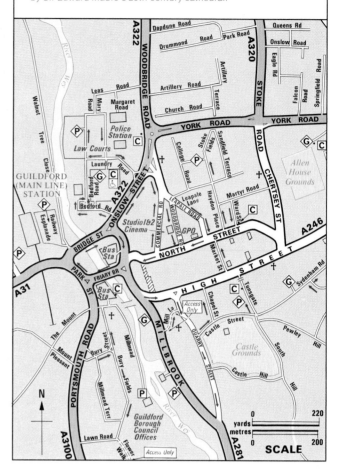

HARWICH & PARKESTON

Harwich stands on a hook of land that extends into a large harbour created by the combining of the Stour and Orwell estuaries. It is an important seaport handling many different types of vessel, from pleasure craft to large Continental traffic, and has close connexions with its sister communities of Parkeston and Dovercourt. Parkeston Quay faces the Stour estuary and deals with the larger craft.

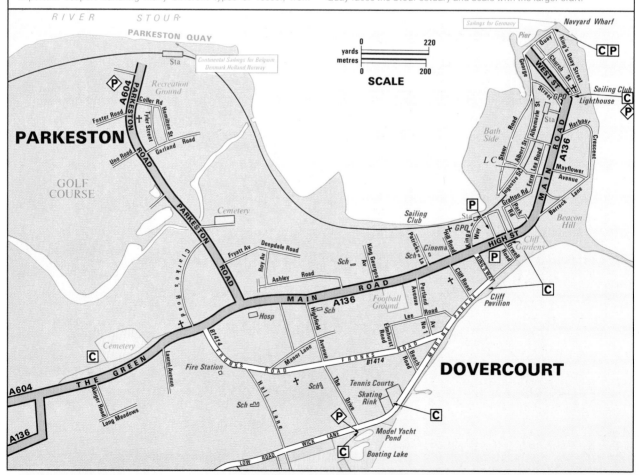

HASTINGS

The twin resorts of Hastings and St Leonards offer 5 miles of shingle beach, with sand at low tide, and good facilities for a variety of sports and amusements. An area known as Old Town lies between East Hill and West Hill, and preserves a number of interesting old houses dominated by the ruins of an 11th-century Norman castle. The Battle of Hastings (1066) was actually fought inland at Battle.

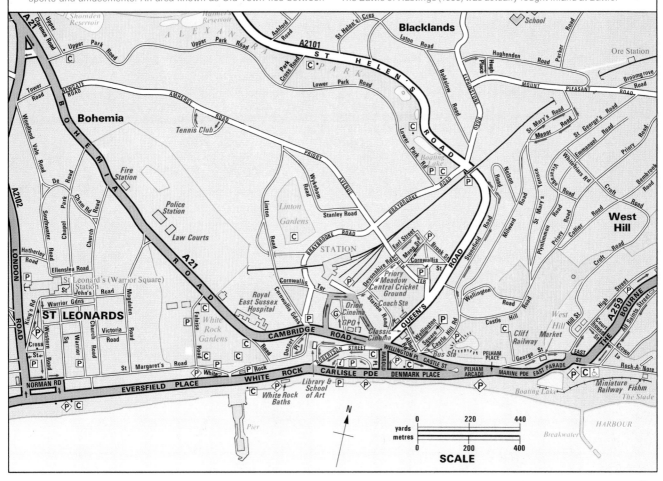

HOLYHEAD

One of Britain's largest passenger ports and the Isle of Anglesy's largest town, Holyhead has survived as the main sea link with Eire despite determined takeover attempts by other termini.

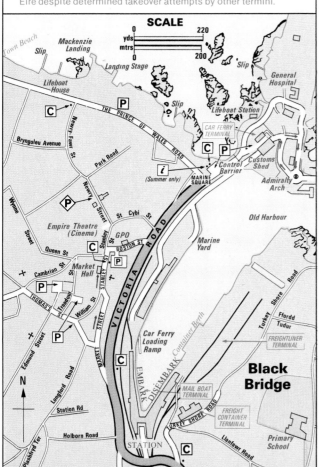

INVERNESS

Attractive and historic Inverness has been dubbed 'The Capital of The Highlands'. It stands at the north-east end of Glen More on the salmon-rich River Ness, near mysterious Loch Ness.

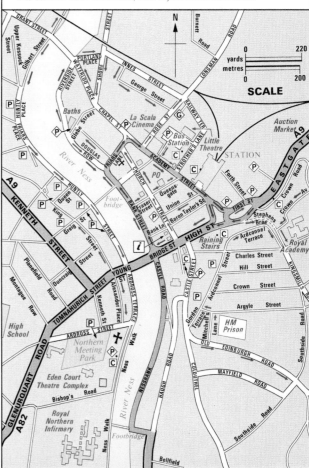

HULL

The name by which this important fishing port is generally known is an abbreviated form of the official designation, which is Kingston-upon-Hull. The town stands at the confluence of the River Hull and the giant Humber estuary, and has port facilities that occupy more than 7 miles of shore and make this one of the premier dock complexes of its type in the world. On-shore processing plants for all types of cargo save time between ship and user.

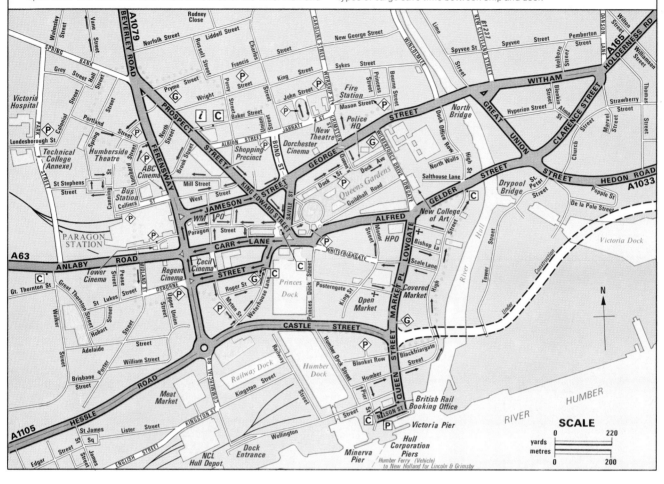

IPSWICH

This thriving port and agricultural centre for East Suffolk stands at the head of the Orwell estuary in largely unspoilt East Anglian countryside. Its maritime activities, through which a long and close association with the Continent has been developed, are now supplemented by light industry. Much of the town's historic past is reflected in the numerous old buildings that survive, and in the local-interest collections exhibited by its museums.

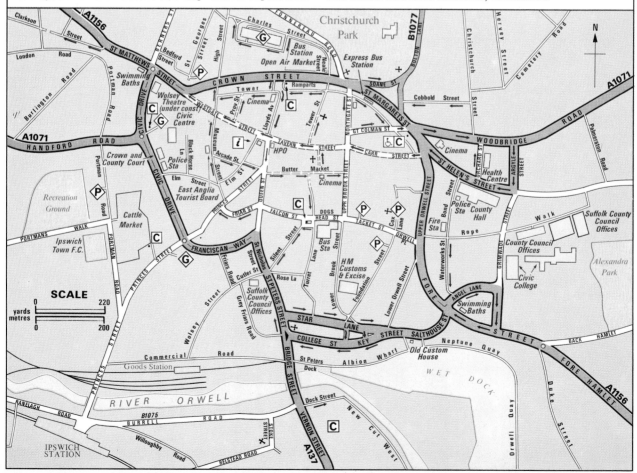

KENDAL

Situated on the southern edge of the Lake District National Park, this pleasant old town stands on the River Kent and makes an ideal base from which to tour Cumbria.

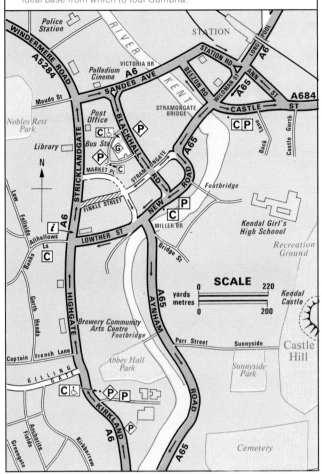

LINCOLN

Old Lincoln, a city of historic and architectural distinction, is built on a slope which rises from the River Witham to a summit crowned by the splendid 11th-century cathedral.

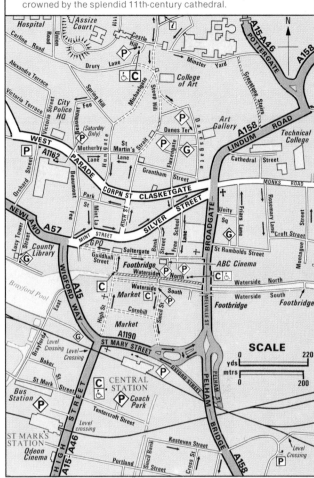

LEEDS

University city and an important manufacturing centre for a number of industries, Leeds has a superb 775-acre park (Roundhay) and preserves several interesting old buildings. Its Quarry Hill flats were one of the country's first large-scale residential complexes, but the town's progressiveness is tempered by a feeling for finer things. Two examples of the latter are the interesting art gallery and the famous triennial music festival. Many ancient buildings survive here.

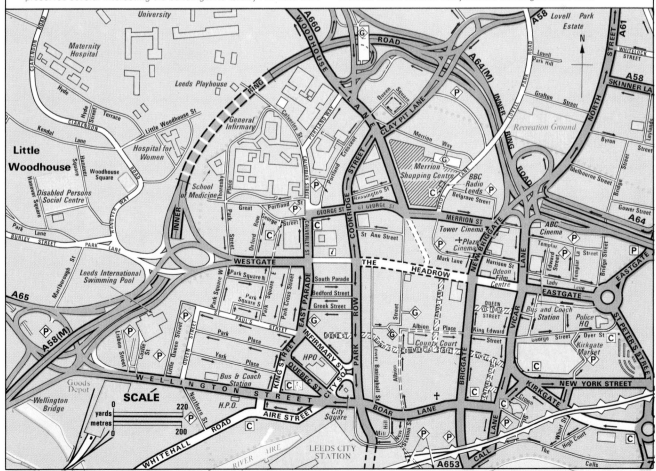

LEICESTER

Traditionally this large county town — a city since its parish church was raised to cathedral status in 1926 — is involved in the manufacture of footwear and hosiery. These old craft industries are now supplemented by light engineering, recent commercial interests, and various activities generated by the modern university. One of the most pleasant parts of the town is New Walk, a tree-shaded pavement bordered by Victorian lamposts.

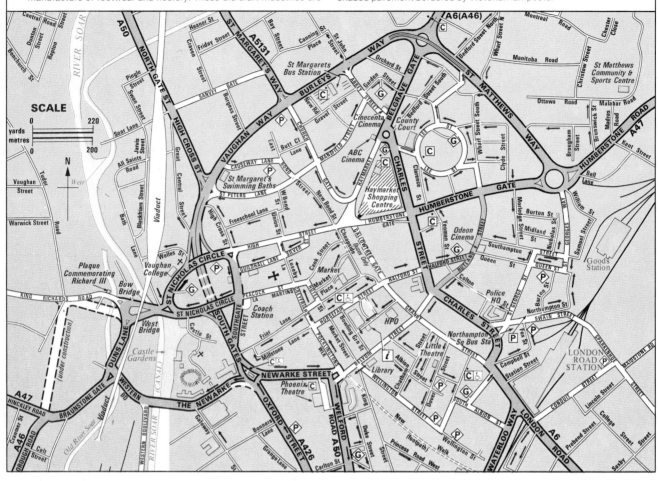

LUTON

Giant car works have made this Bedfordshire town famous as a manufacturing centre, and its airport is one of Great Britain's main termini for world and Continental traffic.

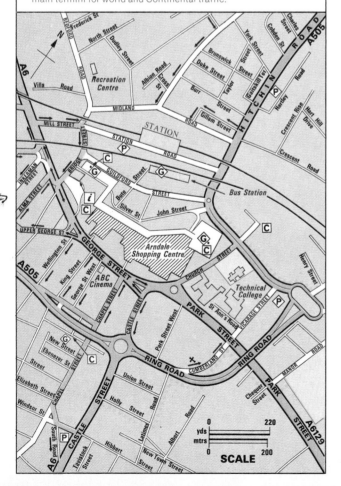

MAIDSTONE

This comfortable county town on the River Medway has a little light industry, but is still fulfills its traditional function as the main agricultural centre in Kent.

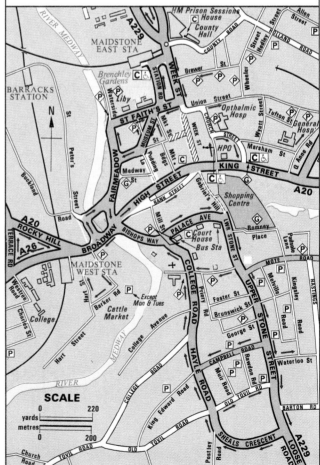

LIVERPOOL

At one time this world-famous port on the Mersey estuary was dwarfed to insignificance by the maritime importance of nearby Chester. This situation started to change as Chester became cut off from the sea by silting in the River Dee. Impetus was given to the port's development by rich West Indian traffic and the slave trade, then in the 19th century the introduction of steamships set the pattern for today. Liverpool's docks are among the world's finest.

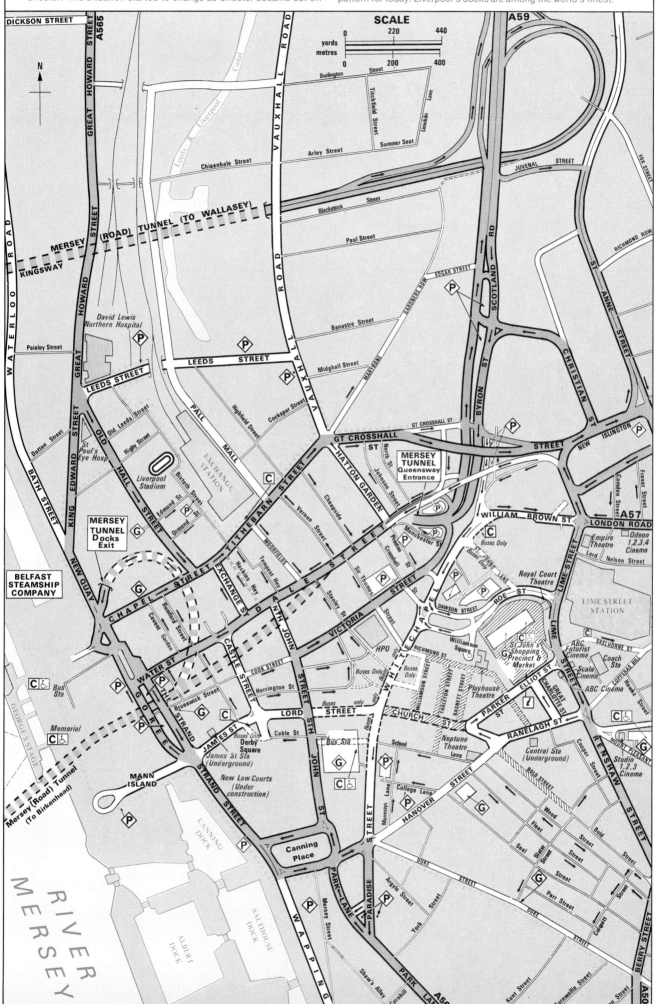

MARGATE

In some ways Margate is for Londoners what Blackpool is for north countrymen. It lies on the south shore of the Thames estuary, within easy reach of the capital, and offers excellent sands complemented by a variety of leisure amenities. The port's one-time importance has declined over the centuries, but this is easily compensated by the high popularity of the town as a resort. High chalk cliffs form impressive seascapes to the east and west.

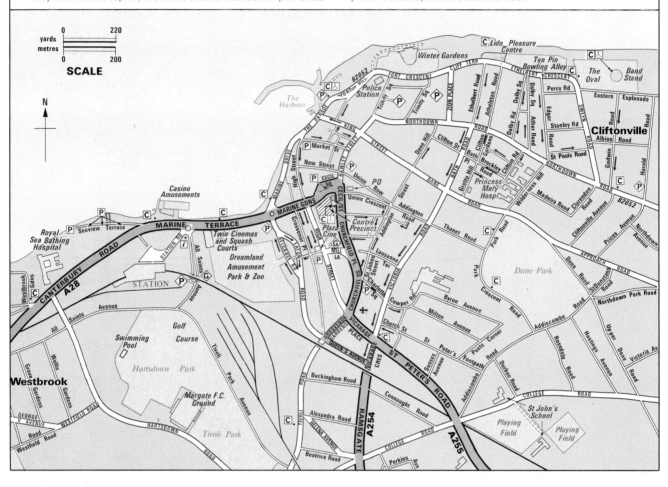

MIDDLESBROUGH

Most of the industry in this Tees-estuary town is involved in the production of iron and steel, or in cargo processing at the extensive dock installations. The development of the town is considered a remarkable example of rapid 19th-century growth, and the whole area is a rich hunting ground for the industrial archaeologist. Two items of particular interest are a vertical lift bridge of 1934 to the west, and a transporter bridge of 1911 over the Tees to the north.

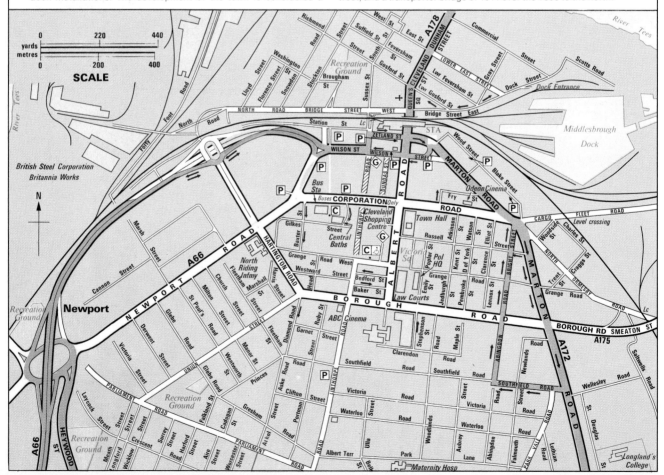

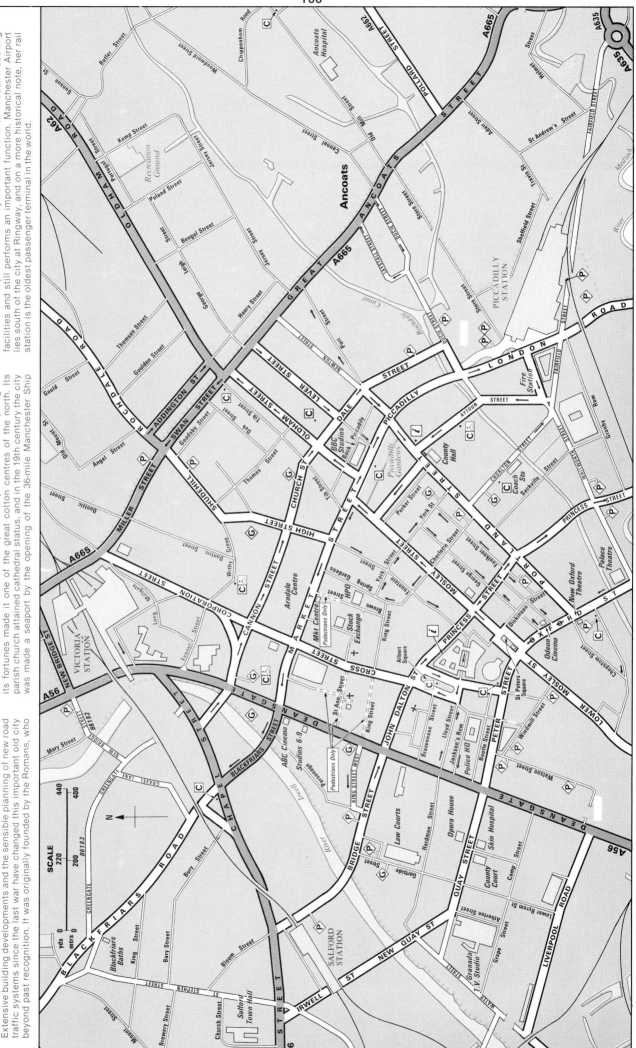

MANCHESTER

Extensive building developments and the sensible planning of new road traffic systems since the last war have changed this important old city beyond past recognition. It was originally founded by the Romans, who knew it as *Mancunium*, and developed slowly until a sudden upsurge in its fortunes made it one of the great cotton centres of the north. Its parish church attained cathedral status, and in the 19th century the city was made a seaport by the opening of the 36-mile Manchester Ship Canal. This important waterway is furnished with modern docking facilities and still performs an important function. Manchester Airport lies south of the city at Ringway, and on a more historical note, her rail station is the oldest passenger terminal in the world.

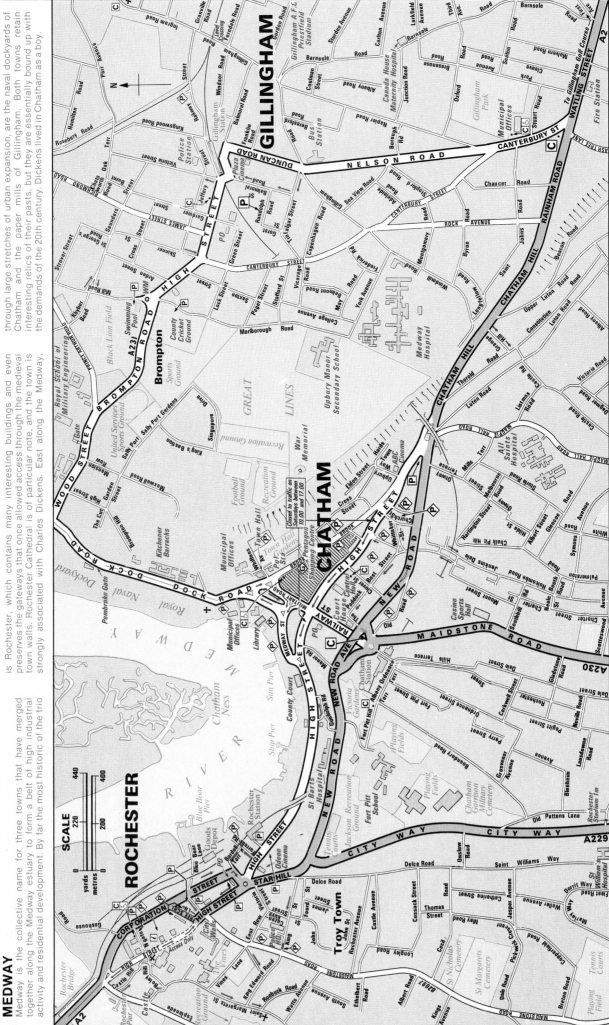

MEDWAY Medway is the collective name for three towns that have merged together along the Medway estuary to form a belt of high industrial activity and residential development. By far the most historic of the trio is Rochester, which contains many interesting buildings and even preserves the gateways that once allowed access through the medieval town walls. Rochester Cathedral is of particular note, and the town is strongly associated with Charles Dickens. East along the Medway, through large stretches of urban expansion, are the naval dockyards of Chatham and the paper mills of Gillingham. Both towns retain interesting relics of their pasts, but they are essentially bound up with the demands of the 20th century. Dickens lived in Chatham as a boy.

ROCHESTER

CHATHAM

GILLINGHAM

Troy Town

Brompton

NORTHAMPTON

The market square in this county town is the largest in England, and has been retained by developers to form a focal point for extensive New Town development. Much of this expansion has been necessary to absorb overspill from centres of high population, like London, and has included the introduction of light industry to supplement the town's traditional footwear concerns. Pleasant walks extend alongside the River Nene and through the town parks.

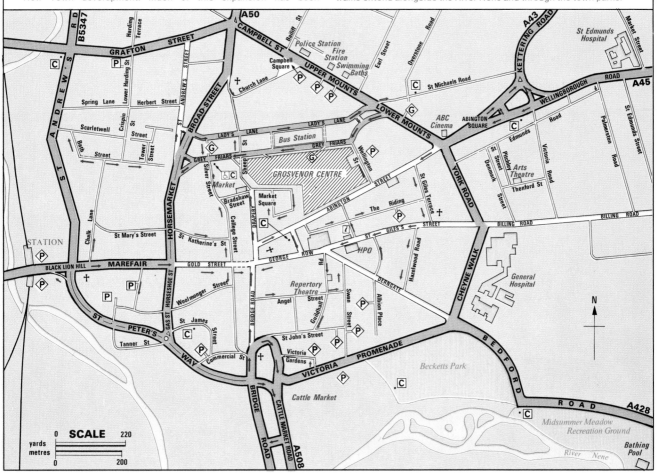

NORWICH

This city is the county town of Norfolk and stands on the River Wensum. During the great textiles boom enjoyed by England in the distant past it was an important centre of the worsted trade, but nowadays it specializes in footwear and has interests in various other industries. The recently-founded University of East Anglia is considered to be one of the best-designed complexes of its type built since the last war; it contrasts well with the Norman cathedral.

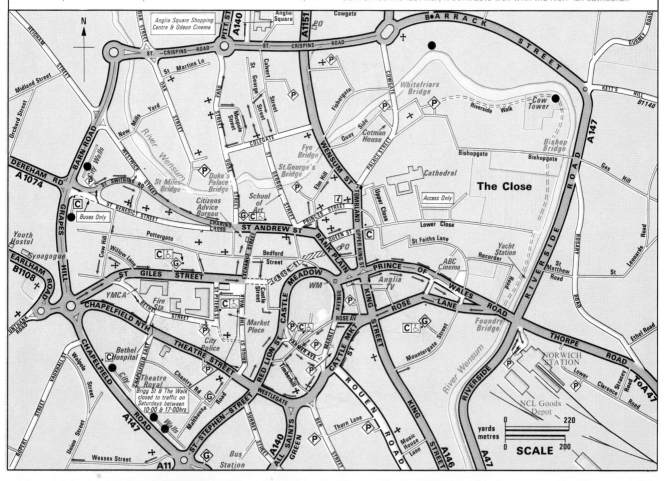

NEWCASTLE-UPON-TYNE

County town and a cathedral city, this important manufacturing centre is traditionally associated with the production of coal, armaments, ships and locomotives. Most of the old trades survive in some form or another, but nowadays they are supplemented by modern concerns such as electrical and petro-chemical works. The cultural cost of industrialization has not been too high here, and parts of the old town survive. Developments include a university.

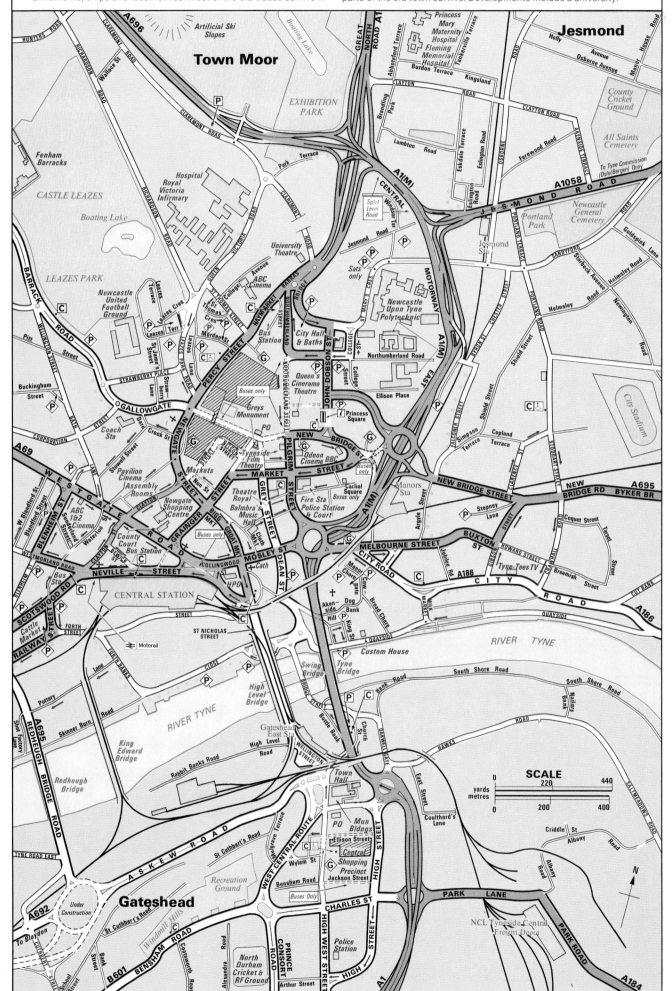

NOTTINGHAM

Early industry in Nottingham suffered severe setbacks at the hands of the anti-machine Luddites, but the local hosiery trade survived the vandalism of their gangs and is still in healthy operation alongside more recent concerns. The famous Nottingham Goose Fair is held in the Forest Recreation Ground during the first week in October. Pleasing modern designs complement the city's many ancient structures, and the River Trent forms a leisure facility to the south.

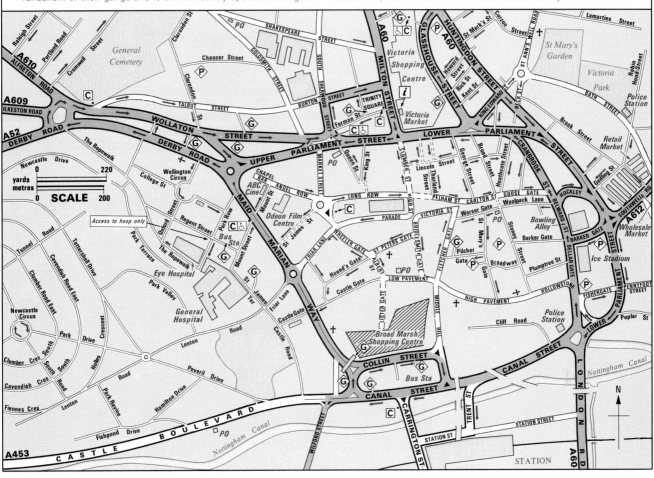

OXFORD

Central Oxford is a friendly combination of mellow stone and fashionable store fronts, where narrow college streets are crowded with students' bicycles and the air of ancient academicism can almost be touched. Outside the centre of town the picture changes dramatically, particularly towards Cowley and the huge British Motor Corporation Works that evolved from William Morris' cycle shop. The Thames, Cherwell, and the Oxford Canal run through the town.

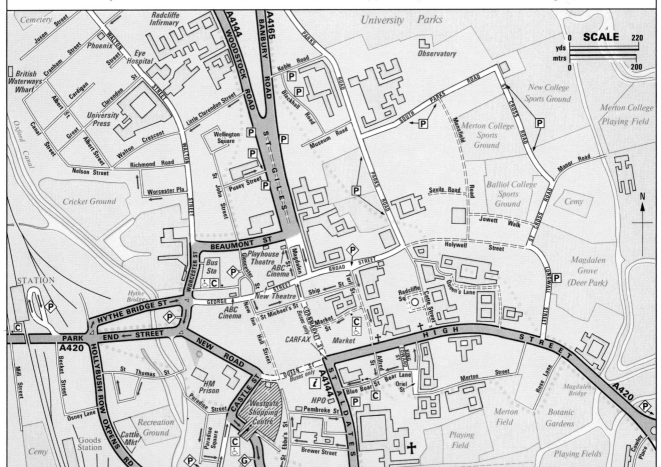

PENZANCE

This popular Mount's Bay holiday resort is situated on the Land's End peninsula of Cornwall, close to several areas designated as being of outstanding natural beauty.

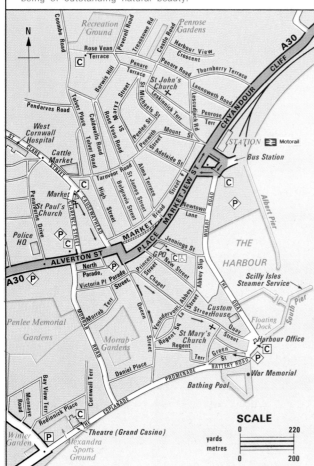

PERTH

One-time capital of Scotland and an historic Royal Burgh, the elegant city of Perth stands on the River Tay and is an ideal base from which to explore the Lowland hills.

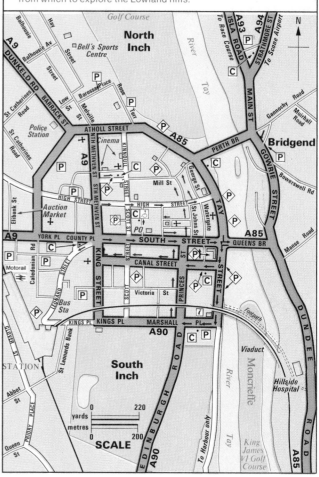

PLYMOUTH

Important naval station, seaport and dockyard. the Plymouth conurbation was largely raised from the ashes of World War II bombing raids and includes one of the finest shopping centres in the country. Several old buildings have survived as reminders of the pre-war town, and Drake's Island still rises from the Sound in much the same way as famous Sir Francis would have seen it while waiting for the Armada. Armada Way is a good example of town planning.

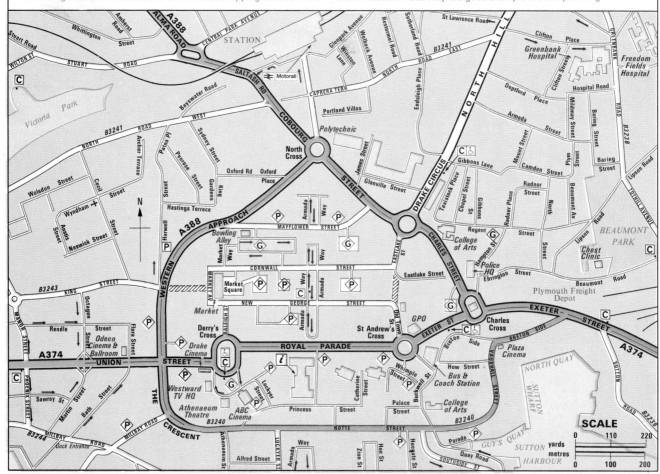

PORTSMOUTH

The Dockyard in Portsmouth comprises some 300 acres of buildings and installations, many of which date from the 18th century. Nelson's *Victory* is preserved here, and the town's present-day connexions with the Royal Navy are demonstrated by special dockyards and educational facilities. Ferry routes between Portsmouth, Gosport and the Isle of Wight are serviced by car and passenger vessels, including hovercraft.

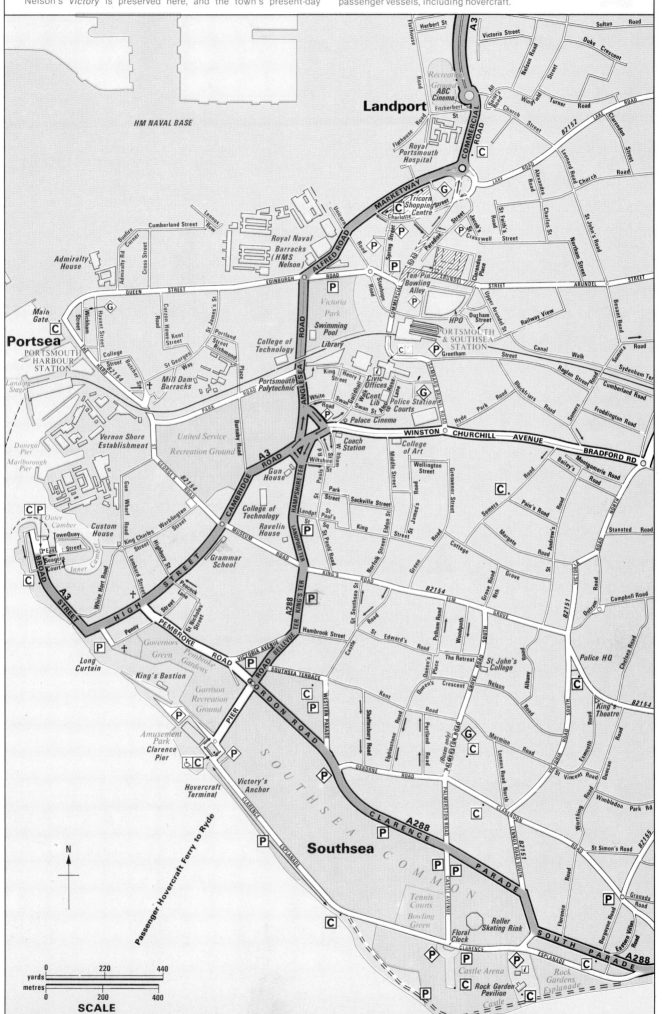

RAMSGATE

The resort and fishing port of Ramsgate occupies the south side of a chalk peninsula that divides Sandwich Bay from the vast bight of the Thames estuary. Its fine sandy beaches are backed by impressive chalk cliffs, and its local Catholic church is considered the ultimate masterpiece of the great architect Pugin. Like Margate, its close neighbour, Ramsgate is close to London and is particularly popular with holidaymakers from the capital.

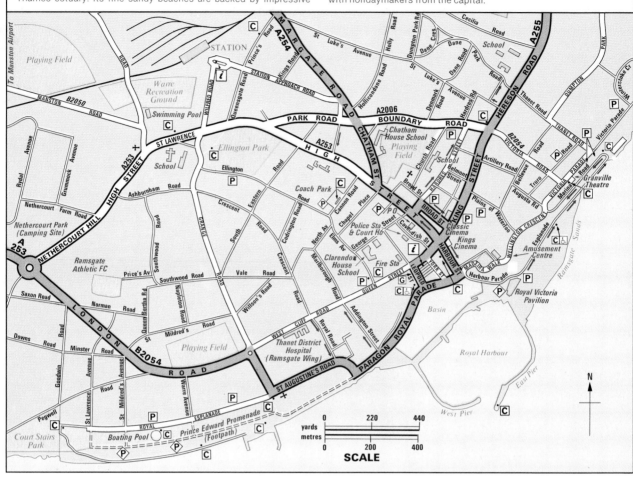

READING

Recent developments in this town have made it one of the best shopping areas in the district, without detracting from the character of its main streets, though its road systems have become somewhat complicated. Its situation on the rivers Kennet and Thames has prompted the laying out of attractive waterside parks which offer fishing and boating facilities. Modern Reading University is situated some distance from the town centre in Whiteknights Park.

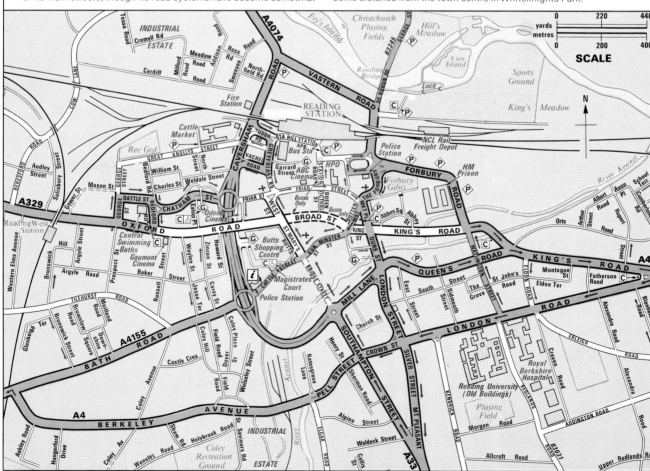

SALISBURY

A copy of the Magna Carta is kept in the library of Salisbury Cathedral. The church itself rises above the city with a lightness that belies the tons of stone in its fabric.

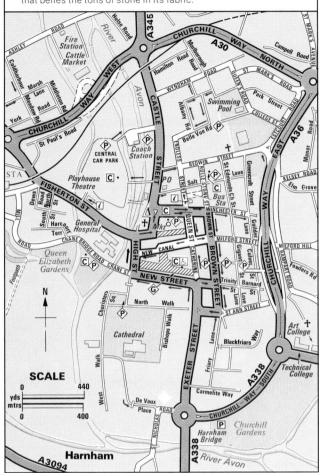

STRANRAER

Situated at the head of Loch Ryan in the Rhinns of Galloway, this large town is a terminal for the 35-mile sea crossing from Larne in Northern Ireland.

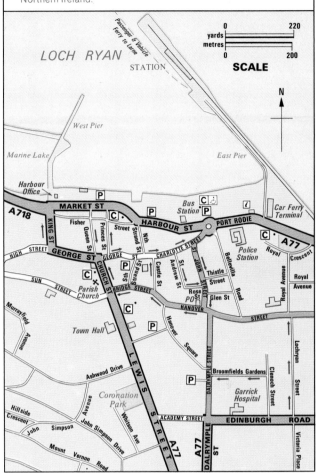

SCARBOROUGH

A large headland laid out with gardens round the ruins of Scarborough's 12th-century castle divides North Bay from South Bay, giving the resort two large areas of sheltered water fringed by sandy beaches. As a touring centre the town is in easy reach of the North Yorks Moors, the Wolds, and some of the best coastal scenery in Yorkshire. Adventurous anglers can embark from here for good deep-water fishing in the unpredictable North Sea.

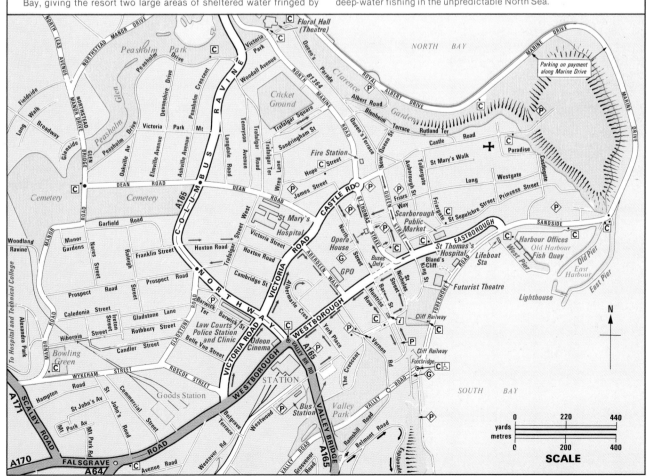

SHEFFIELD

Ever since the early days of its industrialization, this River Don city has been recognised as a premier centre for the production and utilization of fine steel. It has many other similarly successful industries, but the skill of Sheffield's ironmasters and cutlers remains unchallenged. North-east of the city on the M1 motorway is the famous Tinsley viaduct, an impressive piece of civic engineering with eleven carriageways on two levels.

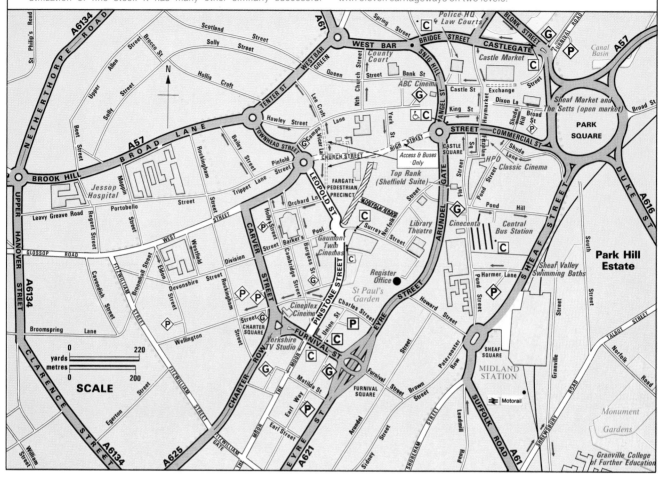

SOUTHEND-ON-SEA

This large London holiday resort lies on the north side of the Thames estuary, slightly east of Canvey Island. Its famous Autumn illuminations are only part of its attractions as a holiday town, and other amenities include swimming baths, golf, a pier, and a mile-long electric railway. As with many other coastal towns, Southend became popular during Regency vogue for seaside holidays, and its old character is retained by elegant period terraces.

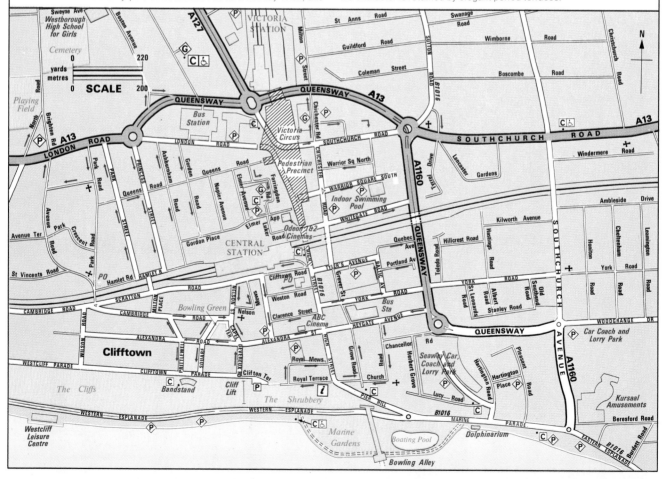

SOUTHAMPTON

Considerable bomb damage during the last war has allowed this major transatlantic port to redesign and pedestrianize much of its city centre. The harbour is noted for its curious double tide, first by way of the Solent and then two hours later by way of Spithead. Several old buildings and sections of the medieval town walls can be seen in the older parts of the city, near the docks, while Sir Basil Spence's modern university design dominates the north suburbs.

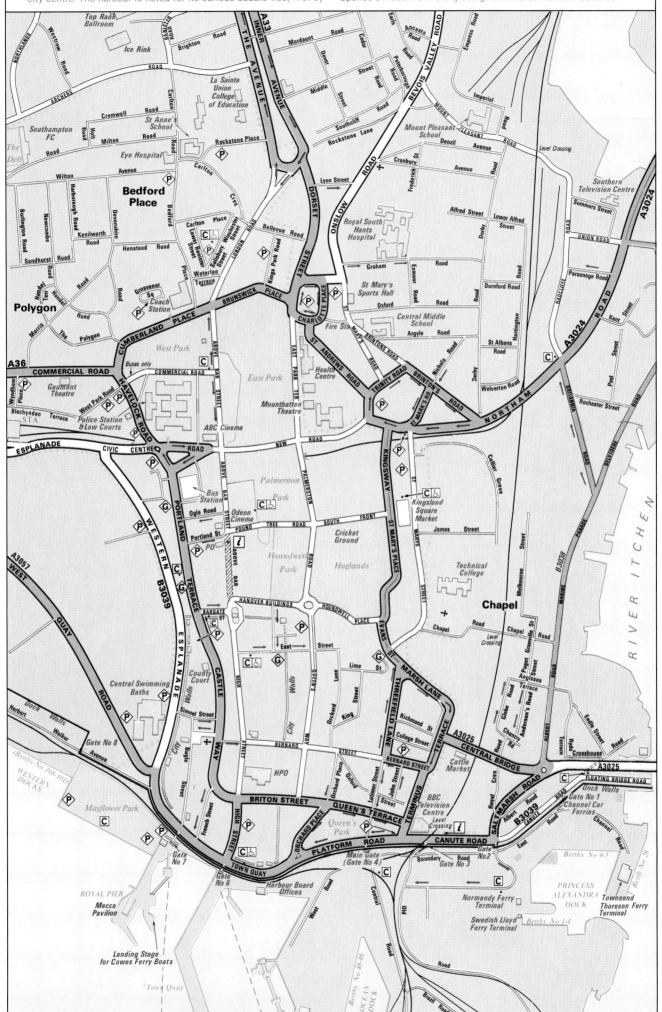

STOCKTON-ON-TEES

This large industrial town faces its sister community of Thornaby-on-Tees across the famous river from which they both derive their names. Farther east the Tees flows through Middlesbrough and joins its wide estuary in the North Sea. Most of Stockton's notable buildings date from the 18th century, a period of growth for many northern towns, and in 1825 a terminal of the Stockton to Darlington railway was opened here. A plaque records the event.

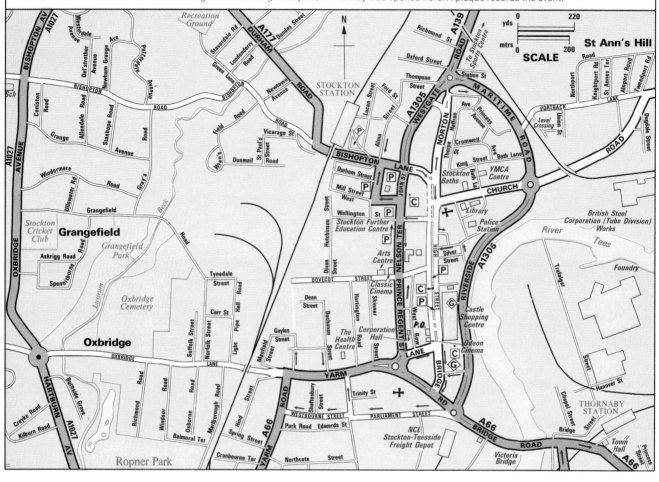

STOKE-ON-TRENT & HANLEY

Stoke-on-Trent is an amalgamation of five towns at the heart of North Staffordshire's coal and pottery district. Novelist Arnold Bennet made the area famous in his 'Anna' books, and local products bearing the names Spode and Wedgewood have won a world-wide reputation for excellence. Hanley has been absorbed by Stoke.

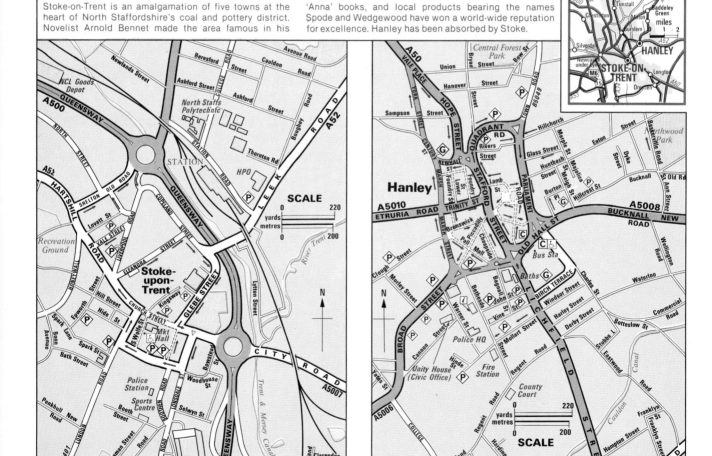

STRATFORD-UPON-AVON

Literary pilgrims from all over the world flock to this town, birthplace of William Shakespeare, to enjoy its quaint old buildings and wide cultural associations.

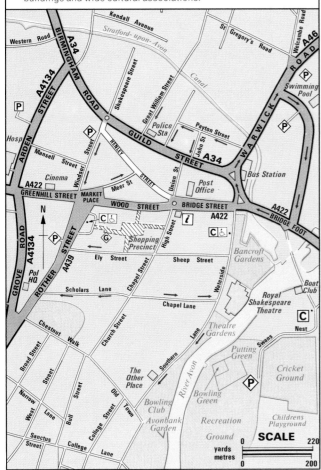

WEYMOUTH

This pleasant port and seaside resort is situated between Weymouth Bay and the naval harbour of Portland, and is an embarkation point for Channel Island car ferries.

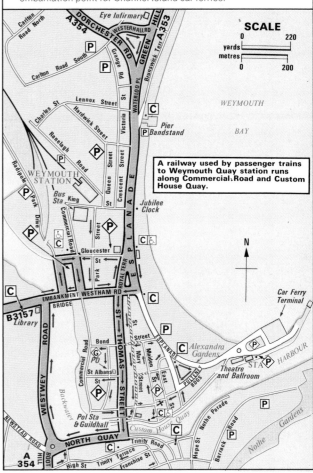

A railway used by passenger trains to Weymouth Quay station runs along Commercial Road and Custom House Quay.

SUNDERLAND

Shipbuilding and coal are the main industries of this Wear-mouth port, though in recent years these activities have been supplemented by various light engineering concerns. The community is very similar to many other northern towns in that hardly any of its buildings predate the 18th century. A little north of the main town is the residential suberb of Roker, where a fine sandy beach allows access for bathing. Hylton Castle lies 3 miles west.

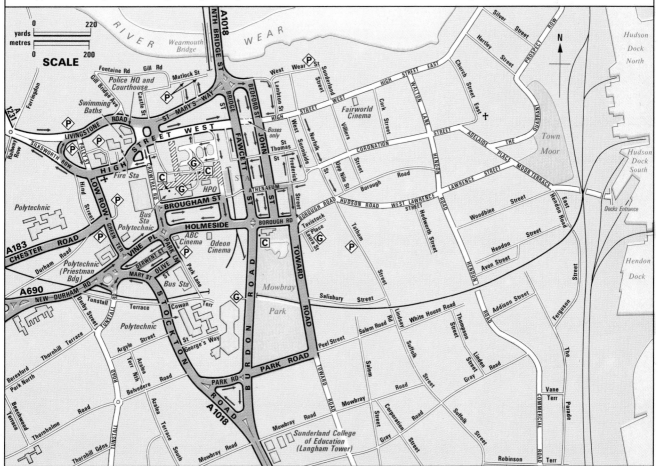

SWANSEA

This is the second largest city and the centre of the biggest industrial complex in Wales. Factories and works of every shape and size, producing a bewildering range of commodities, have been springing up here ever since the coal and iron boom of the 19th century; the population has jumped from 6,000 to 170,000 in little over a century. In complete contrast is the nearby Gower Peninsula, a haven of peace now designated an area of outstanding beauty.

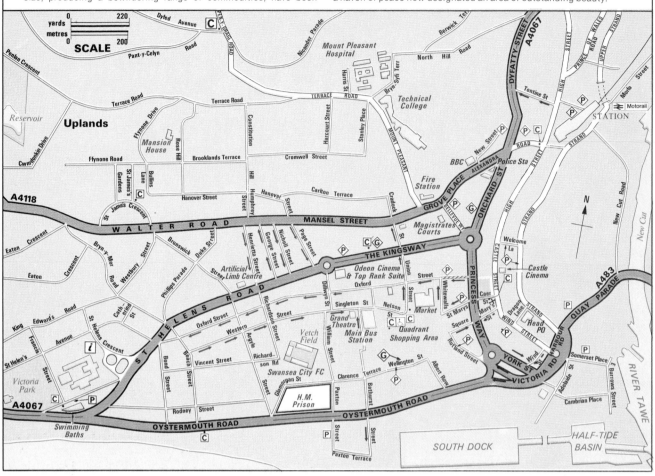

SWINDON

Of particular interest in this Wiltshire town is the Museum of the Great Western Railway, which reflects much of Swindon's importance as a railway centre as well as evoking the nostalgia of enthusiasts. Several miles north in Gloucestershire are the Cotswold Hills, a beautiful limestone range which overlooks the Severn Vale to the west and was once grazed by its own breed of sheep. Many local towns owe their prosperity to Cotswold wool.

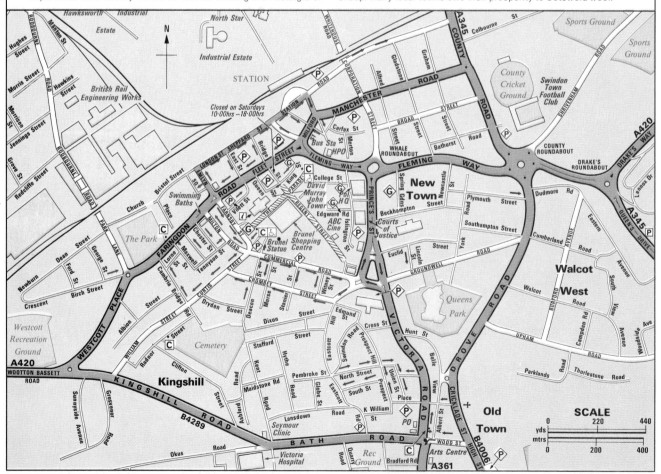

TAUNTON

The cider-making industry for which Taunton has been justly famous for many years still flourishes in this attractive old market town, though the product is somewhat more refined than in the 'old days'.

Many of the streets are shaded by trees, and the town's sheltered situation in the vale of Taunton Dene gives it a warm and equable climate. The River Tone, from which the name Taunton is derived, flows through the town centre and is a valuable leisure amenity.

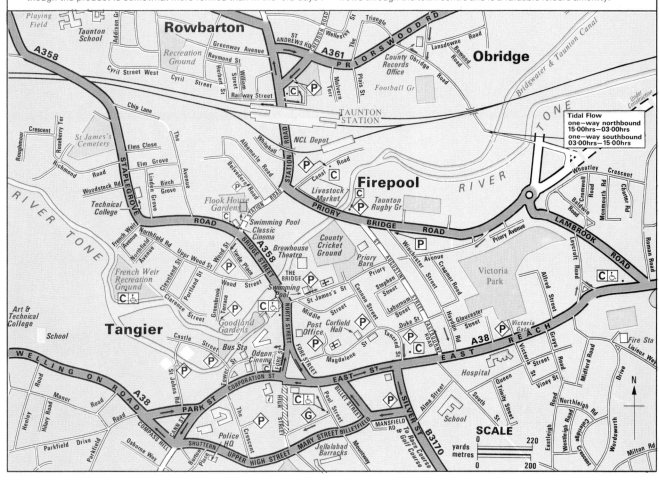

WINCHESTER

Once the capital of Wessex and still one of the most historic cities in Hampshire, Winchester lies between chalk downs in the Itchen Valley and is probably best known for its fine Norman cathedral.

Attractive gardens follow the river alongside well-preserved sections of the city wall, adding an unusual dimension to the town centre. Much of the main street has been pedestrianized in an effort to keep the most interesting areas open and accessible to the public.

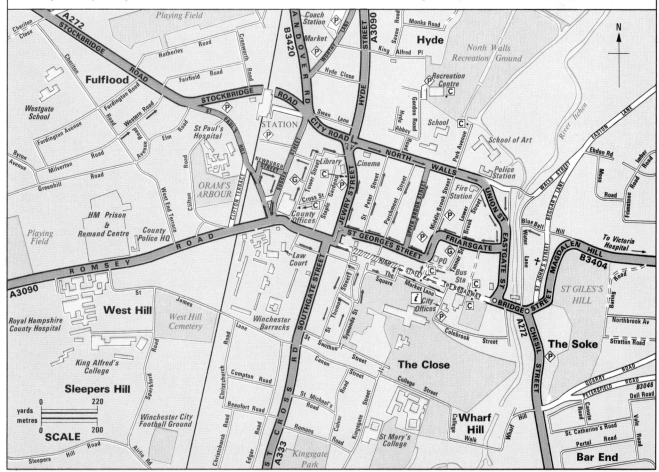

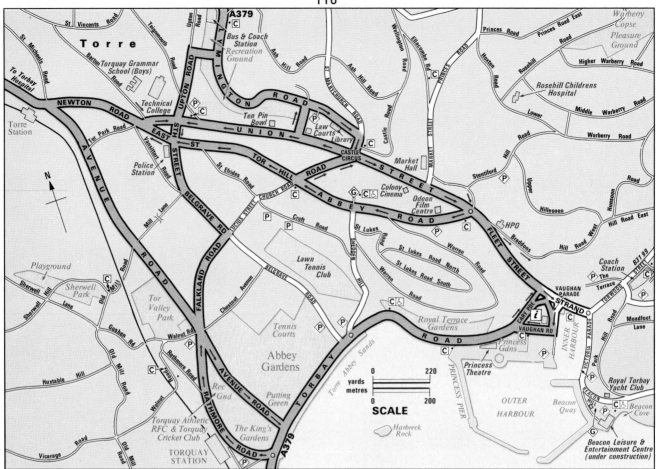

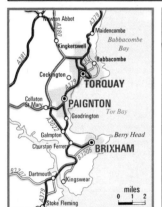

TORBAY

This is the name given to a recently-formed county borough incorporating the well-known Devon resorts of Torquay, Paignton and Brixham. The first two towns are virtually linked by urban development, but Brixham stands on its own in an area of outstanding natural beauty. Mild weather and attractive local scenery are among the main features of the area, and the sheltered waters of Tor Bay are ideal for sailing boats and other small pleasure craft. Torquay is noted for its fine cliff walks, Paignton for good sands and the revived Great Western Railway steam line to the Kingswear ferry terminal, and in summer Brixham is thronged by artists attracted by its picturesque little harbour. Inland and a few miles to the west is the vast Dartmoor National Park, dominated by the high tors of the moor itself.

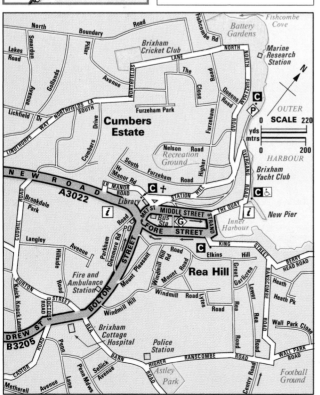

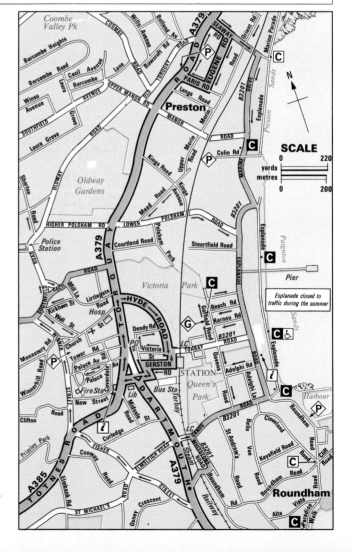

WOLVERHAMPTON

The important manufacturing centre of Wolverhampton is traditionally associated with brass founding and the production of iron and steel. It is situated at the edge of the Midland region known as the Black Country, a name that is self explanatory when the early massive industrialization of the area is considered. In recent years the 'Wolverhampton products' of locks, keys and aircraft parts have been joined by various light engineering commodities.

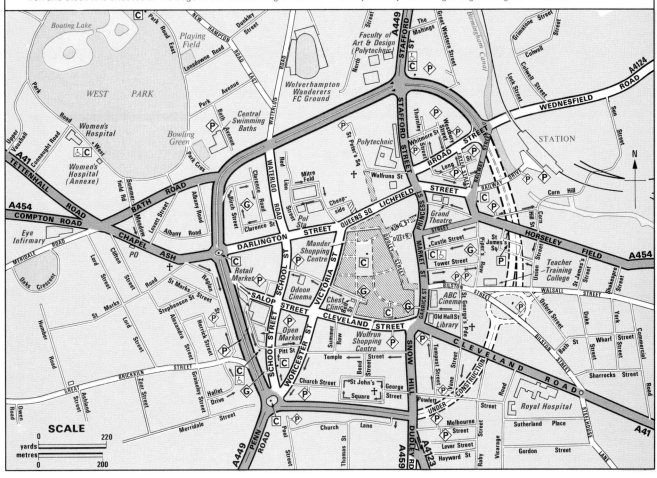

YORK

This city has been described as one of the great historic centres of Western Europe. Inside its superbly preserved medieval town walls numerous examples of long-gone architectural styles cluster together on an arrowhead of land between the rivers Ouse and Wensum. Overall is the dominating completeness of York Minster, certainly one of the finest structures of its type in Europe. The town walls completely encircle York, forming a raised promenade.

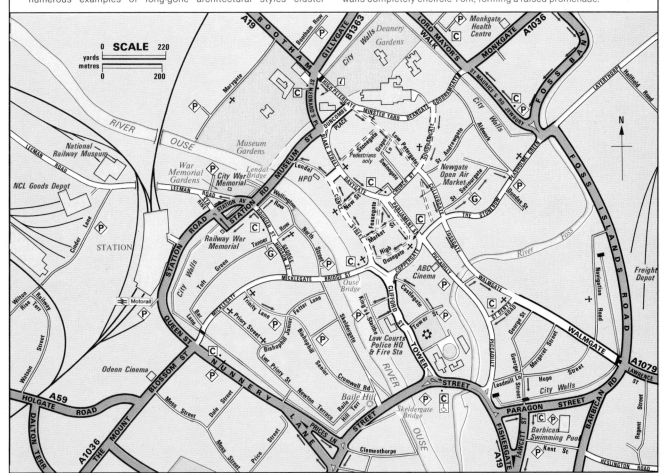

INDEX To Inner London Maps

All the streets shown on the Inner London maps are listed alphabetically in this index. To find a street on the maps use the reference figures given with each street. The relevant page number is shown in italics. The two numbers in the second set of figures are the National Grid reference numbers (the National Grid is explained on page vii), and the two letters indicate in which quarter of the grid square the street is located, (ie north-west, north-east, south-west, or south-east).

120

H

I

J

K

L

M

PRINCIPAL AIRPORTS

Aberdeen	Aberdeen (6 m) (0224) 2331, 574281, 722331
Alderney	St Agnes (048 182) 2886, 2889, 2711
Barra	Island Foreshore, Barra (889 3181) 041
Belfast (Aldergrove)	Belfast (16 m) (0232) 29271
Bembridge	Sandown (098 387) 2511, (098 384) 2646
Benbecula	Benbecula, South Uist (0870) 2051
Biggin Hill	Biggin Hill (09594) 72277
Birmingham (Elmdon)	Birmingham (5½ m) (021) 743 4272, 779 2537
Blackpool (Squires Gate)	Blackpool (2½ m) (0253) 43061
Bournemouth (Hurn)	
	Bournemouth (5 m); Christchurch (3 m) (02015) 6311, 72445
Bristol (Lulsgate)	Bristol (7 m) (027587) 4441
Cambridge	Cambridge (1½ m) (0223) 61133
Carlisle (Crosby)	Carlisle (6 m) (022873) 641
Compton Abbas	Shaftesbury (3 m) Fontmell Magna 767
Coventry	Coventry (3 m) (0203) 301717, 301792
East Midlands	Derby (7 m) (0332) 810621

Edinburgh	Edinburgh (5 m) (031) 334 2351
Elstree	Watford, Herts (2½ m) (01-953) 3502, 4411
Exeter	Exeter (4½ m) (0392) 67433
Fairoaks	Woking, Surrey (2 m) (099 05) 7300, 7700
Glamorgan (Rhoose)	Cardiff (10 m) (0446) 710296
Glasgow (Abbotsinch)	Glasgow (6 m) (041) 887 1111
Glenforsa (Mull)	Salen, Isle of Mull, Aros 377
Gloucester/Cheltenham (Staverton)	
	Gloucester (4 m); Cheltenham (4 m) (0452) 713351, 712285
Guernsey	St Peter Port (2½ m) (0481) 37766
Hawarden	Chester (4 m) (0244) 24646
Humberside	Grimsby (10 m); Scunthorpe (15 m) (065 28) 456
Inverness (Dalcross)	Inverness (7 m) (0463) 32471
Ipswich	Ipswich (2 m) (0473) 70111
Islay (Port Ellen)	Port Ellen, Islay, Port Ellen 2361
Jersey States Airport	St Helier (0534) 22271, 41272
Kirkwall	Kirkwall, Orkney (3 m) (031) 443 8971, (0856) 2421
Lashenden (Headcorn)	Headcorn, Kent (2 m) (0622) 890226, 890671
Leavesden	Watford, Herts (2 m) (09273) 74000
Leeds/Bradford (Yeardon)	Leeds (8 m); Bradford (6 m) (0532) 503431
Liverpool	Liverpool (5½ m) (051) 427 4101
London (Gatwick)	Redhill, Surrey (5 m) (0293) 28822
London (Heathrow)	Central London (12 m) (01-759) 4321
London (Westland Heliport)	London SW11 (01-228) 0181
Luton	Luton (1½ m) (0582) 36061
Lydd	Ashford, Kent (18 m); Folkestone (18 m); Hastings (15 m) (0679) 20401
Manchester International Airport	Manchester (8 m) (061) 437 5233

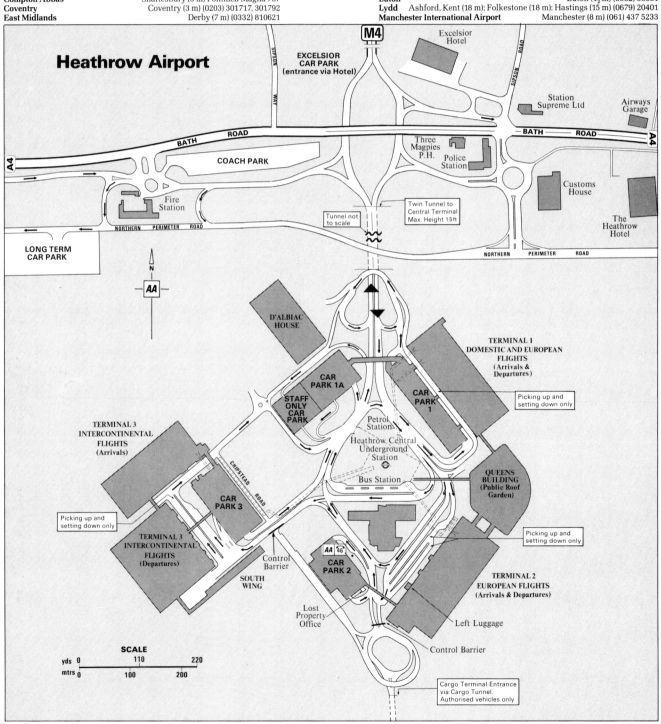

Heathrow Airport

Newcastle (Woolsington)	Newcastle-upon-Tyne (6 m) (0632) 860966
Norwich	Norwich (2½ m) (0603) 45251, 44244
Nottingham (Tollerton)	Nottingham (3 m) (0602) 811327
Oban (North Connel)	Oban (3½ m) Lochgilphead 2233
Penzance Heliport	Penzance (0736) 4296, 3871
Peterborough Business Airport (Conington)	
	Peterborough (8 m) (0487) 830 389
Plymouth (Roborough)	Plymouth (3½ m) (0752) 772752
Prestwick	Glasgow (30 m); Ayr (3 m); Kilmarnock (8 m) (0292) 79822
Ronaldsway	Douglas, Isle of Man (062 482) 3311
St. Mawgan	Newquay (3½ m) (06373) 2201, (06374) 550
Scilly Isle (St. Mary's)	Hugh Town, Scilly Isles (1 m) (072 04) 677
Shoreham	Shoreham-by-Sea (4 m) (079 17) 2304
Skye	Broadford (3 m) (0463) 34121
Southampton (Eastleigh)	Southampton (3½ m) (042126) 2341, 3741
Southend	Southend (2 m) (0702) 40201/6
Stansted	Bishop's Stortford (2½ m) (0279) 502380
Stapleford Tawney	Epping (10 m) (04028) 341
Stornoway	Stornoway (2 m) (0851) 2256
Sumburg	Sumburger Head, Mainland Isle, Shetland (09506) 274
Sunderland (Usworth)	Sunderland (3 m) (078 33) 2718, 2621
Swansea (Fairwood Common)	Swansea (5 m) (0792) 24063
Tees-side	Darlington (5 m); Middlesbrough (12 m) (032 573) 2811
Tiree	Tiree, Inner Hebrides (087 92) 456
Weston-super-Mare	Weston-super-Mare (2 m) (0934) 28726, 28151

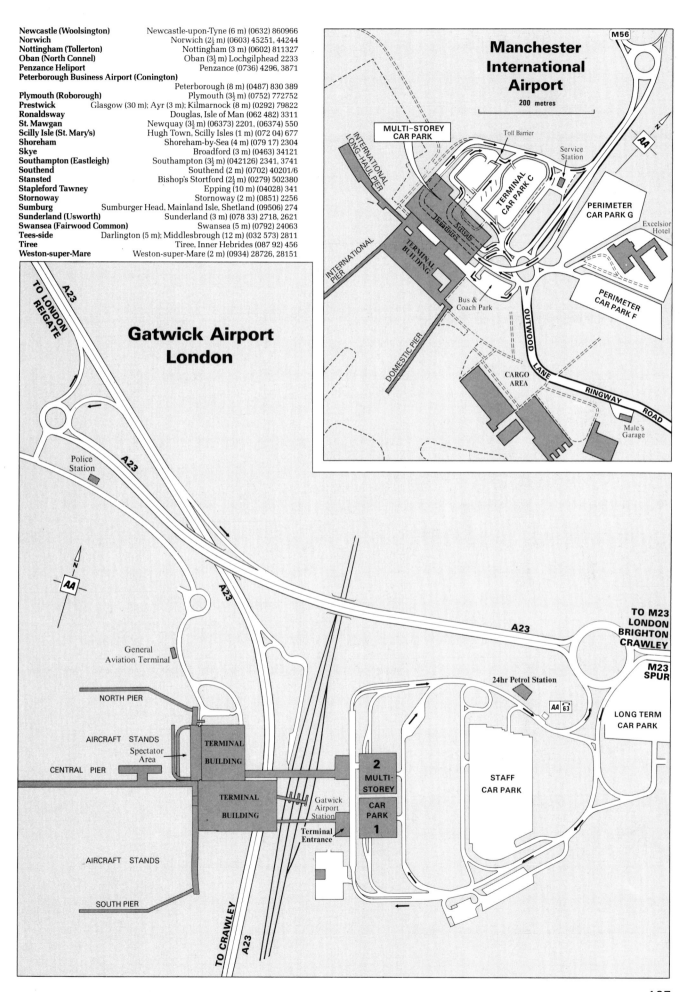

Ashby by Partney Barton Turf

Ashby by Partney 35 TF 4266
Ashby cum Fenby 39 TA 2500
Ashby de la Launde 35 TF 0455
Ashby-de-la-Zouch 33 SK 3516
Ashby Folville 34 SK 7012
Ashby Magna 26 SP 5690
Ashby Parva 26 SP 5288
Ashby St. Ledgers 26 SP 5768
Ashby St. Mary 29 TG 3202
Ashchurch 25 SO 9233
Ashcombe 5 SX 9179
Ashcott 7 ST 4336
Ashdon 20 TL 5842
Asheldham 21 TL 9701
Ashen 20 TL 7442
Ashendon 18 SP 7014
Ashfield (Central) 56 NN 7803
Ashfield (Suff.) 21 TM 2062
Ashfield Green 29 TM 2673
Ashford (Derby.) 33 SK 1969
Ashford (Devon.) 6 SS 5335
Ashford (Kent) 13 TR 0142
Ashford (Surrey) 11 TQ 0671
Ashford Bowdler 24 SO 5170
Ashford Carbonel 24 SO 5270
Ashford Hill 10 SU 5562
Ashgill 50 NS 7849
Ashiesteel Hill 52 NT 4134
Ashill (Devon.) 7 ST 0811
Ashill (Norf.) 28 TF 8804
Ashill (Somer.) 7 ST 3217
Ashingdon 20 TQ 8693
Ashington (Northum.) 47 NZ 2687
Ashington (W Susx) 11 TQ 1315
Ashkirk 52 NT 4722
Ashleworth 17 SO 8125
Ashley (Cambs.) 20 TL 6961
Ashley (Devon.) 6 SS 6411
Ashley (Glos.) 17 ST 9394
Ashley (Hants.) 9 SU 3831
Ashley (Northants.) 26 SP 7991
Ashley (Staffs.) 32 SJ 7536
Ashley Green 19 SP 9705
Ashley Heath 8 SU 1105
Ash Magna 32 SJ 5739
Ashmansworth 10 SU 4156
Ashmansworthy 4 SS 3317
Ash Mill 6 SS 7823
Ashmore 8 ST 9117
Ashorne 26 SP 3057
Ashover 33 SK 3463
Ashow 26 SP 3170
Ashperton 24 SO 6441
Ashprington 5 SX 8157
Ash Priors 7 ST 1429
Ashreigney 6 SS 6213
Ashtead 11 TQ 1858
Ash Thomas 5 ST 0010
Ashton (Ches.) 32 SJ 5069
Ashton (Corn.) 2 SW 6028
Ashton (Devon.) 5 SX 8584
Ashton (Here. and Worc.) 24 SO 5164
Ashton (Northants.) 26 SP 7649
Ashton (Northants.) 27 TL 0588
Ashton Common 17 ST 8958
Ashton-in-Makerfield 32 SJ 5799
Ashton Keynes 17 SU 0494
Ashton under Hill 25 SO 9938
Ashton-under-Lyne 37 SJ 9399
Ashton upon Mersey 37 SJ 7792
Ashurst (Hants.) 9 SU 3310
Ashurst (Kent) 12 TQ 5038
Ashurst (W Susx) 11 TQ 1716
Ashurstwood 12 TQ 4236
Ashwater 4 SX 3895
Ashwell (Herts.) 19 TL 2639
Ashwell (Leic.) 34 SK 8613
Ashwellthorpe 29 TM 1397
Ashwick 8 ST 6447
Ashwicken 28 TF 7018
Askam in Furness 40 SD 2177
Askern 38 SE 5613
Askerswell 7 SY 5292
Askett 18 SP 8105
Askham (Cumbr.) 40 NY 5123
Askham (Notts.) 34 SK 7374
Askham Bryan 38 SE 5548
Askham Richard 38 SE 5347
Askrigg 41 SD 9491
Askwith 37 SE 1648
Aslackby 35 TF 0830
Aslacton 29 TM 1591
Aslockton 34 SK 7440
Asloun 62 NJ 5414
Aspatria 40 NY 1442
Aspenden 20 TL 3528
Aspley Guise 19 SP 9436
Aspley Heath 19 SP 9334
Aspull 36 SD 6108
Asselby 38 SE 7127
Assington 21 TL 9338
Astbury 33 SJ 8461
Astcote 26 SP 6753
Asterley 24 SJ 3707
Asterton 24 SO 3991
Asthall 18 SP 2811
Asthall Leigh 18 SP 3012
Astley (Here. and Worc.) 24 SO 7867
Astley (Salop) 32 SJ 5218
Astley (Warw.) 26 SP 3189
Astley Abbots 24 SO 7096
Astley Cross 24 SO 8069
Astley Green 32 SJ 7099
Aston (Berks.) 18 SU 7884
Aston (Ches.) 32 SJ 5578
Aston (Ches.) 32 SJ 6046
Aston (Derby.) 33 SK 1883
Aston (Here. and Worc.) 24 SO 4571
Aston (Herts.) 19 TL 2722
Aston (Oxon.) 18 SP 3302
Aston (Salop) 32 SJ 5228
Aston (Salop) 24 SJ 6109
Aston (Staffs.) 32 SJ 7540
Aston (Staffs.) 33 SJ 9131
Aston (S Yorks.) 33 SK 4685
Aston (W Mids) 25 SP 0789
Aston Abbotts 19 SP 8420
Aston Blank (Cold Aston) 17 SP 1219
Aston Botterell 24 SO 6284
Aston Cantlow 25 SP 1359
Aston Clinton 19 SP 8812
Aston Crews 17 SO 6723
Aston End 19 TL 2724
Aston Eyre 24 SO 6594
Aston Fields 25 SO 9669
Aston Flamville 26 SP 4692
Aston Ingham 17 SO 6823
Aston juxta Mondrum 32 SJ 6556
Aston le Walls 26 SP 4950
Aston Magna 25 SP 1935
Aston on Clun 24 SO 3981
Aston-on-Trent 33 SK 4129
Aston Rogers 23 SJ 3406
Aston Rowant 18 SU 7299
Aston Sandford 18 SP 7507
Aston Somerville 25 SP 0438
Aston Subedge 25 SP 1341
Aston Tirrold 18 SU 5586
Aston Upthorpe 18 SU 5586
Astwick 19 TL 2138
Astwood 27 SP 9547
Astwood Bank 25 SP 0362
Aswarby (Lincs.) 35 TF 0639
Aswardby (Lincs.) 35 TF 3770
Atcham 24 SJ 5408
Athelington 29 TM 2170
Athelney 7 ST 3428
Athelstaneford 52 NT 5377
Atherington 6 SS 5923
Atherstone 26 SP 3097
Atherstone on Stour 25 SP 2050
Atherton 36 SD 6703
Atlow 33 SK 2248
Attenborough 34 SK 5134
Attleborough (Norf.) 29 TM 0495
Attleborough (Warw.) 26 SP 3790
Attlebridge 29 TG 1216
Atwick 39 TA 1850
Atworth 17 ST 8565
Aubourn 34 SK 9262
Auchagallon 49 NR 8934
Aucharnie 62 NJ 6341
Auchattie 62 NO 6994
Auchenblae 57 NO 7278
Auchenbowie 50 NS 7988
Auchenbreck 49 NS 0281
Auchencairn 45 NX 7951
Auchencarroch 50 NS 4182
Auchencrow 53 NT 8560
Auchendinny 51 NT 2561
Auchengray 51 NS 9953
Auchengruith 45 NS 8209
Auchenhalrig 61 NJ 3661
Auchenheath 50 NS 8043
Auchentiber 50 NS 3647
Auchgourish 60 NH 9315
Auchindrain 55 NN 0303
Auchindrean 64 NH 1980
Auchininna 62 NJ 6446
Auchinleck (Dumf. and Galwy.) 44 NX 4570
Auchinleck (Strath.) 50 NS 5422
Auchinloch 50 NS 6670
Auchintore 55 NN 0972
Auchleuchries 62 NK 0136
Auchleven 62 NJ 6224
Auchlochan 50 NS 8037
Auchlyne 55 NN 5129
Auchmillan 50 NS 5129
Auchmithie 57 NO 6744
Auchmuirbridge 56 NO 2101
Auchnacree 57 NO 4663
Auchnagatt 62 NJ 9341
Auchronie 57 NO 4480
Auchterarder 56 NN 9312
Auchterderran 51 NT 2195
Auchterhouse 57 NO 3337
Auchtermuchty 56 NO 2311
Auchterneed 60 NH 4959
Auchtertool 51 NT 2190
Auchtoo 55 NN 5620
Auckingill 67 ND 3764
Auckley 38 SE 6501
Audenshaw 37 SJ 9196
Audlem 32 SJ 6543
Audley 32 SJ 7950
Auds 62 NJ 6564
Aughton (Humbs.) 38 SE 7038
Aughton (Lancs.) 36 SD 3804
Aughton (Lancs.) 41 SD 5467
Aughton (S Yorks.) 33 SK 4586
Aughton Park 36 SD 4106
Auldearn 60 NH 9155
Aulden 24 SO 4654
Auldhame 52 NT 5984
Auldhouse 50 NS 6250
Ault-a-chrinn 59 NG 9420
Aultbea 64 NG 8789
Aultgrishan 64 NG 7485
Aultiphurst 67 NC 8065
Aultmore (Grampn.) 61 NJ 4053
Aultnagoire 60 NH 5423
Aulton 62 NJ 6028
Aundorach 60 NH 9716
Aunsby 35 TF 0438
Auquhorthies 62 NJ 8329
Aust 17 ST 5789
Austerfield 38 SK 6594
Austonley 37 SE 1207
Austrey 33 SK 2906
Austwick 41 SD 7668
Authorpe 35 TF 3980
Authorpe Row 35 TF 5373
Avebury 17 SU 0969
Aveley 20 TQ 5680
Avening 17 ST 8797
Averham 34 SK 7654
Aveton Gifford 5 SX 6947
Avielochan 60 NH 9016
Aviemore 60 NH 8912
Avington 10 SU 3767
Avoch 60 NH 6955
Avon 8 SZ 1498
Avonbridge 50 NS 9072
Avon Castle 8 SU 1303
Avon Dassett 26 SP 4150
Avonmouth 16 ST 5177
Avonwick 5 SX 7158
Awbridge 9 SU 3323
Awkley 17 ST 5885
Awliscombe 5 ST 1301
Awre 17 SO 7008
Awsworth 33 SK 4843
Axbridge 16 ST 4254
Axford (Hants.) 10 SU 6043
Axford (Wilts.) 10 SU 2369
Axminster 7 SY 2998
Axmouth 5 SY 2591
Aylburton 17 SO 6101
Ayle 46 NY 7149
Aylesbeare 5 SY 0391
Aylesbury 18 SP 8213
Aylesby 39 TA 2007
Aylesford 12 TQ 7359
Aylesham 13 TR 2352
Aylestone 26 SK 5701
Aylmerton 29 TG 1839
Aylsham 29 TG 1926
Aylton 24 SO 6537
Aymestrey 24 SO 4265
Aynho 18 SP 5133
Ayot St. Lawrence 19 TL 1916
Ayot St. Peter 19 TL 2115
Ayr 50 NS 3321
Aysgarth 41 SE 0088
Ayside 40 SD 3983
Ayston 27 SK 8601
Aythorpe Roding 20 TL 5815
Ayton (Berwick.) 53 NT 9260
Ayton (N Yorks.) 43 SE 9884
Aywick (Yell) 63 HU 5386
Azerley 42 SE 2574

Babbinswood 32 SJ 3329
Babcary 7 ST 5628
Babel 15 SN 8235
Babell 31 SJ 1574
Babraham 20 TL 5150
Babworth 34 SK 6880
Back 63 NB 4840
Backaland 63 HY 5630
Backbarrow 40 SD 3584
Backford 32 SJ 3971
Backhill of Clackriach 62 NJ 9246
Backies 67 NC 8302
Backmuir of New Gilston 57 NO 4308
Back of Keppoch 54 NM 6587
Backwell 16 ST 4868
Backworth 47 NZ 2972
Bacon End 20 TL 6018
Baconsthorpe 29 TG 1237
Bacton (Here. and Worc.) 24 SO 3732
Bacton (Norf.) 29 TG 3434
Bacton (Suff.) 21 TM 0466
Bacup 37 SD 8622
Badachro 64 NG 7873
Badbury 17 SU 1980
Badby 26 SP 5559
Badcall (Highld.) 66 NC 1541
Badcall (Highld.) 66 NC 2355
Badcaul 64 NH 0191
Baddeley Green 33 SJ 9250
Baddesley Ensor 26 SP 2798
Baddidarach 64 NC 0923
Badenscoth 62 NJ 7038
Badenyon 61 NJ 3419
Badger 24 SO 7699
Badgers Mount 12 TQ 5061
Badgeworth (Glos.) 17 SO 9019
Badgworth (Somer.) 7 ST 3952
Badingham 21 TM 3067
Badlesmere 13 TR 0154
Badluarach 64 NG 9994
Badminton 17 ST 8082
Badrallach 64 NH 0691
Badsey 25 SP 0743
Badsworth 38 SE 4614
Badwell Ash 29 TL 9969
Bagby 42 SE 4680
Bagendon 17 SP 0006
Bagillt 32 SJ 2175
Baginton 26 SP 3474
Baglan 15 SS 7493
Bagley 32 SJ 4027
Bagnall 33 SJ 9250
Bagshot (Surrey) 11 SU 9163
Bagshot (Wilts.) 10 SU 3165
Bagthorpe (Norf.) 28 TF 7932
Bagthorpe (Notts.) 33 SK 4751
Bagworth 33 SK 4408
Bagwy Llydiart 16 SO 4427
Baildon 37 SE 1539
Bailebeag 60 NH 5018
Baile Boidheach 49 NR 7473
Baile Mor 45 NM 2824
Baillieston 50 NS 6764
Bail Uachdraich 63 NF 8160
Bainbridge 41 SD 9390
Bainton (Cambs.) 35 TF 0906
Bainton (Humbs.) 39 SE 9652
Bairnkine 52 NT 6515
Baker's End 20 TL 3917
Baker Street 20 TQ 6381
Bakewell 33 SK 2168
Bala 31 SH 9236
Balallan 63 NB 2720
Balbeg 60 NH 4924
Balbeggie 56 NO 1629
Balbithan 62 NJ 7917
Balblair 65 NH 7066
Balchladich 64 NC 0330
Balchraggan 60 NH 5343
Balchrick 66 NC 1960
Balcombe 12 TQ 3130
Balcurvie 57 NO 3400
Baldersby 42 SE 3578
Balderstone 36 SD 6332
Balderton 34 SK 8151
Baldhu 2 SW 7743
Baldinnie 57 NO 4311
Baldock 19 TL 2434
Baldrine 43 SC 4281
Baldwin 43 SC 3581
Baldwinholme 46 NY 3351
Baldwin's Gate 32 SJ 7939
Bale 29 TG 0136
Balemartine 48 NL 9841
Balephuil 48 NL 9640
Balerno 51 NT 1666
Balfield 57 NO 5468
Balfour 63 HY 4716
Balfron 50 NS 5488
Balgaveny 62 NJ 6640
Balgavies 57 NO 5351
Balgedie 56 NO 1603
Balgonar 51 NT 0293
Balgove 62 NJ 8133
Balgowan 60 NN 6394
Balgown 58 NG 3868
Balgray 57 NO 4138
Balgrochan 50 NS 6278
Balhalgardy 62 NJ 7623
Balhary 57 NO 2646
Baliasta 63 HP 6009
Baligill 67 NC 8566
Balintore (Highld.) 65 NH 8675
Balintore (Tays.) 57 NO 2859
Balintraid 65 NH 7370
Balivanich 63 NF 7755
Balkeerie 57 NO 3244
Balkholme 38 SE 7828
Balkissock 44 NX 1381
Ball 32 SJ 3026
Ballabeg 43 SC 2470
Ballacannell 43 SC 4382
Ballacarnane Beg 43 SC 3088
Ballajora 43 SC 4790
Ballamodha 43 SC 2773
Ballantrae 44 NX 0882
Ballantrushal 63 NB 3853
Ballasalla (I. of M.) 43 SC 2870
Ballasalla (I. of M.) 43 SC 3497
Ballater 61 NO 3695
Ballaugh 43 SC 3493
Ballchraggan 65 NH 7775
Ballechin 56 NN 9353
Ballencrieff 52 NT 4878
Ballevullin 48 NL 9546
Ball Hill 10 SU 4263
Balliekine 49 NR 8739
Balliemore (Strath.) 54 NM 8228
Ballig 43 SC 2882
Ballinaby 48 NR 2267
Ballindean 57 NO 2529
Ballinger Common 19 SP 9103
Ballingham 24 SO 5731
Ballingry 56 NT 1797
Ballinluig 56 NN 9852
Ballintuim 56 NO 1054
Balloch (Highld.) 60 NH 7346
Balloch (Strath.) 50 NS 3981
Balloch (Tays.) 56 NN 8419
Balloch (Tays.) 57 NO 3557
Ballochan 61 NO 5290
Ballochroy 48 NR 7252
Balls Cross 11 SU 9826
Ballygown 54 NM 4343
Ballygrant 48 NR 3966
Ballymichael 49 NR 9231
Balmacara 59 NG 8028
Balmaclellan 45 NX 6578
Balmacneil 56 NN 9850
Balmae 45 NX 6845
Balmaha 50 NS 4290
Balmalcolm 57 NO 3108
Balmartin 63 NF 7273
Balmedie 62 NJ 9617
Balmerino 57 NO 3524
Balmerlawn 9 SU 3003
Balmore 50 NS 6073
Balmullo 57 NO 4220
Balmungie 60 NH 7359
Balnabodach 63 NF 7101
Balnacra 59 NG 9746
Balnafoich 60 NH 6835
Balnaguard 56 NN 9451
Balnaguisich 65 NH 6771
Balnahard 54 NM 4534
Balnahard 54 NR 4199
Balnakeil 66 NC 3968
Balnaknock 58 NG 4162
Balnamoon 57 NO 5463
Balnapaling 65 NH 7969
Balquhidder 55 NN 5320
Balranald 63 NF 7169
Balsall Common 26 SP 2377
Balscote 26 SP 3841
Balsham 20 TL 5850
Baltasound (Unst) 63 HP 6208
Balterley 32 SJ 7550
Balthangie 62 NJ 8351
Baltonsborough 7 ST 5434
Balvaird 60 NH 5452
Balvarran 56 NO 0762
Balvicar 54 NM 7616
Balvraid 60 NH 8231
Bamburgh 53 NU 1834
Bamford 33 SK 2083
Bampton (Cumbr.) 40 NY 5118
Bampton (Devon.) 6 SS 9522
Bampton (Oxon.) 18 SP 3103
Banavie 55 NN 1177
Banbury 18 SP 4540
Banc Cwmhelen 15 SN 6811
Banchory 62 NO 6995
Banchory-Devenick 62 NJ 9101
Bancyfelin 14 SN 3218
Banc-y-ffordd 15 SN 4037
Banff 62 NJ 6864
Bangor 30 SH 5872
Bangor-is-y-coed 32 SJ 3945
Banham 29 TM 0688
Bank 9 SU 2807
Bankend (Dumf. and Galwy.) 45 NY 0268
Bankend (Strath.) 50 NS 8033
Bankfoot 56 NO 0635
Bankglen 50 NS 5912
Bankhead (Grampn.) 62 NJ 6608
Bankhead (Grampn.) 62 NJ 8910
Bank Newton 37 SD 9152
Banknock 50 NS 7779
Banks (Cumbr.) 46 NY 5664
Banks (Lancs.) 36 SD 3820
Bankshill 46 NY 1981
Bank Street 24 SO 6362
Banningham 29 TG 2129
Bannister Green 20 TL 6920
Bannockburn 50 NS 8190
Banstead 11 TQ 2559
Bantham 5 SX 6643
Banton 50 NS 7479
Banwell 16 ST 3959
Bapchild 13 TQ 9363
Baramore 54 NM 6474
Barassie 50 NS 3232
Barbaraville 65 NH 7471
Barber Booth 33 SK 1184
Barbon 41 SD 6282
Barbrook 6 SS 7147
Barby 26 SP 5470
Barcheston 18 SP 2639
Barcombe 12 TQ 4214
Barcombe Cross 12 TQ 4216
Barden 42 SE 1493
Bardfield Saling 20 TL 6826
Bardister 63 HU 3577
Bardney 35 TF 1169
Bardon Mill 46 NY 7764
Bardowie 50 NS 5873
Bardrainney 50 NS 3372
Bardsea 40 SD 3074
Bardsey 37 SE 3643
Bardsley 37 SD 9201
Bardwell 29 TL 9473
Barewood 24 SO 3856
Barford (Norf.) 29 TG 1007
Barford (Warw.) 26 SP 2660
Barford St. Martin 8 SU 0531
Barford St. Michael 26 SP 4332
Barfreston 13 TR 2650
Bargoed 16 SO 1500
Bargrennan 44 NX 3476
Barham (Cambs.) 27 TL 1375
Barham (Kent) 13 TR 2050
Barham (Suff.) 21 TM 1451
Barholm 35 TF 0811
Barkby 34 SK 6309
Barkestone-le-Vale 34 SK 7734
Barkham 10 SU 7866
Barking (Gtr London) 20 TQ 4785
Barking (Suff.) 21 TM 0653
Barkingside 20 TQ 4489
Barkisland 37 SE 0419
Barkston (Lincs.) 34 SK 9241
Barkston (N Yorks.) 38 SE 4936
Barkway 20 TL 3835
Barkwith 35 TF 1681
Barlaston 33 SJ 8938
Barlavington 11 SU 9716
Barlborough 33 SK 4777
Barlby 38 SE 6334
Barlestone 26 SK 4205
Barley (Herts.) 20 TL 4038
Barley (Lancs.) 37 SD 8240
Barleythorpe 34 SK 8409
Barling 21 TQ 9289
Barlow (Derby.) 33 SK 3474
Barlow (N Yorks.) 38 SE 6428
Barlow (Tyne and Wear) 47 NZ 1560
Barmby Moor 38 SE 7748
Barmby on the Marsh 38 SE 6828
Barmer 28 TF 8133
Barmouth 22 SH 6115
Barmpton 42 NZ 3118
Barmston 39 TA 1659
Barnack 27 TF 0705
Barnacle 26 SP 3884
Barnard Castle 42 NZ 0516
Barnard Gate 18 SP 4010
Barnardiston 20 TL 7148
Barnburgh 38 SE 4803
Barnby 29 TM 4789
Barnby Dun 38 SE 6109
Barnby in the Willows 34 SK 8552
Barnby Moor 34 SK 6684
Barnes 11 TQ 2276
Barnet 19 TQ 2494
Barnetby le Wold 39 TA 0509
Barney 29 TF 9932
Barnham (Suff.) 28 TL 8779
Barnham (W Susx) 11 SU 9604
Barnham Broom 29 TG 0807
Barnhead 57 NO 6657
Barnhill 61 NJ 1457
Barnhills 44 NW 9871
Barningham (Durham) 42 NZ 0810
Barningham (Suff.) 29 TL 9676
Barnoldby le Beck 39 TA 2303
Barnoldswick 37 SD 8746
Barns Green 11 TQ 1227
Barnsley (Glos.) 17 SP 0705
Barnsley (S Yorks.) 37 SE 3406
Barnstaple 6 SS 5533
Barnston (Essex) 20 TL 6519
Barnston (Mers.) 32 SJ 2783
Barnt Green 25 SP 0073
Barnton 32 SJ 6374
Barnwell 27 TL 0485
Barnwood 17 SO 8518
Barr 44 NX 2794
Barrachan 44 NX 3649
Barrack 62 NJ 8942
Barraglom 63 NB 1634
Barrapoll 48 NL 9542
Barras 57 NO 8580
Barrasford 47 NY 9273
Barregarrow 43 SC 3288
Barrhead 50 NS 5058
Barrhill (Strath.) 44 NX 2382
Barrington (Cambs.) 20 TL 3949
Barrington (Somer.) 7 ST 3918
Barripper 2 SW 6338
Barrmill 50 NS 3651
Barrock 67 ND 2571
Barrow (Lancs.) 36 SD 7338
Barrow (Leic.) 34 SK 8815
Barrow (Salop) 24 SJ 6500
Barrow (Somer.) 8 ST 7231
Barrow (Suff.) 20 TL 7663
Barroway Drove 28 TF 5703
Barrowby 34 SK 8736
Barrowden 27 SK 9400
Barrowford 37 SD 8538
Barrow Gurney 16 ST 5267
Barrow-in-Furness 40 SD 1969
Barrow Street 8 ST 8330
Barrow upon Humber 39 TA 0721
Barrow upon Soar 34 SK 5717
Barrow upon Trent 33 SK 3528
Barry (Angus) 57 NO 5334
Barry (S Glam.) 16 ST 1168
Barry Island 16 ST 1168
Barsby 34 SK 6911
Barsham 29 TM 3989
Barston 25 SP 2078
Bartestree 24 SO 5641
Barthol Chapel 62 NJ 8134
Barthomley 32 SJ 7652
Bartley 9 SU 3012
Bartlow 20 TL 5845
Barton (Cambs.) 20 TL 4055
Barton (Ches.) 32 SJ 4454
Barton (Devon.) 5 SX 9067
Barton (Glos.) 17 SP 0925
Barton (Lancs.) 36 SD 5136
Barton (N Yorks.) 42 NZ 2208
Barton (Warw.) 25 SP 1051
Barton Bendish 28 TF 7105
Barton Common 29 TG 3522
Barton Hartshorn 18 SP 6431
Barton in Fabis 34 SK 5232
Barton in the Beans 33 SK 3906
Barton in the Clay 19 TL 0831
Barton-le-Street 38 SE 7274
Barton-le-Willows 38 SE 7163
Barton Mills 28 TL 7273
Barton Moss 32 SJ 7397
Barton on Sea 9 SZ 2493
Barton-on-the-Heath 18 SP 2532
Barton St. David 7 ST 5431
Barton Seagrave 27 SP 8877
Barton Stacey 10 SU 4340
Barton Turf 29 TG 3421

Barton-under-Needwood Blarnaleyoch

Barton-under-Needwood 33 SK 1818
Barton-Upon-Humber 39 TA 0222
Barvas 63 NB 3649
Barway 28 TL 5475
Barwell 26 SP 4496
Barwick 7 ST 5513
Barwick in Elmet 37 SE 3937
Baschurch 32 SJ 4222
Bascote 26 SP 4063
Basford Green 33 SJ 9951
Bashall Eaves 36 SD 6943
Bashley 9 SZ 2496
Basildon (Berks.) 10 SU 6078
Basildon (Essex) 20 TQ 7189
Basing 10 SU 6652
Basingstoke 10 SU 6351
Baslow 33 SK 2572
Bason Bridge 7 ST 3445
Bassenthwaite 40 NY 2332
Bassett 9 SU 4116
Bassingbourn 20 TL 3344
Bassingfield 34 SK 6137
Bassingham 34 SK 9059
Bassingthorpe 34 SK 9628
Basta 63 HU 5294
Baston 35 TF 1114
Bastwick 29 TG 4217
Batcombe (Dorset) 7 ST 6104
Batcombe (Somer.) 8 ST 6838
Bate Heath 32 SJ 6879
Bath 17 ST 7464
Bathampton 17 ST 7765
Bathealton 7 ST 0724
Batheaston 17 ST 7767
Bathford 17 ST 7866
Bathgate 51 NS 9768
Bathley 34 SK 7759
Bathpool 4 SX 2874
Batley 37 SE 2424
Batsford 25 SP 1834
Battersea 11 TQ 2876
Battisford 21 TM 0554
Battisford Tye 21 TM 0254
Battle (E Susx.) 12 TQ 7416
Battle (Powys) 15 SO 0031
Battlefield 24 SJ 5117
Battlesbridge 20 TQ 7794
Battlesden 19 SP 9628
Battleton 6 SS 9127
Battramsley 9 SZ 3099
Baughurst 10 SU 5859
Baulking 18 SU 3190
Baumber 35 TF 2174
Baunton 17 SP 0204
Baverstock 8 SU 0231
Bawburgh 29 TG 1508
Bawdeswell 29 TG 0420
Bawdrip 7 ST 3339
Bawdsey 21 TM 3440
Bawtry 38 SK 6592
Baxenden 37 SD 7726
Baxterley 26 SP 2796
Bayble 63 NB 5231
Baycliff 40 SD 2872
Baydon 10 SU 2877
Bayford 20 TL 3108
Bayhead 63 NF 7468
Bayles 46 NY 7044
Baylham 21 TM 1051
Bayston Hill 24 SJ 4809
Bayton 24 SO 6973
Beachampton 18 SP 7737
Beachley 16 ST 5591
Beacon 5 ST 1705
Beacon End 21 TL 9524
Beacon Hill (Dorset) 8 SY 9794
Beacon's Bottom 18 SU 7895
Beaconsfield 19 SU 9490
Beacontree 20 TQ 4886
Beacravik 63 NG 1190
Beadlam 42 SE 6584
Beadnell 53 NU 2329
Beaford 6 SS 5514
Beal (Northum.) 53 NU 0642
Beal (N Yorks.) 38 SE 5325
Bealings 21 TM 2348
Beaminster 7 ST 4801
Beamish 47 NZ 2253
Beamsley 37 SE 0752
Bean 12 TQ 5972
Beanacre 17 ST 9066
Beanley 53 NU 0818
Beaquoy 63 HY 3022
Beare Green 11 TQ 1842
Bearley 25 SP 1760
Bearpark 42 NZ 2343
Bearsbridge 46 NY 7857
Bearsden 50 NS 5471
Bearsted 12 TQ 8055
Bearwood 8 SZ 0496
Beattock 45 NT 0702
Beauchamp Roding 20 TL 5809
Beauchief 33 SK 3381
Beaufort 16 SO 1611
Beaulieu 9 SU 3801
Beauly 60 NH 5246
Beaumaris 30 SH 6076
Beaumont (Cumbr.) 46 NY 3459
Beaumont (Essex) 21 TM 1725
Beausale 26 SP 2470
Beaworthy 6 SX 4699
Beazley End 20 TL 7428
Bebington 32 SJ 3384
Bebside 47 NZ 2881
Beccles 29 TM 4290
Becconsall 36 SD 4422
Beckbury 24 SJ 7601
Beckenham 12 TQ 3769
Beckermet 40 NY 0206
Beckfoot (Cumbr.) 45 NY 0949
Beckfoot (Cumbr.) 40 NY 1600
Beck Foot (Cumbr.) 41 SD 6196
Beckford 25 SO 9735
Beckhampton 17 SU 0868
Beck Hole 43 NZ 8102
Beckingham (Lincs.) 34 SK 8753
Beckingham (Notts.) 34 SK 7790
Beckington 8 ST 7951
Beckley (E Susx.) 13 TQ 8423
Beckley (Oxon) 18 SP 5611
Beck Row 28 TL 6977
Beck Side 40 SD 2382
Beckton 20 TQ 4381
Beckwithshaw 37 SE 2653
Bedale 42 SE 2688
Bedburn 42 NZ 1031
Beddau 16 ST 0585
Beddgelert 30 SH 5848
Beddingham 12 TQ 4408
Beddington 12 TQ 3165
Bedfield 21 TM 2266
Bedford 27 TL 0449
Bedhampton 9 SU 6906
Bedingfield 21 TM 1768
Bedlington 47 NZ 2581
Bedlinog 16 SO 0901
Bedmond 19 TL 0903
Bednall 25 SJ 9517
Bedrule 52 NT 6017
Bedstone 24 SO 3675
Bedwas 16 ST 1689
Bedworth 26 SP 3587
Beeby 34 SK 6608
Beech (Hants.) 10 SU 6938
Beech (Staffs.) 33 SJ 8538
Beechamwell 28 TF 7405
Beech Hill 10 SU 6964
Beechingstoke 17 SU 0859
Beedon 10 SU 4877
Beeford 39 TA 1254
Beeley 33 SK 2667
Beelsby 39 TA 2001
Beenham 10 SU 5868
Beer 5 SY 2289
Beercrocombe 7 ST 3220
Beer Hackett 7 ST 5911
Beesby 35 TF 4680
Beeson 5 SX 8140
Beeston (Beds.) 27 TL 1648
Beeston (Ches.) 32 SJ 5358
Beeston (Norf.) 28 TF 9015
Beeston (Notts.) 34 SK 5336
Beeston (W Yorks.) 37 SE 2930
Beeston Regis 29 TG 1742
Beeswing 45 NX 8969
Beetham 40 SD 4979
Beetley 29 TF 9718
Begbroke 18 SP 4613
Begelly 14 SN 1107
Beguildy 23 SO 1979
Beighton (Norf.) 29 TG 3808
Beighton (S Yorks.) 33 SK 4483
Beith 50 NS 3454
Bekesbourne 13 TR 1955
Belaugh 29 TG 2818
Belbroughton 25 SO 9177
Belchamp Otten 20 TL 8041
Belchamp St. Paul 20 TL 7942
Belchamp Walter 20 TL 8240
Belchford 35 TF 2975
Belford 53 NU 1033
Belhelvie 62 NJ 9417
Bellabeg 61 NJ 3513
Bellanoch 49 NR 7992
Bellaty 57 NO 2459
Bell Busk 37 SD 9056
Belleau 35 TF 4078
Bellehiglash 61 NJ 1837
Bellerby 42 SE 1192
Belliehill 57 NO 5663
Bellingdon 19 SP 9405
Bellingham 47 NY 8383
Belloch 48 NR 6737
Bellochantuy 48 NR 6632
Bellsbank 44 NS 4804
Bellshill (Northum.) 53 NU 1230
Bellshill (Strath.) 50 NS 7360
Bellspool 51 NT 1635
Bellsquarry 51 NT 0465
Bells Yew Green 12 TQ 6136
Belmaduthy 60 NH 6556
Belmesthorpe 35 TF 0410
Belmont (Lancs.) 36 SD 6715
Belmont (Unst) 63 HP 5600
Belnacraig 61 NJ 3716
Belowda 3 SW 9661
Belper 33 SK 3447
Belsay 47 NZ 1078
Belses 52 NT 5725
Belsford 5 SX 7659
Belstead 21 TM 1341
Belston 50 NS 3820
Belstone 5 SX 6193
Belthorn 36 SD 7124
Beltoft 39 SE 8006
Belton (Humbs.) 38 SE 7806
Belton (Leic.) 33 SK 4420
Belton (Leic.) 26 SK 8101
Belton (Lincs.) 34 SK 9239
Belton (Norf.) 29 TG 4802
Belvedere 12 TQ 4978
Belvoir 34 SK 8133
Bembridge 9 SZ 6488
Bemersyde 52 NT 5933
Bempton 39 TA 1972
Benacre 29 TM 5184
Benenden 13 TQ 8033
Bengate 29 TG 3027
Benholm 57 NO 8069
Beningbrough 38 SE 5257
Benington (Herts.) 20 TL 3023
Benington (Lincs.) 35 TF 3946
Benllech 30 SH 5182
Benmore (Central) 55 NN 4125
Bennacott 4 SX 2991
Bennan (Island of Arran) 49 NR 9821
Bennecarrigan 49 NR 9423
Benniworth 35 TF 2081
Benover 12 TQ 7048
Benson 18 SU 6191
Benthall (Northum.) 53 NU 2328
Benthall (Salop) 24 SJ 6602
Bentham 17 SO 9116
Bentley (Hants.) 10 SU 7844
Bentley (Here. and Worc.) 25 SO 9966
Bentley (Humbs.) 39 TA 0135
Bentley (S Yorks.) 38 SE 5605
Bentley (Warw.) 26 SP 2895
Bentley Heath 26 SP 1676
Benton 6 SS 6536
Bentpath 46 NY 3190
Bentworth 10 SU 6640
Benvie 57 NO 3231
Benwick 27 TL 3490
Beoley 25 SP 0669
Beoraidbeg 58 NM 6793
Bepton 11 SU 8518
Berden 20 TL 4629
Berea 14 SM 7929
Bere Alston 4 SX 4466
Bere Ferrers 4 SX 4563
Berepper 2 SW 6522
Bere Regis 8 SY 8494
Bergh Apton 29 TG 3000
Berinsfield 18 SU 5696
Berkeley 17 ST 6899
Berkhamsted 19 SP 9907
Berkley 8 ST 8049
Berkswell 26 SP 2479
Bermondsey 12 TQ 3579
Bernisdale 58 NG 4050
Berrick Salome 18 SU 6293
Berriedale Water 67 ND 0630
Berriew 23 SJ 1801
Berrington (Northum.) 53 NU 0043
Berrington (Salop) 24 SJ 5206
Berrow 7 ST 2952
Berrow Green 24 SO 7458
Berry Hill 17 SO 5712
Berryhillock 61 NJ 5060
Berrynarbor 6 SS 5546
Berry Pomeroy 5 SX 8261
Bersham 32 SJ 3048
Berstane 63 HY 4610
Bersted 11 SU 9300
Berwick 12 TQ 5105
Berwick Bassett 17 SU 0973
Berwick Hill 47 NZ 1775
Berwick St. James 8 SU 0739
Berwick St. John 8 ST 9421
Berwick St. Leonard 8 ST 9233
Berwick-upon-Tweed 53 NT 9953
Besford 25 SO 9144
Bessacarr 38 SE 6101
Bessels Leigh 18 SP 4501
Bessingham 29 TG 1636
Besthorpe (Norf.) 29 TM 0695
Besthorpe (Notts.) 34 SK 8264
Beswick 39 TA 0148
Betchworth 11 TQ 2149
Bethel 30 SH 5265
Bethersden 13 TQ 9240
Bethesda (Dyfed) 14 SN 0918
Bethesda (Gwyn.) 30 SH 6266
Bethlehem 15 SN 6825
Bethnal Green 20 TQ 3583
Betley 32 SJ 7548
Betsham 12 TQ 6071
Betteshanger 13 TR 3152
Bettiscombe 7 SY 3999
Bettisfield 32 SJ 4535
Betton (Salop) 23 SJ 3102
Betton (Salop) 32 SJ 6836
Bettws (Gwent) 16 ST 2991
Bettws (Mid Glam.) 15 SS 9086
Bettws Bledrws 15 SN 5952
Bettws Cedewain 23 SO 1296
Bettws Evan 14 SN 3047
Bettws Gwerfil Goch 31 SJ 0346
Bettws Malpas 16 ST 3090
Bettws-Newydd 16 SO 3606
Bettyhill 66 NC 7061
Betws 15 SN 6311
Betws Garmon 30 SH 5357
Betws-y-coed 31 SH 7956
Betws-yn-Rhos 31 SH 9073
Beulah (Dyfed) 14 SN 2846
Beulah (Powys) 15 SN 9251
Bevendean 12 TQ 3406
Bevercotes 34 SK 6972
Beverley 39 TA 0339
Beverston 17 ST 8693
Bevington 17 ST 6596
Bewaldeth 40 NY 2134
Bewcastle 46 NY 5674
Bewdley 24 SO 7875
Bewerley 42 SE 1564
Bewholme 39 TA 1650
Bexhill 12 TQ 7407
Bexley 12 TQ 4973
Bexwell 28 TF 6303
Beyton 21 TL 9363
Bibury 17 SP 1106
Bicester 18 SP 5822
Bickenhall 7 ST 2818
Bickenhill 25 SP 1882
Bicker 35 TF 2237
Bickerstaffe 36 SD 4404
Bickerton (Ches.) 32 SJ 5052
Bickerton (N Yorks.) 38 SE 4450
Bickington (Devon.) 6 SS 5332
Bickington (Devon.) 5 SX 7972
Bickleigh (Devon.) 6 SS 9407
Bickleigh (Devon.) 4 SX 5262
Bickleton 6 SS 5031
Bickley 12 TQ 4268
Bickley Moss 32 SJ 5448
Bicknacre 20 TL 7802
Bicknoller 7 ST 1039
Bicknor 13 TQ 8658
Bickton 8 SU 1412
Bicton (Salop) 24 SJ 4415
Bicton (Salop) 23 SO 2882
Bidborough 12 TQ 5643
Biddenden 13 TQ 8538
Biddenham 27 TL 0250
Biddestone 17 ST 8673
Biddisham 7 ST 3853
Biddlesden 18 SP 6340
Biddlestone 47 NT 9508
Biddulph 33 SJ 8857
Biddulph Moor 33 SJ 9057
Bideford 6 SS 4526
Bidford-on-Avon 25 SP 1052
Bielby 38 SE 7843
Bieldside 62 NJ 8702
Bierley 9 SZ 5077
Bierton 19 SP 8415
Bigbury 5 SX 6646
Bigbury-on-Sea 5 SX 6544
Bigby 39 TA 0507
Biggar (Cumbr.) 40 SD 1966
Biggar (Strath.) 51 NT 0437
Biggin (Derby.) 33 SK 1559
Biggin (Derby.) 33 SK 2548
Biggin (N Yorks.) 38 SE 5434
Biggin Hill 12 TQ 4159
Biggleswade 27 TL 1944
Bighouse 67 NC 8964
Bighton 9 SU 6134
Bignor 11 SU 9814
Big Sand 64 NG 7579
Bilberry 3 SX 0159
Bilborough 34 SK 5241
Bilbrook 25 SJ 8703
Bilbrough 38 SE 5246
Bilbster 67 ND 2852
Bildeston 21 TL 9949
Billericay 20 TQ 6794
Billesdon 26 SK 7103
Billesley 25 SP 1456
Billingborough 35 TF 1134
Billinge 36 SD 5300
Billingford (Norf.) 29 TG 0120
Billingford (Norf.) 29 TM 1678
Billingham 42 NZ 4624
Billinghay 35 TF 1554
Billingley 38 SE 4304
Billingshurst 11 TQ 0825
Billingsley 24 SO 7085
Billington (Beds.) 19 SP 9422
Billington (Lancs.) 36 SD 7235
Billockby 29 TG 4213
Billy Row 42 NZ 1637
Bilsborrow 36 SD 5140
Bilsby 35 TF 4776
Bilsington 13 TR 0434
Bilsthorpe 34 SK 6560
Bilston (Lothian) 51 NT 2664
Bilston (W Mids) 25 SO 9496
Bilstone 33 SK 3606
Bilting 13 TR 0549
Bilton (Humbs.) 39 TA 1532
Bilton (Northum.) 53 NU 2210
Bilton (N Yorks.) 38 SE 4750
Bilton (Warw.) 26 SP 4873
Binbrook 39 TF 2093
Bincombe 8 SY 6884
Binegar 7 ST 6149
Binfield 11 SU 8471
Binfield Heath 10 SU 7478
Bingfield 47 NY 9772
Bingham 34 SK 7039
Bingham's Melcombe 8 ST 7701
Bingley 37 SE 1039
Binham 29 TF 9839
Binley (Hants.) 10 SU 4153
Binley (W Mids) 26 SP 3778
Binniehill 50 NS 8572
Binstead (I. of W.) 9 SZ 5792
Binsted (Hants.) 10 SU 7741
Binton 25 SP 1454
Bintree 29 TG 0123
Binweston 23 SJ 3004
Birch (Essex) 21 TL 9419
Birch (Gtr Mches.) 37 SD 8507
Bircham Newton 28 TF 7633
Bircham Tofts 28 TF 7732
Birchanger 20 TL 5122
Bircher 24 SO 4765
Birch Green 21 TL 9418
Birchgrove (S Glam.) 16 ST 1679
Birchgrove (W Glam.) 15 SS 7098
Birchington 13 TR 3069
Birchover 33 SK 2462
Birch Vale 33 SK 0286
Bircotes 38 SK 6391
Birdbrook 20 TL 7041
Bird End 25 SP 0193
Birdham 9 SU 8200
Birdingbury 26 SP 4368
Birdlip 17 SO 9214
Birdsgreen 24 SO 7685
Birdston 50 NS 6575
Birdwell 37 SE 3401
Birdwood 17 SO 7318
Birgham 53 NT 7939
Birkdale 36 SD 3214
Birkenhead 32 SJ 3188
Birkenhills 62 NJ 7445
Birkenshaw (Strath.) 50 NS 6962
Birkenshaw (W Yorks.) 37 SE 2028
Birkhall 61 NO 3493
Birkhill Feus 57 NO 3433
Birkin 38 SE 5226
Birley 24 SO 4553
Birling (Kent) 12 TQ 6860
Birling (Northum.) 47 NU 2406
Birlingham 25 SO 9343
Birmingham 25 SP 0787
Birnam 56 NO 0341
Birness 62 NJ 9933
Birse 62 NO 5596
Birsemore 61 NO 5297
Birstall 34 SK 5809
Birstall Smithies 37 SE 2226
Birstwith 37 SE 2459
Birtley (Here. and Worc.) 24 SO 3669
Birtley (Northum.) 47 NY 8778
Birtley (Tyne and Wear) 47 NZ 2755
Birts Street 24 SO 7836
Bisbrooke 27 SP 8899
Bishampton 25 SO 9851
Bishop Auckland 42 NZ 2029
Bishopbriggs 50 NS 6070
Bishop Burton 39 SE 9839
Bishop Middleham 42 NZ 3231
Bishop Monkton 42 SE 3266
Bishop Norton 39 SK 9892
Bishopsbourne 13 TR 1852
Bishops Cannings 17 SU 0364
Bishop's Castle 23 SO 3288
Bishop's Caundle 8 ST 6912
Bishop's Cleeve 17 SO 9527
Bishop's Frome 24 SO 6648
Bishop's Itchington 26 SP 3857
Bishops Lydeard 7 ST 1629
Bishop's Nympton 6 SS 7523
Bishop's Offley 32 SJ 7729
Bishop's Stortford 20 TL 4821
Bishop's Sutton 9 SU 6031
Bishop's Tachbrook 26 SP 3161
Bishop's Tawton 6 SS 5630
Bishopsteignton 5 SX 9173
Bishopstoke 9 SU 4619
Bishopston 15 SS 5889
Bishopstone (Bucks.) 18 SP 8010
Bishopstone (E Susx) 12 TQ 4701
Bishopstone (Here. and Worc.) 24 SO 4143
Bishopstone (Wilts.) 8 SU 0625
Bishopstone (Wilts.) 18 SU 2483
Bishop Sutton 17 ST 5859
Bishop's Waltham 9 SU 5517
Bishopswood (Somer.) 7 ST 2512
Bishop's Wood (Staffs.) 25 SJ 8309
Bishopsworth 17 ST 5768
Bishop Thornton 38 SE 2663
Bishopthorpe 38 SE 5947
Bishopton (Durham) 42 NZ 3621
Bishopton (Strath.) 50 NS 4371
Bishop Wilton 38 SE 7955
Bishton 16 ST 3887
Bisley (Glos.) 17 SO 9005
Bisley (Surrey) 11 SU 9559
Bispham 36 SD 3139
Bissoe 2 SW 7741
Bisterne Close 9 SU 2202
Bitchfield 34 SK 9828
Bittadon 6 SS 5441
Bittaford 5 SX 6657
Bittering 29 TF 9317
Bitterley 24 SO 5577
Bitterne 9 SU 4513
Bitteswell 26 SP 5385
Bitton 17 ST 6769
Bix 18 SU 7285
Bixter 63 HU 3352
Blaby 26 SP 5697
Blackacre 45 NY 0490
Blackadder 53 NT 8452
Blackawton 5 SX 8050
Blackborough 5 ST 0909
Blackborough End 28 TF 6614
Black Bourton 18 SP 2804
Blackboys 12 TQ 5220
Blackbrook 32 SJ 7639
Blackburn (Grampn.) 62 NJ 8212
Blackburn (Lancs.) 36 SD 6827
Blackburn (Lothian) 51 NS 9865
Black Callerton 47 NZ 1769
Black Clauchrie 44 NX 2984
Black Crofts 54 NM 9234
Blackden Heath 32 SJ 7871
Black Dog (Devon.) 6 SS 8009
Blackdog (Grampn.) 62 NJ 9514
Black Down (Devon.) 5 ST 0907
Black Down (Devon.) 4 SX 5081
Black Down (Dorset) 7 SY 6087
Blackfield 9 SU 4402
Blackford (Cumbr.) 46 NY 3962
Blackford (Somer.) 7 ST 4147
Blackford (Somer.) 8 ST 6526
Blackford (Tays.) 56 NN 8908
Blackfordby 33 SK 3318
Blackgang 9 SZ 4876
Blackhall Colliery 42 NZ 4539
Blackhalls Rocks 42 NZ 4739
Blackham 12 TQ 4839
Blackhaugh 52 NT 4238
Blackheath (Essex) 21 TM 0021
Blackheath (Surrey) 11 TQ 0346
Blackhill (Grampn.) 62 NK 0843
Blackland 17 SU 0168
Blackley 37 SD 8503
Blacklunans 56 NO 1560
Blackmill 15 SS 9386
Blackmoor 9 SU 7833
Blackmoor Gate 6 SS 6443
Blackmore 20 TL 6001
Blackmore End 20 TL 7430
Black Mount (Strath.) 55 NN 2842
Blackness 51 NT 0579
Blacknest 10 SU 7941
Black Notley 20 TL 7620
Blacko 37 SD 8541
Blackpill 15 SS 6290
Blackpool 36 SD 3035
Blackpool Gate 46 NY 5377
Blackridge 50 NS 8967
Blackrock (Gwent) 16 SO 2112
Blackrock (Islay) 48 NR 3063
Blackrod 36 SD 6110
Blackshaw 45 NY 0465
Blacksmith's Corner 21 TM 0131
Blackstone 11 TQ 2416
Blackthorn 18 SP 6219
Blackthorpe 21 TL 9063
Blacktoft 39 SE 8424
Blacktop 62 NJ 8604
Black Torrington 6 SS 4605
Blackwater (Corn.) 2 SW 7346
Blackwater (Hants.) 11 SU 8559
Blackwater (I. of W.) 9 SZ 5086
Blackwater (Suff.) 29 TM 5077
Blackwaterfoot 49 NR 8928
Blackwell (Derby.) 33 SK 1272
Blackwell (Durham.) 42 NZ 2712
Blackwell (Here. and Worc.) 25 SO 9972
Blackwood (Gwent) 16 ST 1797
Blackwood (Strath.) 50 NS 7943
Blackwood Hill 33 SJ 9255
Blacon 32 SJ 3767
Bladnoch 44 NX 4254
Bladon 18 SP 4414
Blaenannerch 14 SN 2449
Blaenau Ffestiniog 30 SH 7045
Blaenavon 16 SO 2509
Blaenawey 16 SO 2919
Blaen Dyryn 15 SN 9336
Blaengarw 15 SS 9092
Blaengwrach 15 SN 8605
Blaengwynfi 15 SS 8996
Blaenpennal 22 SN 6365
Blaenplwyf 22 SN 5775
Blaenporth 14 SN 2648
Blaenrhondda 15 SS 9299
Blaenwaun 14 SN 2327
Blagdon 5 SX 8561
Blagdon Hill 7 ST 2118
Blaich 55 NN 0476
Blaina 16 SO 2008
Blairadam Forest 56 NT 1693
Blair Atholl 56 NN 8765
Blair Castle (Tays.) (ant.) 56 NN 8666
Blairdenon Hill 56 NN 8601
Blair Drummond 56 NS 7398
Blairdrummond Moss 56 NS 7297
Blairfindy Castle (ant.) 61 NJ 1928
Blairgowrie 56 NO 1745
Blairhall 51 NT 0089
Blairingone 56 NS 9896
Blairlogie 56 NS 8396
Blairmore 49 NS 1982
Blairskaith 50 NS 5975
Blaisdon 17 SO 7016
Blakebrook 25 SO 8077
Blakedown 25 SO 8778
Blakelaw 53 NT 7730
Blakemere 24 SO 3641
Blakeney (Glos.) 17 SO 6707
Blakeney (Norf.) 29 TG 0243
Blakenhall (Ches.) 32 SJ 7247
Blakenhall (W Mids) 25 SO 9297
Blakeshall 25 SO 8381
Blakesley 26 SP 6250
Blanchland 47 NY 9650
Blandford Forum 8 ST 8806
Blandford St. Mary 8 ST 8805
Bland Hill 37 SE 2053
Blanefield 50 NS 5579
Blankney 35 TF 0660
Blarghour 55 NM 9913
Blarmachfoldach 55 NN 0969
Blarnaleyoch 64 NH 1490

Blashford Brims

Blashford 8 SU 1406
Blaston 26 SP 8095
Blatherwycke 27 SP 9795
Blawith 40 SD 2888
Blaxhall 21 TM 3657
Blaxton 38 SE 6600
Blaydon 47 NZ 1863
Bleadon 16 ST 3456
Blean 13 TR 1260
Bleasby 34 SK 7049
Blebocraigs 57 NO 4214
Bleddfa 23 SO 2068
Bledington 18 SP 2422
Bledlow 18 SP 7802
Bledlow Ridge 18 SU 7898
Blegbie 52 NT 4861
Blencarn 41 NY 6331
Blencogo 46 NY 1947
Blencow 40 NY 4532
Blendworth 9 SU 7113
Blennerhasset 40 NY 1741
Bletchingdon 18 SP 5017
Bletchingley 12 TQ 3250
Bletchley (Bucks.) 19 SP 8733
Bletchley (Salop) 32 SJ 6233
Bletherston 14 SN 0721
Bletsoe 27 TL 0258
Blewbury 18 SU 5385
Blickling 29 TG 1728
Blidworth 34 SK 5855
Blindburn 53 NT 8310
Blindcrake 40 NY 1434
Blindley Heath 12 TQ 3645
Blisland 4 SX 0973
Blissford 8 SU 1713
Bliss Gate 24 SO 7472
Blisworth 26 SP 7253
Blockley 25 SP 1634
Blofield 29 TG 3309
Blo Norton 29 TM 0179
Blore 33 SK 1349
Bloxham 18 SP 4235
Bloxwich 25 SJ 9902
Bloxworth 8 SY 8894
Blubberhouses 37 SE 1655
Blue Anchor 7 ST 0343
Blue Bell Hill 12 TQ 7462
Blundeston 29 TM 5197
Blunham 27 TL 1551
Blunsdon St. Andrew 17 SU 1389
Bluntisham 27 TL 3674
Blyborough 39 SK 9394
Blyford 29 TM 4276
Blymhill 25 SJ 8112
Blyth (Northum.) 47 NZ 3181
Blyth (Notts.) 34 SK 6287
Blyth Bridge 51 NT 1345
Blythburgh 29 TM 4575
Blythe Bridge 33 SJ 9541
Blyton 39 SK 8594
Boarhills 57 NO 5614
Boarhunt 9 SU 6008
Boarshead 12 TQ 5332
Boarstall 18 SP 6214
Boasley Cross 4 SX 5093
Boath 65 NH 5773
Boat of Garten 60 NH 9419
Bobbing 13 TQ 8865
Bobbington 24 SO 8090
Bobbingworth 20 TL 5305
Bocaddon 4 SX 1758
Bocking 20 TL 7623
Bocking Churchstreet 20 TL 7525
Boconnoc 4 SX 1460
Boddam (Grampn.) 62 NK 1342
Boddam (Shetld.) 63 HU 3915
Boddington 17 SO 8925
Bodedern 30 SH 3380
Bodelwyddan 31 SJ 0075
Bodenham (Here. and Worc.) 24 SO 5251
Bodenham (Wilts.) 8 SU 1626
Bodewryd 30 SH 3990
Bodfari 31 SJ 0970
Bodffordd 30 SH 4276
Bodfuan 30 SH 3237
Bodham Street 29 TG 1240
Bodiam 12 TQ 7826
Bodicote 18 SP 4537
Bodieve 4 SW 9973
Bodior 30 SH 2876
Bodle Street Green 12 TQ 6514
Bodmin 4 SX 0767
Bodney 28 TL 8398
Bodorgan 30 SH 3867
Bogbrae 62 NK 0335
Bogend 50 NS 3932
Boghall 51 NS 9968
Bogmoor 61 NJ 3562
Bogniebrae 62 NJ 5945
Bognor Regis 11 SZ 9399
Bograxie 62 NJ 7119
Bogside 50 NS 8353
Bog, The 24 SO 3597
Bogton 62 NJ 6751
Bogue 45 NX 6481
Bohortha 2 SW 8632
Bohuntine 55 NN 2882
Boisdale 63 NF 7417
Bojewyan 2 SW 3934
Bolam 42 NZ 1922
Bold Heath 32 SJ 5389
Boldon 47 NZ 3661
Boldon Colliery 47 NZ 3462
Boldre 9 SZ 3198
Boldron 42 NZ 0314
Bole 34 SK 7987
Bolehill 33 SK 2955
Boleside 52 NT 4933
Bolham Water 7 ST 1612
Bolingey 2 SW 7653
Bollington (Ches.) 32 SJ 7286
Bollington (Ches.) 33 SJ 9377
Bolney 11 TQ 2622
Bolnhurst 27 TL 0859
Bolshan 57 NO 6252
Bolsover 33 SK 4770
Bolsterstone 37 SK 2696
Bolstone 24 SO 5532
Boltby 42 SE 4886
Bolton (Cumbr.) 41 NY 6323
Bolton (Gtr Mches.) 36 SD 7108
Bolton (Humbs.) 38 SE 7752
Bolton (Lothian) 52 NT 5070
Bolton (Northum.) 53 NU 1013
Bolton Abbey 37 SE 0754
Bolton by Bowland 37 SD 7849
Boltonfellend 46 NY 4768
Boltongate 40 NY 2340
Bolton le Sands 40 SD 4867
Bolton-on-Swale 42 SE 2599
Bolton Percy 38 SE 5341
Bolton Upon Dearne 38 SE 4502
Bolventor 4 SX 1876
Bomere Heath 32 SJ 4719
Bonar Bridge 65 NH 6191
Bonawe 55 NN 0131
Bonawe Quarries 55 NN 0133
Bonby 39 TA 0015
Boncath 14 SN 2038
Bonchester Bridge 52 NT 5811
Bondleigh 6 SS 6504
Bonehill 25 SK 1902
Bo'Ness 51 NS 9981
Bonhill 50 NS 3979
Boningale 25 SJ 8102
Bonjedward 52 NT 6523
Bonkle 50 NS 8356
Bonnington (Kent) 13 TR 0536
Bonnington (Lothian) 51 NT 1269
Bonnington Smiddy 57 NO 5739
Bonnybank 57 NO 3503
Bonnybridge 50 NS 8280
Bonnykelly 62 NJ 8553
Bonnyrigg 51 NT 3065
Bonnyton (Tays.) 57 NO 3338
Bonnyton (Tays.) 57 NO 6655
Bonsall 33 SK 2758
Bont 16 SO 3819
Bontddu 30 SH 6618
Bont-dolgadfan 22 SH 8800
Bontgoch Elerch 22 SN 6886
Bontnewydd (Gwyn.) 30 SH 4859
Bont Newydd (Gwyn.) 31 SH 7720
Bontuchel 31 SJ 0857
Bonvilston 16 ST 0674
Booker 19 SU 8491
Booley 32 SJ 5725
Boosbeck 42 NZ 6516
Boot 40 NY 1700
Boothby Graffoe 34 SK 9859
Boothby Pagnell 34 SK 9730
Boothstown 36 SD 7200
Bootle (Cumbr.) 40 SD 1088
Bootle (Mers.) 32 SJ 3394
Bootle Station 40 SD 0989
Boquhan 50 NS 5387
Boraston 24 SO 6170
Borden 13 TQ 8863
Bordley 41 SD 9465
Boreham (Essex) 20 TL 7509
Boreham (Wilts.) 8 ST 8944
Boreham Street 12 TQ 6611
Borehamwood 19 TQ 1996
Boreland (Dumf. and Galwy.) 46 NY 1790
Boreraig 58 NG 1853
Borgie 66 NC 6759
Borgue (Dumf. and Galwy.) 45 NX 6248
Borgue (Highld.) 67 ND 1325
Borley 20 TL 8442
Bornesketaig 58 NG 3771
Borness 45 NX 6145
Boroughbridge 42 SE 3966
Borough Green 12 TQ 6057
Borras Head 32 SJ 3653
Borrobol Lodge 67 NC 8626
Borrowash 33 SK 4134
Borrowby 42 SE 4289
Borrowdale (Cumbr.) 40 NY 2514
Borth 22 SN 6089
Borthwickbrae 52 NT 4113
Borthwickshiels 52 NT 4315
Borve (Barra) 63 NF 6501
Borve (Berneray) 63 NF 9181
Borve (Island of Skye) 58 NG 4448
Borvemore 63 NG 0294
Borwick 40 SD 5273
Bosavern 2 SW 3730
Bosbury 24 SO 6943
Boscastle 4 SX 0990
Boscombe (Dorset) 8 SZ 1191
Boscombe (Wilts.) 8 SU 2038
Boscoppa 4 SX 0353
Bosham 9 SU 8004
Bosherston 14 SR 9694
Boskednan 2 SW 4434
Bosley 33 SJ 9165
Bossall 38 SE 7160
Bossiney 4 SX 0688
Bossingham 13 TR 1549
Bostock Green 32 SJ 6769
Boston 35 TF 3244
Boston Spa 38 SE 4245
Botallack 2 SW 3632
Botcheston 26 SK 4804
Botesdale 29 TM 0475
Bothal 47 NZ 2386
Bothamsall 34 SK 6773
Bothel 40 NY 1838
Bothenhampton 7 SY 4791
Bothwell 50 NS 7058
Botley (Bucks.) 19 SP 9802
Botley (Hants.) 9 SU 5112
Botley (Oxon.) 18 SP 4806
Botolphs 11 TQ 1909
Bottacks 65 NH 4860
Bottesford (Humbs.) 39 SE 9107
Bottesford (Leic.) 34 SK 8038
Bottisham 20 TL 5460
Bottomcraig 57 NO 3724
Bottoms 37 SD 9321
Botusfleming 4 SX 4061
Botwnnog 30 SH 2631
Boughrood 23 SO 1239
Boughspring 16 ST 5597
Boughton (Norf.) 28 TF 7002
Boughton (Northants.) 26 SP 7565
Boughton (Notts.) 34 SK 6768
Boughton Aluph 13 TR 0348
Boughton Green 12 TQ 7651
Boughton Lees 13 TR 0247
Boughton Malherbe 13 TQ 8849
Boughton Street 13 TR 0559
Boulby 43 NZ 7519
Bouldon 24 SO 5485
Boulmer 53 NU 2614
Boulston 14 SM 9812
Boultham 34 SK 9568
Bourn 20 TL 3256
Bourne 35 TF 0920
Bournebridge 20 TQ 5194
Bourne End (Beds.) 27 SP 9644
Bourne End (Bucks.) 19 SU 8987
Bourne End (Herts.) 19 TL 0206
Bournemouth 8 SZ 0991
Bournes Green 17 SO 9104
Bournheath 25 SO 9474
Bournmoor 47 NZ 3051
Bournville 25 SP 0480
Bourton (Avon) 16 ST 3864
Bourton (Dorset) 8 ST 7630
Bourton (Oxon.) 18 SU 2387
Bourton (Salop) 24 SO 5996
Bourton on Dunsmore 26 SP 4370
Bourton-on-the-Hill 25 SP 1732
Bourton-on-the-Water 17 SP 1620
Bousd 48 NM 2563
Boveney 11 SU 9377
Boverton 15 SS 9868
Bovey Tracey 5 SX 8178
Bovingdon 19 TL 0103
Bovington Camp 8 SY 8389
Bow (Devon.) 6 SS 7201
Bow (Flotta) (Orkney) 63 ND 3593
Bowbank 41 NY 9423
Bow Brickhill 19 SP 9034
Bowburn 42 NZ 3038
Bowcombe 9 SZ 4786
Bowd 5 SY 1190
Bowden (Borders) 52 NT 5530
Bowden (Devon.) 5 SX 8448
Bowden Hill 17 ST 9367
Bowdon 32 SJ 7586
Bower 46 NY 7583
Bowerchalke 8 SU 0122
Bowermadden 67 ND 2364
Bowers Gifford 20 TQ 7588
Bowershall 51 NT 0991
Bowertower 67 ND 2362
Bowes 41 NY 9913
Bowhill 52 NT 4227
Bowland Bridge 40 SD 4189
Bowley 24 SO 5352
Bowlhead Green 11 SU 9138
Bowling 50 NS 4473
Bowling Bank 32 SJ 3948
Bowling Green 25 SO 8151
Bowmanstead 40 SD 3096
Bowmore 48 NR 3159
Bowness-on-Solway 46 NY 2262
Bowness-on-Windermere 40 SD 4097
Bow of Fife 57 NO 3112
Bowsden 53 NT 9941
Bow Street 22 SN 6284
Bowthorpe 29 TG 1709
Box (Glos.) 17 SO 8600
Box (Wilts.) 17 ST 8268
Boxbush 17 SO 7412
Boxford (Berks.) 10 SU 4271
Boxford (Suff.) 21 TL 9640
Boxgrove 11 SU 9007
Boxley 12 TQ 7759
Boxted (Essex) 21 TM 0033
Boxted (Suff.) 20 TL 8250
Boxworth 20 TL 3464
Boyden Gate 13 TR 2264
Boylestone 33 SK 1835
Boyndie 62 NJ 6463
Boyndie Bay 62 NJ 6765
Boyndlie 62 NJ 9162
Boynton 39 TA 1368
Boysack 57 NO 6249
Boyton (Corn.) 4 SX 3192
Boyton (Suff.) 21 TM 3747
Boyton (Wilts.) 8 ST 9539
Bozeat 27 SP 9059
Braaid 43 SC 3176
Brabling Green 21 TM 2964
Brabourne 13 TR 1041
Brabourne Lees 13 TR 0840
Brabstermire 67 ND 3169
Bracadale 58 NG 3538
Braceborough 35 TF 0713
Bracebridge Heath 34 SK 9767
Braceby 34 TF 0135
Bracewell 37 SD 8648
Brackenfield 33 SK 3759
Brackenthwaite 40 NY 1522
Brackletter 55 NN 1882
Brackley (Northants.) 18 SP 5837
Brackley (Strath.) 49 NR 7941
Bracknell 11 SU 8769
Braco 56 NN 8309
Bracobrae 61 NJ 5053
Bracon Ash 29 TM 1899
Bracora 58 NM 7192
Bracorina 58 NM 7292
Bradbourne 33 SK 2052
Bradbury 42 NZ 3128
Bradda 43 SC 1970
Bradden 26 SP 6448
Braddock 4 SX 1662
Bradenham 18 SU 8297
Bradenstoke 17 SU 0079
Bradfield (Berks.) 10 SU 6072
Bradfield (Essex) 21 TM 1430
Bradfield (Norf.) 29 TG 2633
Bradfield (S Yorks.) 37 SK 2692
Bradfield Combust 21 TL 8957
Bradfield Green 32 SJ 6859
Bradfield St. Clare 21 TL 9057
Bradfield St.George 21 TL 9059
Bradford (Devon.) 4 SS 4207
Bradford (Northum.) 53 NU 1532
Bradford (W Yorks.) 37 SE 1633
Bradford Abbas 7 ST 5814
Bradford Leigh 17 ST 8362
Bradford on Avon 17 ST 8260
Bradford-on-Tone 7 ST 1722
Bradford Peverell 7 SY 6592
Brading 9 SZ 6087
Bradley (Derby.) 33 SK 2145
Bradley (Hants.) 10 SU 6341
Bradley (Here. and Worc.) 25 SO 9860
Bradley (Humbs.) 39 TA 2406
Bradley (N Yorks.) 42 SE 0380
Bradley (Staffs.) 25 SJ 8717
Bradley Green 25 SO 9861
Bradley in the Moors 33 SK 0541
Bradmore 34 SK 5831
Bradninch 5 SS 9903
Bradnop 33 SK 0155
Bradpole 7 SY 4794
Bradshaw 36 SD 7312
Bradstone 4 SX 3880
Bradwell (Bucks.) 18 SP 8339
Bradwell (Derby.) 33 SK 1781
Bradwell (Essex) 20 TL 8023
Bradwell (Norf.) 29 TG 5003
Bradwell Green 32 SJ 7563
Bradwell Grove 18 SP 2308
Bradwell-on-Sea 21 TM 0006
Bradwell Waterside 21 TL 9907
Bradworthy 4 SS 3213
Brae (Highld.) 64 NG 8185
Brae (Highld.) 65 NH 6662
Brae (Shetld.) 63 HU 3567
Braedownie 57 NO 2875
Braefield 60 NH 4130
Braegrum 56 NO 0024
Braehead (Orkney) 63 HY 5101
Braehead (Strath.) 50 NS 8134
Braehead (Strath.) 51 NS 9550
Braehead (Tays.) 57 NO 6852
Braehead (Westray) 63 HY 4447
Braehead (Wigtown.) 44 NX 4252
Braehoulland 63 HU 2479
Braemore 67 ND 0630
Brae of Achnahaird 64 NB 9913
Braeside 49 NS 2375
Braeswick 63 HY 6037
Brafferton (Durham) 42 NZ 2921
Brafferton (N Yorks.) 38 SE 4370
Brafield-on-the-Green 26 SP 8158
Bragar 63 NB 2847
Bragbury End 19 TL 2621
Braidwood 50 NS 8448
Braigo 48 NR 2369
Brailes 26 SP 3139
Brailsford 33 SK 2541
Braintree 20 TL 7622
Braiseworth 29 TM 1371
Braishfield 9 SU 3725
Braithwaite 40 NY 2323
Braithwell 38 SK 5394
Bramber 11 TQ 1810
Bramcote 34 SK 5037
Bramdean 9 SU 6127
Bramerton 29 TG 2904
Bramfield (Herts.) 19 TL 2915
Bramfield (Suff.) 29 TM 4073
Bramford 21 TM 1246
Bramhall 33 SJ 8984
Bramham 38 SE 4242
Bramhope 37 SE 2443
Bramley (Hants.) 10 SU 6358
Bramley (Surrey) 11 TQ 0044
Bramley (S Yorks.) 38 SK 4892
Brampford Speke 6 SX 9298
Brampton (Cambs.) 27 TL 2170
Brampton (Cumbr.) 46 NY 5361
Brampton (Cumbr.) 41 NY 6723
Brampton (Lincs.) 34 SK 8479
Brampton (Norf.) 29 TG 2224
Brampton (Suff.) 29 TM 4381
Brampton (S Yorks.) 38 SE 4101
Brampton Abbotts 17 SO 6026
Brampton Ash 26 SP 7887
Brampton Bryan 24 SO 3672
Bramshall 33 SK 0633
Bramshaw 9 SU 2615
Bramshill 10 SU 7461
Bramshott 9 SU 8432
Branault 54 NM 5369
Brancaster 28 TF 7743
Brancepeth 42 NZ 2238
Branchill 61 NJ 0852
Branderburgh 61 NJ 2371
Brandesburton 39 TA 1147
Brandeston 21 TM 2460
Brandiston 29 TG 1321
Brandon (Durham) 42 NZ 2439
Brandon (Lincs.) 34 SK 9048
Brandon (Northum.) 53 NU 0417
Brandon (Suff.) 28 TL 7886
Brandon (Warw.) 26 SP 4076
Brandon Bank 28 TL 6289
Brandon Creek 28 TL 6091
Brandon Parva 29 TG 0708
Brandsby 38 SE 5872
Brands Hatch 12 TQ 5764
Brane 2 SW 4028
Bran End 20 TL 6525
Branksome Park 8 SZ 0490
Branscombe 5 SY 1988
Bransdale 42 SE 6296
Bransford 24 SO 7952
Bransgore 8 SZ 1897
Branston (Leic.) 34 SK 8029
Branston (Lincs.) 34 TF 0167
Branston (Staffs.) 33 SK 2221
Branstone 9 SZ 5583
Brant Broughton 34 SK 9154
Brantham 21 TM 1034
Branthwaite 40 NY 0525
Brantingham 39 SE 9429
Branton 53 NU 0416
Branxholme 52 NT 4611
Branxholm Park 52 NT 4612
Branxton 53 NT 8937
Brassington 33 SK 2354
Brasted 12 TQ 4755
Brasted Chart 12 TQ 4653
Bratoft 35 TF 4765
Brattleby 34 SK 9480
Bratton 8 ST 9152
Bratton Clovelly 4 SX 4691
Bratton Fleming 6 SS 6437
Bratton Seymour 8 ST 6729
Braughing 20 TL 3925
Braunston (Leic.) 34 SK 8306
Braunston (Northants.) 26 SP 5366
Braunstone 26 SK 5502
Braunton 6 SS 4836
Brawby 43 SE 7378
Brawl 67 NC 8066
Brawlbin 67 ND 0757
Bray 11 SU 9079
Braybrooke 26 SP 7684
Brayford 6 SS 6834
Bray Shop 4 SX 3374
Brayton 38 SE 6030
Brazacott 4 SX 2691
Breachwood Green 19 TL 1522
Breaclete 63 NB 1536
Breadsall 33 SK 3639
Breadstone 17 SO 7000
Breage 2 SW 6128
Breakish 58 NG 6723
Bream 17 SO 6005
Breamore 8 SU 1517
Brean 16 ST 2955
Brearton 42 SE 3260
Breasclete 63 NB 2135
Breaston 33 SK 4533
Brechfa 15 SN 5230
Brechin 57 NO 5960
Breckles 29 TL 9594
Breckrey 58 NG 5061
Brecon 16 SO 0428
Bredbury 37 SJ 9292
Brede 12 TQ 8218
Bredenbury 24 SO 6056
Bredfield 21 TM 2653
Bredgar 13 TQ 8860
Bredhurst 12 TQ 7962
Bredon 25 SO 9236
Bredon's Norton 25 SO 9339
Bredwardine 23 SO 3344
Breedon on the Hill 33 SK 4022
Breibister 63 HU 2149
Breich 51 NS 9560
Breighton 38 SE 7033
Breinton 24 SO 4739
Breivig 63 NL 6998
Bremhill 17 ST 9873
Bremia (ant.) 22 SN 6456
Brenchley 12 TQ 6741
Brendon 6 SS 7648
Brenish 63 NA 9926
Brent 19 TQ 2084
Brent Eleigh 21 TL 9447
Brentford 11 TQ 1778
Brent Knoll 7 ST 3350
Brent Pelham 20 TL 4330
Brentwood 20 TQ 5993
Brenzett 13 TR 0027
Brereton 25 SK 0516
Brereton Green 32 SJ 7764
Brereton Heath 32 SJ 8064
Bressingham 29 TM 0780
Bretabister 63 HU 4857
Bretby 33 SK 2923
Bretford 26 SP 4277
Bretforton 25 SP 0943
Bretherton 36 SD 4720
Brettenham (Norf.) 29 TL 9383
Brettenham (Suff.) 21 TL 9653
Bretton 32 SJ 3563
Brewham 8 ST 7136
Brewood 25 SJ 8808
Briantspuddle 8 SY 8193
Bricket Wood 19 TL 1301
Bricklehampton 25 SO 9842
Bride 43 NX 4501
Bridekirk 40 NY 1133
Bridell 14 SN 1742
Bridestowe 4 SX 5189
Brideswell 62 NJ 5739
Bridford 5 SX 8186
Bridge 13 TR 1854
Bridge End (Lincs.) 35 TF 1436
Bridgefoot 40 NY 0529
Bridge Green 20 TL 4636
Bridgemary 9 SU 5702
Bridgend (Cumbr.) 40 NY 3914
Bridgend (Dumf. and Galwy.) 45 NT 0708
Bridgend (Dumf. and Galwy.) 52 NT 5235
Bridgend (Fife.) 57 NO 3911
Bridgend (Grampn.) 61 NJ 3731
Bridgend (Grampn.) 61 NJ 5135
Bridgend (Islay) 48 NR 3362
Bridgend (Lothian) 51 NT 0475
Bridgend (Mid Glam.) 15 SS 9079
Bridgend (Strath.) 49 NR 8592
Bridgend (Strath.) 50 NS 6970
Bridgend (Tays.) 56 NO 1224
Bridgend (Tays.) 57 NO 5368
Bridgend of Lintrathen 57 NO 2854
Bridge of Alford 62 NJ 5617
Bridge of Allan 56 NS 7897
Bridge of Avon 61 NJ 1835
Bridge of Balgie 55 NN 5746
Bridge of Brown 61 NJ 1220
Bridge of Cally 56 NO 1351
Bridge of Canny 62 NO 6597
Bridge of Dee 45 NX 7360
Bridge of Don 62 NJ 9409
Bridge of Dun 57 NO 6658
Bridge of Dye 57 NO 6585
Bridge of Earn 56 NO 1318
Bridge of Feugh 62 NO 7094
Bridge of Gairn 61 NO 3597
Bridge of Gaur 55 NN 5056
Bridge of Muchalls 62 NO 8991
Bridge of Orchy 55 NN 2939
Bridge of Tilt 56 NN 8765
Bridge of Walls 63 HU 2651
Bridge of Weir 50 NS 3865
Bridgerule 4 SS 2803
Bridges 24 SO 3996
Bridge Sollers 24 SO 4142
Bridge Street 21 TL 8749
Bridgetown 6 SS 9233
Bridge Trafford 32 SJ 4471
Bridgeyate 17 ST 6873
Bridgham 29 TL 9686
Bridgnorth 24 SO 7193
Bridgtown 25 SJ 9808
Bridgwater 7 ST 3037
Bridlington 39 TA 1766
Bridport 7 SY 4692
Bridstow 17 SO 5824
Brierfield 37 SD 8436
Brierley (Glos.) 17 SO 6215
Brierley (Here. and Worc.) 24 SO 4956
Brierley (S Yorks.) 38 SE 4011
Brierley Hill 25 SO 9187
Brigg 39 TA 0007
Brigham (Cumbr.) 40 NY 0830
Brigham (Humbs.) 39 TA 0753
Brighouse 37 SE 1423
Brighstone 9 SZ 4282
Brightgate 33 SK 2659
Brighthampton 18 SP 3803
Brightling 12 TQ 6821
Brightlingsea 21 TM 0816
Brighton (Corn.) 2 SW 9054
Brighton (E Susx) 12 TQ 3105
Brightons 51 NS 9277
Brightwalton 10 SU 4278
Brightwell (Oxon.) 18 SU 5790
Brightwell (Suff.) 21 TM 2543
Brightwell Baldwin 18 SU 6594
Brignall 42 NZ 0712
Brig o'Turk 55 NN 5306
Brigsley 39 TA 2501
Brigsteer 40 SD 4889
Brigstock 27 SP 9485
Brill 18 SP 6513
Brilley 23 SO 2549
Brimfield 24 SO 5267
Brimington 33 SK 4073
Brimpsfield 17 SO 9312
Brimpton 10 SU 5564
Brims 63 ND 2888

Chilton Buildings

Copthorne

Chilton Buildings	42	NZ 2929
Chilton Cantelo	7	ST 5621
Chilton Foliat	10	SU 3170
Chilton Polden	7	ST 3739
Chilton Street	20	TL 7547
Chilton Trinity	7	ST 2939
Chilworth	9	SU 4018
Chimney	18	SP 3500
Chineham	10	SU 6554
Chingford	20	TQ 3893
Chinley	33	SK 0382
Chinnor	18	SP 7500
Chipnall	32	SJ 7231
Chippenham (Cambs.)	28	TL 6669
Chippenham (Wilts.)	17	ST 9173
Chipperfield	19	TL 0401
Chipping (Herts.)	20	TL 3532
Chipping (Lancs.)	36	SD 6243
Chipping Campden	25	SP 1539
Chipping Hill	20	TL 8215
Chipping Norton	18	SP 3127
Chipping Ongar	20	TL 5502
Chipping Sodbury	17	ST 7282
Chipping Warden	26	SP 4948
Chipstable	7	ST 0427
Chipstead (Kent)	12	TQ 5056
Chipstead (Surrey)	11	TQ 2756
Chirbury	23	SO 2598
Chirk	32	SJ 2937
Chirmorie	44	NX 2076
Chirnside	53	NT 8756
Chirnsidebridge	53	NT 8556
Chirton	17	SU 0757
Chisbury	10	SU 2766
Chiselborough	7	ST 4614
Chisledon	17	SU 1879
Chislehampton	18	SU 5999
Chislehurst	12	TQ 4470
Chislet	13	TR 2264
Chiswellgreen	19	TL 1303
Chiswick	11	TQ 2077
Chisworth	37	SJ 9991
Chithurst	9	SU 8423
Chittering	28	TL 4970
Chitterne	8	ST 9843
Chittlehamholt	6	SS 6420
Chittlehampton	6	SS 6325
Chittoe	17	ST 9666
Chivelstone	5	SX 7838
Chobham	11	SU 9761
Cholderton	10	SU 2242
Cholesbury	19	SP 9307
Chollerton	47	NY 9372
Cholsey	18	SU 5886
Cholstrey	24	SO 4659
Choppington	47	NZ 2583
Chopwell	47	NZ 1158
Chorley (Ches.)	32	SJ 5650
Chorley (Lancs.)	36	SD 5817
Chorley (Salop)	24	SO 6983
Chorley (Staffs.)	25	SK 0711
Chorleywood	19	TQ 0396
Chorlton	32	SJ 7250
Chorlton-cum-Hardy	37	SJ 8093
Chorlton Lane	32	SJ 4547
Chowley	32	SJ 4756
Chrishall	20	TL 4439
Christchurch (Cambs.)	28	TL 4996
Christchurch (Dorset)	8	SZ 1593
Christchurch (Glos.)	17	SO 5713
Christian Malford	17	ST 9678
Christleton	32	SJ 4365
Christmas Common	18	SU 7193
Christon	16	ST 3956
Christon Bank	53	NU 2122
Christow	5	SX 8385
Chudleigh	5	SX 8679
Chudleigh Knighton	5	SX 8477
Chulmleigh	6	SS 6814
Chunal	37	SK 0391
Church	36	SD 7428
Churcham	17	SO 7618
Church Aston	24	SJ 7317
Church Brampton	26	SP 7165
Church Broughton	33	SK 2033
Church Crookham	10	SU 8152
Churchdown	17	SO 8819
Church Eaton	25	SJ 8417
Church End (Beds.)	19	SP 9921
Church End (Beds.)	19	TL 1937
Church End (Cambs.)	35	TF 3909
Church End (Cambs.)	20	TL 4857
Church End (Essex)	20	TL 5841
Churchend (Essex)	20	TL 6323
Churchend (Essex)	21	TR 0092
Church End (Hants.)	10	SU 6756
Church End (Warw.)	26	SP 2892
Church End (Wilts.)	17	SU 0278
Church Fenton	38	SE 5136
Church Gresley	33	SK 2918
Church Handborough	18	SP 4212
Churchill (Avon)	16	ST 4359
Churchill (Here. and Worc.)	25	SO 8779
Churchill (Oxon.)	18	SP 2824
Churchingford	7	ST 2112
Church Knowle	8	SY 9481
Church Langton	26	SP 7293
Church Lawford	26	SP 4476
Church Lawton	32	SJ 8255
Church Leigh	33	SK 0235
Church Lench	25	SP 0251
Church Minshull	32	SJ 6660
Church Norton	9	SZ 8695
Churchover	26	SP 5080
Church Preen	24	SO 5398
Church Pulverbatch	24	SJ 4303
Churchstanton	7	ST 1914
Church Stoke	23	SO 2694
Churchstow (Devon.)	5	SX 7145
Church Stowe (Northants.)	26	SP 6357
Church Street	12	TQ 7174
Church Stretton	24	SO 4593
Churchtown (I. of M.)	43	SC 4294
Churchtown (Lancs.)	36	SD 4842
Churchtown (Mers.)	36	SD 3618
Church Warsop	34	SK 5668
Churt	11	SU 8538
Churton	32	SJ 4156
Churwell	37	SE 2729
Chwilog	30	SH 4338
Chyandour	2	SW 4731
Cilcain	31	SJ 1765
Cilcennin	22	SN 5160
Cilfor	30	SH 6237
Cilfrew	15	SN 7600
Cilfynydd	16	ST 0892
Cilgerran	14	SN 1943
Cilgwyn	15	SN 7430
Ciliau-Aeron	22	SN 5058
Cilmalieu	54	NM 8955
Cilmery	15	SO 0051
Cilrhedyn	14	SN 2734
Ciltalgarth	31	SH 8840
Cilwendeg	14	SN 2238
Cilybebyll	15	SN 7404
Cilycwm	15	SN 7540
Cinderford	17	SO 6513
Cioch Mhor	65	NH 5063
Cirean Geardail	64	NC 0034
Cirencester	17	SP 0201
City Dulas	30	SH 4687
Clachaig	49	NS 1181
Clachan (Benbecula)	63	NF 7746
Clachan (Lismore Island)	54	NM 8543
Clachan (North Uist)	63	NF 8163
Clachan (Raasay)	58	NG 5436
Clachan (Strath.)	54	NM 7819
Clachan (Strath.)	48	NR 7656
Clachan Mor	48	NL 9847
Clachan of Campsie	50	NS 6179
Clachan of Glendaruel	49	NR 9984
Clachan-Seil	54	NM 7718
Clachbreck	48	NR 7675
Clachtoll	64	NC 0427
Clackavoid	56	NO 1463
Clackmannan	50	NS 9191
Clacton-on-Sea	21	TM 1715
Claddach Kirkibost	63	NF 7865
Cladich	55	NN 0921
Claggan	54	NM 7049
Claigan	58	NG 2354
Claines	25	SO 8559
Clandown	17	ST 6955
Clanfield (Hants.)	9	SU 6916
Clanfield (Oxon.)	18	SP 2801
Clannaborough Barton	6	SS 7402
Clanville	10	SU 3148
Clanyard	44	NX 1037
Claonaig	49	NR 8656
Claonel	66	NC 5604
Clapgate	8	SU 0102
Clapham (Beds.)	27	TL 0252
Clapham (Gtr London)	11	TQ 2875
Clapham (N Yorks.)	41	SD 7469
Clapham (W Susx)	11	TQ 0906
Clappers	53	NT 9455
Clappersgate	40	NY 3603
Clapton (Glos.)	17	SP 1617
Clapton (Somer.)	7	ST 4106
Clapton-in-Gordano	16	ST 4774
Clapworthy	6	SS 6724
Clarbeston	14	SN 0421
Clarbeston Road	14	SN 0121
Clarborough	34	SK 7383
Clardon	67	ND 1468
Clare	20	TL 7645
Clarebrand	45	NX 7666
Claremont Park	11	TQ 1363
Clarencefield	45	NY 0968
Clarkston	50	NS 5757
Clashmore	65	NH 7489
Clashnessie	64	NC 0530
Clathy	56	NN 9919
Clatt	62	NJ 5426
Clatter	23	SN 9994
Clattering Brig	57	NO 6678
Clatworthy	7	ST 0530
Claughton (Lancs.)	36	SD 5242
Claughton (Lancs.)	41	SD 5666
Claverdon	25	SP 1964
Claverham	16	ST 4566
Clavering	20	TL 4832
Claverley	24	SO 7993
Claverton	17	ST 7864
Clawdd-newydd	31	SJ 0852
Clawton	4	SX 3599
Claxby (Lincs.)	39	TF 1194
Claxby (Lincs.)	35	TF 4571
Claxton (Norf.)	29	TG 3303
Claxton (N Yorks.)	38	SE 6960
Claybrooke Magna	26	SP 4988
Clay Common	29	TM 4781
Clay Coton	26	SP 5977
Clay Cross	33	SK 3963
Claydon (Oxon.)	26	SP 4550
Claydon (Suff.)	21	TM 1350
Claygate	11	TQ 1563
Claygate Cross	12	TQ 6155
Clayhanger (Devon.)	7	ST 0223
Clayhanger (W Mids)	25	SK 0404
Clayhidon	7	ST 1615
Clayock	67	ND 1659
Claypole	34	SK 8449
Clays of Allan	65	NH 8376
Clayton (Staffs.)	33	SJ 8443
Clayton (S Yorks.)	38	SE 4507
Clayton (W Susx)	12	TQ 3014
Clayton (W Yorks.)	37	SE 1131
Clayton-le-Moors	36	SD 7431
Clayton-le-Woods	36	SD 5722
Clayton West	37	SE 2511
Clayworth	34	SK 7288
Cleadale	54	NM 4789
Cleadon	47	NZ 3862
Clearwell	17	SO 5708
Cleasby	42	NZ 2713
Cleat	63	ND 4584
Cleatlam	42	NZ 1118
Cleator	40	NY 0113
Cleator Moor	40	NY 0214
Cleckheaton	37	SE 1825
Cleedownton	24	SO 5880
Cleehill	24	SO 5975
Clee St. Margaret	24	SO 5684
Cleethorpes	39	TA 3008
Cleeton St. Mary	24	SO 6178
Cleeve	16	ST 4566
Cleeve Hill	17	SO 9827
Cleeve Prior	25	SP 0849
Clehonger	24	SO 4637
Cleigh	54	NM 8725
Cleish	56	NT 0998
Cleland	50	NS 7958
Clench Common	17	SU 1765
Clenchwarton	28	TF 5820
Clent	25	SO 9179
Cleobury Mortimer	24	SO 6775
Cleobury North	24	SO 6187
Cleongart	48	NR 6734
Clephanton	60	NH 8450
Clerklands	52	NT 5024
Clestrain	63	HY 3006
Cleuchbrae	45	NY 0673
Clevancy	17	SU 0475
Clevedon	16	ST 4071
Cleveleys	36	SD 3142
Cleverton	17	ST 9785
Clewer	7	ST 4350
Cley next the Sea	29	TG 0444
Cliasamol	63	NB 0706
Cliburn	41	NY 5824
Cliddesden	10	SU 6349
Cliffe (Kent)	12	TQ 7376
Cliffe (N Yorks.)	38	SE 6631
Cliff End	13	TQ 8813
Cliffe Woods	12	TQ 7373
Clifford (Here. and Worc.)	23	SO 2445
Clifford (W Yorks.)	38	SE 4244
Clifford Chambers	25	SP 1952
Clifford's Mesne	17	SO 7023
Cliffsend	13	TR 3464
Clifton (Avon)	17	ST 5673
Clifton (Beds.)	27	TL 1739
Clifton (Central)	55	NN 3230
Clifton (Cumbr.)	40	NY 0429
Clifton (Cumbr.)	40	NY 5326
Clifton (Derby.)	33	SK 1644
Clifton (Here. and Worc.)	25	SO 8446
Clifton (Lancs.)	36	SD 4630
Clifton (Northum.)	47	NZ 2082
Clifton (Notts.)	34	SK 5434
Clifton (Oxon.)	18	SP 4831
Clifton Campville	33	SK 2510
Clifton Hampden	18	SU 5495
Clifton Reynes	27	SP 9051
Clifton upon Dunsmore	26	SP 5276
Clifton upon Teme	24	SO 7161
Climping	11	TQ 0002
Clint	37	SE 2559
Clinterty	62	NJ 8311
Clint Green	29	TG 0210
Clintmains	52	NT 6132
Clippesby	29	TG 4214
Clipsham	34	SK 9616
Clipston (Northants.)	26	SP 7181
Clipston (Notts.)	34	SK 6333
Clipstone	34	SK 6064
Clitheroe	36	SD 7441
Clive	32	SJ 5124
Clivocast	63	HP 6000
Clocaenog	31	SJ 0854
Clochan	61	NJ 4060
Clock Face	32	SJ 5291
Clodock	16	SO 3227
Clola	62	NK 0043
Clophill	19	TL 0838
Clopton	27	TL 0680
Clopton Green	20	TL 7654
Closeburn	45	NX 8992
Close Clark	43	SC 2775
Clothall	19	TL 2732
Clothan	63	HU 4581
Clotton	32	SJ 5263
Clough Foot	37	SD 9123
Cloughton	43	TA 0094
Cloughton Newlands	43	TA 0096
Clousta	63	HU 3157
Clova (Grampn.)	61	NJ 4522
Clova (Tays.)	57	NO 3273
Clovelly	4	SS 3124
Clovenfords	52	NT 4436
Clovenstone	62	NJ 7717
Clovulin	55	NN 0063
Clowne	33	SK 4975
Clows Top	24	SO 7171
Cluer	63	NG 1490
Clun	23	SO 3081
Clunas	60	NH 8846
Clunbury	24	SO 3780
Clunes	55	NN 2088
Clungunford	24	SO 3978
Clunie (Grampn.)	62	NJ 6350
Clunie (Tays.)	56	NO 1043
Clunton	23	SO 3381
Cluny	51	NT 2495
Clutton (Avon)	17	ST 6159
Clutton (Ches.)	32	SJ 4654
Clwt-y-bont	30	SH 5763
Clydach (Gwent)	16	SO 2213
Clydach (W Glam.)	15	SN 6801
Clydach Vale	15	SS 9793
Clydebank	50	NS 5069
Clydey	14	SN 2535
Clyffe Pypard	17	SU 0776
Clynder	49	NS 2484
Clynderwen	14	SN 1219
Clynelish	67	NC 8905
Clynnog-fawr	30	SH 4149
Clyro	23	SO 2143
Clyst Honiton	5	SX 9893
Clyst Hydon	5	ST 0301
Clyst St. George	5	SX 9888
Clyst St. Lawrence	5	ST 0200
Clyst St. Mary	5	SX 9890
Clyth	67	ND 2937
Cnwch Coch	22	SN 6775
Coad's Green	4	SX 2976
Coal Aston	33	SK 3679
Coalbrookdale	24	SJ 6604
Coalburn	50	NS 8034
Coalcleugh	46	NY 8045
Coaley	17	SO 7701
Coalpit Heath	17	ST 6780
Coalport	24	SJ 6902
Coalsnaughton	50	NS 9195
Coaltown of Balgonie	57	NT 2999
Coaltown of Wemyss	51	NT 3295
Coalville	33	SK 4214
Coast	64	NG 9290
Coatbridge	50	NS 7265
Coatdyke	50	NS 7464
Coate (Wilts.)	17	SU 0361
Coate (Wilts.)	17	SU 1782
Coates (Cambs.)	27	TL 3097
Coates (Glos.)	17	SO 9700
Coatham	42	NZ 5925
Coatham Mundeville	42	NZ 2919
Coatsgate	45	NT 0605
Cobbaton	6	SS 6127
Coberley	17	SO 9615
Cobham (Kent)	12	TQ 6768
Cobham (Surrey)	11	TQ 1060
Cobnash	24	SO 4560
Cockayne	42	SE 6298
Cockayne Hatley	27	TL 2549
Cock Bridge	61	NJ 2509
Cockburnspath	53	NT 7770
Cock Clarks	20	TL 8102
Cockenzie and Port Seton	52	NT 4075
Cockerham	36	SD 4651
Cockerington	35	TF 3789
Cockermouth	40	NY 1230
Cockernhoe Green	19	TL 1223
Cockfield (Durham)	42	NZ 1224
Cockfield (Suff.)	21	TL 9054
Cockfosters	19	TQ 2896
Cocking	11	SU 8717
Cockington	5	SX 8964
Cocklake	7	ST 4349
Cockley Cley	28	TF 7904
Cockpole Green	10	SU 7981
Cockshutt	32	SJ 4329
Cockthorpe	29	TF 9842
Cockwood	5	SX 9780
Coddenham	21	TM 1354
Coddington (Ches.)	32	SJ 4455
Coddington (Here. and Worc.)	24	SO 7142
Coddington (Notts.)	34	SK 8354
Codford St. Mary	8	ST 9739
Codford St. Peter	8	ST 9640
Codicote	19	TL 2118
Codnor	33	SK 4149
Codrington	17	ST 7278
Codsall	25	SJ 8603
Codsall Wood	25	SJ 8405
Coedana	30	SH 4381
Coedely	15	ST 0285
Coedkernew	16	ST 2783
Coedpoeth	32	SJ 2850
Coed-y-paen	16	ST 3398
Coelbren	15	SN 8411
Coffinswell	5	SX 8868
Cofton Hackett	25	SP 0075
Cogan	16	ST 1772
Cogenhoe	26	SP 8360
Coggeshall	20	TL 8522
Coillaig	55	NN 0120
Coille Coire Chrannaig	55	NN 4888
Coille Mhorgil	59	NH 1001
Coillore	58	NG 3537
Coity	15	SS 9281
Coker	7	ST 5312
Colaboll	66	NC 5610
Colan	2	SW 8661
Colaton Raleigh	5	SY 0787
Colbost	58	NG 2148
Colby (Cumbr.)	41	NY 6620
Colby (I. of M.)	43	SC 2370
Colby (Norf.)	29	TG 2131
Colchester	21	TM 0025
Cold Ash	10	SU 5169
Cold Ashby	26	SP 6576
Cold Ashton	17	ST 7472
Coldbackie	66	NC 6160
Coldblow	12	TQ 5173
Cold Brayfield	27	SP 9252
Coldean	12	TQ 3408
Coldeast	5	SX 8274
Colden Common	9	SU 4822
Coldfair Green	21	TM 4361
Cold Hanworth	35	TF 0383
Coldharbour	11	TQ 1443
Cold Hesledon	47	NZ 4147
Cold Higham	26	SP 6653
Coldingham	53	NT 9065
Cold Kirby	42	SE 5384
Cold Newton	34	SK 7106
Cold Norton	20	TL 8500
Cold Overton	34	SK 8110
Coldrain	56	NO 0700
Coldred	13	TR 2747
Coldridge	6	SS 6907
Coldstream	53	NT 8439
Coldwaltham	11	TQ 0216
Coldwells	62	NK 1039
Cole	8	ST 6633
Colebatch	23	SO 3187
Colebrook	5	ST 0006
Colebrooke	6	SX 7799
Coleby (Humbs.)	39	SE 8919
Coleby (Lincs.)	34	SK 9760
Coleford (Devon.)	6	SS 7701
Coleford (Glos.)	17	SO 5710
Coleford (Somer.)	8	ST 6848
Colehill	8	SU 0300
Coleman's Hatch	12	TQ 4533
Colemere	32	SJ 4232
Colenden	56	NO 1029
Coleorton	33	SK 3917
Colerne	17	ST 8171
Colesbourne	17	SO 9913
Colesden	27	TL 1255
Coleshill (Bucks.)	19	SU 9495
Coleshill (Oxon.)	18	SU 2393
Coleshill (Warw.)	25	SP 1989
Colgate	11	TQ 2332
Colgrain	50	NS 3280
Colinsburgh	57	NO 4703
Colinton	51	NT 2169
Colintraive	49	NS 0374
Colkirk	28	TF 9126
Coll (Isle of Lewis)	63	NB 4739
Collace	56	NO 2032
Collafirth (Shetld.)	63	HU 3482
Collafirth (Shetld.)	63	HU 4368
Collaton St. Mary	5	SX 8660
Collessie	57	NO 2813
Collier Row	20	TQ 4991
Collier's End	20	TL 3720
Collier Street	12	TQ 7145
Colliery Row	47	NZ 3449
Collieston	62	NK 0328
Collin	45	NY 0276
Collingbourne Ducis	10	SU 2453
Collingbourne Kingston	10	SU 2355
Collingham (Notts.)	34	SK 8261
Collingham (W Yorks.)	37	SE 3845
Collington	24	SO 6460
Collingtree	26	SP 7555
Colliston	57	NO 6045
Collynie	62	NJ 8436
Collyweston	27	SK 9903
Colmonell	44	NX 1586
Colmworth	27	TL 1058
Colnabaichin	61	NJ 2908
Colnbrook	11	TQ 0277
Colne (Cambs.)	27	TL 3776
Colne (Lancs.)	37	SD 8839
Colne Engaine	20	TL 8530
Colne Valley	20	TL 8529
Colney	29	TG 1808
Colney Heath	19	TL 2005
Colney Street	19	TL 1502
Coln Rogers	17	SP 0809
Coln St. Aldwyns	17	SP 1405
Coln St. Dennis	17	SP 0810
Colp	62	NJ 7448
Colpy	62	NJ 6432
Colsterdale	42	SE 1280
Colsterworth	34	SK 9224
Colston Bassett	34	SK 7033
Coltfield	61	NJ 1163
Coltishall	29	TG 2619
Colton (Cumbr.)	40	SD 3186
Colton (Norf.)	29	TG 1009
Colton (N Yorks.)	38	SE 5444
Colton (Staffs.)	33	SK 0520
Colvister	63	HU 5196
Colwall Green	24	SO 7541
Colwall Stone	24	SO 7542
Colwell	47	NY 9575
Colwich	33	SK 0121
Colwinston	15	SS 9475
Colworth	11	SU 9102
Colwyn Bay	31	SH 8478
Colyford	5	SY 2492
Colyton	5	SY 2493
Combe (Berks.)	10	SU 3760
Combe (Here. and Worc.)	23	SO 3463
Combe (Oxon.)	18	SP 4115
Combe Florey	7	ST 1531
Combe Hay	17	ST 7359
Combeinteignhead	5	SX 9071
Combe Martin	6	SS 5846
Combe Moor	24	SO 3663
Combe Raleigh	5	ST 1502
Comberbach	32	SJ 6477
Comberton	20	TL 3856
Combe St. Nicholas	7	ST 3011
Comb Hill	46	NT 3900
Combrook	26	SP 3051
Combs (Derby.)	33	SK 0478
Combs (Suff.)	21	TM 0456
Combs Ford	21	TM 0457
Combwich	7	ST 2542
Comers	62	NJ 6707
Commins Coch	22	SH 8403
Commondale	42	NZ 6610
Common Edge	36	SD 3232
Common Moor	4	SX 2369
Common Side	33	SK 3375
Common, The	9	SU 2432
Compstall	33	SJ 9690
Compton (Berks.)	10	SU 5279
Compton (Devon.)	5	SX 8664
Compton (Hants.)	9	SU 4625
Compton (Surrey)	11	SU 9547
Compton (Wilts.)	8	SU 1352
Compton (W Susx)	9	SU 7714
Compton Abbas	8	ST 8718
Compton Abdale	17	SP 0516
Compton Bassett	17	SU 0372
Compton Beauchamp	18	SU 2887
Compton Bishop	16	ST 3955
Compton Chamberlayne	8	SU 0229
Compton Dando	17	ST 6464
Compton Dundon	7	ST 4933
Compton Martin	16	ST 5456
Compton Pauncefoot	8	ST 6425
Compton Valence	7	SY 5993
Comrie	56	NN 7722
Conchra	49	NS 0288
Concraigie	56	NO 1044
Conderton	25	SO 9637
Condicote	17	SP 1528
Condorrat	50	NS 7373
Condover	24	SJ 4906
Coneyhurst Common	11	TQ 1024
Coneysthorpe	38	SE 7171
Coney Weston	29	TL 9578
Congerstone	26	SK 3605
Congham	28	TF 7123
Congleton	33	SJ 8562
Congresbury	16	ST 4363
Coningsby	35	TF 2258
Conington (Cambs.)	27	TL 1785
Conington (Cambs.)	20	TL 3266
Conisbrough	38	SK 5098
Conisby	48	NR 2661
Conisholme	39	TF 3995
Coniston (Cumbr.)	40	SD 3097
Coniston (Humbs.)	39	TA 1535
Coniston Cold	37	SD 9054
Conistone	41	SD 9867
Connah's Quay	32	SJ 2869
Connel	54	NM 9134
Connel Park	50	NS 6012
Connor Downs	2	SW 5939
Cononbridge	60	NH 5455
Cononley	37	SD 9846
Consall	33	SJ 9748
Consett	47	NZ 1150
Constable Burton	42	SE 1690
Constantine	2	SW 7229
Contin	60	NH 4555
Contlaw	62	NJ 8402
Conway	31	SH 7777
Conyer	13	TQ 9664
Cookbury	4	SS 4005
Cookham	19	SU 8985
Cookham Dean	19	SU 8785
Cookham Rise	19	SU 8884
Cookhill	25	SP 0558
Cookley (Here. and Worc.)	25	SO 8480
Cookley (Suff.)	29	TM 3475
Cookley Green	18	SU 6990
Cookney	62	NO 8793
Cooksbridge	12	TQ 4013
Cooksmill Green	20	TL 6306
Coolham	11	TQ 1222
Cooling	12	TQ 7575
Coombe (Corn.)	4	SS 2011
Coombe (Corn.)	2	SW 9551
Coombe Bissett	8	SU 1026
Coombe Hill	17	SO 8827
Coombe Keynes	8	SY 8484
Coombes	11	TQ 1908
Coopersale Common	20	TL 4702
Copdock	21	TM 1141
Copford Green	21	TL 9222
Copister	63	HU 4778
Cople	27	TL 1048
Copley	42	NZ 0825
Coplow Dale	33	SK 1679
Copmanthorpe	38	SE 5646
Coppathorne	4	SS 2000
Coppenhall	33	SJ 9019
Coppingford	27	TL 1680
Copplestone	6	SS 7702
Coppull	36	SD 5613
Copsale	11	TQ 1724
Copster Green	36	SD 6734
Copt Heath	25	SP 1778
Copt Hewick	42	SE 3371
Copthorne	12	TQ 3139

Copt Oak Dalderby

Copt Oak 33 SK 4812
Copythorne 9 SU 3014
Corbridge 47 NY 9964
Corby 27 SP 8988
Corby Glen 34 SK 9925
Coreley 24 SO 6173
Corfe 7 ST 2319
Corfe Castle 8 SY 9681
Corfe Mullen 8 SY 9798
Corfton 24 SO 4985
Corgarff 61 NJ 2708
Corhampton 9 SU 6120
Corley 26 SP 3085
Corley Ash 26 SP 2886
Corley Moor 26 SP 2884
Cornelly 15 SS 8281
Corney 40 SD 1191
Cornforth 42 NZ 3034
Cornhill 62 NJ 5858
Cornhill-on-Tweed 53 NT 8639
Corn Holm (Copinsay) 63 HY 5901
Cornholme (W Yorks.) 37 SD 9025
Cornish Hall End 20 TL 6836
Cornquoy 63 ND 5299
Cornriggs 41 NY 8441
Cornsay 42 NZ 1443
Corntown 60 NH 5555
Cornwell 18 SP 2727
Cornwood 4 SX 6059
Cornworthy 5 SX 8255
Corpach 55 NN 0976
Corpusty 29 TG 1129
Corran (Highld.) 59 NG 8509
Corran (Highld.) 55 NN 0163
Corrany 43 SC 4589
Corrie 49 NS 0243
Corrie Common 46 NY 2085
Corriemoillie 65 NH 3663
Corrimony 60 NH 3830
Corringham (Essex) 20 TQ 7183
Corringham (Lincs.) 39 SK 8691
Corris Uchaf 22 SH 7408
Corry 58 NG 6424
Corry of Ardnagrask 60 NH 5048
Corscombe 7 ST 5105
Corse 62 NJ 6040
Corse of Kinnoir 62 NJ 5443
Corsham 17 ST 8669
Corsindae 62 NJ 6808
Corsley 8 ST 8246
Corsley Heath 8 ST 8245
Corsock 45 NX 7576
Corston (Avon) 17 ST 6965
Corston (Wilts.) 17 ST 9284
Corstorphine 51 NT 1972
Cortachy 57 NO 3959
Corton (Suff.) 29 TM 5497
Corton (Wilts.) 8 ST 9340
Corton Denham 8 ST 6322
Coruanan Lodge 55 NN 0668
Corwen 31 SJ 0743
Coryton (Devon.) 4 SX 4583
Coryton (Essex) 20 TQ 7482
Cosby 26 SP 5495
Coseley 25 SO 9494
Cosgrove 26 SP 7942
Cosham 9 SU 6605
Cosheston 14 SN 0003
Cossall 33 SK 4842
Cosses 44 NX 1182
Cossington (Leic.) 34 SK 6013
Cossington (Somer.) 7 ST 3540
Costa 63 HY 3328
Costessey 29 TG 1712
Costock 34 SK 5726
Coston 34 SK 8422
Cotebrook 32 SJ 5765
Cotehill 46 NY 4750
Cotes (Cumbr.) 40 SD 4886
Cotes (Leic.) 34 SK 5520
Cotes (Staffs.) 33 SJ 8434
Cotesbach 26 SP 5382
Cotgrave 34 SK 6435
Cothall 62 NJ 8716
Cotham 34 SK 7947
Cothelstone 7 ST 1831
Cotherstone 41 NZ 0119
Cothill 18 SU 4699
Cotleigh 5 ST 2002
Coton (Cambs.) 20 TL 4158
Coton (Northants.) 26 SP 6771
Coton (Staffs.) 33 SJ 9832
Coton Clanford 33 SJ 8723
Coton in the Elms 33 SK 2415
Cott 5 SX 7861
Cottam (Lancs.) 36 SD 4932
Cottam (Notts.) 34 SK 8179
Cottartown 61 NJ 0331
Cottenham 20 TL 4567
Cotterdale 41 SD 8393
Cottered 20 TL 3129
Cotterstock 27 TL 0490
Cottesbrooke 26 SP 7073
Cottesmore 34 SK 9013
Cottingham (Humbs.) 39 TA 0532
Cottingham (Northants.) 18 SP 8490
Cottisford 26 SP 5831
Cotton 21 TM 0667
Cotton End 27 TL 0845
Cot-town (Grampn.) 61 NJ 5026
Cottown (Grampn.) 62 NJ 7715
Cot-town (Grampn.) 62 NJ 8140
Cotwalton 33 SJ 9234
Coughton 25 SP 0760
Coulags 59 NG 9645
Coull 61 NJ 5102
Coulport 49 NS 2087
Coulsdon 12 TQ 3059
Coulter 51 NT 0233
Coulton 38 SE 6374
Cound 24 SJ 5504
Coundon 42 NZ 2329
Coundon Grange 42 NZ 2327
Countersett 41 SD 9287
Countess Wear 5 SX 9489
Countesthorpe 26 SP 5895
Countisbury 6 SS 7449
Coupar Angus 56 NO 2139
Coupland 53 NT 9331
Cour 49 NR 8248
Courteachan 58 NM 6897
Courteenhall 26 SP 7653
Court Henry 15 SN 5522
Courtsend 21 TR 0293
Courtway 7 ST 2033
Cousland 51 NT 3768
Cousley Wood 12 TQ 6533
Cove (Devon.) 6 SS 9519
Cove (Hants.) 11 SU 8555
Cove (Highld.) 64 NG 8190
Cove (Strath.) 49 NS 2281
Cove Bay (Grampn.) 62 NJ 9500
Covehithe 29 TM 5281
Coven 25 SJ 9006
Coveney 27 TL 4882
Covenham St. Bartholomew 39 TF 3395
Covenham St. Mary 39 TF 3394
Coventry 26 SP 3379
Cove Point 48 NR 7107
Coverack 2 SW 7818
Coverham 42 SE 1086
Covington 27 TL 0570
Cowan Bridge 41 SD 6476
Cowbeech 12 TQ 6114
Cowbit 35 TF 2618
Cowbridge 15 SS 9974
Cowden 12 TQ 4640
Cowdenbeath 51 NT 1691
Cowdenburn 51 NT 2052
Cowes 9 SZ 4995
Cowesby 42 SE 4689
Cowfold 11 TQ 2122
Cowick 38 SE 6521
Cowie 50 NS 8389
Cowley (Devon.) 6 SX 9095
Cowley (Glos.) 17 SO 9614
Cowley (Gtr London) 19 TQ 0582
Cowley (Oxon.) 18 SP 5404
Cowling (N Yorks.) 37 SD 9743
Cowling (N Yorks.) 42 SE 2387
Cowlinge 20 TL 7154
Cowpen Bewley 42 NZ 4824
Cowplain 9 SU 7011
Cowshill 41 NY 8540
Cowstrandburn 51 NT 0390
Coxbank 32 SJ 6541
Coxbench 33 SK 3743
Cox Common 29 TM 4082
Coxheath 12 TQ 7451
Coxhoe 42 NZ 3235
Coxley 7 ST 5343
Coxwold 42 SE 5377
Coychurch 15 SS 9379
Coylton 50 NS 4119
Coylumbridge 60 NH 9110
Coynach 61 NJ 4405
Crabbs Cross 25 SP 0464
Crabtree 11 TQ 2225
Crabtree Green 32 SJ 3344
Crackenthorpe 41 NY 6622
Crackington Haven 4 SX 1496
Crackleybank 24 SJ 7611
Crackpot 41 SD 9796
Cracoe 41 SD 9760
Cradley 24 SO 7347
Crafthole 4 SX 3654
Cragabus 48 NR 3345
Cragg 37 SE 0023
Craggan (Grampn.) 61 NJ 0226
Craggan (Strath.) 55 NS 2699
Craghead 47 NZ 2150
Craibstone (Grampn.) 62 NJ 8611
Craichie 57 NO 5047
Craig (Dumf. and Galwy.) 45 NX 6875
Craig (Highld.) 59 NH 0349
Craig Castle 61 NJ 4724
Craigcefnparc 15 SN 6703
Craigdallie 57 NO 2428
Craigdam 62 NJ 8430
Craigdarroch 45 NS 6306
Craigearn 62 NJ 7214
Craigellachie (Grampn.) 61 NJ 2844
Craigend 56 NO 1120
Craigendoran 50 NS 3181
Craiggiecat 62 NO 8592
Craighat 50 NS 4984
Craighoar Hill 45 NT 0002
Craighouse 48 NR 5267
Craigie (Grampn.) 62 NJ 9119
Craigie (Strath.) 50 NS 4232
Craigie (Tays.) 56 NO 1143
Craiglockhart 51 NT 2270
Craigmillar 51 NT 2871
Craignant 32 SJ 2535
Craigneuk (Strath.) 50 NS 7656
Craigneuk (Strath.) 50 NS 7764
Craignure 54 NM 7236
Craigo 57 NO 6864
Craigow 56 NO 0806
Craig Penllyn 15 SS 9777
Craigrothie 57 NO 3710
Craigruie 55 NN 5020
Craigton (Grampn.) 62 NJ 8301
Craigton (Tays.) 57 NO 3250
Craigton (Tays.) 57 NO 5138
Craigtown 67 NC 8856
Craig-y-nos 15 SN 8315
Craik 46 NT 3408
Crail 57 NO 6107
Crailing 52 NT 6824
Crailinghall 52 NT 6921
Crakehall 42 SE 2490
Crambe 38 SE 7364
Cramlington 47 NZ 2776
Cramond 51 NT 1876
Cramond Bridge 51 NT 1775
Cranage 32 SJ 7568
Cranberry 32 SJ 8236
Cranborne 8 SU 0513
Cranbourne 11 SU 9272
Cranbrook 12 TQ 7735
Cranbrook Common 12 TQ 7938
Cranfield 27 SP 9542
Cranford 11 TQ 1077
Cranford St. Andrew 27 SP 9277
Cranford St. John 27 SP 9276
Cranham (Essex) 20 TQ 5787
Cranham (Glos.) 17 SO 8912
Crank 32 SJ 5099
Cranleigh 11 TQ 0638
Cranmore (I. of W.) 9 SZ 3990
Cranmore (Somer.) 8 ST 6843
Cranna 62 NJ 6352
Crannach 61 NJ 4954
Cranoe 26 SP 7695
Cransford 21 TM 3164
Cranshaws 52 NT 6961
Cranstal 43 NX 4602
Crantock 2 SW 7860
Cranwell 35 TF 0349
Cranwich 28 TL 7795
Cranworth 29 TF 9804
Crapstone 4 SX 5067
Crarae 55 NR 9897
Craster 53 NU 2519
Cratfield 29 TM 3175
Crathes 62 NO 7596
Crathie (Grampn.) 61 NO 2695
Crathie (Highld.) 60 NN 5893
Crathorne 42 NZ 4407
Craven Arms 24 SO 4382
Crawcrook 47 NZ 1363
Crawford 51 NS 9520
Crawfordjohn 50 NS 8823
Crawick 50 NS 7710
Crawley (Hants.) 9 SU 4234
Crawley (Oxon.) 18 SP 3312
Crawley (W Susx) 11 TQ 2636
Crawley Down 12 TQ 3237
Crawley Side 41 NY 9940
Crawshawbooth 37 SD 8125
Crawton 57 NO 8779
Cray (N Yorks.) 41 SD 9479
Cray (Powys) 15 SN 8924
Crayford 12 TQ 5175
Crayke 38 SE 5670
Crays Hill 20 TQ 7192
Cray's Pond 10 SU 6380
Creacombe 6 SS 8119
Creagan 55 NM 9744
Creagorry 63 NF 7948
Creaton 26 SP 7071
Credenhill 24 SO 4543
Crediton 6 SS 8300
Creech St. Michael 7 ST 2725
Creed 2 SW 9347
Creekmouth 20 TQ 4581
Creeting St. Mary 21 TM 0956
Creeton 34 TF 0120
Creetown 44 NX 4758
Creggans 55 NN 0802
Cregneish 43 SC 1967
Cregrina 23 SO 1252
Creich (Fife.) 57 NO 3221
Creich (Island of Mull) 54 NM 3124
Creigiau 16 ST 0881
Cressage 24 SJ 5904
Cresselly 14 SN 0606
Cressing 20 TL 7920
Cresswell (Dyfed) 14 SN 0506
Cresswell (Northum.) 47 NZ 2993
Cresswell (Staffs.) 33 SJ 9739
Creswell 34 SK 5274
Cretingham 21 TM 2260
Crewe (Ches.) 32 SJ 4253
Crewe (Ches.) 32 SJ 7055
Crew Green 23 SJ 3215
Crewkerne 7 ST 4409
Crianlarich 55 NN 3825
Cribyn 15 SN 5251
Criccieth 30 SH 4938
Crich 33 SK 3554
Crichie 62 NJ 9544
Crichton 51 NT 3862
Crick (Gwent) 16 ST 4890
Crick (Northants.) 26 SP 5872
Crickadarn 23 SO 0942
Cricket St. Thomas 7 ST 3708
Crickheath 32 SJ 2923
Crickhowell 16 SO 2118
Cricklade 17 SU 0993
Cridling Stubbs 38 SE 5221
Crieff 56 NN 8621
Criggion 23 SJ 2915
Crigglestone 37 SE 3116
Crimond 62 NK 0556
Crimplesham 28 TF 6503
Crinaglack 60 NH 4240
Crinan 49 NR 7894
Cringleford 29 TG 1905
Crinow 14 SN 1214
Cripplesease 2 SW 5036
Cripp's Corner 12 TQ 7821
Croachy 60 NH 6527
Crockenhill 12 TQ 5067
Crockernwell 5 SX 7592
Crockerton 8 ST 8642
Crocketford or Ninemile Bar 45 NX 8272
Crockey Hill 38 SE 6246
Crockham Hill 12 TQ 4450
Crockleford Heath 21 TM 0426
Croeserw 15 SS 8695
Croesgoch 14 SM 8330
Croesor 30 SH 6344
Croesyceiliog (Gwent) 15 SN 4016
Croesyceiliog (Gwent) 16 ST 3196
Croes-y-mwyalch 16 ST 3092
Croft (Ches.) 32 SJ 6393
Croft (Leic.) 26 SP 5195
Croft (Lincs.) 35 TF 5162
Croft (N Yorks.) 42 NZ 2909
Croftamie 50 NS 4786
Crofton 37 SE 3717
Crofty 15 SS 5295
Croggan 54 NM 7027
Croglin 46 NY 5747
Croick 65 NH 4591
Croir 63 NB 1539
Cromarty 65 NH 7766
Cromdale 61 NJ 0728
Cromer (Herts.) 19 TL 2928
Cromer (Norf.) 29 TG 2142
Cromford 33 SK 2956
Cromhall 17 ST 6990
Cromhall Common 17 ST 6989
Cromore 63 NB 4021
Cromra 55 NN 5489
Cromwell 34 SK 7961
Cronberry 50 NS 6022
Crondall 10 SU 7948
Cronk, The 43 SC 3495
Cronk-y-Voddy 43 SC 3086
Cronton 32 SJ 4988
Crook (Cumbr.) 40 SD 4694
Crook (Durham) 42 NZ 1635
Crookham (Berks.) 10 SU 5364
Crookham (Northum.) 53 NT 9138
Crookham Village 10 SU 7952
Crookhouse 53 NT 7626
Crooklands 40 SD 5383
Crook of Devon 56 NO 0301
Cropredy 26 SP 4646
Cropston 34 SK 5511
Cropthorne 25 SO 9944
Cropton 43 SE 7589
Cropwell Bishop 34 SK 6835
Cropwell Butler 34 SK 6837
Crosbie 49 NS 2150
Crosby (Cumbr.) 40 NY 0738
Crosby (I. of M.) 43 SC 3279
Crosby (Lincs.) 39 SE 8711
Crosby (Mers.) 32 SJ 3099
Crosby Garrett 41 NY 7309
Crosby Ravensworth 41 NY 6214
Croscombe 7 ST 5844
Cross (Somerset) 16 ST 4154
Cross (W Isles) 63 NB 5061
Crossaig 49 NR 8351
Crossapoll 48 NL 9943
Cross Ash 16 SO 4019
Crossbost 63 NB 3924
Crosscanonby 40 NY 0739
Crossdale Street 29 TG 2239
Crossdougal 63 NF 7520
Crossens 36 SD 3719
Crossford (Fife.) 51 NT 0686
Crossford (Strath.) 50 NS 8246
Crossgates (Fife.) 51 NT 1488
Crossgates (Powys) 23 SO 0865
Crossgill 41 SD 5562
Cross Green (Devon.) 4 SX 3888
Cross Green (Suff.) 21 TL 9952
Cross Hands 15 SN 5612
Crosshill (Fife) 56 NT 1796
Crosshill (Strath.) 44 NS 3206
Crosshouse (Strath.) 50 NS 3938
Cross Houses (Salop) 24 SJ 5307
Crossings 46 NY 5177
Cross in Hand 12 TQ 5621
Cross Inn (Dyfed) 22 SN 3957
Cross Inn (Dyfed) 22 SN 5464
Cross Inn (Mid Glam.) 16 ST 0583
Crosskeys (Gwent) 16 ST 2292
Crosskirk 67 ND 0370
Cross Lanes (Clwyd) 32 SJ 3746
Crosslanes (N Yorks.) 38 SE 5264
Crosslanes (Shrops.) 32 SJ 3218
Crosslee 51 NT 3018
Crossmichael 45 NX 7267
Crossmoor 36 SD 4438
Cross of Jackston 62 NJ 7432
Crossroads 62 NO 7594
Cross Street 29 TM 1876
Crossway 16 SO 4419
Crossway Green 25 SO 8368
Crosswell 14 SN 1236
Crosthwaite 40 SD 4491
Croston 36 SD 4818
Crostwick 29 TG 2515
Crostwight 29 TG 3329
Crouch Hill 8 ST 7010
Croughton 18 SP 5433
Crovie 62 NJ 8065
Crowan 2 SW 6434
Crowborough 12 TQ 5130
Crowcombe 7 ST 1336
Crowfield (Northants.) 26 SP 6141
Crowfield (Suff.) 21 TM 1557
Crow Hill 17 SO 6326
Crowhurst (E Susx) 12 TQ 7512
Crowhurst (Surrey) 12 TQ 3947
Crowland 35 TF 2310
Crowlas 2 SW 5133
Crowle (Here. and Worc.) 25 SO 9256
Crowle (Humbs.) 38 SE 7713
Crowlista 63 NB 0433
Crowmarsh Gifford 18 SU 6189
Crownhill 4 SX 4857
Crownthorpe 29 TG 0803
Crow Rock 14 SR 8894
Crowthorne 11 SU 8464
Crowton 32 SJ 5774
Croxall 25 SK 1913
Croxdale 42 NZ 2636
Croxden 33 SK 0639
Croxley Green 19 TQ 0795
Croxton (Cambs.) 27 TL 2459
Croxton (Humbs.) 39 TA 0912
Croxton (Norf.) 28 TL 8786
Croxton (Staffs.) 32 SJ 7832
Croxton Kerrial 34 SK 8329
Croy (Highld.) 60 NH 7949
Croy (Strath.) 50 NS 7275
Croyde 6 SS 4439
Croydon (Cambs.) 20 TL 3149
Croydon (Gtr London) 12 TQ 3365
Cruban Beag 60 NN 6692
Cruckmeole 24 SJ 4309
Cruckton 24 SJ 4210
Cruden Bay 62 NK 0936
Crudgington 24 SJ 6317
Crudwell 17 ST 9592
Crug 23 SO 1872
Crugmeer 2 SW 9076
Crulivig 63 NB 1733
Crumlin 16 ST 2198
Crundale (Dyfed) 14 SM 9718
Crundale (Kent) 13 TR 0749
Crunwear 14 SN 1810
Cruwys Morchard 6 SS 8712
Crux Easton 10 SU 4256
Crwbin 15 SN 4713
Crymmych 14 SN 1833
Crynant 15 SN 7905
Crystal Palace 12 TQ 3470
Cuaig 58 NG 7057
Cubbington 26 SP 3368
Cubert 2 SW 7857
Cublington 19 SP 8422
Cuckfield 12 TQ 3024
Cucklington 8 ST 7527
Cuckney 34 SK 5671
Cuddesdon 18 SP 5902
Cuddington (Bucks.) 18 SP 7311
Cuddington (Ches.) 32 SJ 5971
Cuddington Heath 32 SJ 4646
Cuddy Hill 36 SD 4937
Cudham 12 TQ 4459
Cudliptown 4 SX 5278
Cudworth (Somer.) 7 ST 3810
Cudworth (S Yorks.) 37 SE 3808
Cuffley 20 TL 3002
Cuiashader 63 NB 5458
Cuier 63 NF 6703
Culbo 65 NH 6360
Culbokie 60 NH 6059
Culburnie 60 NH 4941
Culcabock 60 NH 6844
Culcharry 60 NH 8650
Culcheth 32 SJ 6594
Culdrain 61 NJ 5133
Culduie 58 NG 7140
Culford 28 TL 8370
Culgaith 41 NY 6129
Culham 18 SU 5095
Culkein 64 NC 0333
Culkerton 17 ST 9296
Cullachie 60 NH 9720
Cullen 61 NJ 5166
Cullercoats 47 NZ 3571
Cullerlie 62 NJ 7603
Cullicudden 65 NH 6564
Cullingworth 37 SE 0636
Cullipool 54 NM 7313
Cullisse 65 NH 8274
Cullivoe 63 HP 5402
Culloch 56 NN 7818
Cullompton 5 ST 0207
Culmaily 65 NH 8099
Culmington 24 SO 4982
Culmstock 7 ST 1013
Culnacraig 64 NC 0603
Culrain 65 NH 5794
Culross 51 NS 9885
Culroy 50 NS 3114
Culsh (Grampn.) 62 NJ 8848
Culswick 63 HU 2745
Cultercullen 62 NJ 9124
Cults (Grampn.) 62 NJ 5331
Cults (Grampn.) 62 NJ 8903
Culverstone Green 12 TQ 6363
Culverthorpe 34 TF 0240
Culworth 26 SP 5447
Cumb 63 HU 5292
Cumbernauld 50 NS 7676
Cumberworth 35 TF 5073
Cuminestown 62 NJ 8050
Cummersdale 46 NY 3952
Cummertrees 45 NY 1366
Cummingstown 61 NJ 1368
Cumnock 50 NS 5619
Cumnor 18 SP 4604
Cumrew 46 NY 5550
Cumwhinton 46 NY 4552
Cumwhitton 46 NY 5052
Cundall (N Yorks.) 38 SE 4272
Cunninghamhead 50 NS 3741
Cunningsburgh 63 HU 4330
Cunnister 63 HU 5296
Cupar 57 NO 3714
Cupar Muir 57 NO 3613
Curbar 33 SK 2574
Curbridge (Hants.) 9 SU 5211
Curbridge (Oxon.) 18 SP 3208
Curdridge 9 SU 5313
Curdworth 25 SP 1892
Curland 7 ST 2716
Currie 51 NT 1867
Curry Mallet 7 ST 3221
Curry Rivel 7 ST 3824
Curtisden Green 12 TQ 7440
Cury 2 SW 6721
Cushnie 62 NJ 7962
Cushuish 7 ST 1930
Cusop 23 SO 2341
Cuthill (Highld.) 65 NH 7587
Cutiau 22 SH 6317
Cutnall Green 25 SO 8768
Cutsdean 25 SP 0830
Cutthorpe 33 SK 3473
Cutts 63 HU 4038
Cuxham 18 SU 6695
Cuxton 12 TQ 7166
Cuxwold 39 TA 1701
Cwm (Clwyd) 31 SJ 0677
Cwm (Gwent) 16 SO 1805
Cwm (W Glam.) 15 SS 6895
Cwmaman 15 SS 9999
Cwmavon 15 SS 7892
Cwmbach (Dyfed) 14 SN 2525
Cwmbach (Mid Glam.) 15 SO 0201
Cwmbelan 23 SN 9481
Cwmbran 16 ST 2894
Cwmcarn 16 ST 2293
Cwmcarvan 16 SO 4707
Cwm Ceulan 22 SN 6890
Cwm-Cewydd 22 SH 8713
Cwmcoy 14 SN 2941
Cwmdare 15 SN 9803
Cwmdu (Dyfed) 15 SN 6330
Cwmdu (Powys) 16 SO 1823
Cwmduad 15 SN 3731
Cwmfelin Boeth 14 SN 1919
Cwmfelin Mynach 14 SN 2324
Cwmffrwd 15 SN 4217
Cwmgwrach 15 SN 8605
Cwm Irfon 15 SN 8549
Cwmisfael 15 SN 4915
Cwm-Llinau 22 SH 8407
Cwmllynfell 15 SN 7413
Cwmparc 15 SS 9496
Cwmpengraig 14 SN 3436
Cwmsychpant 15 SN 4746
Cwmtillery 16 SO 2106
Cwmtudu 22 SN 3557
Cwm-y-glo 30 SH 5562
Cwmyoy 16 SO 2923
Cwmystwyth 22 SN 7873
Cwrt-newydd 15 SN 4847
Cwrt-y-gollen 16 SO 2317
Cyffylliog 31 SJ 0557
Cymmer (Mid Glam.) 15 ST 0290
Cymmer (W Glam.) 15 SS 8696
Cynghordy 15 SN 8139
Cynwyd 31 SJ 0541
Cynwyl Elfed 15 SN 3727

Dacre (Cumbr.) 40 NY 4526
Dacre (N Yorks.) 42 SE 1960
Dacre Banks 42 SE 1961
Daddry Shield 41 NY 8937
Dadford 18 SP 6638
Dadlington 26 SP 4098
Dafen 15 SN 5201
Daffy Green 29 TF 9609
Dagenham 20 TQ 5084
Daglingworth 17 SO 9905
Dagnall 19 SP 9916
Daill 48 NR 3662
Dailly 44 NS 2701
Dairsie or Osnaburgh 57 NO 4117
Dalavich 55 NM 9612
Dalbeattie 45 NX 8361
Dalbeg 63 NB 2345
Dalblair 50 NS 6419
Dalbog 57 NO 5871
Dalby 43 SC 2178
Dalcapon 56 NN 9755
Dalchalloch 56 NN 7264
Dalchenna 55 NN 0706
Dalchreichart 59 NH 2912
Dalcross 60 NH 7748
Dalderby 35 TF 2465

Dale Dymock

Dale (Derby.) 33 SK 4338
Dale (Dyfed) 14 SM 8005
Dale (Shetld.) 63 HU 1852
Dale Head 40 NY 4316
Dalelia 54 NM 7369
Dalgarven 50 NS 2945
Dalginross 56 NN 7721
Dalguise 56 NN 9947
Dalhalvaig 67 NC 8954
Dalham 20 TL 7261
Daliburgh 63 NF 7421
Dalkeith 51 NT 3367
Dall 56 NN 5956
Dallas 61 NJ 1252
Dalleagles 50 NS 5710
Dalle Crucis Abbey (ant.) 32 SJ 2044
Dallinghoo 21 TM 2654
Dallington 12 TQ 6519
Dalmally 55 NN 1527
Dalmary 50 NS 5195
Dalmellington 44 NS 4705
Dalmeny 51 NT 1477
Dalmigavie 60 NH 7419
Dalmore (Highld.) 65 NH 6668
Dalmore (Isle of Lewis) 63 NB 2244
Dalnabreck 54 NM 7069
Dalnavie 65 NH 6473
Dalness 55 NN 1751
Dalnessie 66 NC 6315
Dalqueich 56 NO 0704
Dalquharran Castle 44 NS 2702
Dalreavoch 66 NC 7508
Dalry 50 NS 2949
Dalrymple 50 NS 3514
Dalserf 50 NS 7950
Dalston 46 NY 3750
Dalswinton 45 NX 9385
Dalton (Dumf. and Galwy.) 45 NY 1173
Dalton (Lancs.) 36 SD 4907
Dalton (Northum.) 47 NY 9158
Dalton (Northum.) 47 NZ 1172
Dalton (N Yorks.) 42 NZ 1108
Dalton (N Yorks.) 42 SE 4376
Dalton (N Yorks.) 38 SK 4593
Dalton in Furness 40 SD 2374
Dalton-le-Dale 47 NZ 4047
Dalton-on-Tees 42 NZ 2908
Dalton Piercy 42 NZ 4631
Dalveich 56 NN 6124
Dalwhinnie 56 NN 6384
Dalwood 5 ST 2400
Damerham 8 SU 1015
Damgate 29 TG 3909
Damnaglaur 44 NX 1235
Danbury 20 TL 7805
Danby 43 NZ 7009
Danby Wiske 42 SE 3398
Dandaleith 61 NJ 2845
Danderhall 51 NT 3069
Danebridge 33 SJ 9665
Dane End 20 TL 3321
Danehill 12 TQ 4027
Dane Hills 26 SK 5605
Danskine 52 NT 5667
Daren-felen 16 SO 2212
Darenth 12 TQ 5671
Daresbury 32 SJ 5782
Darfield 38 SE 4104
Dargate 13 TR 0861
Darite 4 SX 2569
Darlaston 25 SO 9796
Darlingscott 26 SP 2342
Darlington 42 NZ 2914
Darliston 32 SJ 5833
Darlochan 48 NR 6723
Darlton 34 SK 7773
Darowen 22 SH 8302
Darras Hall 47 NZ 1571
Darrington 38 SE 4919
Darsham 29 TM 4170
Dartford 12 TQ 5474
Dartington 5 SX 7862
Dartmeet 5 SX 6773
Dartmouth 5 SX 8751
Darton 37 SE 3110
Darvel 50 NS 5637
Darwen 36 SD 6922
Datchet 11 SU 9876
Datchworth 19 TL 2619
Dauntsey 17 ST 9882
Davenham 32 SJ 6570
Daventry 26 SP 5762
Davidstow 4 SX 1587
Davington 46 NT 2302
Daviot (Grampn.) 62 NJ 7528
Daviot (Highld.) 60 NH 7139
Davoch of Grange 61 NJ 4951
Dawes Heath 20 TQ 8188
Dawley 24 SJ 6807
Dawlish 5 SX 9676
Dawlish Warren 5 SX 9778
Dawn 31 SH 8672
Dawsmere 35 TF 4430
Daylesford 18 SP 2425
Deadwater 46 NY 6096
Deal 13 TR 3752
Dean (Cumbr.) 40 NY 0725
Dean (Devon.) 5 SX 7364
Dean (Hants.) 9 SU 5619
Dean (Somer.) 8 ST 6743
Deanburnhaugh 51 NT 3911
Deane 10 SU 5450
Deanland 8 ST 9918
Dean Prior 5 SX 7363
Dean Row 33 SJ 8781
Deanscale 40 NY 0926
Deanshanger 26 SP 7639
Deanston 56 NN 7101
Dearham 40 NY 0736
Debach 21 TM 2454
Debden 20 TL 5533
Debden Cross 20 TL 5832
Debenham 21 TM 1763
Dechmont 51 NT 0370
Deddington 18 SP 4631
Dedham 21 TM 0533
Deene 27 SP 9492
Deenethorpe 27 SP 9592
Deepcar 37 SK 2897
Deepcut 11 SU 9057
Deepdale (Cumbr.) 41 SD 7284
Deeping Gate 35 TF 1509
Deeping St. James 35 TF 1609
Deeping St. Nicholas 35 TF 2115
Deerhurst 17 SO 8729
Defford 25 SO 9143
Defynnog 15 SN 9227
Deganwy 31 SH 7779
Deighton (N Yorks.) 42 NZ 3801
Deighton (N Yorks.) 38 SE 6244
Deiniolen 30 SH 5863
Delabole 4 SX 0683
Delamere 32 SJ 5668
Dell 63 NB 4861
Delliefure 61 NJ 0731
Delph 37 SD 9807
Dembleby 35 TF 0437
Denaby 38 SK 4899
Denbigh 31 SJ 0566
Denbury 5 SX 8268
Denby 33 SK 3946
Denby Dale 37 SE 2208
Denchworth 18 SU 3891
Denend 62 NJ 6038
Denford 27 SP 9976
Dengie 21 TL 9801
Denham (Bucks.) 19 TQ 0386
Denham (Suff.) 20 TL 7561
Denham (Suff.) 29 TM 1974
Denham Green 19 TQ 0388
Denhead (Fife.) 57 NO 4613
Denhead (Grampn.) 62 NJ 9952
Denhead of Gray 57 NO 3431
Denholm 52 NT 5718
Denholme 37 SE 0633
Denmead 9 SU 6511
Dennington 21 TM 2866
Denny 50 NS 8182
Dennyloanhead 50 NS 8180
Denny Lodge 9 SU 3305
Denshaw 37 SD 9710
Denside 62 NO 8095
Densole 13 TR 2141
Denston 20 TL 7652
Denstone 33 SK 0940
Dent 41 SD 7087
Den, The 50 NS 3251
Denton (Cambs.) 27 TL 1487
Denton (Durham) 42 NZ 2118
Denton (E Susx) 12 TQ 4502
Denton (Gtr Mches.) 37 SJ 9295
Denton (Kent) 13 TR 2146
Denton (Lincs.) 34 SK 8632
Denton (Norf.) 29 TM 2887
Denton (Northants.) 26 SP 8357
Denton (N Yorks.) 37 SE 1448
Denton (Oxon.) 18 SP 5902
Denver 28 TF 6101
Denwick (Northum.) 53 NU 2014
Deopham 29 TG 0400
Deopham Green 29 TM 0499
Depden Green 20 TL 7756
Deptford (Gtr London) 12 TQ 3676
Deptford (Wilts.) 8 SU 0038
Derby 33 SK 3435
Derbyhaven 43 SC 2867
Deri 16 SO 1202
Derringstone 13 TR 2049
Derrington 33 SJ 8822
Derry Hill 17 ST 9670
Derrythorpe 39 SE 8208
Dersingham 28 TF 6830
Dervaig 54 NM 4351
Derwen 31 SJ 0650
Desborough 26 SP 8083
Desford 26 SK 4703
Detchant 53 NU 0836
Detling 12 TQ 7958
Deuddwr 23 SJ 2317
Devauden 16 ST 4899
Devil's Bridge 22 SN 7477
Devizes 17 SU 0061
Devonport 4 SX 4554
Devonside 56 NS 9296
Devoran 2 SW 7939
Dewlish 8 SY 7798
Dewsall Court 24 SO 4833
Dewsbury 37 SE 2422
Dhoon 43 SC 4586
Dhoor 43 SC 4396
Dhowin 43 NX 4101
Diabaig 64 NG 8060
Dial Post 11 TQ 1519
Dibden 9 SU 3908
Dibden Purlieu 9 SU 4106
Dickleburgh 29 TM 1682
Didbrook 25 SP 0531
Didcot 18 SU 5290
Diddington 27 TL 1965
Diddlebury 24 SO 5085
Didley 24 SO 4432
Didmarton 17 ST 8287
Didsbury 33 SJ 8490
Didworthy 5 SX 6862
Digby 35 TF 0754
Diggle 37 SE 0008
Dihewyd 22 SN 4855
Dilham 29 TG 3325
Dilhorne 33 SJ 9743
Dilston 47 NY 9763
Dilton Marsh 8 ST 8449
Dilwyn 24 SO 4154
Dinas (Dyfed) 14 SN 0139
Dinas (Dyfed) 14 SN 2730
Dinas (Gwyn.) 30 SH 2736
Dinas-Mawddwy 22 SH 8514
Dinas Powis 16 ST 1571
Dinchope 24 SO 4583
Dinder 7 ST 5744
Dinedor 24 SO 5336
Dingley 26 SP 7687
Dingwall 60 NH 5458
Dinnet 61 NO 4698
Dinnington (Somer.) 7 ST 4012
Dinnington (S Yorks.) 34 SK 5386
Dinnington (Tyne and Wear) 47 NZ 2073
Dinorwic 30 SH 5961
Dinton 8 SU 0131
Dinwoodie Mains 45 NY 1090
Dinworthy 4 SS 3015
Dippen 49 NR 7937
Dippin 49 NS 0422
Dipple (Grampn.) 61 NJ 3258
Dipple (Strath.) 44 NS 2002
Diptford 5 SX 7256
Dipton 47 NZ 1554
Dirleton 52 NT 5183
Discoed 23 SO 2764
Diseworth 33 SK 4524
Dishes 63 HY 6523
Dishforth 42 SE 3873
Disley 33 SJ 9784
Diss 29 TM 1179
Disserth 23 SO 0458
Distington 40 NY 0023
Ditcheat 8 ST 6236
Ditchingham 29 TM 3391
Ditchling 12 TQ 3215
Dittisham 5 SX 8655
Ditton (Ches.) 32 SJ 4986
Ditton (Kent) 12 TQ 7158
Ditton Green 20 TL 6658
Ditton Priors 24 SO 6089
Dixton (Glos.) 25 SO 9830
Dixton (Gwent) 16 SO 5114
Dobwalls 4 SX 2165
Doccombe 5 SX 7786
Dochgarroch 60 NH 6140
Docking 28 TF 7637
Docklow 24 SO 5657
Dockray 40 NY 3921
Doddinghurst 20 TQ 5998
Doddington (Cambs.) 27 TL 4090
Doddington (Kent) 13 TQ 9357
Doddington (Lincs.) 34 SK 8970
Doddington (Northum.) 53 NU 0032
Doddington (Salop) 24 SO 6176
Doddiscombsleigh 5 SX 8586
Dodford (Here. and Worc.) 25 SO 9273
Dodford (Northants.) 26 SP 6160
Dodington (Avon) 17 ST 7579
Dodleston 32 SJ 3661
Dodworth 37 SE 3105
Doe Lea 33 SK 4566
Dogdyke 35 TF 2055
Dogmersfield 10 SU 7852
Dog Village 5 SX 9896
Dolanog 23 SJ 0612
Dolau 23 SO 1367
Dolbenmaen 30 SH 5043
Dolfach 22 SN 9077
Dol-for (Powys) 22 SH 8006
Dolfor (Powys) 23 SO 1087
Dolgarrog 31 SH 7766
Dolgellau 22 SH 7217
Doll 67 NC 8803
Dollar 56 NS 9697
Dolphinholme 36 SD 5153
Dolphinton 51 NT 1046
Dolton 6 SS 5712
Dolwen (Clwyd) 31 SH 8874
Dolwen (Powys) 23 SH 9707
Dolwyddelan 30 SH 7352
Dolyhir 23 SO 2458
Domgay 32 SJ 2819
Doncaster 38 SE 5803
Donhead St. Andrew 8 ST 9124
Donhead St. Mary 8 ST 9024
Donibristle 51 NT 1688
Donington 35 TF 2135
Donington on Bain 35 TF 2382
Donisthorpe 33 SK 3114
Donkey Town 11 SU 9460
Donnington (Berks.) 10 SU 4668
Donnington (Glos.) 17 SP 1928
Donnington (Here. and Worc.) 24 SO 7034
Donnington (Salop) 24 SJ 5807
Donnington (Salop) 24 SJ 7114
Donnington (W Susx) 9 SU 8502
Donyatt 7 ST 3313
Doonfoot 50 NS 3218
Dorchester (Dorset) 8 SY 6990
Dorchester (Oxon.) 18 SU 5794
Dordon 26 SK 2600
Dore 33 SK 3081
Dores 60 NH 5934
Dorking 11 TQ 1649
Dormans Land 12 TQ 4042
Dormanstown 42 NZ 5823
Dormington 24 SO 5840
Dorney 11 SU 9379
Dornie 59 NG 8826
Dornoch (Highld.) 65 NH 7989
Dornock (Dumf. and Galwy.) 46 NY 2366
Dorrery 67 ND 0754
Dorridge 25 SP 1774
Dorrington (Lincs.) 35 TF 0752
Dorrington (Salop) 24 SJ 4703
Dorsington 25 SP 1349
Dorstone 23 SO 3142
Dorton 18 SP 6714
Dosthill 25 SP 2199
Doublebois 4 SX 1964
Dougarie 49 NR 8837
Doughton 17 ST 8791
Douglas (I. of M.) 43 SC 3876
Douglas (Strath.) 50 NS 8330
Douglas and Angus 57 NO 4332
Douglas Hill 30 SH 6065
Douglastown 57 NO 4147
Doulting 8 ST 6443
Dounby 63 HY 2920
Doune (Tays.) 56 NN 7201
Douneside 61 NJ 4806
Dounie 65 NH 5590
Dounreay 67 NC 9966
Dousland 4 SX 5368
Dove Holes 33 SK 0778
Dovenby 40 NY 0933
Dover 13 TR 3141
Doverdale 25 SO 8566
Doveridge 33 SK 1134
Dowally 56 NO 0047
Dowdeswell 17 SO 9919
Dowland 6 SS 5610
Dowlish Wake 7 ST 3712
Down Ampney 17 SU 1097
Downderry 4 SX 3153
Downe 12 TQ 4361
Downend (Berks.) 10 SU 4775
Downend (I.of W.) 9 SZ 5387
Downfield 57 NO 3833
Downgate 4 SX 3772
Downham (Cambs.) 28 TL 5284
Downham (Essex) 20 TQ 7395
Downham (Lancs.) 37 SD 7844
Downham (Northum.) 53 NT 8633
Downham Market 28 TF 6003
Down Hatherley 17 SO 8622
Downhead 8 ST 6845
Downhill 2 SW 8669
Downholme 42 SE 1197
Downies 62 NO 9294
Downley 19 SU 8495
Down St. Mary 6 SS 7404
Downton (Hants.) 9 SZ 2693
Downton (Wilts.) 8 SU 1721
Downton on the Rock 24 SO 4273
Dowsby 35 TF 1129
Doxford 53 NU 1823
Doynton 17 ST 7173
Draffan 50 NS 7945
Drakeland Corner 4 SX 5758
Drakemyre 50 NS 2850
Drakes Broughton 25 SO 9248
Draughton (Northants.) 26 SP 7676
Draughton (N Yorks.) 37 SE 0352
Drax 38 SE 6726
Draycote 26 SP 4469
Draycott (Derby) 33 SK 4433
Draycott (Glos.) 25 SP 1836
Draycott (Somer.) 7 ST 4750
Draycott in the Clay 33 SK 1528
Draycott in the Moors 33 SJ 9840
Drayton (Hants.) 9 SU 6605
Drayton (Here. and Worc.) 25 SO 9076
Drayton (Leic.) 26 SP 8392
Drayton (Norf.) 29 TG 1713
Drayton (Oxon.) 26 SP 4241
Drayton (Oxon.) 18 SU 4794
Drayton (Somer.) 7 ST 4024
Drayton Bassett 25 SK 1900
Drayton Parslow 19 SP 8428
Drayton St. Leonard 18 SU 5996
Drefach (Dyfed) 14 SN 3538
Drefach (Dyfed) 15 SN 5045
Drefach (Dyfed) 15 SN 5213
Dreghorn 50 NS 3538
Drem 52 NT 5079
Drewsteignton 5 SX 7391
Driby 35 TF 3874
Driffield 17 SU 0799
Drift 2 SW 4328
Drigg 40 SD 0698
Drighlington 37 SE 2229
Drimnin 54 NM 5553
Drimpton 7 ST 4104
Drinesheader 63 NG 1795
Drinkstone 21 TL 9561
Drinkstone Green 21 TL 9660
Drointon 33 SK 0226
Droitwich 25 SO 8962
Dron 56 NO 1415
Dronfield 33 SK 3578
Dronfield Woodhouse 33 SK 3278
Drongan 50 NS 4418
Dronley 57 NO 3435
Droxford 9 SU 6018
Droylsden 37 SJ 9098
Druid 31 SJ 0343
Druidale 43 SC 3688
Druidston 14 SM 8716
Druimarbin 55 NN 0861
Druimavuic 55 NN 0044
Drum (Grampn.) 62 NJ 8946
Drum (Tays.) 56 NO 0400
Drumbeg 64 NC 1232
Drumblade 62 NJ 5840
Drumbuie (Dumf. and Galwy.) 45 NX 5682
Drumbuie (Highld.) 59 NG 7730
Drumburgh 46 NY 2659
Drumchapel 50 NS 5270
Drumchardine 60 NH 5644
Drumclog 50 NS 6339
Drumeldrie 57 NO 4403
Drumelzier 51 NT 1333
Drumfearn 58 NG 6716
Drumgask 60 NN 6193
Drumgley 57 NO 4250
Drumguish 60 NN 7999
Drumhead 62 NO 6092
Drumlassie 62 NJ 6405
Drumlemble 48 NR 6619
Drumlithie 57 NO 7880
Drummore 44 NX 1336
Drumnadrochit 60 NH 5029
Drumnagorrach 61 NJ 5252
Drumrash 45 NX 6871
Drums 62 NJ 9822
Drumsturdy 57 NO 4935
Drumuie 58 NG 4546
Drumuillie 60 NH 9420
Drumvaich 56 NN 6803
Drumwhindle 62 NJ 9236
Drunkendub 57 NO 6646
Drury 32 SJ 2964
Drybeck 41 NY 6615
Drybridge (Grampn.) 61 NJ 4362
Drybridge (Strath.) 50 NS 3536
Drybrook 17 SO 6416
Dry Doddington 34 SK 8446
Dry Drayton 20 TL 3862
Dryhope 51 NT 2624
Drymen 50 NS 4788
Drymuir 62 NJ 9146
Drynoch 58 NG 4031
Dubford 62 NJ 7963
Dubton 57 NO 5652
Duckington 32 SJ 4851
Ducklington 18 SP 3507
Duck's Cross 27 TL 1156
Duddingston 51 NT 2972
Duddington 27 SK 9800
Duddleswell 12 TQ 4628
Duddo 53 NT 9342
Duddon 32 SJ 5164
Duddon Bridge 40 SD 1988
Dudleston Heath 32 SJ 3636
Dudley 25 SO 9390
Duffield 33 SK 3443
Duffryn 15 SS 8495
Dufftown 61 NJ 3240
Duffus 61 NJ 1668
Dufton 41 NY 6925
Duggleby 39 SE 8766
Duirinish 59 NG 7831
Duisdalemore 58 NG 6913
Duisky 55 NN 0176
Dukestown 16 SO 1410
Dukinfield 37 SJ 9497
Dulas (Gwyn.) 30 SH 4789
Dulcote 7 ST 5644
Dulford 5 ST 0606
Dull 56 NN 8049
Dullatur 50 NS 7476
Dullingham 20 TL 6357
Dulnain Bridge 61 NH 9924
Duloe (Beds.) 27 TL 1560
Duloe (Corn.) 4 SX 2358
Dulsie 60 NH 9341
Dulverton 6 SS 9127
Dulwich 12 TQ 3373
Dumbarton 50 NS 4075
Dumbleton 25 SP 0135
Dumfries 45 NX 9775
Dumgoyne 50 NS 5283
Dummer 10 SU 5845
Dun (Tays.) 57 NO 6659
Dunalastair 56 NN 7159
Dunan (Isle of Skye) 58 NG 5828
Dunan (Strath.) 49 NS 1571
Dunans 49 NS 0491
Dunball 7 ST 3140
Dunbar 52 NT 6878
Dunbeath 67 ND 1629
Dunbeg 54 NM 8734
Dunblane 56 NN 7801
Dunbog 57 NO 2817
Duncanston (Grampn.) 62 NJ 5826
Duncanston (Highld.) 60 NH 5956
Dunchurch 26 SP 4871
Duncote 26 SP 6750
Duncow 45 NX 9683
Duncrievie 56 NO 1309
Duncton 11 SU 9516
Dundee 57 NO 4030
Dundon 7 ST 4732
Dundonald 50 NS 3634
Dundonnell 64 NH 0886
Dundraw 46 NY 2149
Dundreggan 59 NH 3114
Dundrennan 45 NX 7447
Dundry 16 ST 5566
Dundurn 56 NN 7023
Dunecht 62 NJ 7509
Dunfermline 51 NT 0987
Dunford Bridge 37 SE 1602
Dunham 34 SK 8174
Dunham-on-the-Hill 32 SJ 4772
Dunhampton 25 SO 8466
Dunham Town 32 SJ 7488
Dunholme 34 TF 0279
Dunino 57 NO 5311
Dunipace 50 NS 8083
Dunkeld 56 NO 0242
Dunkeswell 5 ST 1407
Dunkirk 13 TR 0758
Dunk's Green 12 TQ 6152
Dunlappie 57 NO 5967
Dunley 24 SO 7869
Dunlop 50 NS 4049
Dunmore (Central.) 50 NS 8989
Dunmore (Strath.) 49 NR 7961
Dunnet 67 ND 2171
Dunnichen 57 NO 5048
Dunning 56 NO 0114
Dunnington (Humbs.) 39 TA 1551
Dunnington (N Yorks.) 38 SE 6652
Dunnington (Warw.) 25 SP 0653
Dunnockshaw 37 SD 8127
Dunollie 54 NM 8532
Dunoon 49 NS 1777
Dunragit 44 NX 1557
Duns 53 NT 7853
Dunsby 35 TF 1026
Dunscore 45 NX 8684
Dunscroft 38 SE 6409
Dunsden Green 10 SU 7477
Dunsfold 11 TQ 0036
Dunsford 5 SX 8089
Dunshelt 57 NO 2410
Dunshillock 62 NJ 9848
Dunsley 43 NZ 8511
Dunsmore 19 SP 8605
Dunsop Bridge 36 SD 6549
Dunstable 19 TL 0221
Dunstall 33 SK 1920
Dunstall Green 20 TL 7460
Dunstan 53 NU 2419
Dunster 7 SS 9943
Duns Tew 18 SP 4528
Dunston (Lincs.) 35 TF 0663
Dunston (Norf.) 29 TG 2302
Dunston (Staffs.) 25 SJ 9217
Dunston (Tyne and Wear) 47 NZ 2263
Dunsville 38 SE 6407
Dunswell 39 TA 0735
Dunsyre 51 NT 0748
Dunterton 4 SX 3779
Duntisbourne Abbots 17 SO 9707
Duntisbourne Leer 17 SO 9707
Duntisbourne Rouse 17 SO 9805
Duntish 8 ST 6906
Duntocher 50 NS 4972
Dunton (Beds.) 27 TL 2344
Dunton (Bucks.) 18 SP 8224
Dunton (Norf.) 28 TF 8730
Dunton Bassett 26 SP 5490
Dunton Green 12 TQ 5157
Dunton Wayletts 20 TQ 6590
Duntulm 58 NG 4174
Dunure 49 NS 2515
Dunvant 15 SS 5993
Dunvegan 58 NG 2548
Dunwich 29 TM 4770
Durdar 46 NY 4051
Durham 42 NZ 2742
Durisdeer 45 NS 8903
Durleigh 7 ST 2736
Durley (Hants.) 9 SU 5115
Durley (Wilts.) 10 SU 2364
Durley Street 9 SU 5217
Durnamuck 64 NH 0192
Durness 66 NC 4067
Durno 62 NJ 7128
Durran 67 ND 1863
Durrington (Wilts.) 8 SU 1544
Durrington (W Susx) 11 TQ 1105
Dursley 17 ST 7597
Durston 7 ST 2828
Durweston 8 ST 8508
Dury 63 HU 4560
Duston 26 SP 7261
Duthil 60 NH 9324
Dutlas 23 SO 2077
Duton Hill 20 TL 6026
Dutton 32 SJ 5779
Duxford 20 TL 4846
Dwygyfylchi 30 SH 7377
Dwyran 30 SH 4466
Dyce 62 NJ 8812
Dyffryn 15 SS 8593
Dyffryn Ardudwy 30 SH 5822
Dyffryn Ceidrych 15 SN 7025
Dyffryn Cellwen 15 SN 8509
Dyke (Devon.) 4 SS 3123
Dyke (Grampn.) 60 NH 9858
Dyke (Lincs.) 35 TF 1022
Dykehead (Central) 56 NS 5997
Dykehead (Strath.) 50 NS 8759
Dykehead (Tays.) 57 NO 3860
Dykends 57 NO 2557
Dylife 22 SN 8594
Dymchurch 13 TR 1029
Dymock 24 SO 6931

Evertown	46	NY 3576
Evesbatch	24	SO 6848
Evesham	25	SP 0344
Evington	26	SK 6203
Ewden Village	37	SK 2796
Ewe Hill	51	NT 0540
Ewell	11	TQ 2262
Ewell Minnis	13	TR 2643
Ewelme	18	SU 6491
Ewen	17	SU 0097
Ewenny	15	SS 9077
Ewerby	35	TF 1247
Ewesley	47	NZ 0592
Ewhurst (E Susx)	12	TQ 7924
Ewhurst (Surrey)	11	TQ 0940
Ewloe	32	SJ 3066
Eworthy	4	SX 4494
Ewshot	10	SU 8149
Ewyas Harold	16	SO 3828
Exbourne	6	SS 6002
Exbury	9	SU 4200
Exebridge	6	SS 9324
Exelby	42	SE 2986
Exeter	5	SX 9292
Exford	6	SS 8538
Exhall	25	SP 1055
Exminster	5	SX 9487
Exmouth	5	SY 0080
Exnaboe	63	HU 3912
Exning	20	TL 6265
Exton (Devon.)	5	SX 9886
Exton (Hants.)	9	SU 6121
Exton (Leic.)	34	SK 9211
Exton (Somer.)	6	SS 9233
Eyam	33	SK 2176
Eydon	26	SP 5450
Eye (Here. and Worc.)	24	SO 4963
Eye (Northants.)	27	TF 2202
Eye (Suffolk)	29	TM 1473
Eyemouth	53	NT 9464
Eyeworth	27	TL 2545
Eyhorne Street	12	TQ 8354
Eyke	21	TM 3151
Eynesbury	27	TL 1859
Eynsford	12	TQ 5365
Eynsham	18	SP 4309
Eype	7	SY 4491
Eyre	58	NG 4152
Eythorne	13	TR 2849
Eyton (Here. and Worc.)	24	SO 4761
Eyton (Salop)	24	SO 3687
Eyton upon the Weald Moors	24	SJ 6414
Faccombe	10	SU 3857
Faceby	42	NZ 4903
Faddiley	32	SJ 5752
Fadmoor	42	SE 6789
Faifley	50	NS 5073
Failand	16	ST 5272
Failford	50	NS 4526
Failsworth	37	SD 9002
Fairbourne	22	SH 6113
Fairburn	38	SE 4727
Fairfield	25	SO 9475
Fairford	17	SP 1501
Fairlie	49	NS 2155
Fairlight	13	TQ 8612
Fairmile	5	SY 0997
Fairmilehead	51	NT 2567
Fair Oak (Hants.)	9	SU 4918
Fairoak (Staffs.)	32	SJ 7632
Fairseat	12	TQ 6261
Fairstead (Essex)	20	TL 7616
Fairstead (Norf.)	29	TG 2723
Fairwarp	12	TQ 4626
Fairy Cross	4	SS 4024
Fakenham	29	TF 9229
Fala	52	NT 4361
Fala Dam	52	NT 4261
Falahill	51	NT 3956
Faldingworth	35	TF 0684
Falfield	17	ST 6893
Falkenham	21	TM 2939
Falkirk	50	NS 8880
Falkland	57	NO 2507
Falla	52	NT 7013
Fallin	50	NS 8391
Falmer	12	TQ 3508
Falmouth	2	SW 8032
Falstone	46	NY 7287
Fanagmore	66	NC 1750
Fangdale Beck	42	SE 5694
Fangfoss	38	SE 7653
Fan Hill	23	SN 9388
Fan Llia	15	SN 9318
Fanmore	54	NM 4244
Fans	52	NT 6140
Farcet	27	TL 2094
Far Cotton	26	SP 7458
Farden	24	SO 5776
Fareham	9	SU 5806
Farewell	25	SK 0811
Faringdon	18	SU 2895
Farington	36	SD 5425
Farlam	46	NY 5558
Farleigh	12	TQ 3660
Farleigh Hungerford	17	ST 7957
Farleigh Wallop	10	SU 6246
Farlesthorpe	35	TF 4774
Farleton	40	SD 5380
Farley (Salop)	24	SJ 3808
Farley (Staffs.)	33	SK 0644
Farley (Wilts.)	9	SU 2229
Farley Green	11	TQ 0645
Farley Hill	10	SU 7564
Farleys End	17	SO 7615
Farlington	38	SE 6167
Farlow	24	SO 6380
Farmborough	17	ST 6560
Farmcote	17	SP 0629
Farmers	15	SN 6444
Farmington	17	SP 1315
Farmoor	18	SP 4407
Farmtown	61	NJ 5051
Farnborough (Berks.)	10	SU 4381
Farnborough (Gtr London)	12	TQ 4464
Farnborough (Hants.)	11	SU 8753
Farnborough (Warw.)	26	SP 4349
Farncombe	11	SU 9755
Farndish	27	SP 9263
Farndon (Ches.)	32	SJ 4154
Farndon (Notts.)	34	SK 7651
Farnell	57	NO 6255
Farnham (Dorset)	8	ST 9514
Farnham (Essex)	20	TL 4724
Farnham (N Yorks.)	42	SE 3460
Farnham (Suff.)	21	TM 3660
Farnham (Surrey)	11	SU 8446
Farnham Common	19	SU 9584
Farnham Green	20	TL 4625
Farnham Royal	19	SU 9682
Farningham	12	TQ 5566
Farnley	37	SE 2147
Farnley Tyas	37	SE 1612
Farnsfield	34	SK 6456
Farnworth (Ches.)	32	SJ 5187
Farnworth (Gtr Mches.)	36	SD 7305
Farr (Highld.)	66	NC 7163
Farr (Highld.)	60	NH 6833
Farr (Highld.)	60	NH 8203
Farringdon	5	SY 0191
Farrington Gurney	17	ST 6255
Farsley	37	SE 2135
Farthinghoe	18	SP 5339
Farthingstone	26	SP 6155
Farway	5	SY 1895
Fasnacloich	55	NN 0247
Fasque	57	NO 6475
Fassfern	55	NN 0278
Fatfield	47	NZ 3053
Fattahead	62	NJ 6657
Faugh	46	NY 5154
Fauldhouse	51	NS 9260
Faulkbourne	20	TL 7917
Faulkland	17	ST 7354
Fauls	32	SJ 5933
Faversham	13	TR 0161
Favillar	61	NJ 2734
Fawfieldhead	33	SK 0763
Fawkham Green	12	TQ 5865
Fawler	18	SP 3717
Fawley (Berks.)	10	SU 3981
Fawley (Bucks.)	18	SU 7586
Fawley (Hants.)	9	SU 4503
Fawley Chapel	17	SO 5829
Faxfleet	39	SE 8624
Faygate	11	TQ 2134
Fazeley	25	SK 2001
Fearby	42	SE 1981
Fearnan	56	NN 7244
Fearnhead	32	SJ 6290
Fearnmore	64	NG 7260
Featherstone (Staffs.)	25	SJ 9305
Featherstone (W Yorks.)	38	SE 4222
Feckenham	25	SP 0061
Fedderate	62	NJ 8949
Feering	21	TL 8720
Feetham	41	SD 9898
Feizor	41	SD 7968
Felbridge	12	TQ 3739
Felbrigg	29	TG 2039
Felcourt	12	TQ 3841
Felden	19	TL 0404
Felindre (Dyfed)	15	SN 7027
Felindre (Powys)	23	SO 1681
Felindre (W Glam.)	15	SN 6302
Felinfach	23	SO 0933
Felinfoel	15	SN 5202
Felingwm Uchaf	15	SN 5024
Felixkirk	42	SE 4684
Felixstowe	21	TM 3034
Felkington	53	NT 9444
Felling	47	NZ 2762
Felmersham	27	SP 9957
Felmingham	29	TG 2529
Felpham	11	SZ 9599
Felsham	21	TL 9457
Felsted	20	TL 6720
Feltham	11	TQ 1072
Felthorpe	29	TG 1618
Felton (Avon)	16	ST 5165
Felton (Here. and Worc.)	24	SO 5748
Felton (Northum.)	47	NU 1800
Felton Butler	24	SJ 3917
Feltwell	28	TL 7190
Feltwell Anchor	28	TL 6789
Fence	37	SD 8237
Fendike Corner	35	TF 4560
Fen Ditton	20	TL 4860
Fen Drayton	20	TL 3468
Fen End	26	SP 2274
Feniscowles	36	SD 6425
Feniton	5	SY 1199
Fenny Bentley	33	SK 1750
Fenny Bridges	5	SY 1198
Fenny Compton	26	SP 4152
Fenny Drayton	26	SP 3597
Fenny Stratford	19	SP 8834
Fenrother	47	NZ 1792
Fenstanton	20	TL 3168
Fenton (Cambs.)	27	TL 3279
Fenton (Lincs.)	34	SK 8476
Fenton (Lincs.)	34	SK 8750
Fenton (Staffs.)	33	SJ 8944
Fenton Town	53	NT 9733
Fenwick (Northum.)	53	NU 0639
Fenwick (Northum.)	47	NZ 0572
Fenwick (Strath.)	50	NS 4643
Fenwick (S Yorks.)	38	SE 5916
Feock	2	SW 8238
Feolin Ferry	48	NR 4469
Feriniquarrie	58	NG 1750
Fern	57	NO 4861
Ferndale	15	SS 9997
Ferndown	8	SU 0700
Ferness	60	NH 9645
Fernham	18	SU 2991
Fernhill Heath	25	SO 8659
Fernhurst	11	SU 9028
Fernie	57	NO 3115
Fernilee	33	SK 0178
Fernlea	58	NG 3732
Ferrensby	42	SE 3660
Ferring	11	TQ 0902
Ferrybridge	38	SE 4824
Ferryden	57	NO 7156
Ferryhill	42	NZ 2832
Ferryside	15	SN 3610
Fersfield	29	TM 0682
Fersit	55	NN 3577
Feshiebridge	60	NH 8504
Fetcham	11	TQ 1555
Fetterangus	62	NJ 9850
Fettercairn	57	NO 6573
Fewston	37	SE 1954
Ffairfach	15	SN 6220
Ffestiniog	30	SH 7042
Fforest	15	SN 5804
Fforest-fach (W Glam.)	15	SS 6396
Ffostrasol	15	SN 3747
Ffrith	32	SJ 2855
Ffrwdgrech	15	SO 0227
Ffynnonddrain	15	SN 4021
Ffynnongroew	31	SJ 1382
Fiddes	57	NO 8181
Fiddington (Glos.)	25	SO 9231
Fiddington (Somer.)	7	ST 2140
Fiddlers Hamlet	20	TL 4701
Field	33	SK 0233
Field Broughton	40	SD 3881
Field Dalling	29	TG 0039
Field Head	33	SK 4909
Fifehead Magdalen	8	ST 7721
Fifehead Neville	8	ST 7610
Fifield (Berks.)	11	SU 9076
Fifield (Oxon.)	18	SP 2318
Figheldean	8	SU 1547
Fighting Cocks	42	NZ 3414
Filby	29	TG 4613
Filey	43	TA 1180
Filgrave	27	SP 8748
Filkins	18	SP 2304
Filleigh (Devon.)	6	SS 6628
Filleigh (Devon.)	6	SS 7410
Fillingham	34	SK 9485
Fillongley	26	SP 2787
Filton	17	ST 6079
Fimber	39	SE 8960
Finavon	57	NO 4957
Finavon Castle	57	NO 4956
Fincham	28	TF 6806
Finchampstead	10	SU 7963
Fincharn	54	NM 9003
Finchdean	9	SU 7312
Finchingfield	20	TL 6832
Finchley	19	TQ 2890
Findern	33	SK 3030
Findhorn	61	NJ 0464
Findhorn Bridge	60	NH 8027
Findochty	61	NJ 4667
Findo Gask	56	NO 0020
Findon (Grampn.)	62	NO 9397
Findon (W Susx)	11	TQ 1208
Findon Mains	65	NH 6060
Finedon	27	SP 9272
Fingal Street	29	TM 2169
Fingask	62	NJ 7827
Fingest	18	SU 7791
Finghall	42	SE 1889
Fingringhoe	21	TM 0220
Finmere	18	SP 6333
Finnart	55	NN 5157
Finningham	29	TM 0669
Finningly	38	SK 6699
Finnygaud	62	NJ 6054
Finsbay	63	NG 0786
Finsbury	20	TQ 3282
Finstall	25	SO 9869
Finsthwaite	40	SD 3687
Finstock	18	SP 3516
Finstown	63	HY 3514
Fintry (Central)	50	NS 6186
Fintry (Grampn.)	62	NJ 7554
Fionnphort (Island of Mull)	54	NM 2923
Firbeck	34	SK 5688
Firgrove	37	SD 9113
Firsby	35	TF 4563
Firth	63	HU 4473
Fir Tree	42	NZ 1334
Fishbourne (I of W)	9	SZ 5592
Fishbourne (W Susx)	9	SU 8304
Fishburn	42	NZ 3632
Fishcross	50	NS 8995
Fisherford	62	NJ 6635
Fisher's Pond	9	SU 4820
Fisherstreet	11	SU 9531
Fisherton (Highld.)	60	NH 7451
Fisherton (Strath.)	50	NS 2717
Fishguard	14	SM 9637
Fishlake	38	SE 6513
Fishpool	37	SD 8009
Fishtoft	35	TF 3642
Fishtoft Drove	35	TF 3148
Fishtown of Usan	57	NO 7254
Fishwick	53	NT 9151
Fiskavaig	58	NG 3234
Fiskerton (Lincs.)	35	TF 0472
Fiskerton (Notts.)	34	SK 7351
Fittleton	8	SU 1449
Fittleworth	11	TQ 0119
Fitton End	35	TF 4312
Fitz	24	SJ 4417
Fitzhead	7	ST 1228
Fitzwilliam	38	SE 4115
Five Ashes	12	TQ 5525
Fivehead	7	ST 3522
Five Oak Green	12	TQ 6445
Five Oaks	11	TQ 0928
Five Penny Borve	63	NB 4055
Five Penny Ness	63	NB 5364
Five Roads	15	SN 4905
Flackwell Heath	19	SU 8890
Fladbury	25	SO 9946
Fladdabister	63	HU 4332
Flagg	33	SK 1368
Flamborough	39	TA 2270
Flamstead	19	TL 0814
Flansham	11	SU 9601
Flasby	37	SD 9456
Flash	33	SK 0267
Flashader	58	NG 3553
Flatt, The	46	NY 5678
Flaunden	19	TL 0100
Flawborough	34	SK 7842
Flawith	38	SE 4865
Flax Bourton	16	ST 5069
Flaxby	37	SE 3957
Flaxley	17	SO 6915
Flaxpool	7	ST 1435
Flaxton	38	SE 6762
Fleckney	26	SP 6493
Flecknoe	26	SP 5163
Fleet (Hants.)	10	SU 8054
Fleet (Lincs.)	35	TF 3823
Fleetham	53	NU 1928
Fleet Hargate	35	TF 3925
Fleetwood	36	SD 3247
Flemingston	15	ST 0170
Flemington	50	NS 6559
Flempton	28	TL 8169
Fletching	12	TQ 4323
Flexford	11	SU 9350
Flimby	40	NY 0233
Flimwell	12	TQ 7131
Flint	32	SJ 2472
Flintham	34	SK 7446
Flint Mountain	32	SJ 2369
Flinton	39	TA 2136
Flitcham	28	TF 7226
Flitton	19	TL 0536
Flitwick	19	TL 0335
Flixborough	39	SE 8715
Flixton (Gtr Mches.)	32	SJ 7494
Flixton (N Yorks.)	43	TA 0479
Flixton (Suff.)	29	TM 3186
Flockton	37	SE 2314
Flodda (Benbecula)	63	NF 8455
Flodden	53	NT 9235
Flodigarry	58	NG 4671
Flookburgh	40	SD 3675
Flordon	29	TM 1897
Flore	26	SP 6460
Flotterton	47	NT 9902
Flowton	21	TM 0847
Flushing (Corn.)	2	SW 8034
Flushing (Grampn.)	62	NK 0546
Flyford Flavell	25	SO 9754
Fobbing	20	TQ 7183
Fochabers	61	NJ 3458
Fochriw	16	SO 1005
Fockerby	39	SE 8419
Fodder Fen	28	TL 5287
Fodderletter	61	NJ 1421
Fodderty	60	NH 5159
Foel	23	SH 9911
Foffarty	57	NO 4145
Foggathorpe	38	SE 7537
Fogo	53	NT 7749
Foindle	66	NC 1948
Folda	56	NO 1964
Fole	33	SK 0437
Foleshill	26	SP 3582
Folke	8	ST 6513
Folkestone	13	TR 2336
Folkingham	35	TF 0433
Folkington	12	TQ 5604
Folksworth	27	TL 1490
Folkton	43	TA 0579
Folla Rule	62	NJ 7333
Follifoot	37	SE 3452
Folly Gate	6	SX 5797
Fonthill Bishop	8	ST 9332
Fonthill Gifford	8	ST 9231
Fontmell Magna	8	ST 8616
Fontwell	11	SU 9407
Foolow	33	SK 1976
Foots Cray	12	TQ 4770
Forcett	42	NZ 1712
Ford (Bucks.)	18	SP 7709
Ford (Glos.)	17	SP 0829
Ford (Mers.)	32	SJ 3598
Ford (Northum.)	53	NT 9437
Ford (Salop)	24	SJ 4113
Ford (Staffs.)	33	SK 0654
Ford (Strath.)	54	NM 8603
Ford (Wilts.)	17	ST 8475
Ford (W Susx)	11	TQ 0003
Fordcombe	12	TQ 5240
Fordell	51	NT 1588
Forden	23	SJ 2201
Ford End	20	TL 6716
Fordham (Cambs.)	28	TL 6370
Fordham (Essex)	21	TL 9228
Fordham (Norf.)	28	TL 6199
Fordingbridge	8	SU 1413
Fordon	39	TA 0475
Fordoun	57	NO 7475
Fordstreet (Essex)	21	TL 9227
Ford Street (Somer.)	7	ST 1518
Fordwells	18	SP 3013
Fordwich	13	TR 1859
Fordyce	62	NJ 5563
Foremark	33	SK 3326
Forest	41	NY 8629
Forestburn Gate	47	NZ 0696
Forestfield	50	NS 8566
Forest Gate	20	TQ 4085
Forest Green	11	TQ 1241
Forest Hall	41	NY 5401
Forest Head	46	NY 5857
Forest Hill	18	SP 5807
Forest Mill	51	NS 9594
Forest Moor	37	SE 2256
Forest Row	12	TQ 4235
Forestside	9	SU 7512
Forest Town	34	SK 5662
Forfar	57	NO 4550
Forgandenny	56	NO 0818
Forgie	61	NJ 3954
Formby	36	SD 2907
Forncett End	29	TM 1493
Forncett St. Mary	29	TM 1694
Forncett St. Peter	29	TM 1693
Forneth	56	NO 0945
Fornham All Saints	20	TL 8367
Fornham St. Martin	20	TL 8566
Forres	61	NJ 0358
Forsbrook	33	SJ 9641
Forse	67	ND 2234
Forsinard	67	NC 8842
Forstal, The	13	TQ 8946
Forston	8	SY 6695
Fort Augustus	59	NH 3709
Forter	56	NO 1864
Forteviot	56	NO 0517
Fort George	60	NH 7656
Forth	51	NS 9453
Forthampton	25	SO 8532
Fortingall	56	NN 7447
Forton (Lancs.)	36	SD 4851
Forton (Salop)	24	SJ 4216
Forton (Somer.)	7	ST 3306
Forton (Staffs.)	32	SJ 7521
Fortree	62	NJ 9640
Fortrie	62	NJ 6645
Fortrose	60	NH 7256
Fortuneswell	8	SY 6873
Fort William	55	NN 1074
Forty Hill	20	TQ 3398
Forward Green	21	TM 1059
Fosbury	10	SU 3157
Fosdyke	35	TF 3133
Foss	56	NN 7958
Fossebridge	17	SP 0811
Foss-y-ffin	22	SN 4460
Foster Street	20	TL 4909
Foston (Derby.)	33	SK 1831
Foston (Lincs.)	34	SK 8542
Foston (N Yorks.)	38	SE 6965
Foston on the Wolds	39	TA 1055
Fotherby	39	TF 3191
Fotheringhay	27	TL 0593
Foulden (Borders)	53	NT 9355
Foulden (Norf.)	28	TL 7699
Foulis Castle	65	NH 5964
Foul Mile	12	TQ 6215
Foulridge	37	SD 8942
Foulsham	29	TG 0324
Fountainhall	52	NT 4349
Four Ashes	29	TM 0070
Fourcrosses (Gwyn.)	30	SH 3939
Four Crosses (Powys)	23	SJ 0508
Four Crosses (Powys)	32	SJ 2718
Four Crosses (Staffs.)	25	SJ 9509
Four Elms	12	TQ 4648
Four Forks	7	ST 2336
Four Gotes	35	TF 4516
Four Lanes	2	SW 6838
Fourlanes End	32	SJ 8059
Four Marks	9	SU 6634
Four Mile Bridge	30	SH 2778
Four Oaks (E Susx)	13	TQ 8624
Four Oaks (W Mids)	25	SP 1198
Four Oaks (W Mids)	26	SP 2480
Fourstones	47	NY 8967
Four Throws	12	TQ 7729
Fovant	8	SU 0028
Foveran	62	NJ 9824
Fowey	4	SX 1251
Fowlis	57	NO 3133
Fowlis Wester	56	NN 9223
Fowlmere	20	TL 4245
Fownhope	24	SO 5734
Foxdale	43	SC 2878
Foxearth	20	TL 8344
Foxfield	40	SD 2085
Foxham	17	ST 9777
Foxhole (Corn.)	2	SW 9654
Foxholes (N Yorks.)	39	TA 0173
Fox Lane	11	SU 8557
Foxley (Norf.)	29	TG 0321
Foxley (Wilts.)	17	ST 8985
Foxt	33	SK 0348
Foxton (Cambs.)	20	TL 4148
Foxton (Leic.)	26	SP 7090
Foxup	41	SD 8676
Foxwist Green	32	SJ 6168
Foy	17	SO 5928
Foyers	60	NH 4921
Fraddon	2	SW 9158
Fradley	25	SK 1513
Fradswell	33	SJ 9831
Fraisthorpe	39	TA 1561
Framfield	12	TQ 4920
Framingham Earl	29	TG 2702
Framingham Pigot	29	TG 2703
Framlingham	21	TM 2863
Frampton (Dorset)	8	SY 6294
Frampton (Lincs.)	35	TF 3239
Frampton Cotterell	17	ST 6582
Frampton Mansell	17	SO 9202
Frampton on Severn	17	SO 7407
Frampton West End	35	TF 3040
Framsden	21	TM 1959
Framwellgate Moor	47	NZ 2644
Franche	25	SO 8178
Frankby	32	SJ 2486
Frankley	25	SO 9980
Frankton	26	SP 4270
Frant	12	TQ 5835
Fraserburgh	62	NJ 9966
Frating Green	21	TM 0923
Fratton	9	SU 6600
Freathy	4	SX 3952
Freckenham	28	TL 6672
Freckleton	36	SD 4228
Freeby	34	SK 8020
Freeland	18	SP 4112
Freester	63	HU 4553
Freethorpe	29	TG 4105
Freethorpe Common	29	TG 4004
Freiston	35	TF 3743
Fremington	6	SS 5132
Frenchay	17	ST 6377
Frenchbeer	5	SX 6785
Frensham	11	SU 8441
Fresgoe	67	NC 9566
Freshfield	36	SD 2807
Freshford	17	ST 7860
Freshwater	9	SZ 3487
Freshwater Bay	9	SZ 3485
Freshwater West	14	SR 8899
Fressingfield	29	TM 2677
Freston	21	TM 1739
Freswick	67	ND 3667
Frettenham	29	TG 2417
Freuchie	57	NO 2806
Friar's Gate	12	TQ 4933
Friday Bridge	27	TF 4605
Fridaythorpe	39	SE 8759
Friern Barnet	19	TQ 2892
Friesthorpe	35	TF 0683
Frieth	18	SU 7990
Frilford	18	SU 4497
Frilsham	10	SU 5373
Frimley	11	SU 8758
Frindsbury	12	TQ 7369
Fring	28	TF 7334
Fringford	18	SP 6028
Frinsted	13	TQ 8957
Frinton-on-Sea	21	TM 2319
Friockheim	57	NO 5949
Frisby on the Wreake	34	SK 6917
Friskney	35	TF 4555
Friston (E Susx)	12	TV 5498
Friston (Suff.)	21	TM 4160
Fritchley	33	SK 3553
Fritham	9	SU 2413
Frith Bank	35	TF 3147
Frith Common	24	SO 6969
Frithelstock	6	SS 4619
Frithville	35	TF 3250
Frittenden	12	TQ 8141
Fritton (Norf.)	29	TG 4700
Fritton (Norf.)	29	TM 2293
Fritwell	18	SP 5229
Frizington	40	NY 0316
Frocester	17	SO 7803
Frodesley	24	SJ 5101
Frodsham	32	SJ 5177
Froggatt	33	SK 2476
Froghall	33	SK 0247
Frogmore	10	SU 8360
Frolesworth	26	SP 5090
Frome	8	ST 7747
Frome St. Quintin	7	ST 5902
Fromes Hill	24	SO 6846
Fron (Gwyn.)	30	SH 3539
Fron (Powys)	23	SJ 2203
Fron (Powys)	23	SO 0865
Fron Cysyllte	32	SJ 2741
Fron-goch	31	SH 9039
Frosterley	42	NZ 0237

Froxfield

Great Horkesley

Froxfield	10	SU 2967
Froxfield Green	9	SU 7025
Fryerning	20	TL 6400
Fryton	38	SE 6875
Fulbeck	34	SK 9450
Fulbourn	20	TL 5256
Fulbrook	18	SP 2513
Fulford (N Yorks.)	38	SE 6149
Fulford (Somer.)	7	ST 2129
Fulford (Staffs.)	33	SJ 9438
Fulham	11	TQ 2576
Fulking	11	TQ 2411
Fuller's Moor	32	SJ 4953
Fuller Street	20	TL 7415
Fullerton	10	SU 3739
Fulletby	35	TF 2973
Full Sutton	38	SE 7455
Fullwood	50	NS 4450
Fulmer	19	SU 9985
Fulmodeston	29	TF 9931
Fulnetby	35	TF 0979
Fulstow	39	TF 3297
Fulwell	47	NZ 3959
Fulwood (Lancs.)	36	SD 5331
Fulwood (S Yorks.)	33	SK 3085
Funtington	9	SU 7908
Funzie	63	HU 6689
Furnace	55	NN 0200
Furneux Pelham	20	TL 4327
Furzehill	6	SS 7245
Fyfett	7	ST 2314
Fyfield (Essex)	20	TL 5707
Fyfield (Glos.)	17	SP 2003
Fyfield (Hants.)	10	SU 2946
Fyfield (Oxon.)	18	SU 4298
Fyfield (Wilts.)	17	SU 1468
Fylingthorpe	43	NZ 9405
Fyvie	62	NJ 7637
Gabroc Hill	50	NS 4551
Gaddesby	34	SK 6813
Gaer	16	SO 1721
Gaerwen	30	SH 4871
Gagingwell	18	SP 4025
Gailey	25	SJ 9110
Gainford	42	NZ 1716
Gainsborough	34	SK 8189
Gainsford End	20	TL 7235
Gairloch	64	NG 8076
Gairlochy	55	NN 1784
Gairney Bank	56	NT 1299
Gaitsgill	46	NY 3946
Galashiels	52	NT 4936
Galby	26	SK 6901
Galgate	36	SD 4855
Galhampton	8	ST 6329
Gall	56	NO 0734
Gallanach (Strath.)	54	NM 8226
Gallatown	51	NT 2994
Galley Common	26	SP 3192
Galleyend	20	TL 7103
Galleywood	20	TL 7002
Gallowfauld	57	NO 4342
Galltair	59	NG 8120
Galmisdale	54	NM 4784
Galmpton (Devon.)	5	SX 6940
Galmpton (Devon.)	5	SX 8856
Galphay	42	SE 2572
Galson	63	NB 4358
Galston	50	NS 5036
Galtrigill	58	NG 1854
Gamblesby	41	NY 6039
Gamlingay	27	TL 2452
Gamrie	62	NJ 7962
Gamston (Notts.)	34	SK 6037
Gamston (Notts.)	34	SK 7076
Ganarew	16	SO 5216
Ganavan	54	NM 8632
Ganllwyd	30	SH 7224
Gannachy	57	NO 5970
Ganstead	39	TA 1434
Ganthorpe	38	SE 6870
Ganton	43	SE 9877
Garbhallt (Strath.)	49	NS 0295
Garboldisham	29	TM 0081
Gardenstown	62	NJ 7964
Garderhouse	63	HU 3347
Gare Hill	8	ST 7840
Garelochhead	49	NS 2491
Garford	18	SU 4296
Garforth	38	SE 4033
Gargrave	37	SD 9354
Gargunnock	50	NS 7094
Garinin	63	NB 1944
Garlieston	44	NX 4746
Garlogie	62	NJ 7805
Garmond	62	NJ 8052
Garmouth	61	NJ 3364
Garn	30	SH 2734
Garnant	15	SN 6813
Garn-Dolbenmaen	30	SH 4944
Garnett Bridge	40	SD 5299
Garnkirk	50	NS 6768
Garrabost	63	NB 5133
Garraron	54	NM 8008
Garras	2	SW 7023
Garreg	30	SH 6141
Garreg Bank	23	SJ 2811
Garrick	56	NN 8412
Garrigill	41	NY 7441
Garros	58	NG 4963
Garrow	56	NN 8240
Garrynamonie	63	NF 7416
Garsdale	41	SD 7389
Garsdon	17	ST 9687
Garshall Green	33	SJ 9633
Garsington	18	SP 5802
Garstang	36	SD 4945
Garston	32	SJ 4083
Garswood	32	SJ 5599
Gartcosh	50	NS 6968
Garth (Clwyd)	32	SJ 2542
Garth (I. of M.)	43	SC 3177
Garth (Mid Glam.)	15	SS 8690
Garth (Powys)	15	SN 9549
Garth (Shetld.)	63	HU 2157
Garthbrengy	23	SO 0433
Gartheli	22	SN 5956
Garthmyl	23	SO 1999
Garthorpe (Humbs.)	39	SE 8419
Garthorpe (Leic.)	34	SK 8320
Gartmore	55	NS 5297
Gartness (Central)	50	NS 5086
Gartness (Strath.)	50	NS 7864
Gartocharn	50	NS 4286
Garton	39	TA 2635
Garton-on-the-Wolds	39	SE 9859
Gartymore	67	ND 0114
Garvald	52	NT 5870
Garvan	55	NM 9777
Garvard	48	NR 3691
Garve	65	NH 3961
Garveston	29	TG 0207
Garvock	49	NS 2571
Garway	16	SO 4522
Garynahine	63	NB 2331
Gastard	17	ST 8868
Gasthorpe	29	TL 9780
Gatcombe	9	SZ 4885
Gatebeck	41	SD 5485
Gate Burton	34	SK 8382
Gateforth	38	SE 5528
Gatehead	50	NS 3936
Gate Helmsley	38	SE 6955
Gatehouse	46	NY 7988
Gatehouse of Fleet	45	NX 5956
Gatelawbridge	45	NX 9096
Gateley	29	TF 9624
Gatenby	42	SE 3287
Gateshead	47	NZ 2562
Gatesheath	32	SJ 4760
Gateside (Fife.)	56	NO 1809
Gateside (Strath.)	50	NS 3653
Gateside (Tays.)	57	NO 3749
Gateside (Tays.)	57	NO 4344
Gathurst	36	SD 5307
Gatley	32	SJ 8387
Gattonside	52	NT 5435
Gauldry	57	NO 3723
Gaunt's Common	8	SU 0205
Gautby	35	TF 1772
Gavinton	53	NT 7652
Gawber	37	SE 3207
Gawcott	18	SP 6831
Gawsworth	33	SJ 8869
Gawthrop	41	SD 6987
Gawthwaite	40	SD 2784
Gaydon	26	SP 3654
Gayhurst	27	SP 8446
Gayles	42	NZ 1207
Gay Street	11	TQ 0820
Gayton (Mers.)	32	SJ 2680
Gayton (Norf.)	28	TF 7219
Gayton (Northants.)	26	SP 7054
Gayton (Staffs.)	33	SJ 9728
Gayton le Marsh	35	TF 4284
Gayton Thorpe	28	TF 7418
Gaywood	28	TF 6320
Gazeley	20	TL 7264
Geary	58	NG 2661
Gedding	21	TL 9457
Geddington	27	SP 8983
Gedintailor	58	NG 5235
Gedney	35	TF 4024
Gedney Broadgate	35	TF 4022
Gedney Drove End	35	TF 4629
Gedney Dyke	35	TF 4126
Gedney Hill	35	TF 3311
Gee Cross	37	SJ 9593
Geilston	50	NS 3477
Geise	67	ND 1064
Geldeston	29	TM 3891
Gell	31	SH 8569
Gelligaer	16	ST 1397
Gelli Gynan	32	SJ 1854
Gellilydan	30	SH 6839
Gellioedd	31	SH 9344
Gelly	14	SN 0819
Gellyburn	56	NO 0939
Gellywen	14	SN 2723
Gelston	45	NX 7758
Genoch Mains	44	NX 1356
Gentleshaw	25	SK 0511
Geocrab	63	NG 1190
Georgeham	6	SS 4639
George Nympton	6	SS 7023
Georgetown	50	NS 4567
Georgia	2	SW 4836
Georth	63	HY 3625
Germansweek	4	SX 4394
Germoe	2	SW 5829
Gerrans	2	SW 8735
Gerrards Cross	19	TQ 0088
Geshader	63	NB 1131
Gestingthorpe	20	TL 8138
Geufford	23	SJ 2114
Gibraltar	35	TF 5558
Gidea Park	20	TQ 5390
Gidleigh	5	SX 6788
Gifford	52	NT 5368
Giggleswick	41	SD 8163
Gilberdyke	39	SE 8329
Gilchriston	52	NT 4865
Gilcrux	40	NY 1138
Gildersome	37	SE 2429
Gildingwells	34	SK 5585
Gileston	15	ST 0167
Gilfach	16	ST 1598
Gilfach Goch	15	SS 9890
Gilfachrheda	22	SN 4058
Gillamoor	43	SE 6890
Gilling East	42	SE 6176
Gillingham (Dorset)	8	ST 8026
Gillingham (Kent)	12	TQ 7768
Gillingham (Norf.)	29	TM 4191
Gilling West	42	NZ 1805
Gillow Heath	33	SJ 8858
Gills	67	ND 3172
Gilmerton (Lothian)	51	NT 2968
Gilmerton (Tays.)	56	NN 8823
Gilmorton	26	SP 5787
Gilsland	46	NY 6366
Gilsland Spa	46	NY 6367
Gilston	52	NT 4456
Gilwern	16	SO 2414
Gimingham	29	TG 2836
Gipping	21	TM 0763
Gipsey Bridge	35	TF 2850
Girlsta	63	HU 4250
Girsby	42	NZ 3508
Girthon	45	NX 6053
Girton (Cambs.)	20	TL 4262
Girton (Notts.)	34	SK 8266
Girvan	44	NX 1897
Gisburn	37	SD 8248
Gisleham	29	TM 5188
Gislingham	29	TM 0771
Gissing	29	TM 1485
Gittisham	5	SY 1398
Glackossian	60	NH 5938
Gladestry	23	SO 2355
Gladsmuir	52	NT 4573
Glais	15	SN 7000
Glaisdale (N Yorks.)	43	NZ 7705
Glamis	57	NO 3846
Glanaber Terrace	30	SH 7547
Glanaman	15	SN 6713
Glan-Conwy	31	SH 8352
Glandford	29	TG 0441
Glandwr (Dyfed)	14	SN 1928
Glandwr (Gwent)	16	SO 2101
Glangrwyne	16	SO 2316
Glan-Mule	23	SO 1690
Glanrhyd	14	SN 1442
Glanton	53	NU 0714
Glanton Pike	53	NU 0514
Glanvilles Wootton	8	ST 6708
Glan-y-don	31	SJ 1679
Glan-yr-afon (Clwyd-Gwyn.)	31	SJ 0242
Glan-yr-afon (Gwyn.)	31	SH 9141
Glapthorn	27	TL 0290
Glapwell	33	SK 4766
Glasbury	23	SO 1739
Glascote	26	SK 2203
Glascwm	23	SO 1553
Glasdrum	55	NN 0046
Glasfryn	31	SH 9150
Glasgow	50	NS 5865
Glasinfryn	30	SH 5868
Glaspwll	22	SN 7397
Glasserton	44	NX 4238
Glassford	50	NS 7247
Glasshouse Hill	17	SO 7020
Glasshouses	42	SE 1764
Glasslaw	62	NJ 8659
Glasslie	56	NO 2305
Glasson (Cumbr.)	46	NY 2560
Glasson (Lancs.)	36	SD 4455
Glassonby	41	NY 5738
Glasterlaw	57	NO 6051
Glaston	27	SK 8900
Glastonbury	7	ST 4938
Glatton	27	TL 1586
Glazebury	32	SJ 6796
Glazeley	24	SO 7088
Gleadless Townend	33	SK 3883
Gleadsmoss	33	SJ 8469
Gleaston	40	SD 2570
Glemsford	20	TL 8247
Glenalmond (Tays.)	56	NN 9627
Glenancross	58	NM 6691
Glen Auldyn	43	SC 4393
Glenbarr	48	NR 6736
Glen Barry	62	NJ 5554
Glen Bernisdale	58	NG 4048
Glenbervie	57	NO 7680
Glenboig	50	NS 7268
Glenbranter	55	NS 1097
Glen Breackerie	48	NR 6511
Glenbreck	51	NT 0521
Glenbuck	50	NS 7429
Glenburn	50	NS 4761
Glencaple	45	NX 9968
Glencarse	56	NO 1922
Glencloy	49	NS 0036
Glencoe (Highld.)	55	NN 1058
Glencraig	51	NT 1795
Glendaruel	49	NR 9985
Glendevon (Tays.)	56	NN 9804
Glendoick	56	NO 2022
Glenduckie	57	NO 2818
Glenegedale	48	NR 3351
Glenelg	59	NG 8119
Glenfarg (Tays.)	56	NO 1310
Glenfield	34	SK 5306
Glenfinnan (Highld.)	54	NM 9080
Glenfoot	56	NO 1715
Glengarnock	50	NS 3252
Glengrasco	58	NG 4444
Glenkindie	61	NJ 4313
Glenlee (Dumf. and Galwy.)	45	NX 6080
Glenlivet	61	NJ 2126
Glenluce	44	NX 1957
Glenmaye	43	SC 2380
Glenmore (Island of Skye)	58	NG 4340
Glenmore (Strath.)	54	NM 8412
Glen Parva	26	SP 5798
Glenridding	40	NY 3817
Glenrothes	57	NO 2600
Glensaugh	57	NO 6778
Glenshee (Tays.)	56	NN 9834
Glensluain	55	NS 0999
Glenstockadale	44	NX 0061
Glenstriven	49	NS 0878
Glentham	34	TF 0090
Glentress	51	NT 2839
Glentrool Village	44	NX 3578
Glentworth	34	SK 9488
Glen Village	50	NS 8878
Glen Vine	43	SC 3378
Glespin	50	NS 8028
Gletness	63	HU 4651
Glewstone	16	SO 5522
Glinton	35	TF 1506
Glooston	26	SP 7596
Glossop	37	SK 0393
Gloster Hill	47	NU 2504
Gloucester	17	SO 8318
Gloup	63	HP 5004
Glusburn	37	SE 0344
Gluss	63	HU 3477
Glympton	18	SP 4221
Glyn	30	SH 7457
Glynarthen	14	SN 3148
Glyn Ceiriog	32	SJ 2038
Glyncorrwg	15	SS 8799
Glyn-Cywarch	30	SH 6034
Glynde	12	TQ 4509
Glyndebourne	12	TQ 4510
Glyn Dyfrdwy	31	SJ 1542
Glyn-Neath	15	SN 8806
Glyntaff	16	ST 0889
Glynteg	15	SN 3637
Glyntrefnant	22	SN 9192
Gnosall	32	SJ 8220
Gnosall Heath	33	SJ 8419
Goadby	26	SP 7598
Goadby Marwood	34	SK 7826
Goatacre	17	SU 0176
Goathill	8	ST 6717
Goathland	43	NZ 8301
Goathurst	7	ST 2534
Gobowen	32	SJ 3033
Godalming	11	SU 9743
Godmanchester	27	TL 2470
Godmanstone	8	SY 6697
Godmersham	13	TR 0650
Godney	7	ST 4842
Godolphin Cross	2	SW 6031
Godre'r-graig	15	SN 7507
Godshill (Hants.)	8	SU 1714
Godshill (I. of W.)	9	SZ 5281
Godstone	12	TQ 3551
Goetre	16	SO 3205
Goff's Oak	20	TL 3202
Gogar	51	NT 1672
Goginan	22	SN 6981
Golan	30	SH 5242
Golant	4	SX 1254
Golberdon	4	SX 3271
Golborne	32	SJ 6097
Golcar	37	SE 0915
Goldcliff	16	ST 3683
Golden Cross	12	TQ 5312
Golden Green	12	TQ 6348
Golden Grove	15	SN 5919
Goldenhill	33	SJ 8553
Golden Pot	10	SU 7143
Golden Valley (Glos.)	17	SO 9022
Golders Green	19	TQ 2488
Goldhanger	21	TL 9009
Golding	24	SJ 5403
Goldsborough (N Yorks.)	43	NZ 8314
Goldsborough (N Yorks.)	37	SE 3856
Goldsithney	2	SW 5430
Goldthorpe	38	SE 4604
Gollanfield	60	NH 8052
Golspie	65	NH 8399
Golval	67	NC 8962
Gomersal	37	SE 2026
Gomshall	11	TQ 0847
Gonalston	34	SK 6847
Gonfirth (Shetld.)	63	HU 3661
Good Easter	20	TL 6212
Gooderstone	28	TF 7602
Goodleigh	6	SS 5934
Goodmanham	39	SE 8842
Goodnestone (Kent)	13	TR 0461
Goodnestone (Kent)	13	TR 2554
Goodrich	17	SO 5719
Goodrington	5	SX 8958
Goodwick	14	SM 9438
Goodworth Clatford	10	SU 3642
Goodyers End	26	SP 3385
Goole	38	SE 7423
Goole Fields	38	SE 7519
Goonbell	2	SW 7249
Goonhavern	2	SW 7953
Gooseham	4	SS 2316
Goosetrey	32	SJ 7769
Goosey	18	SU 3591
Goosnargh	36	SD 5536
Gordon	52	NT 6443
Gordonbush	67	NC 8409
Gordonstoun	61	NJ 1368
Gordonstown (Grampn.)	62	NJ 5656
Gordonstown (Grampn.)	62	NJ 7138
Gorebridge	51	NT 3461
Gorefield	35	TF 4112
Goring	10	SU 6080
Goring-by-Sea	11	TQ 1102
Gorleston on Sea	29	TG 5203
Gorley	8	SU 1511
Gorrachie	62	NJ 7358
Gorran Haven	4	SX 0141
Gors	22	SN 6277
Gorsedd	31	SJ 1476
Gorseinon	15	SS 5998
Gors-goch	23	SN 9393
Gorslas	15	SN 5713
Gorsley	17	SO 6826
Gorsness	63	HY 4119
Gorstan	65	NH 3862
Gorsty Common	24	SO 4537
Gorton	37	SJ 8996
Gosbeck	21	TM 1555
Gosberton	35	TF 2331
Gosfield	20	TL 7829
Gosforth (Cumbr.)	40	NY 0603
Gosforth (Tyne and Wear)	47	NZ 2467
Gosmore	19	TL 1927
Gosport	9	SZ 6199
Gossabrough	63	HU 5383
Goswick	53	NU 0545
Gotham	34	SK 5330
Gotherington	17	SO 9629
Gott Bay	48	NM 0546
Goudhurst	12	TQ 7337
Goulceby	35	TF 2579
Gourdas	62	NJ 7741
Gourdon	57	NO 8270
Gourock	49	NS 2477
Govan	50	NS 5464
Gowanhill	62	NK 0363
Gowdall	38	SE 6122
Gowerton	15	SS 5896
Gowkhall	51	NT 0589
Goxhill (Humbs.)	39	TA 1021
Goxhill (Humbs.)	39	TA 1844
Graffham (W Susx)	11	SU 9216
Grafham (Cambs.)	27	TL 1669
Grafton (Here. and Worc.)	24	SO 4937
Grafton (Here. and Worc.)	24	SO 5761
Grafton (N Yorks.)	38	SE 4163
Grafton (Oxon.)	18	SP 2600
Grafton Flyford	25	SO 9655
Grafton Regis	26	SP 7546
Grafton Underwood	27	SP 9280
Grafty Green	13	TQ 8748
Graianrhyd	32	SJ 2156
Graig (Clwyd)	31	SJ 0872
Graig (Gwyn.)	31	SH 8071
Graig-fechan	31	SJ 1454
Grain	13	TQ 8876
Grainsby	39	TF 2799
Grainthorpe	39	TF 3896
Graizelound	38	SK 7798
Grampound	2	SW 9348
Grampound Road	2	SW 9150
Gramsdale	63	NF 8255
Granborough	18	SP 7625
Granby	34	SK 7536
Grandborough	26	SP 4866
Grandtully	56	NN 9152
Grange (Cumbr.)	40	NY 2517
Grange (Mers.)	32	SJ 2286
Grange (N Yorks.)	42	SE 5796
Grange (Tays.)	57	NO 2725
Grange Crossroads	61	NJ 4754
Grange Hill	20	TQ 4492
Grange Moor	37	SE 2216
Grangemouth	51	NS 9281
Grange of Lindores	57	NO 2516
Grange-over-Sands	40	SD 4077
Grangepans	51	NT 0282
Grangetown	42	NZ 5420
Grange Villa	47	NZ 2352
Granish	60	NH 8914
Gransmoor	39	TA 1259
Granston	14	SM 8934
Grantchester	20	TL 4355
Grantham	34	SK 9135
Grantlodge	62	NJ 7017
Granton (Dumf. and Galwy.)	45	NT 0709
Granton (Lothian)	51	NT 2277
Grantown-on-Spey	61	NJ 0327
Grantshouse	53	NT 8065
Grappenhall	32	SJ 6385
Grasby	39	TA 0804
Grasmere (Cumbr.)	40	NY 3307
Grasscroft	37	SD 9804
Grassendale	32	SJ 3985
Grassholme	41	NY 9221
Grassington	41	SE 0064
Grassmoor	33	SK 4067
Grassthorpe	34	SK 7967
Grateley	10	SU 2741
Gratwich	33	SK 0231
Graveley (Cambs.)	27	TL 2564
Graveley (Herts.)	19	TL 2328
Gravelly Hill	25	SP 1090
Gravels	23	SJ 3300
Graveney	13	TR 0562
Gravesend	12	TQ 6473
Gravir	63	NB 3715
Grayingham	39	SK 9395
Grayrigg	41	SD 5797
Grays	12	TQ 6177
Grayshott	11	SU 8735
Grayswood	11	SU 9234
Grazeley	10	SU 6966
Greasbrough	38	SK 4195
Greasby	32	SJ 2587
Great Abington	20	TL 5348
Great Addington	27	SP 9575
Great Alne	25	SP 1159
Great Altcar	36	SD 3206
Great Amwell	20	TL 3712
Great Asby	41	NY 6813
Great Ashfield	21	TM 0068
Great Ayton	42	NZ 5510
Great Baddow	20	TL 7204
Great Badminton	17	ST 8082
Great Bardfield	20	TL 6730
Great Barford	27	TL 1352
Great Barr	25	SP 0495
Great Barrington	17	SP 2013
Great Barrow	32	SJ 4668
Great Barton	21	TL 8967
Great Barugh	43	SE 7478
Great Bavington	47	NY 9880
Great Bedwyn	10	SU 2764
Great Bentley	21	TM 1121
Great Billing	26	SP 8162
Great Bircham	28	TF 7632
Great Blakenham	21	TM 1150
Great Bolas	32	SJ 6421
Great Bookham	11	TQ 1454
Great Bosullow	2	SW 4133
Great Bourton	26	SP 4545
Great Bowden	26	SP 7488
Great Bradley	20	TL 6753
Great Braxted	20	TL 8614
Great Bricett	21	TM 0350
Great Brickhill	19	SP 9030
Great Bridgeford	33	SJ 8827
Great Brington	26	SP 6665
Great Bromley	21	TM 0826
Great Broughton	42	NZ 5406
Great Budworth	32	SJ 6677
Great Burdon	42	NZ 3116
Great Burstead	20	TQ 6892
Great Busby	42	NZ 5105
Great Canfield	20	TL 5917
Great Carlton	35	TF 4185
Great Casterton	34	TF 0009
Great Chart	13	TQ 9842
Great Chatwell	24	SJ 7914
Great Chesterford	20	TL 5042
Great Cheverell	17	ST 9858
Great Chishill	20	TL 4238
Great Clacton	21	TM 1716
Great Coates	39	TA 2310
Great Comberton	25	SO 9542
Great Corby	46	NY 4754
Great Cornard	21	TL 8840
Great Coxwell	18	SU 2693
Great Cransley	26	SP 8376
Great Cressingham	28	TF 8501
Great Crosby	32	SJ 3199
Great Cubley	33	SK 1637
Great Dalby	34	SK 7414
Great Doddington	27	SP 8864
Great Driffield	39	TA 0257
Great Dunham	28	TF 8714
Great Dunmow	20	TL 6221
Great Durnford	8	SU 1338
Great Easton (Essex)	20	TL 6125
Great Easton (Leic.)	27	SP 8493
Great Eccleston	36	SD 4240
Great Edstone	43	SE 7084
Great Ellingham	29	TM 0196
Great Elm	8	ST 7449
Great Eversden	20	TL 3653
Great Fen	28	TL 5978
Great Finborough	21	TM 0157
Greatford	35	TF 0811
Great Fransham	28	TF 8913
Great Gaddesden	19	TL 0211
Great Gidding	27	TL 1183
Great Givendale	39	SE 8153
Great Glemham	21	TM 3361
Great Glen	26	SP 6597
Great Gonerby	34	SK 8938
Great Gransden	27	TL 2756
Great Green (Norf.)	29	TM 2789
Great Green (Suff.)	21	TL 9155
Great Habton	43	SE 7576
Great Hallingbury	20	TL 5119
Greatham (Cleve.)	42	NZ 4927
Greatham (Hants.)	9	SU 7730
Greatham (W Susx)	11	TQ 0415
Great Hanwood	24	SJ 4309
Great Harrowden	27	SP 8871
Great Harwood	36	SD 7332
Great Haseley	18	SP 6401
Great Hatfield	39	TA 1842
Great Heck	38	SE 5920
Great Henny	21	TL 8738
Great Hinton	17	ST 9058
Great Hockham	29	TL 9592
Great Holland	21	TM 2119
Great Horkesley	21	TL 9731

Great Hormead Haselbech

Great Hormead 20 TL 4030
Great Horwood 18 SP 7731
Great Houghton (Northants.) 26 SP 7958
Great Houghton (S Yorks.) 38 SE 4206
Great Hucklow 33 SK 1777
Great Kelk 39 TA 1058
Great Kingshill 19 SU 8798
Great Langton 42 SE 2996
Great Leighs 20 TL 7317
Great Limber 39 TA 1308
Great Linford 27 SP 8542
Great Livermere 28 TL 8871
Great Longstone 33 SK 1971
Great Lumley 47 NZ 2949
Great Lyth 24 SJ 4507
Great Malvern 24 SO 7845
Great Maplestead 20 TL 8034
Great Marton 36 SD 3335
Great Massingham 28 TF 7922
Great Milton 18 SP 6302
Great Missenden 19 SP 8901
Great Mitton 36 SD 7138
Great Mongeham 13 TR 3451
Great Moulton 29 TM 1690
Great Musgrave 41 NY 7613
Great Ness 32 SJ 3918
Great Oakley (Essex) 21 TM 1927
Great Oakley (Northants.) 27 SP 8686
Great Offley 19 TL 1427
Great Ormside 41 NY 7017
Great Orton 46 NY 3254
Great Oxendon 26 SP 7383
Great Palgrave 28 TF 8312
Great Parndon 20 TL 4308
Great Paxton 27 TL 2164
Great Plumstead 29 TG 2910
Great Ponton 34 SK 9230
Great Postland 35 TF 2612
Great Preston 38 SE 4029
Great Raveley 27 TL 2581
Great Rissington 17 SP 1917
Great Rollright 18 SP 3231
Great Ryburgh 29 TF 9527
Great Ryle 53 NU 0212
Great Saling 20 TL 7025
Great Salkeld 41 NY 5536
Great Sampford 20 TL 6435
Great Sankey 32 SJ 5688
Great Saxham 20 TL 7862
Great Shefford 10 SU 3875
Great Shelford 20 TL 4652
Great Smeaton 42 NZ 3404
Great Snoring 29 TF 9434
Great Somerford 17 ST 9682
Great Soudley 32 SJ 7228
Great Stainton 42 NZ 3322
Great Stambridge 21 TQ 8991
Great Staughton 27 TL 1264
Great Steeping 35 TF 4364
Great Stonar 13 TR 3359
Greatstone-on-Sea 13 TR 0822
Great Strickland 41 NY 5522
Great Stukeley 27 TL 2275
Great Sturton 35 TF 2176
Great Swinburne 47 NY 9375
Great Tew 18 SP 3929
Great Tey 21 TL 8925
Great Torrington 6 SS 4919
Great Tosson 47 NU 0300
Great Totham (Essex) 20 TL 8511
Great Totham (Essex) 20 TL 8613
Great Wakering 21 TQ 9487
Great Waldingfield 21 TL 9143
Great Walsingham 29 TF 9437
Great Waltham 20 TL 6913
Great Warley 20 TQ 5890
Great Washbourne 25 SO 9834
Great Welnetham 21 TL 8759
Great Wenham 21 TM 0738
Great Whittington 47 NZ 0070
Great Wigborough 21 TL 9615
Great Wilbraham 20 TL 5557
Great Wishford 8 SU 0835
Great Witcombe 17 SO 9014
Great Witley 24 SO 7566
Great Wolford 18 SP 2434
Greatworth 26 SP 5542
Great Wratting 20 TL 6848
Great Wyrley 25 SJ 9907
Great Wytheford 32 SJ 5719
Great Yarmouth 29 TG 5207
Great Yeldham 20 TL 7638
Greenbank 36 SD 5254
Greenburn 51 NS 9360
Greendikes 53 NU 0628
Greenfield (Beds.) 19 TL 0534
Greenfield (Clwyd) 32 SJ 1977
Greenfield (Gtr Mches.) 37 SD 9904
Greenfield (Highld.) 59 NH 2000
Greenfield (Oxon.) 18 SU 7191
Greenford 19 TQ 1382
Greengairs 50 NS 7870
Greenham 10 SU 4865
Green Hammerton 38 SE 4656
Greenhaugh 46 NY 7987
Greenhead (Northum.) 46 NY 6665
Greenhill (Central) 50 NS 8278
Greenhill (Gtr London) 19 TQ 1688
Green Hill (Northum.) 47 NY 8647
Greenhill (S Yorks.) 33 SK 3481
Green Hill (Wilts.) 17 SU 0686
Greenhithe 12 TQ 5974
Greenholm 50 NS 5637
Greenholme 41 NY 5905
Greenhow Hill 42 SE 1164
Greenigo 63 HY 4107
Greenland 67 ND 2367
Greenlaw (Borders) 52 NT 7145
Greenloaning 56 NN 8307
Greenmount 37 SD 7714
Greenock 50 NS 2776
Greenodd 40 SD 3182
Green Ore 7 ST 5749
Greenside 47 NZ 1362
Greenskairs 62 NJ 7863
Greens Norton 26 SP 6649
Greenstead Green 20 TL 8227
Greensted 20 TL 5302
Green Street 19 TQ 1998
Green Street Green 12 TQ 4563
Green, The (Cumbr.) 40 SD 1784
Green, The (Wilts.) 8 ST 8731
Greenwich 12 TQ 4077
Greet 25 SP 0230
Greete 24 SO 5770
Greetham (Leic.) 34 SK 9214
Greetham (Lincs.) 35 TF 3070
Greetland 37 SE 0821
Greinton 7 ST 4136
Grendon (Northants.) 27 SP 8760
Grendon (Warw.) 26 SK 2800
Grendon Common 26 SP 2799
Grendon Green 24 SO 5957
Grendon Underwood 18 SP 6720
Grenitote 63 NF 8274
Grenoside 37 SK 3394
Gresford 32 SJ 3454
Gresham 29 TG 1738
Greshornish 58 NG 3454
Gress 63 NB 4842
Gressenhall 29 TF 9615
Gressenhall Green 29 TF 9616
Gressingham 41 SD 5769
Greta Bridge 42 NZ 0813
Gretna 46 NY 3167
Gretna Green 46 NY 3268
Gretton (Glos.) 25 SP 0030
Gretton (Northants.) 27 SP 8994
Gretton (Salop) 24 SO 5195
Grewelthorpe 42 SE 2276
Greysouthen 40 NY 0729
Greystoke 40 NY 4330
Greystone 57 NO 5343
Greywell 10 SU 7151
Gribun 54 NM 4533
Griff 26 SP 3588
Griffithstown 16 ST 2999
Grigghall 40 SD 4691
Grimeford Village 36 SD 6112
Grimethorpe 38 SE 4109
Griminish 63 NF 7851
Grimista 63 HU 4643
Grimley 25 SO 8360
Grimness (S. Ronaldsay) 63 ND 4793
Grimoldby 35 TF 3988
Grimsargh 36 SD 5834
Grimsby 39 TA 2810
Grimscote 26 SP 6553
Grimscott 4 SS 2606
Grimshader 63 NB 4025
Grimsthorpe 35 TF 0423
Grimston (Leic.) 34 SK 6821
Grimston (Norf.) 28 TF 7221
Grimstone 8 SY 6393
Grindale 39 TA 1371
Grindle 24 SJ 7403
Grindleford 33 SK 2477
Grindleton 37 SD 7545
Grindlow 33 SK 1877
Grindon (Northum.) 53 NT 9144
Grindon (Staffs.) 33 SK 0854
Gringley on the Hill 34 SK 7390
Grinsdale 46 NY 3758
Grinshill 32 SJ 5223
Grinton 42 SE 0498
Gristhorpe 43 TA 0882
Griston 29 TL 9499
Gritley 63 HY 5605
Grittenham 17 SU 0382
Grittleton 17 ST 8579
Grizebeck 40 SD 2384
Grizedale 40 SD 3394
Grobister 63 HY 6524
Groby 34 SK 5207
Groes (Clwyd) 31 SJ 0064
Groes (W Glam.) 15 SS 7986
Groes-faen 16 ST 0780
Groesffordd Marli 31 SJ 0073
Groeslon 30 SH 4755
Grogport 49 NR 8044
Gronant 31 SJ 0883
Groombridge 12 TQ 5337
Grosebay 63 NG 1592
Grosmont (Gwent) 16 SO 4024
Grosmont (N Yorks.) 43 NZ 8205
Groton 21 TL 9641
Grove (Dorset) 8 SY 6972
Grove (Kent) 13 TR 2362
Grove (Notts.) 34 SK 7379
Grove (Oxon.) 18 SU 4090
Grovely Wood 8 SU 0534
Grove Park 12 TQ 4172
Grovesend 15 SN 5900
Gruids 66 NC 5604
Gruinart 48 NR 2866
Grula 58 NG 3826
Gruline 54 NM 5440
Grunasound 63 HU 3733
Grundisburgh 21 TM 2251
Gruting 63 HU 2748
Grutness 63 HU 4009
Grwyne Fechan 16 SO 2324
Gualachulain 55 NN 1145
Guardbridge 57 NO 4519
Guarlford 25 SO 8145
Guay 56 NO 0049
Guestling Green 13 TQ 8513
Guestwick 29 TG 0627
Gugh 2 SV 8908
Guide Post 47 NZ 2585
Guilden Morden 27 TL 2744
Guilden Sutton 32 SJ 4468
Guildford 11 TQ 0049
Guildtown 56 NO 1331
Guilsborough 26 SP 6773
Guilsfield 23 SJ 2111
Guisborough 42 NZ 6115
Guiseley 37 SE 1941
Guist 29 TF 9925
Guiting Power 17 SP 0924
Gulberwick 63 HU 4437
Gulf of Corryvreckan 54 NM 6901
Gullane 52 NT 4882
Gulval 2 SW 4831
Gumfreston 14 SN 1101
Gumley 26 SP 6890
Gunby (Humbs.) 38 SE 7135
Gunby (Lincs.) 34 SK 9021
Gundleton 9 SU 6133
Gunn 6 SS 6333
Gunnerside 41 SD 9598
Gunnerton 47 NY 9074
Gunness 39 SE 8411
Gunnislake 4 SX 4371
Gunnista 63 HU 5043
Gunthorpe (Norf.) 29 TG 0135
Gunthorpe (Notts.) 34 SK 6844
Gurnard 9 SZ 4795
Gurney Slade 8 ST 6249
Gurnos 15 SN 7709
Gussage All Saints 8 SU 0010
Gussage St. Michael 8 ST 9811
Guston 13 TR 3244
Gutcher 63 HU 5498
Guthrie 57 NO 5650
Guyhirn 27 TF 3903
Guy's Head 35 TF 4825
Guy's Marsh 8 ST 8420
Guyzance 47 NU 2103
Gwaenysgor 31 SJ 0780
Gwalchmai 30 SH 3975
Gwaun-Cae-Gurwen 15 SN 7011
Gwbert-on-Sea 14 SN 1650
Gweek 2 SW 7026
Gwehelog 16 SO 3804
Gwenddwr 23 SO 0643
Gwennap 2 SW 7340
Gwenter 2 SW 7418
Gwernaffield 32 SJ 2064
Gwernesney 16 SO 4101
Gwernogle 15 SN 5234
Gwernymynydd 32 SJ 2162
Gwespyr 31 SJ 1183
Gwinear 2 SW 5937
Gwithian 2 SW 5841
Gwrhyd 15 SN 9339
Gwrych Castle 31 SH 9277
Gwyddelwern 31 SJ 0746
Gwyddgrug 15 SN 4635
Gwytherin 31 SH 8761
Gylchedd 31 SH 8644
Gypsey Race 39 TA 0970

Habberley (Here. and Worc.) 24 SO 8077
Habberley. (Salop) 24 SJ 3903
Habost (Isle of Lewis) 63 NB 3219
Habost (Isle of Lewis) 63 NB 5362
Habrough 39 TA 1514
Haccombe 5 SX 8970
Hacconby 35 TF 1025
Haceby 34 TF 0236
Hacheston 21 TM 3059
Hackenthorpe 33 SK 4183
Hackets 20 TL 3208
Hackford 29 TG 0502
Hackforth 42 SE 2493
Hackland 63 HY 3920
Hacklete 63 NB 1534
Hackleton 26 SP 8055
Hackness (N Yorks.) 43 SE 9690
Hackness (South Walls) 63 ND 3391
Hackney 20 TQ 3585
Hackthorn 34 SK 9882
Hackthorpe 41 NY 5423
Hadden 53 NT 7836
Haddenham (Bucks.) 18 SP 7408
Haddenham (Cambs.) 27 TL 4675
Haddington 52 NT 5174
Haddiscoe 29 TM 4497
Haddon 27 TL 1392
Hademore 25 SK 1708
Hadfield 37 SK 0296
Hadham Cross 20 TL 4218
Hadham Ford 20 TL 4321
Hadleigh (Essex) 20 TQ 8087
Hadleigh (Suff.) 21 TM 0242
Hadley 24 SJ 6712
Hadley End 33 SK 1320
Hadlow 12 TQ 6349
Hadlow Down 12 TQ 5324
Hadnall 32 SJ 5120
Hadstock 20 TL 5645
Hadzor 25 SO 9162
Haffenden Quarter 13 TQ 8841
Hafod-Dinbych 31 SH 8953
Hafodunos 31 SH 8666
Haggbeck 46 NY 4774
Hagley (Here. and Worc.) 24 SO 5641
Hagley (Here. and Worc.) 25 SO 9181
Hagworthingham 35 TF 3469
Haigh 36 SD 6108
Haighton Green 36 SD 5634
Haile 40 NY 0308
Hailes 25 SP 0530
Hailey (Herts.) 20 TL 3710
Hailey (Oxon.) 18 SP 3512
Hailsham 12 TQ 5909
Hail Weston 27 TL 1662
Hainault 20 TQ 4691
Hainford 29 TG 2218
Hainton 35 TF 1784
Haisthorpe 39 TA 1264
Halam 34 SK 6754
Halberton 7 ST 0012
Halcro 67 ND 2260
Hale (Ches.) 32 SJ 4682
Hale (Gtr Mches.) 32 SJ 7786
Hale (Hants.) 8 SU 1919
Hale (Lincs.) 35 TF 1443
Hale Bank 32 SJ 4784
Halebarns 32 SJ 7985
Hales (Norf.) 29 TM 3897
Hales (Staffs.) 32 SJ 7134
Halesowen 25 SO 9683
Hales Place 13 TR 1459
Hale Street 12 TQ 6749
Halesworth 29 TM 3877
Halewood 32 SJ 4585
Halford (Salop) 24 SO 4383
Halford (Warw.) 26 SP 2545
Halfpenny Green 25 SO 8292
Halfway (Berks.) 10 SU 4068
Halfway (Dyfed) 15 SN 6430
Halfway (Dyfed) 15 SN 8232
Halfway House 23 SJ 3411
Halfway Houses 13 TQ 9373
Halifax 37 SE 0825
Halistra 58 NG 2459
Halket 50 NS 4252
Halkirk 67 ND 1359
Halkyn 32 SJ 2071
Halland 12 TQ 5016
Hallaton 26 SP 7896
Hallatrow 17 ST 6356
Hallbankgate 46 NY 5859
Hall Dunnerdale 40 SD 2195
Hallen 16 ST 5479
Hall Green 25 SP 1181
Hallin 58 NG 2559
Halling 12 TQ 7063
Hallington 47 NY 9875
Halloughton 34 SK 6744
Hallow 25 SO 8258
Hallrule 52 NT 5914
Halls 52 NT 6572
Hallsands 5 SX 8138
Hall's Green 19 TL 2728
Halltoft End 35 TF 3645
Hallworthy 4 SX 1787
Hallyburton 52 NT 6748
Hallyne 51 NT 1940
Halmer End 32 SJ 7949
Halmore 17 SO 6902
Halmyre Mains 51 NT 1749
Halnaker 11 SU 9108
Halsall 36 SD 3710
Halse (Northants.) 18 SP 5640
Halse (Somer.) 7 ST 1327
Halsetown 2 SW 5038
Halsham 39 TA 2627
Halsinger 6 SS 5138
Halstead (Essex) 20 TL 8130
Halstead (Kent) 12 TQ 4961
Halstead (Leic.) 26 SK 7505
Halstock 7 ST 5308
Haltham 35 TF 2463
Halton (Bucks.) 19 SP 8710
Halton (Ches.) 32 SJ 5381
Halton (Clwyd) 32 SJ 3039
Halton (Lancs.) 40 SD 5065
Halton East 37 SE 0454
Halton Gill 41 SD 8876
Halton Holegate 35 TF 4165
Halton Lea Gate 46 NY 6558
Halton West 37 SD 8454
Haltwhistle 46 NY 7064
Halvergate 29 TG 4206
Halwell 5 SX 7753
Halwill 4 SX 4299
Halwill Junction 4 SS 4400
Ham (Bressay) 63 HU 4939
Ham (Foula) 63 HT 9739
Ham (Glos.) 17 ST 6898
Ham (Gtr London) 11 TQ 1672
Ham (Highld.) 67 ND 2373
Ham (Kent) 13 TR 3354
Ham (Wilts.) 10 SU 3262
Hamble 9 SU 4806
Hambleden (Bucks.) 18 SU 7886
Hambledon (Hants.) 9 SU 6414
Hambledon (Surrey) 11 SU 9638
Hambleton (Lancs.) 36 SD 3742
Hambleton (N Yorks.) 38 SE 5430
Hambridge 7 ST 3921
Hambrook (Avon) 17 ST 6378
Hambrook (W Susx) 9 SU 7806
Hameringham 35 TF 3167
Hamerton 27 TL 1379
Ham Green (Avon) 16 ST 5575
Ham Green (Here. and Worc.) 25 SP 0063
Hamilton 50 NS 7255
Hammersmith 11 TQ 2279
Hammerwich 25 SK 0707
Hammoon 8 ST 8114
Hamnavoe (Shetld.) 63 HU 4971
Hamnavoe (West Burra) 63 HU 3635
Hamnavoe (Yell) 63 HU 4980
Hampden 19 SP 8603
Hampden Park 12 TQ 6002
Hampden Row 19 SP 8402
Hampnett 17 SP 0915
Hampole 38 SE 5010
Hampreston 8 SZ 0598
Hampstead 19 TQ 2485
Hampstead Norris 10 SU 5276
Hampsthwaite 37 SE 2558
Hampton (Gtr London) 11 TQ 1369
Hampton (Salop) 24 SO 7486
Hampton Bishop 24 SO 5538
Hampton Heath 32 SJ 4949
Hampton in Arden 25 SP 2081
Hampton Lovett 25 SO 8865
Hampton Lucy 26 SP 2557
Hampton on the Hill 26 SP 2564
Hampton Poyle 18 SP 5015
Hamsey 12 TQ 4112
Hamstall Ridware 33 SK 1019
Hamstead (I. of W.) 9 SZ 3991
Hamstead (W Mids) 25 SP 0593
Hamstead Marshall 10 SU 4165
Hamsterley (Durham) 42 NZ 1131
Hamsterley (Durham) 47 NZ 1156
Hamstreet (Kent) 13 TR 0034
Ham Street (Somer.) 7 ST 5534
Hamtoun 63 HT 9637
Hamworthy 8 SY 9990
Hanbury (Here and Worc.) 25 SO 9663
Hanbury (Staffs.) 33 SK 1727
Hanchurch 33 SJ 8441
Handbridge 32 SJ 4164
Handcross 11 TQ 2630
Handforth 33 SJ 8883
Handley 32 SJ 4657
Handsacre 25 SK 0916
Handsworth (S Yorks.) 33 SK 4086
Handsworth (W Mids) 25 SP 0490
Hanford 33 SJ 8642
Hanging Langford 8 SU 0237
Hanham 17 ST 6372
Hankelow 32 SJ 6645
Hankerton 17 ST 9690
Hankham 12 TQ 6105
Hanley 33 SJ 8847
Hanley Castle 25 SO 8342
Hanley Childe 24 SO 6565
Hanley Swan 25 SO 8143
Hanley William 24 SO 6765
Hanlith 41 SD 9061
Hanmer 32 SJ 4540
Hannington (Hants.) 10 SU 5355
Hannington (Northants.) 26 SP 8171
Hannington (Wilts.) 17 SU 1793
Hannington Wick 17 SU 1795
Hanslope 26 SP 8046
Hanthorpe 35 TF 0824
Hanwell 26 SP 4343
Hanworth (Gtr London) 11 TQ 1271
Hanworth (Norf.) 29 TG 1935
Happendon 50 NS 8533
Happisburgh 29 TG 3731
Happisburgh Common 29 TG 3729
Hapsford 32 SJ 4774
Hapton (Lancs.) 37 SD 7931
Hapton (Norf.) 29 TM 1796
Harberton 5 SX 7758
Harbertonford 5 SX 7856
Harbledown 13 TR 1358
Harborne 25 SP 0384
Harborough Magna 26 SP 4779
Harbottle 47 NT 9304
Harbury 26 SP 3759
Harby (Leic.) 34 SK 7431
Harby (Notts.) 34 SK 8770
Harcombe 5 SY 1590
Harden 37 SE 0838
Hardenhuish 17 ST 9074
Hardgate 62 NJ 7801
Hardham 11 TQ 0317
Hardingham 29 TG 0403
Hardingstone 26 SP 7657
Hardings Wood 32 SJ 8054
Hardington 8 ST 7452
Hardington Mandeville 7 ST 5111
Hardington Marsh 7 ST 5009
Hardley 9 SU 4205
Hardley Street 29 TG 3801
Hardmead 27 SP 9347
Hardrow 41 SD 8691
Hardstoft 33 SK 4463
Hardway (Hants.) 9 SU 6101
Hardway (Somer.) 8 ST 7134
Hardwick (Bucks.) 18 SP 8019
Hardwick (Cambs.) 20 TL 3758
Hardwick (Norf.) 29 TM 2290
Hardwick (Northants.) 27 SP 8569
Hardwick (Oxon.) 18 SP 3706
Hardwick (Oxon.) 18 SP 5729
Hardwicke (Glos.) 17 SO 7912
Hardwicke (Glos.) 17 SO 9127
Hareby 35 TF 3365
Hareden 36 SD 6350
Harefield 19 TQ 0590
Hare Hatch 10 SU 8077
Harehope 53 NU 0920
Harescombe 17 SO 8410
Haresfield 17 SO 8110
Hare Street 20 TL 3929
Harewood 37 SE 3245
Harford 5 SX 6359
Hargrave (Ches.) 32 SJ 4862
Hargrave (Northants.) 27 TL 0370
Hargrave Green 20 TL 7759
Haringey 20 TQ 3290
Harker 46 NY 3960
Harkstead 21 TM 1935
Harlaston 25 SK 2111
Harlaxton 34 SK 8832
Harlech 30 SH 5831
Harlesden 19 TQ 2383
Harleston (Norf.) 29 TM 2483
Harleston (Suff.) 21 TM 0160
Harlestone 26 SP 7064
Harle Syke 37 SD 8634
Harley 24 SJ 5901
Harling Road 29 TL 9788
Harlington 19 TL 0330
Harlosh 58 NG 2841
Harlow 20 TL 4711
Harlow Hill 47 NZ 0768
Harlthorpe 38 SE 7337
Harlton 20 TL 3852
Harman's Cross 8 SY 9880
Harmby 42 SE 1289
Harmer Green 19 TL 2516
Harmer Hill 32 SJ 4822
Harmston 34 SK 9762
Harnhill 17 SP 0600
Harold Hill 20 TQ 5391
Haroldston West 14 SM 8615
Haroldswick (Unst) 63 HP 6312
Harold Wood 20 TQ 5590
Harome 42 SE 6482
Harpenden 19 TL 1314
Harpford 5 SY 0890
Harpham 39 TA 0961
Harpley (Here. and Worc.) 24 SO 6861
Harpley (Norf.) 28 TF 7826
Harpole 26 SP 6961
Harpsdale 67 ND 1256
Harpsden 10 SU 7680
Harpswell 34 SK 9389
Harpurhey 37 SD 8701
Harpur Hill 33 SK 0671
Harrapool 58 NG 6523
Harrietfield 56 NN 9829
Harrietsham 13 TQ 8753
Harrington (Cumbr.) 40 NX 9926
Harrington (Lincs.) 35 TF 3671
Harrington (Northants.) 26 SP 7780
Harringworth 27 SP 9197
Harriseahead 33 SJ 8656
Harrogate 37 SE 3055
Harrold 27 SP 9456
Harrow 19 TQ 1388
Harrowbarrow 4 SX 3969
Harrowden 27 TL 0646
Harrow on the Hill 19 TQ 1586
Harsgeir 63 NB 1040
Harston (Cambs.) 20 TL 4251
Harston (Leic.) 34 SK 8331
Hart 42 NZ 4735
Hartburn 47 NZ 0886
Hartest 20 TL 8352
Hartfield 12 TQ 4735
Hartford (Cambs.) 27 TL 2572
Hartford (Ches.) 32 SJ 6372
Hartfordbridge 10 SU 7757
Hartford End 20 TL 6817
Harthill (Ches.) 32 SJ 4955
Harthill (Lothian) 50 NS 9064
Harthill (S Yorks.) 33 SK 4980
Hartington 33 SK 1360
Hartland 4 SS 2624
Hartland Quay 4 SS 2224
Hartlebury 25 SO 8470
Hartlepool 42 NZ 5032
Hartley (Cumbr.) 41 NY 7808
Hartley (Kent) 12 TQ 6166
Hartley (Kent) 12 TQ 7634
Hartley (Northum.) 47 NZ 3475
Hartley Wespall 10 SU 6958
Hartley Wintney 10 SU 7756
Hartlip 12 TQ 8364
Harton (N Yorks.) 38 SE 7061
Harton (Salop) 24 SO 4888
Harton (Tyne and Wear) 47 NZ 3864
Hartpury 17 SO 7924
Hartshill 26 SP 3293
Hartshorne 33 SK 3221
Hartsop 40 NY 4013
Hartwell 26 SP 7850
Hartwood 50 NS 8459
Harvel 12 TQ 6563
Harvington 25 SP 0548
Harvington Cross 25 SP 0549
Harwell 18 SU 4989
Harwich 21 TM 2431
Harwood (Durham) 41 NY 8133
Harwood (Gtr Mches.) 36 SD 7411
Harwood Dale 43 SE 9595
Harworth 38 SK 6291
Hascombe 11 TQ 0039
Haselbech 26 SP 7177

Haselbury Plucknett Holland-on-Sea

Haselbury Plucknett 7 ST 4711
Haseley 26 SP 2368
Haselor 25 SP 1257
Hasfield 17 SO 8227
Hasguard 14 SM 8509
Haskayne 36 SD 3507
Hasketon 21 TM 2550
Hasland 33 SK 3969
Haslemere 11 SU 9032
Haslingden 37 SD 7823
Haslingden Grane 37 SD 7523
Haslingfield 20 TL 4052
Haslington 32 SJ 7355
Hassall 32 SJ 7657
Hassall Green 32 SJ 7758
Hassell Street 13 TR 0946
Hassendean 52 NT 5420
Hassingham 29 TG 3605
Hassocks 12 TQ 3015
Hassop 33 SK 2272
Hastigrow 67 ND 2661
Hastingleigh 13 TR 0945
Hastings 12 TQ 8009
Hastingwood 20 TL 4807
Hastoe 19 SP 9209
Haswell 42 NZ 3743
Hatch (Beds.) 27 TL 1547
Hatch (Hants.) 10 SU 6752
Hatch (Wilts.) 8 ST 9228
Hatch Beauchamp 7 ST 3020
Hatch End 19 TQ 1391
Hatching Green 19 TL 1313
Hatchmere 32 SJ 5571
Hatcliffe 39 TA 2100
Hatfield (Here. and Worc.) 24 SO 5859
Hatfield (Herts.) 19 TL 2309
Hatfield (S Yorks.) 38 SE 6609
Hatfield Broad Oak 20 TL 5516
Hatfield Heath 20 TL 5215
Hatfield Peverel 20 TL 7911
Hatfield Woodhouse 38 SE 6708
Hatford 18 SU 3394
Hatherden 10 SU 3450
Hatherleigh 6 SS 5404
Hathern 34 SK 5022
Hatherop 17 SP 1505
Hathersage 33 SK 2381
Hatherton (Ches.) 32 SJ 6847
Hatherton (Staffs.) 25 SJ 9610
Hatley St. George 27 TL 2851
Hattingley 10 SU 6437
Hatton (Ches.) 32 SJ 5982
Hatton (Derby.) 33 SK 2130
Hatton (Grampn.) 62 NK 0537
Hatton (Gtr London) 11 TQ 1075
Hatton (Lincs.) 35 TF 1776
Hatton (Salop) 24 SO 4690
Hatton (Warw.) 26 SP 2367
Hattoncrook 62 NJ 8424
Hatton Heath 32 SJ 4561
Hatton of Fintray 62 NJ 8316
Haugham 35 TF 3381
Haugh Head 53 NU 0026
Haughley 21 TM 0262
Haughley Green 21 TM 0364
Haugh of Urr 45 NX 8066
Haughton (Notts.) 34 SK 6772
Haughton (Salop) 32 SJ 3727
Haughton (Salop) 24 SJ 5516
Haughton (Salop) 24 SO 6795
Haughton (Staffs.) 33 SJ 8620
Haughton Green 37 SJ 9393
Haughton Moss 32 SJ 5756
Haunton 33 SK 2411
Hauxley 47 NU 2703
Hauxton 20 TL 4351
Havant 9 SU 7106
Haven 24 SO 4054
Havenstreet 9 SZ 5690
Haverfordwest 14 SM 9515
Haverhill 20 TL 6745
Haverigg 40 SD 1578
Havering 20 TQ 5587
Havering-atte-Bower 20 TQ 5193
Havering's Grove 20 TQ 6594
Haversham 26 SP 8343
Haverthwaite 40 SD 3483
Hawarden 32 SJ 3165
Hawes 41 SD 8789
Hawford 25 SO 8460
Hawick (Borders) 52 NT 5014
Hawkchurch 7 ST 3400
Hawkedon 20 TL 7952
Hawkeridge 8 ST 8653
Hawkerland 5 SY 0588
Hawkesbury 17 ST 7687
Hawkesbury Upton 17 ST 7786
Hawkes End 26 SP 2983
Hawkhill 53 NU 2212
Hawkhope 46 NY 7188
Hawkhurst 12 TQ 7630
Hawkinge 13 TR 2139
Hawkley 9 SU 7429
Hawkridge 6 SS 8630
Hawkshead 40 SD 3598
Hawksland 50 NS 8439
Hawkstone 32 SJ 5830
Hawkswick 41 SD 9570
Hawksworth (Notts.) 34 SK 7543
Hawksworth (W Yorks.) 37 SE 1641
Hawkwell 20 TQ 8691
Hawley (Hants.) 11 SU 8558
Hawley (Kent) 12 TQ 5571
Hawling 17 SP 0623
Hawnby 42 SE 5389
Haworth 37 SE 0337
Hawsker 43 NZ 9207
Hawstead 20 TL 8559
Hawthorn Hill 11 SU 8873
Hawton 34 SK 7851
Haxby 38 SE 6057
Haxey 38 SK 7699
Haydock 32 SJ 5696
Haydon 8 ST 6615
Haydon Bridge 47 NY 8464
Haydon Wick 17 SU 1388
Haye 4 SX 3570
Hayes (Gtr London) 19 TQ 0980
Hayes (Gtr London) 12 TQ 4165
Hayfield 33 SK 0386
Hayhillock 57 NO 5242
Hayle 2 SW 5537
Hayling Island 9 SU 7201
Haynes 27 TL 0841
Hay-on-Wye 23 SO 2342
Hayscastle 14 SM 8925
Hayscastle Cross 14 SM 9125
Hayton (Cumbr.) 40 NY 1041
Hayton (Cumbr.) 46 NY 5057
Hayton (Humbs.) 39 SE 8145
Hayton (Notts.) 34 SK 7284
Hayton's Bent 24 SO 5280
Haytor Vale 5 SX 7677
Haywards Heath 12 TQ 3324
Haywood Oaks 34 SK 6055
Hazelbank 50 NS 8344
Hazelbury Bryan 8 ST 7408
Hazeley 10 SU 7459
Hazel Grove 33 SJ 9287
Hazelrigg 53 NU 0533
Hazelslade 25 SK 0212
Hazelton Walls 57 NO 3321
Hazelwood 33 SK 3245
Hazlemere 19 SU 8895
Hazlerigg 47 NZ 2472
Hazleton 17 SP 0718
Heacham 28 TF 6737
Headbourne Worthy 9 SU 4831
Headcorn 12 TQ 8344
Headington 18 SP 5407
Headlam 42 NZ 1818
Headless Cross 25 SP 0365
Headley (Hants.) 10 SU 5162
Headley (Hants.) 9 SU 8236
Headley (Surrey) 11 TQ 2054
Head of Muir 50 NS 8080
Headon 34 SK 7476
Heads Nook 46 NY 4955
Heage 33 SK 3650
Healaugh (N Yorks.) 41 SE 0198
Healaugh (N Yorks.) 38 SE 4947
Heale 6 SS 6446
Healey (Lancs.) 37 SD 8817
Healey (Northum.) 47 NZ 0158
Healey (N Yorks.) 42 SE 1780
Healeyfield 47 NZ 0648
Healing 39 TA 2110
Heamoor 2 SW 4631
Heanish 48 NM 0343
Heanor 33 SK 4346
Heanton Punchardon 6 SS 5035
Heapham 34 SK 8788
Hearthstane 51 NT 1125
Heaste 58 NG 6417
Heath 33 SK 4467
Heath and Reach 19 SP 9228
Heathcote 33 SK 1460
Heath End (Hants.) 10 SU 5762
Heath End (Hants.) 11 SU 8550
Heather 33 SK 3910
Heathfield (Devon.) 5 SX 8376
Heathfield (E Susx) 12 TQ 5821
Heathfield (Somer.) 7 ST 1526
Heath Hayes 25 SK 0110
Heath Hill 24 SJ 7614
Heath House 7 ST 4146
Heath, The 21 TL 9043
Heathton 25 SO 8192
Heatley 32 SJ 6988
Heaton (Lancs.) 40 SD 4460
Heaton (Staffs.) 33 SJ 9462
Heaton (Tyne and Wear) 47 NZ 2665
Heaton Moor 37 SJ 8691
Heaverham 12 TQ 5758
Heaviley 33 SJ 9088
Hebburn 47 NZ 3265
Hebden 42 SE 0263
Hebden Bridge 37 SD 9927
Hebden Green 32 SJ 6365
Hebron 47 NZ 1989
Heckfield 10 SU 7260
Heckfield Green 29 TM 1875
Heckington 35 TF 1444
Heckmondwike 37 SE 2123
Heddington 17 ST 9966
Heddle 63 HY 3512
Heddon-on-the-Wall 47 NZ 1366
Hedenham 29 TM 3193
Hedge End 9 SU 4812
Hedgerley 19 SU 9787
Hedging 7 ST 3029
Hedley on the Hill 47 NZ 0759
Hednesford 25 SK 0012
Hedon 39 TA 1828
Hedsor 19 SU 9086
Hegdon Hill 24 SO 5854
Heglibister 63 HU 3852
Heighington (Durham) 42 NZ 2522
Heighington (Lincs.) 34 TF 0269
Heights of Brae 65 NH 5161
Heights of Kinlochewe 64 NH 0764
Heilam 66 NC 4659
Heiton 52 NT 7130
Heldon Hill 61 NJ 1257
Hele (Devon.) 6 SS 5347
Hele (Devon.) 5 SS 9902
Helensburgh 50 NS 2982
Helford 2 SW 7526
Helhoughton 28 TF 8626
Helions Bumpstead 20 TL 6541
Helland 4 SX 0770
Hellesdon 29 TG 1810
Hellidon 26 SP 5158
Hellifield 37 SD 8556
Hellingly 12 TQ 5812
Hellington 29 TG 3103
Hellister 63 HU 3949
Helmdon 26 SP 5843
Helmingham 21 TM 1857
Helmsdale 67 ND 0215
Helmshore 37 SD 7821
Helmsley 42 SE 6183
Helperby 38 SE 4369
Helperthorpe 39 SE 9570
Helpringham 35 TF 1340
Helpston 27 TF 1205
Helsby 32 SJ 4875
Helston 2 SW 6527
Helstone 4 SX 0881
Helton 40 NY 5122
Helwith Bridge 41 SD 8169
Hemblington 29 TG 3411
Hemel Hempstead 19 TL 0506
Hemingbrough 38 SE 6730
Hemingby 35 TF 2374
Hemingford Abbots 27 TL 2870
Hemingford Grey 27 TL 2970
Hemingstone 21 TM 1453
Hemington (Northants.) 27 TL 0985
Hemington (Somer.) 8 ST 7253
Hemley 21 TM 2842
Hempholme 39 TA 0850
Hempnall 29 TM 2494
Hempnall Green 29 TM 2593
Hempriggs 61 NJ 1064
Hempstead (Essex) 20 TL 6338
Hempstead (Norf.) 29 TG 4124
Hempsted (Glos.) 17 SO 8117
Hempsted (Norf.) 29 TG 1037
Hempton (Norf.) 28 TF 9129
Hempton (Oxon.) 18 SP 4431
Hemsby 29 TG 4917
Hemswell 34 SK 9290
Hemsworth 38 SE 4213
Hemyock 7 ST 1313
Henbury (Avon) 16 ST 5478
Henbury (Ches.) 33 SJ 8873
Hendon (Gtr London) 19 TQ 2389
Hendon (Tyne and Wear) 47 NZ 4055
Hendy 15 SN 5804
Heneglwys 30 SH 4276
Henfield 11 TQ 2116
Hengoed (Mid Glam.) 16 ST 1495
Hengoed (Powys) 23 SO 2253
Hengoed (Salop) 32 SJ 2833
Hengrave 20 TL 8268
Henham 20 TL 5428
Heniarth 23 SJ 1108
Henley (Salop) 24 SO 5476
Henley (Somer.) 7 ST 4232
Henley (Suff.) 21 TM 1551
Henley (W Susx) 11 SU 8926
Henley-in-Arden 25 SP 1465
Henley on Thames 10 SU 7682
Henley Park 11 SU 9352
Henllan (Clwyd) 31 SJ 0268
Henllan (Dyfed) 14 SN 3540
Henllan Amgoed 14 SN 1820
Henllys 16 ST 2693
Henlow 19 TL 1738
Hennock 5 SX 8380
Henryd 31 SH 7674
Henry's Moat (Castell Hendre) 14 SN 0428
Hensall 38 SE 5923
Henshaw 46 NY 7664
Henstead 29 TM 4986
Henstridge 8 ST 7219
Henstridge Marsh 8 ST 7420
Henton (Oxon.) 18 SP 7602
Henton (Somer.) 7 ST 4845
Henwick 25 SO 8354
Henwood 4 SX 2673
Heogan 63 HU 4743
Heol Senni 15 SN 9223
Heol-y-Cyw 15 SS 9484
Hepburn 53 NU 0724
Hepple 47 NT 9800
Hepscott 47 NZ 2284
Heptonstall 37 SD 9827
Hepworth (Suff.) 29 TL 9874
Hepworth (W Yorks.) 37 SE 1606
Herbrandston 14 SM 8707
Hereford 24 SO 5040
Hergest 23 SO 2655
Heriot 51 NT 3952
Hermitage (Berks.) 10 SU 5072
Hermitage (Borders) 46 NY 5095
Hermitage (Dorset.) 8 ST 6306
Hermitage (Hants.) 9 SU 7505
Hermitage, The 11 TQ 2253
Hermon (Dyfed) 14 SN 2032
Hermon (Dyfed) 15 SN 3630
Hermon (Gwyn.) 30 SH 3868
Herne 13 TR 1866
Herne Bay 13 TR 1768
Herner 6 SS 5926
Hernhill 13 TR 0660
Herodsfoot 4 SX 2160
Herongate 20 TQ 6391
Heronsgate 19 TQ 0294
Herriard 10 SU 6645
Herringfleet 29 TM 4797
Herringswell 28 TL 7170
Herrington 47 NZ 3553
Hersden 13 TR 1961
Hersham 11 TQ 1164
Herstmonceux 12 TQ 6312
Hertford 20 TL 3212
Hertford Heath 20 TL 3510
Hertingfordbury 20 TL 3112
Hesketh Bank 36 SD 4323
Hesketh Lane 36 SD 6141
Hesket Newmarket 40 NY 3438
Heskin Green 36 SD 5315
Hesleden 42 NZ 4438
Hesleyside 46 NY 8183
Heslington 38 SE 6250
Hessay 38 SE 5253
Hessenford 4 SX 3057
Hessett 21 TL 9361
Hessle 39 TA 0326
Hest Bank 40 SD 4566
Heston 11 TQ 1277
Heswall 32 SJ 2682
Hethe 18 SP 5929
Hethersett 29 TG 1505
Hethersgill 46 NY 4767
Hethpool 53 NT 8928
Hett 42 NZ 2836
Hetton 37 SD 9658
Hetton-le-Hole 47 NZ 3548
Heugh 47 NZ 0873
Heugh-Head 61 NJ 3711
Heveningham 29 TM 3372
Hever 12 TQ 4744
Heversham 40 SD 4983
Hevingham 29 TG 2022
Hewelsfield 17 SO 5602
Hewish (Avon) 16 ST 4064
Hewish (Somer.) 7 ST 4108
Hexham 47 NY 9364
Hextable 12 TQ 5170
Hexton 19 TL 1030
Hexworthy 5 SX 6572
Heybridge (Essex) 20 TL 8508
Heybridge (Essex) 20 TQ 6498
Heybridge Basin 21 TL 8707
Heybrook Bay 4 SX 4948
Heydon (Cambs.) 20 TL 4340
Heydon (Norf.) 29 TG 1127
Heydour 34 TF 0039
Heyford 26 SP 6558
Heylipoll 48 NL 9643
Heylor 63 HU 2881
Heysham 40 SD 4161
Heyshott 11 SU 8918
Heytesbury 8 ST 9242
Heythrop 18 SP 3527
Heywood (Gtr Mches.) 37 SD 8510
Heywood (Wilts.) 8 ST 8753
Hibaldstow 39 SE 9702
Hickleton 38 SE 4805
Hickling (Norf.) 29 TG 4124
Hickling (Notts.) 34 SK 6929
Hickling Green 29 TG 4023
Hickling Heath 29 TG 4022
Hidcote Boyce 25 SP 1742
High Ackworth 38 SE 4317
Higham (Derby.) 33 SK 3959
Higham (Kent) 12 TQ 7171
Higham (Lancs.) 37 SD 8036
Higham (Suff.) 20 TL 7465
Higham (Suff.) 21 TM 0335
Higham Dykes 47 NZ 1375
Higham Ferrers 27 SP 9669
Higham Gobion 19 TL 1033
Higham on the Hill 26 SP 3895
Highampton 6 SS 4804
Higham Wood 12 TQ 6048
High Banton 50 NS 7480
High Beach 20 TQ 4097
High Bentham 41 SD 6669
High Bickington 6 SS 5920
High Birkwith 41 SD 8076
High Blantyre 50 NS 6756
High Bonnybridge 50 NS 8378
Highbridge 7 ST 3147
Highbrook 12 TQ 3630
Highburton 37 SE 1813
Highbury 8 ST 6849
High Buston 47 NU 2308
High Callerton 47 NZ 1670
High Catton 38 SE 7153
Highclere 10 SU 4360
Highcliffe 9 SZ 2193
High Cogges 18 SP 3709
High Coniscliffe 42 NZ 2215
High Cross (Hants.) 9 SU 7126
High Cross (Herts.) 20 TL 3618
High Cross Bank 33 SK 3018
High Easter 20 TL 6214
High Ellington 42 SE 1983
Higher Ansty 8 ST 7603
Higher Ballam 36 SD 3630
High Ercall 24 SJ 5917
Higher Penwortham 36 SD 5128
Higher Tale 5 ST 0601
Higher Walreddon 4 SX 4771
Higher Walton (Ches.) 32 SJ 5985
Higher Walton (Lancs.) 36 SD 5727
Higher Wych 32 SJ 4943
High Etherley 42 NZ 1628
Highfield (Strath.) 50 NS 3050
Highfield (Tyne and Wear) 47 NZ 1459
Highfields 20 TL 3559
High Garrett 20 TL 7726
High Grange 42 NZ 1731
High Grantley 42 SE 2369
High Green (Here. and Worc.) 25 SO 8745
High Green (Norf.) 29 TG 1305
High Green (S Yorks.) 37 SK 3397
High Halden 13 TQ 9037
High Halstow 12 TQ 7875
High Ham 7 ST 4231
High Hatton 32 SJ 6024
High Hesket 46 NY 4744
High Hoyland 37 SE 2710
High Hunsley 39 SE 9535
High Hurstwood 12 TQ 4926
High Lane 24 SO 6760
High Laver 20 TL 5208
Highleadon 17 SO 7623
High Legh 32 SJ 6984
Highleigh 9 SZ 8498
Highley 24 SO 7483
High Littleton 17 ST 6458
High Lorton 40 NY 1625
High Melton 38 SE 5001
Highmoor Cross 18 SU 7084
Highmoor Hill 16 ST 4689
Highnam 17 SO 7919
High Newton 40 SD 4082
High Newton-by-the-Sea 53 NU 2325
High Offley 32 SJ 7826
High Ongar 20 TL 5603
High Onn 25 SJ 8216
High Roding 20 TL 6017
High Salvington 11 TQ 1206
High Shaw 41 SD 8791
High Spen 47 NZ 1359
Highsted 13 TQ 9161
High Street (Corn.) 2 SW 9753
High Street (Suff.) 21 TM 4355
High Street Green 21 TM 0055
Hightae 45 NY 0979
Hightown (Ches.) 33 SJ 8762
Hightown (Mers.) 36 SD 2903
High Toynton 35 TF 2869
High Trewhitt 47 NU 0105
Highway 17 SU 0474
Highweek 5 SX 8472
Highworth 17 SU 2092
High Wray 40 SD 3799
High Wych 20 TL 4614
High Wycombe 19 SU 8593
Hilborough (Norf.) 28 TF 8200
Hildenborough 12 TQ 5648
Hildersham 20 TL 5448
Hilderstone 33 SJ 9434
Hilderthorpe 39 TA 1765
Hilgay 28 TL 6298
Hill 17 ST 6495
Hillam 38 SE 5028
Hillbeck 41 NY 7915
Hillberry 43 SC 3879
Hillborough (Kent) 13 TR 2168
Hillbrae (Grampn.) 62 NJ 6047
Hillbrae (Grampn.) 62 NJ 7923
Hill Brow 9 SU 7926
Hill Dyke 35 TF 3447
Hill End (Durham) 41 NZ 0135
Hill End (Fife.) 51 NT 0495
Hillend (Fife.) 51 NT 1483
Hillesden 18 SP 6828
Hillesley 17 ST 7689
Hillfarrance 7 ST 1624
Hillhead (Devon.) 5 SX 9053
Hill Head (Hants.) 9 SU 5402
Hillhead (Strath.) 50 NS 4219
Hillhead of Auchentumb 62 NJ 9258
Hillhead of Cocklaw 62 NK 0844
Hilliard's Cross 25 SK 1412
Hilliclay 67 ND 1764
Hillingdon 19 TQ 0882
Hillington 28 TF 7225
Hillmorton 26 SP 5374
Hillockhead 61 NJ 3809
Hill of Beath 51 NT 1690
Hill of Fearn 65 NH 8377
Hill of Maud Crofts 61 NJ 4661
Hill Ridware 33 SK 0718
Hill Row 27 TL 4475
Hillside (Grampn.) 62 NO 9298
Hillside (Shetld.) 63 HU 4063
Hillside (Tays.) 57 NO 7061
Hillswick 63 HU 2877
Hill, The 40 SD 1783
Hill Top (Hants.) 9 SU 4002
Hill Top (W Yorks.) 37 SE 3315
Hillwell 63 HU 3714
Hilmarton 17 SU 0175
Hilperton 17 ST 8759
Hilsea 9 SU 6503
Hilton (Cambs.) 27 TL 2966
Hilton (Cleve.) 42 NZ 4611
Hilton (Cumbr.) 41 NY 7320
Hilton (Derby.) 33 SK 2430
Hilton (Dorset) 8 ST 7802
Hilton (Durham) 42 NZ 1621
Hilton (Grampn.) 62 NJ 9434
Hilton (Salop) 24 SO 7795
Hilton of Cadboll 65 NH 8776
Himbleton 25 SO 9458
Himley 25 SO 8891
Hincaster 40 SD 5184
Hinckley 26 SP 4294
Hinderclay 29 TM 0276
Hinderwell 43 NZ 7916
Hindford 32 SJ 3333
Hindhead 11 SU 8736
Hindley 36 SD 6104
Hindley Green 36 SD 6403
Hindlip 25 SO 8758
Hindolveston 29 TG 0329
Hindon 8 ST 9032
Hindringham 29 TF 9836
Hingham 29 TG 0202
Hinstock 32 SJ 6926
Hintlesham 21 TM 0843
Hinton (Avon) 17 ST 7376
Hinton (Hants.) 8 SZ 2095
Hinton (Northants.) 26 SP 5352
Hinton (Salop) 24 SJ 4008
Hinton Ampner 9 SU 5927
Hinton Blewett 17 ST 5956
Hinton Charterhouse 17 ST 7758
Hinton-in-the-Hedges 18 SP 5537
Hinton Marsh 9 SU 5827
Hinton Martell 8 SU 0106
Hinton on the Green 25 SP 0240
Hinton Parva 18 SU 2283
Hinton St. George 7 ST 4212
Hinton St. Mary 8 ST 7816
Hinton Waldrist 18 SU 3799
Hints (Salop) 24 SO 6175
Hints (Staffs.) 25 SK 1503
Hinwick 27 SP 9361
Hinxhill 13 TR 0442
Hinxton 20 TL 4945
Hinxworth 19 TL 2340
Hipperholme 37 SE 1225
Hirn 62 NJ 7300
Hirnant 31 SJ 0423
Hirst 47 NZ 2787
Hirst Courtney 38 SE 6124
Hirwaun 15 SN 9505
Hiscott 6 SS 5426
Histon 20 TL 4363
Hitcham 21 TL 9851
Hitchin 19 TL 1829
Hither Green 12 TQ 3874
Hittisleigh 6 SX 7395
Hixon 33 SK 0026
Hoaden 13 TR 2759
Hoaldalbert 16 SO 3923
Hoar Cross 33 SK 1223
Hoarwithy 16 SO 5429
Hoath 13 TR 2064
Hobarris 23 SO 3078
Hobbister 63 HY 3807
Hobkirk 52 NT 5810
Hobson 47 NZ 1755
Hoby 34 SK 6617
Hockering 29 TG 0713
Hockerton 34 SK 7156
Hockley 20 TQ 8293
Hockley Heath 25 SP 1572
Hockliffe 19 SP 9726
Hockwold cum Wilton 28 TL 7288
Hockworthy 7 ST 0319
Hoddesdon 20 TL 3709
Hoddlesden 36 SD 7122
Hodgeston 14 SS 0399
Hodnet 32 SJ 6128
Hodthorpe 34 SK 5476
Hoe 29 TF 9916
Hoe Gate 9 SU 6213
Hoff 41 NY 6717
Hoggeston 18 SP 8025
Hoghton 36 SD 6125
Hognaston 33 SK 2350
Hogsthorpe 35 TF 5372
Holbeach 35 TF 3625
Holbeach Bank 35 TF 3627
Holbeach Drove 35 TF 3212
Holbeach Hurn 35 TF 3927
Holbeach St. Johns 35 TF 3418
Holbeach St. Marks 35 TF 3731
Holbeach St. Matthew 35 TF 4132
Holbeck 34 SK 5473
Holberrow Green 25 SP 0259
Holbeton 5 SX 6150
Holborn 20 TQ 3181
Holbrook (Derby.) 33 SK 3645
Holbrook (Suff.) 21 TM 1636
Holburn 53 NU 0436
Holbury 9 SU 4303
Holcombe (Devon.) 5 SX 9574
Holcombe (Somer.) 8 ST 6649
Holcombe Rogus 7 ST 0519
Holcot 26 SP 7969
Holden 37 SD 7749
Holdenby 26 SP 6967
Holdgate 24 SO 5589
Holdingham 35 TF 0547
Holestane 45 NX 8799
Holford 7 ST 1541
Holker 40 SD 3577
Holkham 28 TF 8944
Hollacombe 4 SS 3702
Holland (Papa Westray) 63 HY 4851
Holland (Stronsay) 63 HY 6622
Holland Fen 35 TF 2445
Holland-on-Sea 21 TM 2016

Hollandstoun Jurby West

Hollandstoun 63 HY 7553
Hollesley 21 TM 3544
Hollingbourne 13 TQ 8455
Hollington (Derby.) 33 SK 2239
Hollington (E Susx) 12 TQ 7911
Hollington (Staffs.) 33 SK 0538
Hollingworth 37 SK 0096
Hollins 37 SD 8108
Hollinsclough 33 SK 0666
Hollins Green 32 SJ 6990
Hollinswood 24 SJ 6909
Hollinwood 32 SJ 5236
Hollocombe 6 SS 6311
Holloway 33 SK 3256
Hollowell 26 SP 6972
Hollybush (Gwent) 16 SO 1603
Hollybush (Here. and Worc.) 24 SO 7636
Hollybush (Strath.) 50 NS 3914
Holly End 28 TF 4906
Hollym 39 TA 3425
Holm (Isle of Lewis) 63 NB 4531
Holmbury St. Mary 11 TQ 1144
Holme (Cambs.) 27 TL 1987
Holme (Cumbr.) 40 SD 5278
Holme (Notts.) 34 SK 8059
Holme (W Yorks.) 37 SE 1005
Holme Chapel 37 SD 8728
Holme Hale 28 TF 8807
Holme Lacy 24 SO 5535
Holme Marsh 23 SO 3354
Holme next the Sea 28 TF 7043
Holme on the Wolds 39 SE 9646
Holmer 24 SO 5042
Holmer Green 19 SU 9097
Holmes Chapel 32 SJ 7667
Holmesfield 33 SK 3277
Holmeswood 36 SD 4316
Holme upon Spalding Moor 39 SE 8138
Holmewood 33 SK 4365
Holmfirth 37 SE 1408
Holmhead 50 NS 5620
Holmpton 39 TA 3623
Holmrook 40 SD 0799
Holmsgarth 63 HU 4642
Holne 5 SX 7069
Holnest 8 ST 6509
Holsworthy 4 SS 3403
Holsworthy Beacon 4 SS 3508
Holt (Clwyd) 32 SJ 4053
Holt (Dorset) 8 SU 0203
Holt (Here. and Worc.) 25 SO 8262
Holt (Norf.) 29 TG 0738
Holt (Wilts.) 17 ST 8661
Holtby 38 SE 6754
Holt End 25 SP 0769
Holt Heath 25 SO 8163
Holton (Lincs.) 35 TF 1181
Holton (Oxon.) 18 SP 6006
Holton (Somerset) 8 ST 6826
Holton (Suff.) 29 TM 4077
Holton Heath 8 SY 9491
Holton le Clay 39 TA 2802
Holton le Moor 39 TF 0797
Holton St. Mary 21 TM 0537
Holwell (Herts.) 19 TL 1633
Holwell (Leic.) 34 SK 7323
Holwell (Oxon.) 18 SP 2309
Holwick 41 NY 9026
Holworth 8 SY 7683
Holybourne 10 SU 7341
Holy Cross 25 SO 9279
Holyhead 30 SH 2482
Holymoorside 33 SK 3369
Holyport 11 SU 8977
Holystone 47 NT 9502
Holytown 50 NS 7760
Holywell (Cambs.) 27 TL 3370
Holywell (Clwyd) 32 SJ 1875
Holywell (Corn.) 2 SW 7658
Holywell (Dorset) 7 ST 5904
Holywell Green 37 SE 0918
Holywell Lake 7 ST 1020
Holywell Row 28 TL 7077
Holywood 45 NX 9480
Homer 24 SJ 6101
Homersfield 29 TM 2885
Hom Green 17 SO 5822
Homington 8 SU 1226
Honeyborough 14 SM 9506
Honeybourne 25 SP 1144
Honeychurch 6 SS 6202
Honey Hill 13 TR 1161
Honiley 26 SP 2472
Honing 29 TG 3227
Honingham 29 TG 1011
Honington (Lincs.) 34 SK 9443
Honington (Suff.) 28 TL 9174
Honington (Warw.) 26 SP 2642
Honiton 5 ST 1600
Honley 37 SE 1311
Hoo (Kent) 12 TQ 7872
Hooe (Devon.) 4 SX 5052
Hooe (E Susx) 12 TQ 6809
Hoo Green 21 TM 2559
Hook (Dyfed) 14 SM 9811
Hook (Hants.) 10 SU 7254
Hook (Humbs.) 38 SE 7525
Hook (Surrey) 11 TQ 1764
Hook (Wilts.) 17 SU 0784
Hooke (Dorset) 7 ST 5300
Hookgate 32 SJ 7435
Hook Norton 18 SP 3533
Hookway 6 SX 8598
Hookwood 11 TQ 2643
Hoole 32 SJ 4367
Hooton 32 SJ 3679
Hooton Levitt 38 SK 5291
Hooton Pagnell 38 SE 4808
Hooton Roberts 38 SK 4897
Hope (Clwyd) 32 SJ 3058
Hope (Derby.) 33 SK 1783
Hope (Devon.) 5 SX 6740
Hope (Powys) 23 SJ 2507
Hope (Salop) 23 SJ 3401
Hope Bagot 24 SO 5874
Hope Bowdler 24 SO 4792
Hopeman 61 NJ 1469
Hope Mansell 17 SO 6219
Hopesay 24 SO 3883
Hope under Dinmore 24 SO 5052
Hopton (Norf.) 29 TG 5200
Hopton (Salop) 32 SJ 5926
Hopton (Staffs.) 33 SJ 9426
Hopton (Suff.) 29 TL 9979
Hopton Cangeford 24 SO 5480
Hopton Castle 24 SO 3678
Hopton Wafers 24 SO 6476
Hopwas 25 SK 1705
Hopwood 25 SP 0375
Horam 12 TQ 5717
Horbling 35 TF 1135
Horbury 37 SE 2918
Horden 42 NZ 4441
Horderley 24 SO 4086
Hordle 9 SZ 2795
Hordley 32 SJ 3730
Horeb 15 SN 3942
Horham 29 TM 2172
Horkesley Heath 21 TL 9829
Horkstow 39 SE 9818
Horley (Oxon.) 26 SP 4143
Horley (W Susx) 11 TQ 2843
Hornblotton Green 7 ST 5833
Hornby (Lancs.) 41 SD 5868
Hornby (N Yorks) 42 NZ 3605
Horncastle 35 TF 2669
Hornchurch 20 TQ 5487
Horncliffe 53 NT 9249
Horndean 9 SU 7013
Horndon on the Hill 20 TQ 6683
Horne 12 TQ 3344
Horn Hill 19 TQ 0292
Horning 29 TG 3417
Horninghold 26 SP 8097
Horninglow 33 SK 2324
Horningsea 20 TL 4962
Horningsham 8 ST 8241
Horningtoft 29 TF 9323
Hornsby 46 NY 5150
Hornsea 39 TA 2047
Hornsey 20 TQ 3089
Hornton 26 SP 3945
Horrabridge 4 SX 5169
Horringer 20 TL 8261
Horsebridge (E Susx) 12 TQ 5911
Horsebridge (Hants.) 9 SU 3430
Horse Bridge (Staffs.) 33 SJ 9553
Horsebrook 25 SJ 8810
Horsehay 24 SJ 6707
Horseheath 20 TL 6147
Horsehouse 42 SE 0481
Horsell 11 SU 9959
Horseman's Green 32 SJ 4441
Horseway 27 TL 4287
Horsey 29 TG 4523
Horsford 29 TG 1915
Horsforth 37 SE 2337
Horsham (Here. and Worc.) 24 SO 7357
Horsham (W Susx) 11 TQ 1730
Horsham St. Faith 29 TG 2114
Horsington (Lincs.) 35 TF 1868
Horsington (Somer.) 8 ST 7023
Horsley (Derby.) 33 SK 3744
Horsley (Glos.) 17 ST 8398
Horsley (Northum.) 47 NY 8496
Horsley (Northum.) 47 NZ 0966
Horsley Cross 21 TM 1227
Horsleycross Street 21 TM 1228
Horsleyhill 52 NT 5319
Horsley Woodhouse 33 SK 3945
Horsmonden 12 TQ 7040
Horspath 18 SP 5704
Horstead 29 TG 2619
Horsted Keynes 12 TQ 3828
Horton (Avon) 17 ST 7684
Horton (Berks.) 11 TQ 0175
Horton (Bucks.) 19 SP 9219
Horton (Dorset) 8 SU 0307
Horton (Lancs.) 37 SD 8550
Horton (Northants.) 26 SP 8254
Horton (Northum.) 53 NU 0230
Horton (Staffs.) 33 SJ 9457
Horton (W Glam.) 15 SS 4785
Horton (Wilts.) 17 SU 0463
Horton Green 32 SJ 4549
Horton Heath 9 SU 4916
Horton in Ribblesdale 41 SD 8172
Horton Kirby 12 TQ 5668
Horwich 36 SD 6311
Horwood 6 SS 5027
Hose 34 SK 7329
Hosh 56 NN 8523
Hoswick 63 HU 4124
Hotham 39 SE 8934
Hothfield 13 TQ 9644
Hoton 34 SK 5722
Houbie 63 HU 6390
Hough 32 SJ 7151
Hougham 34 SK 8844
Hougharry 63 NF 7071
Hough Green 32 SJ 4885
Hough-on-the-Hill 34 SK 9246
Houghton (Cambs.) 27 TL 2871
Houghton (Cumbr.) 46 NY 4159
Houghton (Dyfed) 14 SM 9807
Houghton (Hants.) 9 SU 3331
Houghton (W Susx) 11 TQ 0111
Houghton Conquest 27 TL 0441
Houghton le Spring 47 NZ 3450
Houghton on the Hill 26 SK 6703
Houghton Regis 19 TL 0224
Houghton St. Giles 29 TF 9235
Houlsyke 43 NZ 7308
Hound Green 10 SU 7259
Houndslow 52 NT 6347
Houndwood 53 NT 8464
Hounslow 11 TQ 1276
Housetter 63 HU 3684
Houston 50 NS 4067
Houstry 67 ND 1534
Hove 11 TQ 2805
Hoveringham 34 SK 6946
Hoveton 29 TG 3018
Hovingham 38 SE 6675
How 46 NY 5056
How Caple 24 SO 6030
Howden 38 SE 7428
Howden-le-Wear 42 NZ 1633
Howe (Cumbr.) 40 SD 4588
Howe (Highld.) 67 ND 3062
Howe (Norf.) 29 TM 2799
Howe Green 20 TL 7403
Howell 35 TF 1346
Howe of Teuchar 62 NJ 7947
Howe Street (Essex) 20 TL 6914
Howe Street (Essex) 20 TL 6934
Howe, The 43 SC 1967
Howey 23 SO 0558
Howgate 51 NT 2457
Howick 53 NU 2517
Howlaws 52 NT 7242
Howle 32 SJ 6823
Howlett End 20 TL 5834
Howmore 63 NF 7636
Hownam 53 NT 7719
Hownam Law 53 NT 7921
Hownam Mains 53 NT 7820
Howsham (Humbs.) 39 TA 0404
Howsham (N Yorks.) 38 SE 7362
Howton 16 SO 4129
Howwood 50 NS 3960
Hoxne 29 TM 1877
Hoylake 32 SJ 2189
Hoyland Nether 37 SE 3600
Hoyland Swaine 37 SE 2604
Hubbert's Bridge 35 TF 2643
Huby 38 SE 5665
Hucclecote 17 SO 8717
Hucking 12 TQ 8358
Hucknall 34 SK 5349
Huddersfield 37 SE 1416
Huddington 25 SO 9457
Hudswell 42 NZ 1400
Huggate 39 SE 8855
Hughenden Valley 19 SU 8695
Hughley 24 SO 5697
Hugh Town 2 SV 9010
Hugmore 32 SJ 3752
Huish (Devon.) 6 SS 5311
Huish (Wilts.) 17 SU 1463
Huish Champflower 7 ST 0429
Huish Episcopi 7 ST 4226
Hulcott 19 SP 8516
Hulland 33 SK 2447
Hullavington 17 ST 8982
Hullbridge 20 TQ 8194
Hulme End 33 SK 1059
Hulme Walfield 33 SJ 8465
Hulne Park 53 NU 1514
Hulver Street 29 TM 4686
Humber Court 24 SO 5356
Humberston 39 TA 3105
Humberstone 34 SK 6206
Humbie 52 NT 4562
Humbleton (Humbs.) 39 TA 2234
Humbleton (Northum.) 53 NT 9728
Hume 52 NT 7041
Humshaugh 47 NY 9171
Huna 67 ND 3573
Huncoat 37 SD 7730
Huncote 26 SP 5197
Hundalee 52 NT 6418
Hunderthwaite 41 NY 9821
Hundleby 35 TF 3966
Hundleton 14 SM 9600
Hundon 20 TL 7348
Hundred Acres 9 SU 5911
Hundred End 36 SD 4122
Hundred, The 24 SO 5264
Hungarton 34 SK 6807
Hungerford (Berks.) 10 SU 3368
Hungerford (Hants.) 8 SU 1612
Hungerford Newtown 10 SU 3571
Hunmanby 43 TA 0977
Hunningham 26 SP 3768
Hunsdon 20 TL 4114
Hunsingore 38 SE 4253
Hunsonby 41 NY 5835
Hunspow 67 ND 2172
Hunstanton 28 TF 6741
Hunstanworth 47 NY 9449
Hunston (Suff.) 21 TL 9768
Hunston (W Susx) 9 SU 8601
Hunstrete 17 ST 6462
Hunt End 25 SP 0364
Hunter's Quay 49 NS 1879
Huntingdon 27 TL 2371
Huntingfield 29 TM 3374
Huntington (Here. and Worc.) 23 SO 2553
Huntington (Lothian) 52 NT 4875
Huntington (N Yorks.) 38 SE 6156
Huntington (Staffs.) 25 SJ 9713
Huntingtower 56 NO 0725
Huntley 17 SO 7219
Huntly 62 NJ 5339
Hunton (Kent) 12 TQ 7149
Hunton (N Yorks.) 42 SE 1892
Hunt's Cross 32 SJ 4385
Huntsham 7 ST 0020
Huntspill 7 ST 3045
Huntworth 7 ST 3134
Hunwick 42 NZ 1832
Hunworth 29 TG 0635
Hurdsfield 33 SJ 9274
Hurley (Berks.) 18 SU 8283
Hurley (Warw.) 26 SP 2495
Hurlford 50 NS 4536
Hurliness 63 ND 2888
Hurn 8 SZ 1296
Hursley 9 SU 4225
Hurst (Berks.) 10 SU 7972
Hurst (Gtr Mches.) 37 SD 9400
Hurst (N Yorks.) 42 NZ 0402
Hurstbourne Priors 10 SU 4346
Hurstbourne Tarrant 10 SU 3853
Hurst Green (E Susx) 12 TQ 7327
Hurst Green (Lancs.) 36 SD 6838
Hurst Green (Surrey) 12 TQ 3951
Hurstpierpoint 11 TQ 2816
Hurtwood Common 11 TQ 0743
Hurworth 42 NZ 3010
Hury 41 NY 9619
Husbands Bosworth 26 SP 6484
Husborne Crawley 19 SP 9535
Husinish 63 NA 9812
Husthwaite 38 SE 5175
Huthwaite 33 SK 4659
Huttoft 35 TF 5176
Hutton (Avon) 16 ST 3458
Hutton (Borders) 53 NT 9053
Hutton (Cumbr.) 40 NY 4326
Hutton (Essex) 20 TQ 6394
Hutton (Lancs.) 36 SD 4926
Hutton (N Yorks.) 38 SE 7667
Hutton Bonville 42 NZ 3300
Hutton Buscel 43 SE 9784
Hutton Conyers 42 SE 3273
Hutton Cranswick 39 TA 0252
Hutton End 40 NY 4538
Hutton Henry 42 NZ 4236
Hutton-le-Hole 43 SE 7090
Hutton Magna 42 NZ 1212
Hutton Roof (Cumbr.) 40 NY 3734
Hutton Roof (Cumbr.) 41 SD 5777
Hutton Rudby 42 NZ 4606
Hutton Sessay 42 SE 4776
Hutton Wandesley 38 SE 5050
Huxley 32 SJ 5061
Huxter (Shetld.) 63 HU 5662
Huyton 32 SJ 4490
Hycemoor 40 SD 0989
Hyde (Glos.) 17 SO 8801
Hyde (Gtr Mches.) 37 SJ 9294
Hyde Heath 19 SP 9300
Hydestile 11 SU 9740
Hynish 48 NL 9839
Hyssington 23 SO 3194
Hythe (Hants.) 9 SU 4207
Hythe (Kent) 13 TR 1635
Hythe End 11 TQ 0172
Hythie 62 NK 0051

Ibberton 8 ST 7807
Ible 33 SK 2457
Ibsley 8 SU 1509
Ibstock 33 SK 4010
Ibstone 18 SU 7593
Ibthorpe 10 SU 3753
Ibworth 10 SU 5654
Ickburgh 28 TL 8195
Ickenham 19 TQ 0786
Ickford 18 SP 6407
Ickham 13 TR 2258
Ickleford 19 TL 1831
Icklesham 13 TQ 8816
Ickleton 20 TL 4943
Icklingham 28 TL 7772
Ickwell Green 27 TL 1545
Icomb 17 SP 2122
Idbury 18 SP 2320
Iddesleigh 6 SS 5608
Ide 5 SX 8990
Ideford 5 SX 8977
Ide Hill 12 TQ 4851
Iden 13 TQ 9123
Iden Green 12 TQ 8031
Idlicote 26 SP 2844
Idmiston 8 SU 1937
Idridgehay 33 SK 2849
Idrigil 58 NG 3863
Idstone 18 SU 2584
Idvies 57 NO 5347
Ifield (W Susx) 11 TQ 2537
Ifield or Singlewell (Kent) 12 TQ 6471
Ifold 11 TQ 0231
Iford 12 TQ 4007
Ifton Heath 32 SJ 3236
Ightfield 32 SJ 5938
Ightham 12 TQ 5956
Iken 21 TM 4155
Ilam 33 SK 1351
Ilchester 7 ST 5222
Ilderton 53 NU 0121
Ilford 20 TQ 4586
Ilfracombe 6 SS 5147
Ilkeston 33 SK 4642
Ilketshall St. Andrew 29 TM 3887
Ilketshall St. Margaret 29 TM 3485
Ilkley 37 SE 1147
Illey 25 SO 9881
Illingworth 37 SE 0728
Illogan 2 SW 6643
Illston on the Hill 26 SP 7099
Ilmer 18 SP 7605
Ilmington 25 SP 2143
Ilminster 7 ST 3614
Ilsington 5 SX 7876
Ilston 15 SS 5590
Ilton (N Yorks.) 42 SE 1878
Ilton (Somer.) 7 ST 3517
Imachar 49 NR 8640
Imber 8 ST 9648
Immingham 39 TA 1714
Impington 20 TL 4463
Ince 32 SJ 4476
Ince Blundell 36 SD 3203
Ince-in-Makerfield 36 SD 5903
Inchbare 57 NO 6065
Inchberry 61 NJ 3155
Inchinnan 50 NS 4768
Inchlaggan 59 NH 1801
Inchnacardoch 59 NH 3710
Inchnadamph 64 NC 2522
Inchture 57 NO 2728
Inchyra 56 NO 1820
Indian Queens 2 SW 9158
Ingatestone 20 TQ 6499
Ingbirchworth 37 SE 2205
Ingestre 33 SJ 9724
Ingham (Lincs.) 34 SK 9483
Ingham (Norf.) 29 TG 3825
Ingham (Suff.) 28 TL 8570
Ingleby Arncliffe 42 NZ 4400
Ingleby Greenhow 42 NZ 5806
Inglesbatch 17 ST 7061
Inglesham 17 SU 2098
Ingleton (Durham) 42 NZ 1720
Ingleton (N Yorks.) 41 SD 6972
Inglewhite 36 SD 5439
Ingoe 47 NZ 0374
Ingoldisthorpe 28 TF 6832
Ingoldmells 35 TF 5668
Ingoldsby 34 TF 0030
Ingram 53 NU 0116
Ingrave 20 TQ 6292
Ings 40 SD 4498
Ingst 17 ST 5887
Ingworth 29 TG 1929
Inkberrow 25 SP 0157
Inkhorn 62 NJ 9239
Inkpen 10 SU 3564
Inkstack 67 ND 2570
Innellan 49 NS 1469
Innerleithen 51 NT 3336
Innerleven 57 NO 3700
Innermessan 44 NX 0863
Innerwick (Lothian) 52 NT 7273
Innerwick (Tays.) 56 NN 5947
Insch 62 NJ 6327
Insh 60 NH 8101
Inskip 36 SD 4537
Instow 6 SS 4730
Inver (Grampn.) 61 NO 2393
Inver (Highld.) 65 NH 8682
Inver (Tays.) 56 NO 0142
Inverailort 54 NM 7681
Inveralligin 59 NG 8457
Inverallochy 62 NK 0464
Inveramsay 62 NJ 7424
Inveran 65 NH 5797
Inveraray 55 NN 0908
Inverarish 58 NG 5535
Inverarity 57 NO 4444
Inverarnan 55 NN 3118
Inverasdale 64 NG 8286
Inverbervie 57 NO 8372
Invercreran 55 NN 0147
Inverdruie 60 NH 9010
Inverebrie 62 NJ 9233
Inveresk 51 NT 3471
Inverey 56 NO 0889
Inverfarigaig 60 NH 5224
Invergarry 59 NH 3101
Invergeldie 56 NN 7427
Invergordon 65 NH 7168
Invergowrie 57 NO 3430
Inverguseran 58 NG 7407
Inverhadden 56 NN 6757
Inverharroch 61 NJ 3831
Inverie 59 NG 7600
Inverinan 55 NM 9917
Inverinate 59 NG 9122
Inverkeilor 57 NO 6649
Inverkeithing 51 NT 1383
Inverkeithny 62 NJ 6246
Inverkip 49 NS 2071
Inverkirkaig 64 NC 0819
Inverlael 64 NH 1885
Inverlochlarig 55 NN 4318
Inver Mallie 55 NN 1388
Invermoriston 60 NH 4117
Invernaver 66 NC 7060
Inverness 60 NH 6645
Invernoaden 55 NS 1197
Inverquharity 57 NO 4057
Inverquhomery 62 NK 0246
Inverroy 55 NN 2581
Inverugie 62 NK 0947
Inveruglas 55 NN 3109
Inverurie 62 NJ 7721
Invervar 56 NN 6648
Inwardleigh 6 SX 5599
Inworth 21 TL 8717
Iping 9 SU 8522
Ipplepen 5 SX 8366
Ipsden 18 SU 6385
Ipstones 33 SK 0249
Ipswich 21 TM 1744
Irby 32 SJ 2584
Irby in the Marsh 35 TF 4763
Irby upon Humber 39 TA 1904
Irchester 27 SP 9265
Ireby (Cumbr.) 40 NY 2338
Ireby (Lancs.) 41 SD 6575
Ireland (Shetld.) 63 HU 3722
Ireleth 40 SD 2277
Ireshopeburn 41 NY 8638
Irlam 32 SJ 7194
Irnham 34 TF 0226
Iron Acton 17 ST 6783
Iron-Bridge 24 SJ 6703
Iron Cross 25 SP 0552
Ironside 62 NJ 8852
Ironville 33 SK 4351
Irstead 29 TG 3620
Irthington 46 NY 4961
Irthlingborough 27 SP 9470
Irton 43 TA 0084
Irvine 50 NS 3239
Isauld 67 NC 9765
Isbister (Shetld.) 63 HU 3791
Isbister (Whalsay) 63 HU 5763
Isfield 12 TQ 4417
Isham 27 SP 8873
Islawr-dref 22 SH 6815
Isle Abbotts 7 ST 3520
Isle Brewers 7 ST 3621
Isleham 28 TL 6474
Isle of Whithorn 44 NX 4736
Isleornsay 58 NG 6912
Islesburgh 63 HU 3369
Isleworth 11 TQ 1675
Isley Walton 33 SK 4225
Islington 20 TQ 3085
Islip (Northants.) 27 SP 9879
Islip (Oxon.) 18 SP 5214
Islivig 63 NA 9927
Istead Rise 12 TQ 6369
Itchen Abbas 9 SU 5332
Itchen Stoke 9 SU 5532
Itchingfield 11 TQ 1328
Itchington 17 ST 6586
Itteringham 29 TG 1430
Itton (Devon.) 6 SX 6898
Itton (Gwent) 16 ST 4896
Ivegill 40 NY 4143
Ivelet 41 SD 9398
Iver 19 TQ 0381
Iver Heath 19 TQ 0283
Iveston 47 NZ 1350
Ivinghoe 19 SP 9416
Ivinghoe Aston 19 SP 9518
Ivington 24 SO 4756
Ivington Green 24 SO 4656
Ivybridge 5 SX 6356
Ivychurch 13 TR 0227
Ivy Hatch 12 TQ 5854
Iwade 13 TQ 9067
Iwerne Courtney or Shroton 8 ST 8512
Iwerne Minster 8 ST 8614
Ixworth 29 TL 9370
Ixworth Thorpe 28 TL 9172

Jack Hill 37 SE 1951
Jackstown 62 NJ 7531
Jackton 50 NS 5953
Jacobstow (Corn.) 4 SX 1995
Jacobstowe (Devon.) 6 SS 5801
Jameston 14 SS 0599
Jamestown (Dumf. and Galwy.) 46 NY 2996
Jamestown (Highld.) 60 NH 4756
Jamestown (Strath.) 50 NS 3981
Janetstown 67 ND 1932
Jarrow 47 NZ 3265
Jawcraig 50 NS 8475
Jaywick 21 TM 1513
Jedburgh 52 NT 6520
Jeffreyston 14 SN 0906
Jemimaville 65 NH 7165
Jevington 12 TQ 5601
Johnby 40 NY 4333
Johnshaven 57 NO 7966
Johnston (Dyfed) 14 SM 9310
Johnstone (Strath.) 50 NS 4263
Johnstonebridge 45 NY 1091
Jordans 19 SU 9791
Jordanston 14 SM 9132
Jump 37 SE 3701
Juniper Green 51 NT 2068
Jurby East 43 SC 3899
Jurby West 43 SC 3598

Knelston Little Gaddesden

Knelston 15 SS 4689
Knightacott 6 SS 6439
Knightcote 26 SP 3954
Knighton (Devon.) 4 SX 5249
Knighton (Leic.) 26 SK 6001
Knighton (Powys) 23 SO 2872
Knighton (Staffs.) 32 SJ 7240
Knighton (Staffs.) 32 SJ 7427
Knightwick 24 SO 7355
Knill 23 SO 2960
Knipton 34 SK 8231
Knitsley 47 NZ 1148
Kniveton 33 SK 2050
Knock (Cumbr.) 41 NY 6826
Knock (Grampn.) 62 NJ 5452
Knock (Island of Mull) 54 NM 5438
Knock (Isle of Lewis) 63 NB 4931
Knockally 67 ND 1428
Knockan 64 NC 2110
Knockando 61 NJ 1941
Knockbain 60 NH 6255
Knockbrex 45 NX 5849
Knockdee 67 ND 1761
Knockdolian Castle 44 NX 1285
Knockenkelly 49 NS 0426
Knockentiber 50 NS 3939
Knockholt 12 TQ 4658
Knockholt Pound 12 TQ 4859
Knockie Lodge 60 NH 4413
Knockin 32 SJ 3322
Knocknaha 48 NR 6817
Knockrome 48 NR 5571
Knocksharry 43 SC 2785
Knodishall 21 TM 4261
Knolls Green 32 SJ 8079
Knolton 32 SJ 3738
Knook 8 ST 9341
Knossington 34 SK 8008
Knott End-on-Sea 36 SD 3548
Knotting 27 TL 0063
Knottingley 38 SE 5023
Knotty Green 19 SU 9392
Knowbury 24 SO 5774
Knowe 44 NX 3171
Knowehead 45 NX 6090
Knowesgate 47 NY 9885
Knoweside 49 NS 2512
Knowetownhead 52 NT 5418
Knowle (Avon) 17 ST 6170
Knowle (Devon.) 6 SS 4938
Knowle (Devon.) 6 SS 7801
Knowle (W Mids) 25 SP 1876
Knowle Green 36 SD 6337
Knowl Hill 10 SU 8279
Knowlton 13 TR 2853
Knowsley 32 SJ 4395
Knowstone 6 SS 8223
Knucklas 23 SO 2574
Knutsford 32 SJ 7578
Knypersley 33 SJ 8856
Kyleakin (Highld.) 58 NG 7526
Kyle of Lochalsh 59 NG 7627
Kylerhea (Highld.) 59 NG 7820
Kyles 63 NG 1391
Kylesmorar 59 NM 8093
Kylestrome 64 NC 2234
Kyloe 53 NU 0540
Kynnersley 24 SJ 6716
Kyre Park 24 SO 6263

Labost 63 NB 2748
Laceby 39 TA 2106
Lacey Green 18 SP 8200
Lach Dennis 32 SJ 7071
Lackalee 63 NG 1292
Lackford 28 TL 7970
Lacock 17 ST 9168
Ladbroke 26 SP 4158
Laddingford 12 TQ 6948
Lade Bank 35 TF 3954
Ladock 2 SW 8950
Ladybank (Fife.) 57 NO 3009
Ladybank (Strath.) 44 NS 2102
Ladykirk 53 NT 8847
Ladysford 62 NJ 9060
Lagavulin 48 NR 4045
Lagg (Island of Arran) 49 NR 9521
Lagg (Jura) 48 NR 5978
Laggan (Highld.) 59 NN 2997
Laggan (Highld.) 60 NN 6194
Lagganulva 54 NM 4541
Laid 66 NC 4159
Laide 64 NG 8992
Laindon 20 TQ 6889
Lair 59 NH 0148
Lairg 66 NC 5806
Lake 8 SU 1239
Lakenham 29 TG 2307
Lakenheath 28 TL 7182
Lakesend 28 TL 5196
Lake Side 40 SD 3787
Laleham 11 TQ 0568
Laleston 15 SS 8779
Lamarsh 21 TL 8935
Lamas 29 TG 2423
Lamberhurst 12 TQ 6735
Lamberton 53 NT 9657
Lambeth 12 TQ 3074
Lambfell Moar 43 SC 2984
Lambley (Northum.) 46 NY 6758
Lambley (Notts.) 34 SK 6245
Lambourn 10 SU 3278
Lambourne End 20 TQ 4894
Lambs Green 11 TQ 2136
Lambston 14 SM 9016
Lamerton 4 SX 4476
Lamesley 47 NZ 2557
Lamington (Highld.) 65 NH 7577
Lamington (Strath.) 51 NS 9730
Lamlash 49 NS 0231
Lamonby 40 NY 4135
Lamorna 2 SW 4524
Lamorran 2 SW 8741
Lampeter 15 SN 5748
Lampeter-Velfrey 14 SN 1514
Lamphey 14 SN 0100
Lamplugh 40 NY 0820
Lamport 26 SP 7574
Lamyatt 8 ST 6535
Lana 4 SX 3496
Lanark 50 NS 8843
Lancaster 40 SD 4761
Lanchester 47 NZ 1647
Landbeach 20 TL 4765
Landcross 4 SS 4524
Landerberry 62 NJ 7404
Landewednack 2 SW 7012
Landford 9 SU 2519
Landimore 15 SS 4693
Landkey 6 SS 5931
Landore 15 SS 6595
Landrake 4 SX 3760
Landscove 5 SX 7766
Landshipping 14 SN 0211
Landulph 4 SX 4261
Landwade 20 TL 6268
Landywood 25 SJ 9806
Laneast 4 SX 2283
Lane End 18 SU 8091
Lane Green 25 SJ 8802
Laneham 34 SK 8076
Laneshawbridge 37 SD 9240
Langar 34 SK 7234
Langbank 50 NS 3873
Langbar 37 SE 0951
Langcliffe 41 SD 8264
Langdale End 43 SE 9391
Langdon Hills 20 TQ 6786
Langdyke 57 NO 3304
Langenhoe 21 TM 0018
Langford (Beds.) 27 TL 1841
Langford (Devon.) 5 ST 0203
Langford (Essex) 20 TL 8408
Langford (Notts.) 34 SK 8258
Langford (Oxon.) 18 SP 2402
Langford Budville 7 ST 1122
Langford End 27 TL 1654
Langham (Essex) 21 TM 0233
Langham (Leic.) 34 SK 8411
Langham (Norf.) 29 TG 0041
Langham (Suff.) 29 TL 9769
Langho 36 SD 7034
Langholm 46 NY 3684
Langley (Berks.) 11 TQ 0078
Langley (Ches.) 33 SJ 9471
Langley (Essex) 20 TL 4435
Langley (Hants.) 9 SU 4400
Langley (Herts.) 19 TL 2122
Langley (Kent) 12 TQ 8051
Langley (Warw.) 25 SP 1962
Langley (W Susx) 9 SU 8029
Langley Burrell 17 ST 9275
Langley Hill 17 SP 0028
Langley Marsh 7 ST 0729
Langley Park 47 NZ 2144
Langley Street 29 TG 3601
Langney 12 TQ 6302
Langold 34 SK 5887
Langore 4 SX 3086
Langport 7 ST 4226
Langrick 35 TF 2648
Langridge 17 ST 7369
Langrigg 45 NY 1645
Langrish 9 SU 7023
Langsett 37 SE 2100
Langshaw 52 NT 5139
Langstone 9 SU 7104
Langthorne 42 SE 2491
Langthorpe 42 SE 3867
Langthwaite 41 NZ 0002
Langtoft (Humbs.) 39 TA 0166
Langtoft (Lincs.) 35 TF 1212
Langton (Durham) 42 NZ 1719
Langton (Lincs.) 35 TF 2368
Langton (Lincs.) 35 TF 3970
Langton (N Yorks.) 38 SE 7967
Langton by Wragby 35 TF 1476
Langton Green 12 TQ 5439
Langton Herring 7 SY 6182
Langton Matravers 8 SY 9978
Langtree 4 SS 4415
Langwathby 41 NY 5733
Langworth 35 TF 0676
Lanivet 4 SX 0364
Lanlivery 4 SX 0759
Lanner 2 SW 7139
Lanreath 4 SX 1756
Lansallos 4 SX 1751
Lanteglos Highway 4 SX 1453
Lanton (Borders) 52 NT 6221
Lanton (Northum.) 53 NT 9231
Lapford 6 SS 7308
Laphroaig 48 NR 3845
Lapley 25 SJ 8713
Lapworth 25 SP 1671
Larachbeg 54 NM 6948
Larbert 50 NS 8582
Largie 62 NJ 6131
Largiemore 49 NR 9486
Largoward 57 NO 4607
Largs 49 NS 2058
Largybeg 49 NS 0423
Largymore 49 NS 0424
Larkfield 49 NS 2376
Larkhall 50 NS 7651
Larkhill 8 SU 1243
Larling 29 TL 9889
Larriston 46 NY 5494
Lartington 41 NZ 0117
Lasham 10 SU 6742
Lassodie 51 NT 1292
Lasswade 51 NT 3066
Lastingham 43 SE 7290
Latchingdon 21 TL 8800
Latchley 4 SX 4173
Lately Common 32 SJ 6797
Lathbury 27 SP 8745
Latheron 67 ND 1933
Lathones 57 NO 4708
Latimer 19 TQ 0099
Latteridge 17 ST 6684
Lattiford 8 ST 6926
Latton 17 SU 0995
Lauder 52 NT 5347
Laugharne 14 SN 3011
Laughterton 34 SK 8375
Laughton (E Susx) 12 TQ 4913
Laughton (Leic.) 26 SP 6589
Laughton (Lincs.) 39 SK 8497
Laughton-en-le-Morthen 34 SK 5188
Launcells 4 SS 2405
Launceston 4 SX 3384
Launton 18 SP 6022
Laurencekirk 57 NO 7171
Laurieston 45 NX 6864
Lavant 9 SU 8608
Lavendon 27 SP 9153
Lavenham 21 TL 9149
Laverhay 45 NY 1498
Laverstock 8 SU 1530
Laverstoke 10 SU 4948
Laverton (Glos.) 25 SP 0735
Laverton (N Yorks.) 42 SE 2273
Laverton (Somer.) 8 ST 7753
Law 50 NS 8252
Lawers (Tays.) 56 NN 6739
Lawford 21 TM 0830
Lawhitton 4 SX 3582
Lawkland 41 SD 7766
Lawley 24 SJ 6608
Lawnhead 32 SJ 8224
Lawrenny 14 SN 0107
Lawshall 20 TL 8654
Lawton 24 SO 4459
Laxay 63 NB 3321
Laxdale 63 NB 4234
Laxey 43 SC 4384
Laxfield 29 TM 2972
Laxford Bridge 66 NC 2347
Laxo 63 HU 4463
Laxobigging 63 HU 4172
Laxton (Humbs.) 38 SE 7825
Laxton (Northants.) 27 SP 9496
Laxton (Notts.) 34 SK 7266
Laycock 37 SE 0340
Layer Breton 21 TL 9417
Layer-de-la-Haye 21 TL 9620
Layham 21 TM 0340
Layland's Green 10 SU 3866
Laysters Pole 24 SO 5563
Laytham 38 SE 7439
Lazenby 42 NZ 5719
Lazonby 41 NY 5439
Lea (Derby.) 33 SK 3357
Lea (Here. and Worc.) 17 SO 6521
Lea (Lincs.) 34 SK 8286
Lea (Salop) 24 SJ 4108
Lea (Salop) 24 SO 3589
Lea (Wilts.) 17 ST 9586
Leachkin 60 NH 6344
Leadburn 51 NT 2355
Leadenham 34 SK 9452
Leaden Roding 20 TL 5913
Leadgate (Cumbr.) 41 NY 7043
Leadgate (Durham) 47 NZ 1251
Leadhills 50 NS 8814
Leafield 18 SP 3115
Leake Common Side 35 TF 3952
Leake Hurn's End 35 TF 4248
Lealholm 43 NZ 7607
Lealt (Island of Skye) 58 NG 5060
Lea Marston 25 SP 2093
Leamington Hastings 26 SP 4467
Leargybreck 48 NR 5371
Learmouth 53 NT 8537
Leasgill 40 SD 4984
Leasingham 35 TF 0548
Leask 62 NK 0232
Leatherhead 11 TQ 1656
Leathley 37 SE 2346
Leaton 32 SJ 4618
Lea Town 36 SD 4930
Leaveland 13 TQ 9854
Leavening 38 SE 7863
Leaves Green 12 TQ 4162
Lea Yeat 41 SD 7587
Lebberston 43 TA 0882
Lechlade 17 SU 2199
Leckford 10 SU 3737
Leckfurin 66 NC 7059
Leckgruinart 48 NR 2769
Leckhampstead (Berks.) 10 SU 4375
Leckhampstead (Bucks.) 18 SP 7237
Leckhampton 17 SO 9419
Leckmelm 64 NH 1690
Leckwith 16 ST 1574
Leconfield 39 TA 0143
Ledaig 54 NM 9037
Ledburn 19 SP 9022
Ledbury 24 SO 7037
Ledgemoor 24 SO 4150
Ledicot 24 SO 4162
Ledmore 64 NC 2412
Ledsham (Ches.) 32 SJ 3574
Ledsham (W Yorks.) 38 SE 4529
Ledston 38 SE 4328
Ledwell 18 SP 4128
Lee (Devon.) 6 SS 4846
Lee (Hants.) 9 SU 3517
Lee (Island of Mull) 54 NM 4022
Lee (Lancs.) 36 SD 5655
Lee (Salop) 32 SJ 4032
Leebotwood 24 SO 4798
Lee Brockhurst 32 SJ 5426
Leece 40 SD 2469
Lee Clump 19 SP 9004
Leeds (Kent) 12 TQ 8253
Leeds (W Yorks.) 37 SE 3034
Leedstown 2 SW 6034
Lee Green 32 SJ 6561
Leek 33 SJ 9856
Leek Wootton 26 SP 2868
Leeming 42 SE 2989
Leeming Bar 42 SE 2889
Lee Moor 4 SX 5862
Lee-on-the-Solent 9 SU 5600
Lees (Derby.) 33 SK 2637
Lees (Gtr Mches) 37 SD 9504
Leeswood 32 SJ 2759
Lee, The 19 SP 8904
Legbourne 35 TF 3684
Legerwood 52 NT 5843
Legsby 35 TF 1385
Leicester 26 SK 5904
Leicester Forest East 26 SK 5203
Leigh (Dorset) 7 ST 6108
Leigh (Glos.) 17 SO 8725
Leigh (Gtr Mches) 32 SJ 6699
Leigh (Here. and Worc.) 24 SO 7853
Leigh (Kent) 12 TQ 5546
Leigh (Salop) 23 SJ 3303
Leigh (Surrey) 11 TQ 2246
Leigh (Wilts.) 17 SU 0692
Leigh Beck 20 TQ 8182
Leigh Common 8 ST 7329
Leigh Delamere 17 ST 8879
Leigh Green 13 TQ 8933
Leigh-on-Sea 20 TQ 8385
Leigh Sinton 24 SO 7750
Leighterton 17 ST 8290
Leighton (Powys) 23 SJ 2405
Leighton (Salop) 24 SJ 6105
Leighton (Somer.) 8 ST 7043
Leighton Bromswold 27 TL 1175
Leighton Buzzard 19 SP 9225
Leigh upon Mendip 8 ST 6847
Leigh Woods 16 ST 5572
Leinthall Earls 24 SO 4467
Leinthall Starkes 24 SO 4369
Leintwardine 24 SO 4074
Leire 26 SP 5290
Leirinmore 66 NC 4267
Leishmore 60 NH 3940
Leiston 21 TM 4462
Leitfie 57 NO 2545
Leith 51 NT 2676
Leitholm 53 NT 7944
Lelant 2 SW 5437
Lelley 39 TA 2032
Lem Hill 24 SO 7274
Lempitlaw 53 NT 7832
Lemreway 63 NB 3711
Lendalfoot 44 NX 1390
Lenham 13 TQ 8952
Lenham Heath 13 TQ 9249
Lenie 60 NH 5127
Lennel 53 NT 8540
Lennoxtown 50 NS 6277
Lenton 34 TF 0230
Lenwade 29 TG 0918
Lenzie 50 NS 6571
Leoch 57 NO 3636
Leochel-Cushnie 61 NJ 5210
Leominster 24 SO 4959
Leonard Stanley 17 SO 8003
Lepe 9 SZ 4498
Leperstone Resr. 50 NS 3571
Lephin 58 NG 1749
Lephinmore 49 NR 9892
Leppington 38 SE 7661
Lepton 37 SE 2015
Lerryn 4 SX 1356
Lerwick (Shetld.) 63 HU 4741
Lesbury 53 NU 2311
Leslie (Fife.) 57 NO 2401
Leslie (Grampn.) 62 NJ 5924
Lesmahagow 50 NS 8139
Lesnewth 4 SX 1390
Lessingham 29 TG 3928
Lessonhall 46 NY 2250
Leswalt 44 NX 0263
Letchmore Heath 19 TQ 1597
Letchworth 19 TL 2132
Letcombe Bassett 18 SU 3785
Letcombe Regis 18 SU 3786
Letham (Fife.) 57 NO 3014
Letham (Tays.) 57 NO 5248
Letham Grange 57 NO 6245
Lethenty 62 NJ 8041
Letheringham 21 TM 2757
Letheringsett 29 TG 0638
Lettaford 5 SX 7084
Letterewe 64 NG 9571
Letterfearn 59 NG 8823
Lettermore 54 NM 4948
Letters 64 NH 1687
Letterston 14 SM 9429
Lettoch (Grampn.) 61 NJ 0932
Letton (Here. and Worc.) 23 SO 3346
Letton (Here. and Worc.) 24 SO 3770
Letty Green 19 TL 2810
Letwell 34 SK 5587
Leuchars 57 NO 4521
Leurbost 63 NB 3725
Levedale 25 SJ 8916
Leven (Fife.) 57 NO 3700
Leven (Humbs.) 39 TA 1045
Levens 40 SD 4886
Levenshulme 37 SJ 8794
Levenwick 63 HU 4021
Leverburgh 63 NG 0186
Leverington 35 TF 4411
Leverton 35 TF 3947
Levington 21 TM 2339
Levisham 43 SE 8390
Lew 18 SP 3206
Lewannick 4 SX 2780
Lewdown 4 SX 4486
Lewes 12 TQ 4110
Leweston 14 SM 9422
Lewisham 12 TQ 3674
Lewiston 60 NH 5029
Lewknor 18 SU 7197
Leworthy 6 SS 6638
Lewtrenchard 4 SX 4586
Ley (Corn.) 4 SX 1766
Leybourne 12 TQ 6858
Leyburn 42 SE 1190
Leycett 32 SJ 7846
Leyland 36 SD 5421
Leylodge 62 NJ 7713
Leys (Grampn.) 62 NK 0052
Leys (Tays.) 57 NO 2537
Leysdown-on-Sea 13 TR 0370
Leysmill 57 NO 6047
Leys of Cossans 57 NO 3749
Leyton 20 TQ 3886
Lezant 4 SX 3378
Lhanbryde 61 NJ 2761
Lhen, The 43 NX 3801
Libberton 51 NS 9943
Liberton 51 NT 2769
Lichfield 25 SK 1209
Lickey 25 SO 9975
Lickey End 25 SO 9772
Lickfold 11 SU 9225
Liddel 63 ND 4683
Liddington 17 SU 2081
Lidgate 20 TL 7258
Lidlington 19 SP 9939
Lidstone 18 SP 3524
Liff 57 NO 3332
Lifton 4 SX 3885
Lighthazles 37 SE 0220
Lighthorne 26 SP 3355
Lightwater 11 SU 9262
Lightwood 33 SJ 9041
Lightwood Green 32 SJ 3840
Likisto 63 NG 1292
Lilbourne 26 SP 5677
Lilleshall 24 SJ 7315
Lilley 19 TL 1226
Lilliesleaf 52 NT 5325
Lillingstone Dayrell 18 SP 7039
Lillingstone Lovell 18 SP 7140
Lillington 8 ST 6212
Lilstock 7 ST 1644
Limbrick 36 SD 6016
Limefield 37 SD 8012
Limekilnburn 50 NS 7050
Limekilns 51 NT 0783
Limerigg 50 NS 8570
Limington 7 ST 5422
Limpenhoe 29 TG 3903
Limpley Stoke 17 ST 7760
Limpsfield 12 TQ 4152
Linby 34 SK 5350
Linchmere 9 SU 8630
Lincoln 34 SK 9771
Lincomb 25 SO 8268
Lincombe 5 SX 7458
Lindale 40 SD 4180
Lindal in Furness 40 SD 2575
Lindean 52 NT 4931
Lindfield 12 TQ 3425
Lindford 9 SU 8136
Lindores 57 NO 2616
Lindridge 24 SO 6769
Lindsell 20 TL 6427
Lindsey 21 TL 9744
Linford (Essex) 12 TQ 6779
Linford (Hants.) 8 SU 1707
Lingague 43 SC 2172
Lingdale 42 NZ 6716
Lingen 24 SO 3667
Lingfield 12 TQ 3943
Lingwood 29 TG 3609
Liniclett 63 NF 7949
Linicro 58 NG 3967
Linkenholt 10 SU 3657
Linkinhorne 4 SX 3173
Linksness (Hoy) 63 HY 2403
Linktown 51 NT 2790
Linley 24 SO 3593
Linley Green 24 SO 6953
Linlithgow 51 NS 9977
Linlithgow Bridge 51 NS 9877
Linshader (Isle of Lewis) 63 NB 2031
Linsidemore 65 NH 5498
Linslade 19 SP 9125
Linstead Parva 29 TM 3377
Linstock 46 NY 4258
Linthwaite 37 SE 0913
Lintlaw 53 NT 8258
Lintmill 61 NJ 5165
Linton (Borders) 53 NT 7726
Linton (Cambs.) 20 TL 5646
Linton (Derby.) 33 SK 2716
Linton (Here. and Worc.) 17 SO 6625
Linton (Kent) 12 TQ 7550
Linton (N Yorks.) 41 SD 9962
Linton-on-Ouse 38 SE 4960
Linwood (Hants.) 8 SU 1809
Linwood (Lincs.) 35 TF 1186
Linwood (Strath.) 50 NS 4464
Lionel 63 NB 5263
Liphook 9 SU 8431
Liscombe 6 SS 8732
Lisgear Mhor HW 8133
Liskeard 4 SX 2564
Liss 9 SU 7727
Lissett 39 TA 1458
Liss Forest 9 SU 7929
Lissington 35 TF 1083
Lisvane 16 ST 1983
Liswerry 16 ST 3487
Litcham 28 TF 8817
Litchborough 26 SP 6354
Litchfield 10 SU 4553
Litherland 32 SJ 3397
Litlington (Cambs.) 20 TL 3142
Litlington (E Susx) 12 TQ 5201
Little Abington 20 TL 5349
Little Addington 27 SP 9573
Little Alne 25 SP 1361
Little Amwell 20 TL 3511
Little Aston 25 SK 0900
Little Atherfield 9 SZ 4680
Little Ayre 63 ND 3091
Little Ayton 42 NZ 5710
Little Baddow 20 TL 7807
Little Badminton 17 ST 8084
Little Ballinluig 56 NN 9152
Little Bardfield 20 TL 6530
Little Barford 27 TL 1857
Little Barningham 29 TG 1333
Little Barrington 17 SP 2012
Little Barugh 43 SE 7579
Little Bedwyn 10 SU 2966
Little Bentley 21 TM 1125
Little Berkhamsted 19 TL 2907
Little Billing 26 SP 8061
Little Birch 24 SO 5031
Little Blakenham 21 TM 1048
Littleborough (Gtr Mches) 37 SD 9316
Littleborough (Notts.) 34 SK 8282
Littlebourne 13 TR 2057
Little Bowden 26 SP 7487
Little Bradley 20 TL 6852
Little Brampton 24 SO 3681
Little Brechin 57 NO 5862
Littlebredy 7 SY 5888
Little Brickhill 19 SP 9032
Little Brington 26 SP 6663
Little Bromley 21 TM 0928
Little Budworth 32 SJ 5965
Little Burstead 20 TQ 6691
Littlebury 20 TL 5139
Littlebury Green 20 TL 4938
Little Bytham 34 TF 0118
Little Carlton 35 TF 3985
Little Casterton 34 TF 0109
Little Cawthorpe 35 TF 3583
Little Chalfont 19 SU 9997
Little Chart 13 TQ 9245
Little Chesterford 20 TL 5141
Little Cheverell 8 ST 9853
Little Chishill 20 TL 4237
Little Clacton 21 TM 1618
Little Comberton 25 SO 9643
Little Common 12 TQ 7107
Little Compton 18 SP 2530
Little Cowarne 24 SO 6051
Little Coxwell 18 SU 2893
Little Cressingham 28 TF 8600
Little Dalby 34 SK 7714
Littledean 17 SO 6713
Little Dens 62 NK 0744
Little Dewchurch 24 SO 5231
Little Dunham 28 TF 8613
Little Dunkeld 56 NO 0242
Little Dunmow 20 TL 6521
Little Easton 20 TL 6023
Little Eaton 33 SK 3641
Little Ellingham 29 TM 0099
Little End 20 TL 5400
Little Eversden 20 TL 3752
Little Fakenham 28 TL 9076
Little Faringdon 18 SP 2201
Little Fenton 38 SE 5135
Littleferry 65 NH 8095
Little Fransham 28 TF 9011
Little Gaddesden 19 SP 9913

Lootcherbrae Melvaig

Lootcherbrae ... 62 ... NJ 6054
Lopcombe Corner ... 9 ... SU 2435
Lopen ... 7 ... ST 4214
Loppington ... 32 ... SJ 4629
Lorbottle ... 47 ... NU 0306
Lornty ... 56 ... NO 1746
Loscoe ... 33 ... SK 4247
Lossiemouth ... 61 ... NJ 2370
Lossit ... 48 ... NR 1856
Lostock Gralam ... 32 ... SJ 6874
Lostwithiel ... 4 ... SX 1059
Lothbeg ... 67 ... NC 9410
Lothersdale ... 37 ... SD 9545
Lothmore ... 67 ... NC 9611
Loudwater ... 19 ... SU 8990
Loughborough ... 34 ... SK 5319
Loughor ... 15 ... SS 5898
Loughton (Bucks.) ... 19 ... SP 8337
Loughton (Essex) ... 20 ... TQ 4296
Loughton (Salop) ... 24 ... SO 6183
Lound (Lincs.) ... 35 ... TF 0618
Lound (Notts.) ... 34 ... SK 6986
Lound (Suff.) ... 29 ... TM 5099
Lount ... 33 ... SK 3819
Louth ... 35 ... TF 3287
Love Clough ... 37 ... SD 8126
Lover ... 9 ... SU 2120
Loversall ... 38 ... SK 5798
Loves Green ... 20 ... TL 6404
Loveston ... 14 ... SN 0808
Lovington ... 7 ... ST 5931
Low Bradfield ... 37 ... SK 2691
Low Bradley ... 37 ... SE 0048
Low Braithwaite ... 40 ... NY 4242
Low Brunton ... 47 ... NY 9269
Low Burnham ... 38 ... SE 7702
Lowca ... 40 ... NX 9821
Low Catton ... 38 ... SE 7053
Low Coniscliffe ... 42 ... NZ 2514
Low Crosby ... 46 ... NY 4459
Lowdham ... 34 ... SK 6646
Low Dinsdale ... 42 ... NZ 3411
Low Eggborough ... 38 ... SE 5522
Lower Aisholt ... 7 ... ST 2035
Lower Assendon ... 18 ... SU 7484
Lower Beeding ... 11 ... TQ 2227
Lower Benefield ... 27 ... SP 9888
Lower Bentham ... 41 ... SD 6469
Lower Boddington ... 26 ... SP 4752
Lower Bullingham ... 24 ... SO 5038
Lower Cam ... 17 ... SO 7401
Lower Chapel ... 15 ... SO 0235
Lower Chute ... 10 ... SU 3153
Lower Cwmtwrch ... 15 ... SN 7710
Lower Darwen ... 36 ... SD 6824
Lower Down ... 23 ... SO 3384
Lower Dunsforth ... 38 ... SE 4464
Lower Farringdon ... 9 ... SU 7035
Lower Frankton ... 32 ... SJ 3732
Lower Froyle ... 10 ... SU 7544
Lower Gledfield ... 65 ... NH 5990
Lower Green ... 29 ... TF 9837
Lower Halstow ... 13 ... TQ 8567
Lower Hardres ... 13 ... TR 1453
Lower Heyford ... 18 ... SP 4824
Lower Higham ... 12 ... TQ 7172
Lower Hordley ... 32 ... SJ 3929
Lower Killeyan ... 48 ... NR 2743
Lower Langford ... 16 ... ST 4660
Lower Largo ... 57 ... NO 4102
Lower Lemington ... 18 ... SP 2134
Lower Lye ... 24 ... SO 4067
Lower Maes-coed ... 23 ... SO 3431
Lower Mayland ... 21 ... TL 9101
Lower Moor ... 25 ... SO 9847
Lower Nazeing ... 20 ... TL 3906
Lower Penarth ... 16 ... ST 1869
Lower Penn ... 25 ... SO 8696
Lower Pennington ... 9 ... SZ 3193
Lower Peover ... 32 ... SJ 7474
Lower Pitcalzean ... 65 ... NH 8070
Lower Quinton ... 25 ... SP 1847
Lower Shader ... 63 ... NB 3854
Lower Shelton ... 27 ... SP 9942
Lower Shiplake ... 10 ... SU 7779
Lower Shuckburgh ... 26 ... SP 4862
Lower Slaughter ... 17 ... SP 1622
Lower Stanton St. Quintin ... 17 ... ST 9180
Lower Sundon ... 19 ... TL 0526
Lower Swanwick ... 9 ... SU 4909
Lower Swell ... 17 ... SP 1725
Lower Tysoe ... 26 ... SP 3445
Lower Upham ... 9 ... SU 5219
Lower Vexford ... 7 ... ST 1135
Lower Weare ... 7 ... ST 4053
Lower Wield ... 10 ... SU 6340
Lower Winchendon ... 18 ... SP 7312
Lower Woodend ... 18 ... SU 8088
Lower Woodford ... 8 ... SU 1235
Lowesby ... 34 ... SK 7207
Lowestoft ... 29 ... TM 5493
Lowestoft End ... 29 ... TM 5394
Loweswater ... 40 ... NY 1421
Low Gate ... 47 ... NY 9064
Lowgill (Cumbr.) ... 41 ... SD 6297
Lowgill (Lancs.) ... 41 ... SD 6564
Low Ham ... 7 ... ST 4329
Low Hartsop ... 40 ... NY 4013
Low Hesket ... 46 ... NY 4646
Low Hesleyhurst ... 47 ... NZ 0997
Lowick (Cumbr.) ... 40 ... SD 2985
Lowick (Northants.) ... 27 ... SP 9781
Lowick (Northum.) ... 53 ... NU 0139
Low Mill ... 42 ... SE 6795
Low Moor ... 36 ... SD 7241
Lownie Moor ... 57 ... NO 4848
Low Redford ... 42 ... NZ 0731
Low Row (Cumbr.) ... 46 ... NY 5863
Low Row (N Yorks.) ... 41 ... SD 9897
Low Santon ... 39 ... SE 9312
Lowsonford ... 25 ... SP 1867
Low Street ... 29 ... TG 3424
Lowthorpe ... 39 ... TA 0860
Low Thurlton ... 29 ... TM 4299
Lowton ... 32 ... SJ 6197
Lowton Common ... 32 ... SJ 6397
Low Torry ... 51 ... NT 0086
Low Waters ... 50 ... NS 7353
Low Worsall ... 42 ... NZ 3909
Loxbeare ... 6 ... SS 9116
Loxhill ... 11 ... TQ 0037
Loxhore ... 6 ... SS 6138
Loxley ... 26 ... SP 2553
Loxton ... 16 ... ST 3755
Loxwood ... 11 ... TQ 0431
Lubenham ... 26 ... SP 7087
Luccombe ... 6 ... SS 9144
Luccombe Village ... 9 ... SZ 5880
Lucker ... 53 ... NU 1530
Luckett ... 4 ... SX 3873
Luckington ... 17 ... ST 8383
Lucklawhill ... 57 ... NO 4222
Luckwell Bridge ... 6 ... SS 9038
Lucton ... 24 ... SO 4364
Ludag ... 63 ... NF 7714
Ludborough ... 39 ... TF 2995
Ludchurch ... 14 ... SN 1411
Luddenden ... 37 ... SE 0425
Luddesdown ... 12 ... TQ 6766
Luddington ... 39 ... SE 8216
Ludford (Lincs.) ... 35 ... TF 1989
Ludford (Salop) ... 24 ... SO 5173
Ludgershall (Bucks.) ... 18 ... SP 6617
Ludgershall (Wilts.) ... 10 ... SU 2650
Ludgvan ... 2 ... SW 5033
Ludham ... 29 ... TG 3818
Ludlow ... 24 ... SO 5175
Ludwell ... 8 ... ST 9122
Ludworth ... 42 ... NZ 3641
Luffincott ... 4 ... SX 3394
Luffness ... 52 ... NT 4780
Lugar ... 50 ... NS 5821
Luggiebank ... 50 ... NS 7672
Lugton ... 50 ... NS 4152
Lugwardine ... 24 ... SO 5441
Luib ... 58 ... NG 5628
Lulham ... 24 ... SO 4041
Lullingstone Castle ... 12 ... TQ 5364
Lullington (Derby.) ... 33 ... SK 2513
Lullington (Somer.) ... 8 ... ST 7851
Lulsgate Bottom ... 16 ... ST 5065
Lulsley ... 24 ... SO 7455
Lumb ... 37 ... SE 0221
Lumby ... 38 ... SE 4830
Lumloch ... 50 ... NS 6369
Lumphanan ... 62 ... NJ 5804
Lumphinnans ... 51 ... NT 1692
Lumsdaine ... 53 ... NT 8769
Lumsden ... 61 ... NJ 4722
Lunan ... 57 ... NO 6851
Lunanhead ... 57 ... NO 4752
Luncarty ... 56 ... NO 0929
Lund (Humbs.) ... 39 ... SE 9648
Lund (N Yorks.) ... 38 ... SE 6532
Lundie (Tays.) ... 57 ... NO 2836
Lundin Links ... 57 ... NO 4002
Lunna ... 63 ... HU 4869
Lunning ... 63 ... HU 5066
Lunsford's Cross ... 12 ... TQ 7210
Lunt ... 36 ... SD 3401
Luntley ... 24 ... SO 3955
Luppitt ... 5 ... ST 1606
Lupton ... 41 ... SD 5581
Lurgashall ... 11 ... SU 9326
Lurgmore ... 60 ... NH 5937
Lusby ... 35 ... TF 3367
Luskentyre ... 63 ... NG 0699
Luss ... 50 ... NS 3592
Lusta ... 58 ... NG 2756
Lustleigh ... 5 ... SX 7881
Luston ... 24 ... SO 4863
Luthermuir ... 57 ... NO 6568
Luthrie ... 57 ... NO 3219
Luton (Beds.) ... 19 ... TL 0821
Luton (Devon.) ... 5 ... SX 9076
Luton (Kent) ... 12 ... TQ 7766
Lutterworth ... 26 ... SP 5484
Lutton (Devon.) ... 4 ... SX 5959
Lutton (Lincs.) ... 35 ... TF 4325
Lutton (Northants.) ... 27 ... TL 1187
Luxborough ... 7 ... SS 9738
Luxulyan ... 4 ... SX 0458
Lybster ... 67 ... ND 2435
Lydbury North ... 23 ... SO 3486
Lydcott ... 6 ... SS 6936
Lydd ... 13 ... TR 0421
Lydden ... 13 ... TR 2645
Lyddington ... 27 ... SP 8797
Lydd-on-Sea ... 13 ... TR 0819
Lydeard St. Lawrence ... 7 ... ST 1232
Lydford (Devon.) ... 4 ... SX 5084
Lydford (Somer.) ... 7 ... ST 5731
Lydgate ... 37 ... SD 9225
Lydham ... 23 ... SO 3391
Lydiard Millicent ... 17 ... SU 0986
Lydiate ... 36 ... SD 3604
Lydlinch ... 8 ... ST 7413
Lydney ... 17 ... SO 6203
Lydstep ... 14 ... SS 0898
Lye ... 25 ... SO 9284
Lye Green ... 19 ... SP 9703
Lyford ... 18 ... SU 3994
Lymbridge Green ... 13 ... TR 1243
Lyme Regis ... 7 ... SY 3492
Lyminge ... 13 ... TR 1641
Lymington ... 9 ... SZ 3295
Lyminster ... 11 ... TQ 0204
Lymm ... 32 ... SJ 6786
Lymore ... 9 ... SZ 2992
Lympne ... 13 ... TR 1235
Lympsham ... 16 ... ST 3454
Lympstone ... 5 ... SX 9984
Lynchat ... 60 ... NH 7801
Lyndhurst ... 9 ... SU 2907
Lyndon ... 27 ... SK 9004
Lyne ... 11 ... TQ 0166
Lyneal ... 32 ... SJ 4433
Lyneham (Oxon.) ... 18 ... SP 2720
Lyneham (Wilts.) ... 17 ... SU 0179
Lynemouth ... 47 ... NZ 2991
Lyne of Gorthleck ... 60 ... NH 5420
Lyne of Skene ... 62 ... NJ 7610
Lyness ... 63 ... ND 3094
Lyng (Norf.) ... 29 ... TG 0617
Lyng (Somer.) ... 7 ... ST 3328
Lynmouth ... 6 ... SS 7249
Lynsted ... 13 ... TQ 9461
Lynton ... 6 ... SS 7149
Lyon's Gate ... 8 ... ST 6605
Lyonshall ... 23 ... SO 3356
Lytchett Matravers ... 8 ... SY 9495
Lytchett Minster ... 8 ... SY 9593
Lyth ... 67 ... ND 2763
Lytham ... 36 ... SD 3727
Lytham St. Anne's ... 36 ... SD 3427
Lythe ... 43 ... NZ 8413
Lythes ... 63 ... ND 4589

Maaruig ... 63 ... NB 1906
Mabe Burnthouse ... 2 ... SW 7634
Mabie ... 45 ... NX 9570
Mablethorpe ... 35 ... TF 5085
Macclesfield ... 33 ... SJ 9173
Macduff ... 62 ... NJ 7064
Machany ... 56 ... NN 9015
Macharioch ... 48 ... NR 7309
Machen ... 16 ... ST 2189
Machrihanish ... 48 ... NR 6220
Machynlleth ... 22 ... SH 7401
Mackworth ... 33 ... SK 3137
Macmerry ... 52 ... NT 4372
Madderty ... 56 ... NN 9522
Maddiston ... 51 ... NS 9476
Madehurst ... 11 ... SU 9810
Madeley (Salop) ... 24 ... SJ 6904
Madeley (Staffs.) ... 32 ... SJ 7744
Madingley ... 20 ... TL 3960
Madley ... 24 ... SO 4138
Madresfield ... 24 ... SO 8047
Madron ... 2 ... SW 4532
Maenclochog ... 14 ... SN 0827
Maendy ... 15 ... ST 0176
Maentwrog ... 30 ... SH 6640
Mær ... 32 ... SJ 7938
Maerdy (Clwyd) ... 31 ... SJ 0144
Maerdy (Mid Glam.) ... 15 ... SS 9798
Maesbrook ... 32 ... SJ 3121
Maesbury Marsh ... 32 ... SJ 3125
Maes-glas ... 16 ... ST 2985
Maesgwynne ... 14 ... SN 2024
Maeshafn ... 32 ... SJ 2061
Maesllyn ... 15 ... SN 3644
Maesmynis ... 15 ... SO 0148
Maesteg ... 15 ... SS 8591
Maesybont ... 15 ... SN 5616
Maes-y-cwmmer ... 16 ... ST 1794
Magdalen Laver ... 20 ... TL 5108
Maggieknockater ... 61 ... NJ 3145
Magham Down ... 12 ... TQ 6111
Maghull ... 36 ... SD 3702
Magor ... 16 ... ST 4287
Maiden Bradley ... 8 ... ST 8038
Maidencombe ... 5 ... SX 9268
Maidenhead ... 19 ... SU 8881
Maiden Law ... 47 ... NZ 1749
Maiden Newton ... 7 ... SY 5997
Maidens ... 44 ... NS 2107
Maidford ... 26 ... SP 6052
Maids' Moreton ... 18 ... SP 7035
Maidstone ... 12 ... TQ 7656
Maidwell ... 26 ... SP 7477
Mail ... 63 ... HU 4228
Mains ... 60 ... NH 4239
Mains of Ardestie ... 57 ... NO 5034
Mains of Balhall ... 57 ... NO 5163
Mains of Ballindarg ... 57 ... NO 4051
Mains of Dalvey ... 61 ... NJ 1132
Mains of Drum ... 62 ... NO 8099
Mains of Melgund ... 57 ... NO 5456
Mains of Thornton ... 57 ... NO 6871
Mains of Throsk ... 50 ... NS 8690
Mainstone ... 23 ... SO 2687
Maisemore ... 17 ... SO 8121
Malborough ... 5 ... SX 7039
Malden ... 11 ... TQ 2166
Maldon ... 20 ... TL 8506
Malham ... 41 ... SD 9062
Mallaig ... 58 ... NM 6796
Malleny Mills ... 51 ... NT 1665
Mallwyd ... 22 ... SH 8612
Malmesbury ... 17 ... ST 9387
Malpas (Ches.) ... 32 ... SJ 4847
Malpas (Cornwall) ... 2 ... SW 8442
Maltby (Cleve.) ... 42 ... NZ 4613
Maltby (S Yorks.) ... 38 ... SK 5392
Maltby le Marsh ... 35 ... TF 4681
Malting Green ... 21 ... TL 9720
Maltman's Hill ... 13 ... TQ 9043
Malton ... 38 ... SE 7871
Malvern Link ... 24 ... SO 7848
Malvern Wells ... 24 ... SO 7742
Mamble ... 24 ... SO 6871
Manaccan ... 2 ... SW 7625
Manafon ... 23 ... SJ 1102
Manaton ... 5 ... SX 7481
Manby ... 35 ... TF 3986
Mancetter ... 26 ... SP 3196
Manchester ... 37 ... SJ 8397
Mancot ... 32 ... SJ 3267
Mandally ... 59 ... NH 2900
Manea ... 27 ... TL 4789
Manfield ... 42 ... NZ 2213
Mangersta ... 63 ... NB 0131
Mangotsfield ... 17 ... ST 6676
Manish (Harris) ... 63 ... NG 1089
Manish (Isle of Lewis) ... 63 ... NA 9513
Mankinholes ... 37 ... SD 9523
Manley ... 32 ... SJ 5071
Manmoel ... 16 ... SO 1703
Mannel ... 48 ... NL 9840
Manningford Bohune ... 17 ... SU 1357
Manningford Bruce ... 17 ... SU 1359
Manning's Heath ... 11 ... TQ 2028
Mannington ... 8 ... SU 0605
Manningtree ... 21 ... TM 1031
Mannofield ... 62 ... NJ 9104
Manorbier ... 14 ... SS 0698
Manorhill ... 52 ... NT 6632
Manorowen ... 14 ... SM 9336
Mansell Gamage ... 24 ... SO 3944
Mansell Lacy ... 24 ... SO 4245
Mansergh ... 41 ... SD 6082
Mansfield (Notts.) ... 34 ... SK 5361
Mansfield (Strath.) ... 50 ... NS 6214
Mansfield Woodhouse ... 34 ... SK 5363
Mansriggs ... 40 ... SD 2880
Manston ... 8 ... ST 8115
Manthorpe ... 35 ... TF 0616
Manton (Humbs.) ... 39 ... SE 9302
Manton (Leic.) ... 27 ... SK 8704
Manton (Wilts.) ... 17 ... SU 1768
Manuden ... 20 ... TL 4926
Maplebeck ... 34 ... SK 7160
Maple Cross ... 19 ... TQ 0392
Mapledurham ... 10 ... SU 6776
Mapledurwell ... 10 ... SU 6851
Maplehurst ... 11 ... TQ 1924
Mapleton ... 33 ... SK 1648
Mapperley ... 33 ... SK 4343
Mapperton ... 7 ... SY 5099
Mappleborough Green ... 25 ... SP 0866
Mappleton ... 39 ... TA 2244
Mappowder ... 8 ... ST 7105
Marazion ... 2 ... SW 5130
Marbury ... 32 ... SJ 5545
March ... 27 ... TL 4197
Marcham ... 18 ... SU 4596
Marchamley ... 32 ... SJ 5929
Marchbankwood ... 45 ... NY 0899
Marchington ... 33 ... SK 1330
Marchington Woodlands ... 33 ... SK 1128
Marchwiel ... 32 ... SJ 3547
Marchwood ... 9 ... SU 3809
Marcross ... 15 ... SS 9269
Marden (Here. and Worc.) ... 24 ... SO 5247
Marden (Kent) ... 12 ... TQ 7444
Marden (Wilts.) ... 17 ... SU 0857
Mardy ... 16 ... SO 3016
Marefield ... 34 ... SK 7408
Mare Green ... 7 ... ST 3326
Mareham le Fen ... 35 ... TF 2761
Mareham on the Hill ... 35 ... TF 2867
Maresfield ... 12 ... TQ 4624
Marfleet ... 39 ... TA 1329
Margam ... 15 ... SS 7887
Margaret Marsh ... 8 ... ST 8218
Margaret Roding ... 20 ... TL 5912
Margaretting ... 20 ... TL 6601
Margate ... 13 ... TR 3670
Margnaheglish ... 49 ... NS 0331
Marham ... 28 ... TF 7110
Marhamchurch ... 4 ... SS 2203
Marholm ... 27 ... TF 1402
Marian-glas ... 30 ... SH 5084
Mariansleigh ... 6 ... SS 7422
Marishader ... 58 ... NG 4963
Maristow ... 4 ... SX 4764
Mariveg ... 63 ... NB 4119
Mark ... 7 ... ST 3747
Markbeech ... 12 ... TQ 4842
Markby ... 35 ... TF 4878
Mark Causeway ... 7 ... ST 3547
Mark Cross ... 12 ... TQ 5831
Market Bosworth ... 26 ... SK 4003
Market Deeping ... 35 ... TF 1310
Market Drayton ... 32 ... SJ 6734
Market Harborough ... 26 ... SP 7387
Markethill ... 56 ... NO 2239
Market Lavington ... 17 ... SU 0154
Market Overton ... 34 ... SK 8816
Market Rasen ... 35 ... TF 1089
Market Stainton ... 35 ... TF 2279
Market Street ... 29 ... TG 2921
Market Weighton ... 39 ... SE 8741
Market Weston ... 29 ... TL 9877
Markfield ... 33 ... SK 4810
Markham ... 16 ... SO 1600
Markinch ... 57 ... NO 2901
Markington ... 42 ... SE 2864
Marksbury ... 17 ... ST 6662
Marks Tey ... 21 ... TL 9123
Markwell ... 4 ... SX 3658
Markyate ... 19 ... TL 0616
Marlborough ... 17 ... SU 1869
Marlcliff ... 25 ... SP 0950
Marldon ... 5 ... SX 8663
Marlesford ... 21 ... TM 3258
Marley Green ... 32 ... SJ 5745
Marlingford ... 29 ... TG 1208
Marloes ... 14 ... SM 7908
Marlow ... 19 ... SU 8587
Marlpit Hill ... 12 ... TQ 4447
Marnhull ... 8 ... ST 7718
Marnoch ... 62 ... NJ 5950
Marple ... 33 ... SJ 9588
Marr ... 38 ... SE 5105
Marrick ... 42 ... SE 0798
Marrister ... 63 ... HU 5464
Marros ... 14 ... SN 2008
Marsden ... 37 ... SE 0411
Marsett ... 41 ... SD 9086
Marsh ... 5 ... ST 2410
Marshall's Heath ... 19 ... TL 1515
Marsham ... 29 ... TG 1924
Marshaw ... 36 ... SD 5853
Marsh Baldon ... 18 ... SU 5699
Marshborough ... 13 ... TR 2958
Marshbrook ... 24 ... SO 4389
Marshchapel ... 39 ... TF 3598
Marshfield (Avon) ... 17 ... ST 7773
Marshfield (Gwent) ... 16 ... ST 2582
Marshgate ... 4 ... SX 1592
Marsh Gibbon ... 18 ... SP 6423
Marsh Green (Devon.) ... 5 ... SY 0493
Marsh Green (Kent) ... 12 ... TQ 4344
Marsh Green (Salop) ... 24 ... SJ 6014
Marshside ... 36 ... SD 3419
Marsh, The ... 23 ... SO 3197
Marshwood ... 7 ... SY 3899
Marske ... 42 ... NZ 1000
Marske-by-the-Sea ... 42 ... NZ 6322
Marston (Ches.) ... 32 ... SJ 6474
Marston (Here. and Worc.) ... 24 ... SO 3657
Marston (Lincs.) ... 34 ... SK 8943
Marston (Oxon.) ... 18 ... SP 5208
Marston (Staffs.) ... 25 ... SJ 8314
Marston (Staffs.) ... 33 ... SJ 9227
Marston (Warw.) ... 25 ... SP 2095
Marston (Wilts.) ... 17 ... ST 9656
Marston Green ... 25 ... SP 1685
Marston Magna ... 7 ... ST 5922
Marston Meysey ... 17 ... SU 1297
Marston Montgomery ... 33 ... SK 1338
Marston Moretaine ... 27 ... SP 9941
Marston on Dove ... 33 ... SK 2329
Marston St. Lawrence ... 26 ... SP 5342
Marston Stannett ... 24 ... SO 5655
Marston Trussell ... 26 ... SP 6986
Marstow ... 16 ... SO 5519
Marsworth ... 19 ... SP 9214
Marten ... 10 ... SU 2860
Marthall ... 32 ... SJ 8076
Martham ... 29 ... TG 4518
Martin (Hants.) ... 8 ... SU 0719
Martin (Lincs.) ... 35 ... TF 1259
Martin Drove End ... 8 ... SU 0420
Martinhoe ... 6 ... SS 6648
Martin Hussingtree ... 25 ... SO 8860
Martinscroft ... 32 ... SJ 6589
Martinstown ... 8 ... SY 6488
Martlesham ... 21 ... TM 2547
Martletwy ... 14 ... SN 0310
Martley ... 24 ... SO 7559
Martock ... 7 ... ST 4619
Marton (Ches.) ... 33 ... SJ 8468
Marton (Cleve.) ... 42 ... NZ 5115
Marton (Lincs.) ... 34 ... SK 8381
Marton (N Yorks.) ... 38 ... SE 4162
Marton (N Yorks.) ... 43 ... SE 7383
Marton (Salop) ... 23 ... SJ 2802
Marton (Warw.) ... 26 ... SP 4069
Marwood ... 6 ... SS 5437
Marybank ... 60 ... NH 4753
Maryburgh ... 60 ... NH 5456
Marygold ... 53 ... NT 8160
Maryhill ... 62 ... NJ 8245
Marykirk ... 57 ... NO 6865
Marylebone ... 36 ... SD 5807
Marypark ... 61 ... NJ 1938
Maryport ... 44 ... NX 1434
Maryport ... 40 ... NY 0336
Marystow ... 4 ... SX 4382
Mary Tavy ... 4 ... SX 5079
Maryton ... 57 ... NO 6856
Marywell (Grampn.) ... 62 ... NO 5896
Marywell (Tays.) ... 57 ... NO 6544
Masham ... 42 ... SE 2280
Mashbury ... 20 ... TL 6511
Mason ... 47 ... NZ 2073
Mastrick ... 62 ... NJ 9007
Matching ... 20 ... TL 5212
Matching Green ... 20 ... TL 5311
Matching Tye ... 20 ... TL 5111
Matfen ... 47 ... NZ 0371
Matfield ... 12 ... TQ 6541
Mathern ... 16 ... ST 5291
Mathon ... 24 ... SO 7345
Mathry ... 14 ... SM 8832
Matlaske ... 29 ... TG 1534
Matlock ... 33 ... SK 3060
Matlock Bath ... 33 ... SK 2958
Matson ... 17 ... SO 8316
Matterdale End ... 40 ... NY 3923
Mattersey ... 34 ... SK 6889
Mattingley ... 10 ... SU 7357
Mattishall ... 29 ... TG 0510
Mattishall Burgh ... 29 ... TG 0511
Mauchline ... 50 ... NS 4927
Maud ... 62 ... NJ 9247
Maugersbury ... 17 ... SP 1925
Maughold ... 43 ... SC 4991
Maulden ... 19 ... TL 0538
Maulds Meaburn ... 41 ... NY 6216
Maunby ... 42 ... SE 3486
Maund Bryan ... 24 ... SO 5550
Mautby ... 29 ... TG 4712
Mavesyn Ridware ... 25 ... SK 0817
Mavis Enderby ... 35 ... TF 3666
Mawbray ... 45 ... NY 0846
Mawdesley ... 36 ... SD 4914
Mawgan ... 2 ... SW 7024
Maw Green ... 25 ... SP 0197
Mawla ... 2 ... SW 6945
Mawnan ... 2 ... SW 7827
Mawnan Smith ... 2 ... SW 7728
Maxey ... 35 ... TF 1208
Maxstoke ... 26 ... SP 2386
Maxton ... 52 ... NT 6129
Maxwellheugh ... 52 ... NT 7333
Maxwellston ... 44 ... NS 2600
Maybole ... 44 ... NS 3009
Mayfield (E Susx) ... 12 ... TQ 5827
Mayfield (Staffs.) ... 33 ... SK 1545
Mayford ... 11 ... SU 9956
Maypole ... 16 ... SO 4716
Maypole Green ... 29 ... TM 4195
Maywick ... 63 ... HU 3724
Meadle ... 18 ... SP 8005
Meadowtown ... 23 ... SJ 3101
Meal Bank ... 41 ... SD 5495
Mealsgate ... 40 ... NY 2141
Mearbeck ... 41 ... SD 8160
Meare ... 7 ... ST 4541
Mears Ashby ... 26 ... SP 8366
Measham ... 33 ... SK 3312
Meathop ... 40 ... SD 4380
Meaux ... 39 ... TA 0939
Meavag ... 63 ... NG 1596
Meavy ... 4 ... SX 5467
Medbourne ... 26 ... SP 7993
Meddon ... 4 ... SS 2717
Medmenham ... 18 ... SU 8084
Medstead ... 10 ... SU 6537
Meerbrook ... 33 ... SJ 9860
Meer End ... 26 ... SP 2474
Meesden ... 20 ... TL 4432
Meeth ... 6 ... SS 5408
Meidrim ... 14 ... SN 2820
Meifod ... 23 ... SJ 1513
Meigle ... 57 ... NO 2844
Meikle Earnock ... 50 ... NS 7253
Meikleour ... 56 ... NO 1539
Meikle Strath ... 57 ... NO 6471
Meikle Tarty ... 62 ... NJ 9928
Meikle Wartle ... 62 ... NJ 7230
Meinciau ... 15 ... SN 4610
Meir ... 33 ... SJ 9342
Melbost ... 63 ... NB 4632
Melbourn (Cambs.) ... 20 ... TL 3844
Melbourne (Derby.) ... 33 ... SK 3825
Melbourne (Humbs.) ... 38 ... SE 7543
Melbury Bubb ... 7 ... ST 5906
Melbury Osmond ... 7 ... ST 5707
Melbury Sampford ... 7 ... ST 5705
Melchbourne ... 27 ... TL 0265
Melcombe Bingham ... 8 ... ST 7602
Meldon (Devon) ... 4 ... SX 5592
Meldon (Northum.) ... 47 ... NZ 1284
Meldreth ... 20 ... TL 3746
Melfort ... 54 ... NM 8314
Meliden ... 31 ... SJ 0580
Melin Court ... 15 ... SN 8201
Melin-y-coed ... 31 ... SH 8160
Melin-y-ddol ... 23 ... SJ 0807
Melin-y-grug ... 23 ... SJ 0507
Melin-y-wig ... 31 ... SJ 0448
Melkinthorpe ... 41 ... NY 5525
Melkridge ... 46 ... NY 7363
Melksham ... 17 ... ST 9063
Melldalloch ... 49 ... NR 9375
Melling (Lancs.) ... 41 ... SD 5970
Melling (Mers.) ... 36 ... SD 3800
Mellis ... 29 ... TM 0974
Mellon Charles ... 64 ... NG 8491
Mellon Udrigle ... 64 ... NG 8895
Mellor (Gtr Mches.) ... 33 ... SJ 9888
Mellor (Lancs.) ... 36 ... SD 6530
Mellor Brook ... 36 ... SD 6331
Mells ... 8 ... ST 7249
Melmerby (Cumbr.) ... 41 ... NY 6137
Melmerby (N Yorks.) ... 42 ... SE 0785
Melmerby (N Yorks.) ... 42 ... SE 3376
Melplash ... 7 ... SY 4797
Melrose ... 52 ... NT 5433
Melsetter ... 63 ... ND 2689
Melsonby ... 42 ... NZ 1908
Meltham ... 37 ... SE 0910
Melton ... 21 ... TM 2850
Meltonby ... 38 ... SE 7952
Melton Constable ... 29 ... TG 0433
Melton Mowbray ... 34 ... SK 7518
Melton Ross ... 39 ... TA 0610
Melvaig ... 64 ... NG 7486

Melverley Nailstone

Melverley 23 SJ 3316
Melvich 67 NC 8864
Membury 7 ST 2703
Memsie 62 NJ 9762
Memus 57 NO 4258
Menabilly 4 SX 0951
Menai Bridge 30 SH 5572
Mendham 29 TM 2783
Mendlesham 21 TM 1065
Mendlesham Green 21 TM 0963
Menheniot 4 SX 2862
Mennock 45 NS 8008
Menston 37 SE 1743
Menstrie 56 NS 8596
Mentmore 19 SP 9019
Meole Brace 24 SJ 4811
Meonstoke 9 SU 6119
Meopham 12 TQ 6466
Meopham Station 12 TQ 6467
Mepal 27 TL 4481
Meppershall 19 TL 1336
Merbach 23 SO 3045
Mere (Ches.) 32 SJ 7281
Mere (Wilts.) 8 ST 8132
Mere Brow 36 SD 4118
Mereclough 37 SD 8730
Mere Green 25 SP 1298
Merevale 26 SP 2897
Mereworth 12 TQ 6553
Mergie 57 NO 7988
Meriden 26 SP 2482
Merkadale 58 NG 3831
Merkland 44 NX 2491
Merlin's Bridge 14 SM 9414
Merrington 32 SJ 4621
Merriott 7 ST 4412
Merrivale 4 SX 5475
Merrymeet 4 SX 2766
Mersham 13 TR 0539
Merstham 11 TQ 2953
Merston 11 SU 8903
Merstone 9 SZ 5285
Merther 2 SW 8644
Merthyr 14 SN 3520
Merthyr Cynog 15 SN 9837
Merthyr Dyfan 16 ST 1169
Merthyr Mawr 15 SS 8877
Merthyr Tydfil 16 SO 0406
Merthyr Vale 16 ST 0899
Merton (Devon.) 6 SS 5212
Merton (Gtr London) 11 TQ 2569
Merton (Norf.) 28 TL 9098
Merton (Oxon.) 18 SP 5717
Mervinslaw 52 NT 6713
Meshaw 6 SS 7519
Messing 21 TL 8918
Messingham 39 SE 8904
Metfield 29 TM 2980
Metheringham 35 TF 0661
Methil 57 NT 3699
Methley 37 SE 3826
Methlick 62 NJ 8537
Methven 56 NO 0225
Methwold 28 TL 7394
Methwold Hithe 28 TL 7195
Mettingham 29 TM 3689
Mevagissey 4 SX 0144
Mexborough 38 SK 4799
Mey 67 ND 2872
Meysey Hampton 17 SU 1199
Miavaig 63 NB 0834
Michaelchurch 16 SO 5125
Michaelchurch Escley 23 SO 3134
Michaelchurch-on-Arrow 23 SO 2450
Michaelston-le-Pit 16 ST 1573
Michaelston-y-Fedw 16 ST 2484
Michaelstow 4 SX 0778
Micheldever 10 SU 5138
Michelmersh 9 SU 3426
Mickfield 21 TM 1361
Mickleby 43 NZ 8013
Micklefield 38 SE 4433
Mickleham 11 TQ 1753
Mickleover 33 SK 3034
Mickleton (Durham) 41 NY 9623
Mickleton (Glos.) 25 SP 1543
Mickle Trafford 32 SJ 4469
Mickley 42 SE 2576
Mickley Square 47 NZ 0761
Mid Ardlaw 62 NJ 9464
Midbea 63 HY 4444
Mid Beltie 62 NJ 6200
Mid Cairncross 57 NO 4979
Middle Assendon 18 SU 7385
Middle Aston 18 SP 4726
Middle Barton 18 SP 4326
Middlebie 46 NY 2176
Middle Claydon 18 SP 7125
Middle Drums 57 NO 5957
Middleham 42 SE 1287
Middlehope 24 SO 4988
Middle Littleton 25 SP 0747
Middle Maes-coed 23 SO 3334
Middlemarsh 8 ST 6707
Middle Mill 14 SM 8025
Middle Rasen 35 TF 0889
Middlesbrough 42 NZ 4920
Middlesmoor 42 SE 0974
Middlestone Moor 42 NZ 2532
Middlestown 37 SE 2617
Middleton (Cumbr.) 41 SD 6286
Middleton (Derby.) 33 SK 1963
Middleton (Derby.) 33 SK 2755
Middleton (Essex) 20 TL 8639
Middleton (Grampn.) 62 NJ 8419
Middleton (Gtr Mches.) 37 SD 8606
Middleton (Hants.) 10 SU 4243
Middleton (Here. and Worc.) 24 SO 5469
Middleton (Lancs.) 36 SD 4258
Middleton (Lothian) 51 NT 3657
Middleton (Norf.) 28 TF 6616
Middleton (Northants.) 27 SP 8489
Middleton (Northum.) 53 NU 0024
Middleton (Northum.) 53 NU 1035
Middleton (Northum.) 47 NZ 0585
Middleton (N Yorks.) 43 SE 7885
Middleton (N Yorks. - W Yorks.) 37 SE 1249
Middleton (Salop) 32 SJ 3128
Middleton (Salop) 23 SO 2999
Middleton (Salop) 24 SO 5377
Middleton (Suff.) 21 TM 4267
Middleton (Tays.) 56 NO 1206
Middleton (Tiree) 48 NL 9443
Middleton (Warw.) 25 SP 1798
Middleton (W Yorks.) 37 SE 3027
Middleton Cheney 26 SP 4941
Middleton Green 33 SJ 9935
Middleton Hall 53 NT 9825
Middleton in Teesdale 41 NY 9425
Middleton-on-Sea 11 SU 9800
Middleton on the Hill 24 SO 5464
Middleton-on-the-Wolds 39 SE 9449
Middleton Priors 24 SO 6290
Middleton St. George 42 NZ 3412
Middleton Scriven 24 SO 6787
Middleton Stoney 18 SP 5323
Middleton Tyas 42 NZ 2205
Middletown 23 SJ 3012
Middle Tysoe 26 SP 3344
Middle Wallop 10 SU 2937
Middlewich 32 SJ 7066
Middle Winterslow 9 SU 2432
Middle Witchyburn 62 NJ 6356
Middle Woodford 8 SU 1136
Middlewood Green 21 TM 0961
Middleyard 50 NS 5132
Middlezoy 7 ST 3733
Middridge 42 NZ 2526
Midfield 66 NC 5864
Midge Hall 36 SD 5123
Midgeholme 46 NY 6458
Midgham 10 SU 5567
Midgley 37 SE 0226
Midhopestones 37 SK 2399
Midhurst 11 SU 8821
Midlem 52 NT 5227
Mid Sannox 49 NS 0145
Midsomer Norton 17 ST 6654
Mid Thundergay 49 NR 8846
Midtown 64 NG 8285
Midville 35 TF 3857
Mid Yell 63 HU 4991
Migvie 61 NJ 4306
Milborne Port 8 ST 6718
Milborne St. Andrew 8 SY 7997
Milborne Wick 8 ST 6620
Milbourne 47 NZ 1175
Milburn (Cumbr.) 41 NY 6529
Milbury Heath 17 ST 6690
Milcombe 18 SP 4134
Milden 21 TL 9546
Mildenhall (Suff.) 28 TL 7074
Mildenhall (Wilts.) 17 SU 2069
Milebrook 23 SO 3172
Milebush 12 TQ 7546
Mile Elm 17 ST 9968
Mile End 21 TL 9827
Mileham 28 TF 9119
Milesmark 51 NT 0688
Milfield 53 NT 9333
Milford (Derby.) 33 SK 3445
Milford (Staffs.) 33 SJ 9721
Milford (Surrey) 11 SU 9442
Milford Haven (Dyfed) 14 SM 9006
Milford on Sea 9 SZ 2891
Milkwall 17 SO 5809
Milland 9 SU 8228
Milland Marsh 9 SU 8326
Mill Bank 37 SE 0321
Millbounds 63 HY 5635
Millbreck 62 NK 0045
Millbridge 11 SU 8542
Millbrook (Beds.) 19 TL 0138
Millbrook (Corn.) 4 SX 4252
Millbrook (Hants.) 9 SU 4012
Millburn (Strath.) 50 NS 4429
Millcorner 12 TQ 8223
Milldens 57 NO 5450
Mill End (Bucks.) 18 SU 7885
Mill End (Herts.) 20 TL 3332
Millerhill 51 NT 3269
Miller's Dale 33 SK 1373
Mill Green (Essex) 20 TL 6400
Millgreen (Salop) 32 SJ 6727
Millheugh 50 NS 7551
Mill Hill 19 TQ 2292
Millholme 41 SD 5690
Millhouse 49 NR 9570
Millikenpark 50 NS 4162
Millington 39 SE 8351
Mill Lane 10 SU 7850
Millmeece 32 SJ 8333
Mill of Kingoodie 62 NJ 8425
Millom 40 SD 1780
Millport 49 NS 1655
Mill Street 29 TG 0118
Millthrop 41 SD 6691
Milltimber 62 NJ 8501
Millton of Auchriachan 61 NJ 1718
Millton of Corsindae 62 NJ 6809
Millton of Murtle 62 NJ 8702
Milltown (Derby.) 33 SK 3561
Milltown (Dumf. and Galwy.) 46 NY 3375
Milltown (Grampn.) 61 NJ 4616
Milltown (Grampn.) 62 NJ 5447
Milltown of Aberdalgie 56 NO 0720
Milltown of Auchindown 61 NJ 3540
Milltown of Campfield 62 NJ 6400
Milltown of Craigston 62 NJ 7655
Milltown of Edinvillie 61 NJ 2639
Milltown of Towie 61 NJ 4612
Milnathort 56 NO 1204
Milngavie 50 NS 5574
Milnrow 37 SD 9212
Milnthorpe 40 SD 4981
Milovaig 58 NG 1550
Milson 24 SO 6372
Milstead 13 TQ 9058
Milston 8 SU 1645
Milton (Cambs.) 20 TL 4762
Milton (Central) 55 NN 5001
Milton (Central) 50 NS 4490
Milton (Cumbr.) 46 NY 5560
Milton (Dumf. and Galwy.) 44 NX 2154
Milton (Dumf. and Galwy.) 45 NX 8470
Milton (Grampn.) 61 NJ 5163
Milton (Highld.) 67 ND 3451
Milton (Highld.) 59 NH 3055
Milton (Highld.) 60 NH 4930
Milton (Highld.) 60 NH 5749
Milton (Highld.) 65 NH 7674
Milton (Highld.) 60 NH 9553
Milton (Oxon.) 18 SP 4535
Milton (Oxon.) 18 SU 4892
Milton (Staffs.) 33 SJ 9050
Milton (Strath.) 50 NS 4274
Milton (Tays.) 56 NN 9138
Milton (Tays.) 57 NO 3843
Milton Abbas 8 ST 8001
Milton Abbot 4 SX 4079
Milton Bridge 51 NT 2363
Milton Bryan 19 SP 9730
Milton Clevedon 8 ST 6637
Milton Coldwells 62 NJ 9538
Milton Combe 4 SX 4866
Milton Damerel 4 SS 3810
Miltonduff 61 NJ 1760
Milton Ernest 27 TL 0156
Milton Green 32 SJ 4558
Milton Hill 18 SU 4790
Milton Keynes 27 SP 8939
Milton Lilbourne 17 SU 1860
Milton Malsor 26 SP 7355
Milton Morenish 56 NN 6135
Milton of Auchinhove 62 NJ 5503
Milton of Balgonie 57 NO 3100
Milton of Braicklaich 60 NH 7851
Milton of Campsie 50 NS 6576
Milton of Cushnie 61 NJ 5111
Milton of Lesmore 61 NJ 4628
Milton of Noth 61 NJ 5028
Milton of Potterton 62 NJ 9415
Milton of Tullich 61 NO 3897
Milton on Stour 8 ST 7928
Milton Regis 13 TQ 9064
Milton-under-Wychwood 18 SP 2618
Milverton 7 ST 1225
Milwich 33 SJ 9632
Milwr 32 SJ 1974
Minard 55 NR 9796
Minchinhampton 17 SO 8600
Mindrum 53 NT 8432
Minehead 7 SS 9746
Minera 32 SJ 2651
Minety 17 SU 0290
Minffordd 30 SH 5938
Mingary 63 NF 7426
Miningsby 35 TF 3264
Minions 4 SX 2671
Minishant 50 NS 3314
Minley Manor 10 SU 8157
Minnes 62 NJ 9423
Minnigaff 44 NX 4166
Minskip 42 SE 3864
Minstead 9 SU 2811
Minster (Kent) 13 TQ 9573
Minster (Kent) 13 TR 3164
Minsteracres 47 NZ 0255
Minsterley 24 SJ 3705
Minster Lovell 18 SP 3111
Minsterworth 17 SO 7717
Minterne Magna 8 ST 6504
Minting 35 TF 1873
Mintlaw 62 NK 0048
Minto 52 NT 5620
Minton 24 SO 4290
Minwear 14 SN 0413
Minworth 25 SP 1592
Mirbister 63 HY 3019
Mireland 67 ND 3160
Mirfield 37 SE 2019
Miserden 17 SO 9308
Miskin 16 ST 0481
Misson 38 SK 6895
Misterton (Leic.) 26 SP 5584
Misterton (Notts.) 38 SK 7694
Misterton (Somer.) 7 ST 4508
Mistley 21 TM 1231
Mitcham 11 TQ 2868
Mitcheldean 17 SO 6618
Mitchell 2 SW 8554
Mitchel Troy 16 SO 4910
Mitford 47 NZ 1786
Mithian 2 SW 7450
Mixbury 18 SP 6033
Mixon 33 SK 0457
Mobberley 32 SJ 7880
Moccas 24 SO 3542
Mochdre (Clwyd) 31 SH 8278
Mochdre (Powys) 23 SO 0788
Mochrum 44 NX 3446
Mockerkin 40 NY 0823
Modbury 5 SX 6551
Moddershall 33 SJ 9236
Moelfre (Clwyd) 32 SJ 1828
Moelfre (Gwyn.) 30 SH 5186
Moel Tryfan 30 SH 5155
Moffat 45 NT 0805
Mogerhanger 27 TL 1349
Moira 33 SK 3216
Molash 13 TR 0251
Mold 32 SJ 2363
Molehill Green 20 TL 5624
Molescroft 39 TA 0140
Molesworth 27 TL 0775
Molland 6 SS 8028
Mollington (Ches.) 32 SJ 3870
Mollington (Northants.) 26 SP 4347
Mollinsburn 50 NS 7171
Monachty 22 SN 5062
Monboddo 57 NO 7478
Mondynes 57 NO 7879
Monewden 21 TM 2358
Moneydie 56 NO 0629
Moniaive 45 NX 7791
Monifieth 57 NO 4932
Monikie 57 NO 4938
Monimail 57 NO 2914
Monington 14 SN 1344
Monken Hadley 19 TQ 2497
Monk Fryston 38 SE 5029
Monkhopton 24 SO 6293
Monkland 24 SO 4557
Monkleigh 4 SS 4520
Monknash 15 SS 9270
Monkokehampton 6 SS 5805
Monks Eleigh 21 TL 9647
Monks' Heath 33 SJ 8873
Monk Sherborne 10 SU 6056
Monkshill 62 NJ 7941
Monksilver 7 ST 0737
Monks Kirby 26 SP 4683
Monk Soham 21 TM 2165
Monkswood 16 SO 3403
Monkton (Devon.) 5 ST 1803
Monkton (Kent) 13 TR 2865
Monkton (Strath.) 50 NS 3527
Monkton (Tyne and Wear) 47 NZ 3463
Monkton Combe 17 ST 7761
Monkton Deverill 8 ST 8537
Monkton Farleigh 17 ST 8065
Monkton Heathfield 7 ST 2526
Monkton Up Wimborne 8 SU 0113
Monkwood 9 SU 6730
Monmouth 16 SO 5113
Monnington on Wye 23 SO 3743
Monreith 44 NX 3641
Monreith Mains 44 NX 3643
Montacute 7 ST 4916
Montford 24 SJ 4114
Montgarrie 62 NJ 5717
Montgomery 23 SO 2296
Montgreenan 50 NS 3343
Montrave 57 NO 3706
Montrose 57 NO 7157
Monxton 10 SU 3144
Monyash 33 SK 1566
Monymusk 62 NJ 6815
Monzie 56 NN 8725
Moonzie 57 NO 3317
Moorby 35 TF 2964
Moorcot 24 SO 3555
Moor Crichel 8 ST 9908
Moordown 8 SZ 0994
Moore 32 SJ 5584
Moorends 38 SE 6915
Moorhall 33 SK 3175
Moorhampton 24 SO 3846
Moorhouse (Cumbr.) 46 NY 3356
Moorhouse (Notts.) 34 SK 7566
Moorland or Northmoor Green 7 ST 3332
Moorlinch 7 ST 3936
Moor Monkton 38 SE 5056
Moor Nook 36 SD 6537
Moorsholm 43 NZ 6814
Moorside 37 SD 9507
Moor, The 12 TQ 7529
Moortown (Hants.) 9 SZ 4283
Moortown (Lincs.) 39 TF 0699
Morar 58 NM 6792
Morborne 27 TL 1391
Morchard Bishop 6 SS 7607
Morcombelake 7 SY 4093
Morcott 27 SK 9200
Morda 32 SJ 2827
Morden (Dorset) 8 SY 9195
Morden (Gtr London) 11 TQ 2567
Mordiford 24 SO 5637
Mordon 42 NZ 3326
More 23 SO 3491
Morebath 6 SS 9525
Morebattle 53 NT 7724
Morecambe 40 SD 4364
Morefield 64 NH 1195
Moreleigh 5 SX 7652
Morenish 56 NN 6035
Moresby 40 NX 9821
Morestead 9 SU 5125
Moreton (Dorset) 8 SY 8089
Moreton (Essex) 20 TL 5307
Moreton (Mers.) 32 SJ 2689
Moreton (Oxon.) 18 SP 6904
Moreton Corbet 32 SJ 5523
Moretonhampstead 5 SX 7586
Moreton-in-Marsh 25 SP 2032
Moreton Jeffries 24 SO 6048
Moreton Morrell 26 SP 3155
Moreton on Lugg 24 SO 5045
Moreton Pinkney 26 SP 5749
Moreton Say 32 SJ 6234
Moreton Valence 17 SO 7809
Morfa Bychan 30 SH 5437
Morfa Glas 15 SN 8606
Morfa Nefyn 30 SH 2840
Morgan's Vale 8 SU 1921
Morland 41 NY 6022
Morley (Derby.) 33 SK 3941
Morley (Durham) 42 NZ 1227
Morley (W Yorks.) 37 SE 2627
Morley Green 32 SJ 8282
Morley St. Botolph 29 TM 0799
Morningside 51 NT 2471
Morningthorpe 29 TM 2192
Morpeth 47 NZ 2085
Morphie 57 NO 7164
Morrey 33 SK 1218
Morriston 15 SS 6698
Morston 29 TG 0043
Mortehoe 6 SS 4545
Mortimer 10 SU 6564
Mortimer's Cross 24 SO 4263
Mortimer West End 10 SU 6363
Mortlake 11 TQ 2075
Morton (Avon) 17 ST 6491
Morton (Derby.) 33 SK 4060
Morton (Lincs.) 39 SK 8091
Morton (Lincs.) 35 TF 0924
Morton (Norf.) 29 TG 1217
Morton (Salop) 32 SJ 2824
Morton Bagot 25 SP 1164
Morton-on-Swale 42 SE 3292
Morvah 2 SW 4035
Morval 4 SX 2556
Morvich 59 NG 9621
Morville 24 SO 6694
Morwenstow 4 SS 2015
Morwick Hall 47 NU 2303
Mosborough 33 SK 4281
Moscow 50 NS 4840
Mosedale 40 NY 3532
Moseley (Here. and Worc.) 25 SO 8159
Moseley (W Mids) 25 SP 0883
Moss (Clwyd) 32 SJ 3052
Moss (Highld.) 54 NM 6868
Moss (S Yorks.) 38 SE 5914
Moss (Tiree) 48 NL 9644
Mossat 61 NJ 4719
Moss Bank (Cumbr.) 32 SJ 5198
Mossbank (Shetld.) 63 HU 4475
Mossburnford 52 NT 6616
Mossdale 45 NX 6571
Mossend 50 NS 7460
Mosside 57 NO 4252
Mossley 37 SD 9702
Moss Nook 32 SJ 8385
Moss of Barmuckity 61 NJ 2461
Moss Side 36 SD 3830
Mosston 57 NO 5444
Mosterton 7 ST 4505
Mostyn 31 SJ 1680
Motcombe 8 ST 8425
Motherwell 50 NS 7557
Mottingham 12 TQ 4272
Mottisfont 9 SU 3226
Mottistone 9 SZ 4083
Mottram in Longdendale 37 SJ 9995
Mouldsworth 32 SJ 5171
Moulin 56 NN 9459
Moulsecoomb 12 TQ 3307
Moulsford 18 SU 5984
Moulsoe 27 SP 9041
Moulton (Ches.) 32 SJ 6569
Moulton (Lincs.) 35 TF 3023
Moulton (Northants.) 26 SP 7866
Moulton (N Yorks.) 42 NZ 2303
Moulton (Suff.) 20 TL 6964
Moulton Chapel 35 TF 2918
Moulton Seas End 35 TF 3227
Mount (Corn.) 2 SW 7856
Mount (Corn.) 4 SX 1467
Mountain Ash 16 ST 0498
Mountain Cross 51 NT 1446
Mountain Water 14 SM 9224
Mountbenger 51 NT 3125
Mount Bures 21 TL 9032
Mountfield 12 TQ 7320
Mountgerald 65 NH 5661
Mount Hawke 2 SW 7147
Mountjoy 2 SW 8760
Mountnessing 20 TQ 6297
Mounton 16 ST 5193
Mount Pleasant 29 TM 5077
Mountsorrel 34 SK 5814
Mountstuart (Strath.) 49 NS 1059
Mousehole 2 SW 4626
Mouswald 45 NY 0672
Mow Cop 33 SJ 8557
Mowhaugh 53 NT 8120
Mowsley 26 SP 6489
Mowtie 57 NO 8388
Moy 55 NN 4282
Moy Hall 60 NH 7635
Moy House 61 NJ 0159
Moylgrove 14 SN 1244
Muasdale 48 NR 6840
Muchalls 62 NO 9091
Much Birch 24 SO 5030
Much Cowarne 24 SO 6147
Much Dewchurch 24 SO 4831
Muchelney 7 ST 4224
Much Hadham 20 TL 4319
Much Hoole 36 SD 4723
Muchlarnick 4 SX 2156
Much Marcle 24 SO 6533
Much Wenlock 24 SO 6199
Muckfoot 44 NX 2185
Mucking 20 TQ 6881
Mucklestone 32 SJ 7237
Muckleton 32 SJ 5821
Muckletown 62 NJ 5621
Muckton 35 TF 3781
Muddiford 6 SS 5638
Mudeford 8 SZ 1892
Mudford 7 ST 5719
Mudgley 7 ST 4445
Mugdock Resr. 50 NS 5576
Mugeary 58 NG 4438
Mugginton 33 SK 2843
Muggleswick 47 NZ 0450
Muie 66 NC 6704
Muirdrum 57 NO 5637
Muirhead (Fife.) 57 NO 2805
Muirhead (Strath.) 50 NS 3530
Muirhead (Strath.) 50 NS 6869
Muirhead (Tays.) 57 NO 3434
Muirhouses 51 NT 0180
Muirkirk 50 NS 6927
Muir of Fowlis 62 NJ 5612
Muir of Ord 60 NH 5250
Muirshearlich 55 NN 1380
Muirskie 62 NO 8295
Muirtack (Grampn.) 62 NJ 8146
Muirtack (Grampn.) 62 NJ 9937
Muirton 65 NH 7463
Muirton of Ardblair 56 NO 1743
Muirton of Ballochy 57 NO 6462
Muirtown 56 NN 9211
Muiryfold 62 NJ 7651
Muker 41 SD 9198
Mulbarton 29 TG 1901
Mulben 61 NJ 3450
Mulgrave Castle 43 NZ 8412
Mulindry 48 NR 3659
Mullion 2 SW 6719
Mumbles, The 15 SS 6287
Mumby 35 TF 5174
Muncaster Castle 40 SD 1096
Munderfield Row 24 SO 6451
Munderfield Stocks 24 SO 6550
Mundesley 29 TG 3136
Mundford 28 TL 8093
Mundham (Norf.) 29 TM 3298
Mundham (W. Susx) 11 SU 8701
Mundon Hill 21 TL 8702
Mundurno 62 NJ 9413
Munerigie 59 NH 2602
Mungrisdale 40 NY 3630
Munlochy 60 NH 6453
Munsley 24 SO 6640
Munslow 24 SO 5187
Munslow Aston 24 SO 5086
Murcott 18 SP 5815
Murkle 67 ND 1668
Murlaggan (Highld.) 55 NN 3181
Murrow 35 TF 3707
Mursley 18 SP 8128
Murthill 57 NO 4657
Murthly 56 NO 0938
Murton (Cumbr.) 41 NY 7221
Murton (Durham) 47 NZ 3947
Murton (Northum.) 53 NT 9748
Murton (N Yorks.) 38 SE 6452
Musbury 7 SY 2794
Muscoates 43 SE 6880
Musselburgh 51 NT 3472
Muston (Leic.) 34 SK 8237
Muston (N Yorks.) 43 TA 0979
Mustow Green 25 SO 8774
Mutford 29 TM 4888
Muthill 56 NN 8616
Mutterton 5 ST 0304
Mybster 67 ND 1652
Myddfai 15 SN 7730
Myddle 32 SJ 4623
Mydroilyn 22 SN 4555
Mylor Bridge 2 SW 8036
Mynachlog-ddu 14 SN 1430
Myndtown 24 SO 3889
Mynytho 30 SH 3031
Myrebird 62 NO 7498
Mytchett 11 SU 8855
Mytholm 37 SD 9827
Mytholmroyd 37 SE 0125
Myton-on-Swale 38 SE 4366

Naburn 38 SE 5945
Nackington 13 TR 1554
Nacton 21 TM 2240
Nafferton 39 TA 0559
Nailsea 16 ST 4670
Nailstone 33 SK 4107

Nailsworth
North Tamerton

Nailsworth 17 ST 8499
Nairn 60 NH 8756
Nancegollan 2 SW 6632
Nanhoron 30 SH 2831
Nannau 30 SH 7420
Nannerch 31 SJ 1669
Nanpantan 34 SK 5017
Nanpean 2 SW 9556
Nant-ddu 15 SO 0015
Nanternis 22 SN 3756
Nantgaredig 15 SN 4921
Nantgarw 16 ST 1285
Nant-glas 23 SN 9965
Nantglyn 31 SJ 0061
Nantlle 30 SH 5053
Nantmawr 32 SJ 2424
Nantmel 23 SO 0366
Nantmor 30 SH 6046
Nantwich 32 SJ 6552
Nant-y-derry 16 SO 3306
Nantyffyllon 15 SS 8492
Nantyglo 16 SO 1911
Nant-y-moel 15 SS 9393
Naphill 19 SU 8496
Nappa 37 SD 8553
Napton on the Hill 26 SP 4661
Narberth 14 SN 1114
Narborough (Leic.) 26 SP 5497
Narborough (Norf.) 28 TF 7413
Nasareth 30 SH 4749
Naseby 26 SP 6878
Nash (Bucks.) 18 SP 7734
Nash (Gwent) 16 ST 3483
Nash (Here. and Worc.) 23 SO 3062
Nash (Salop) 24 SO 6071
Nash Lee 19 SP 8408
Nassington 27 TL 0696
Nasty 20 TL 3624
Nateby (Cumbr.) 41 NY 7706
Nateby (Lancs.) 36 SD 4644
Natland 40 SD 5289
Naughton 21 TM 0249
Naunton (Glos.) 17 SP 1123
Naunton (Here. and Worc.) 25 SO 8739
Naunton Beauchamp 25 SO 9652
Naust 64 NG 8283
Navenby 34 SK 9857
Navestock 20 TQ 5397
Navestock Side 20 TQ 5697
Nawton 42 SE 6584
Nayland 21 TL 9734
Nazeing 20 TL 4106
Neacroft 8 SZ 1897
Neal's Green 26 SP 3384
Neap 63 HU 5060
Near Cotton 33 SK 0646
Neasham 42 NZ 3210
Neath 15 SS 7597
Neatishead 29 TG 3421
Nebo (Dyfed) 22 SN 5465
Nebo (Gwyn.) 30 SH 4750
Nebo (Gwyn.) 31 SH 8356
Necton 28 TF 8709
Nedd 64 NC 1332
Nedging Tye 21 TM 0149
Needham 29 TM 2281
Needham Market 21 TM 0855
Needingworth 27 TL 3472
Neen Savage 24 SO 6777
Neen Sollars 24 SO 6572
Neenton 24 SO 6487
Nefyn 30 SH 3040
Neilston 50 NS 4657
Nelson (Lancs.) 37 SD 8737
Nelson (Mid Glam.) 16 ST 1195
Nelson Village 47 NZ 2577
Nemphlar 50 NS 8544
Nempnett Thrubwell 16 ST 5360
Nenthead 41 NY 7743
Nenthorn 52 NT 6837
Nercwys 32 SJ 2260
Nereabolls 48 NR 2255
Nerston 50 NS 6457
Nesbit 53 NT 9833
Ness (Ches.) 32 SJ 3075
Ness (N Yorks.) 43 SE 6878
Nesscliffe 32 SJ 3819
Neston (Ches.) 32 SJ 2877
Neston (Wilts.) 17 ST 8667
Nether Alderley 33 SJ 8476
Netheravon 8 SU 1448
Nether Blainslie 52 NT 5443
Netherbrae 62 NJ 7959
Nether Broughton 34 SK 6925
Netherburn 50 NS 7947
Nether Burrow 41 SD 6174
Netherbury 7 SY 4799
Netherby 46 NY 3971
Nether Cerne 8 SY 6698
Nether Compton 7 ST 5907
Nether Crimond 62 NJ 8222
Nether Dallachy 61 NJ 3663
Netherend 17 SO 5900
Nether Exe 6 SS 9300
Netherfield 12 TQ 7018
Netherhampton 8 SU 1029
Nether Handwick 57 NO 3641
Nether Haugh 38 SK 4196
Nether Howecleuch 51 NT 0312
Nether Kellet 40 SD 5067
Nether Kinmundy 62 NK 0444
Nether Kirkton 50 NS 4757
Nether Langwith 34 SK 5371
Netherlaw 45 NX 7445
Netherley 62 NO 8593
Nethermill 45 NY 0487
Nethermuir 62 NJ 9143
Nether Padley 33 SK 2478
Netherplace 50 NS 5155
Nether Poppleton 38 SE 5654
Netherseal 33 SK 2813
Nether Silton 42 SE 4592
Nether Stowey 7 ST 1939
Netherstreet 17 ST 9764
Netherthird 50 NS 5818
Netherthong 37 SE 1309
Netherton (Central) 50 NS 5579
Netherton (Devon.) 5 SX 8971
Netherton (Here. and Worc.) 25 SO 9941
Netherton (Mers.) 36 SD 3500
Netherton (Northum.) 47 NT 9907
Netherton (Tays.) 56 NO 1452
Netherton (Tays.) 57 NO 5457
Netherton (W Yorks.) 37 SE 2716
Nethertown (Cumbr.) 40 NX 9807
Nethertown (Island of Stroma) 67 ND 3578
Nether Wallop 9 SU 3036
Nether Whitacre 26 SP 2393
Netherwitton 47 NZ 1090
Nether Worton 18 SP 4230
Nethy Bridge 61 NJ 0020
Netley 9 SU 4508
Netley Marsh 9 SU 3312
Nettlebed 18 SU 7086
Nettlebridge 8 ST 6448
Nettlecombe 7 SY 5195
Nettleden 19 TL 0210
Nettleham 34 TF 0075
Nettlestead 12 TQ 6852
Nettlestead Green 12 TQ 6850
Nettlestone 9 SZ 6290
Nettleton (Lincs.) 39 TA 1000
Nettleton (Wilts.) 17 ST 8178
Neuk, The 62 NO 7397
Nevendon 20 TQ 7390
Nevern 14 SN 0840
New Abbey 45 NX 9665
New Aberdour 62 NJ 8863
New Addington 12 TQ 3863
New Alresford 9 SU 5832
New Alyth 57 NO 2447
New Annesley 34 SK 5153
Newark (Northants.) 27 TF 2100
Newark (Sanday) 63 HY 7242
Newark-on-Trent 34 SK 7953
Newarthill 50 NS 7859
Newbald 39 SE 9136
New Bewick 53 NU 0620
Newbiggin (Cumbr.) 46 NY 5649
Newbiggin (Cumbr.) 41 NY 6228
Newbiggin (Cumbr.) 40 SD 2669
Newbiggin (Durham) 41 NY 9127
Newbiggin (N Yorks.) 41 SD 9591
Newbiggin (N Yorks.) 41 SD 9985
Newbiggin Common 41 NY 9131
Newbiggin-by-the Sea 47 NZ 3187
Newbigging (Strath.) 51 NT 0145
Newbigging (Tays.) 57 NO 2841
Newbigging (Tays.) 57 NO 4237
Newbigging (Tays.) 57 NO 4936
Newbiggin on Lune 41 NY 7005
Newbold (Derby.) 33 SK 3773
Newbold (Leic.) 33 SK 4018
Newbold on Avon 26 SP 4877
Newbold on Stour 26 SP 2446
Newbold Pacey 26 SP 2957
Newbold Verdon 26 SK 4403
New Bolingbroke 35 TF 3058
Newborough (Gwyn.) 30 SH 4265
Newborough (Northants.) 35 TF 2006
Newborough (Staffs.) 33 SK 1325
Newbottle 18 SP 5236
Newbourn 21 TM 2743
Newbridge (Clwyd) 32 SJ 2841
Newbridge (Corn.) 2 SW 4231
Newbridge (Gwent) 16 ST 2197
Newbridge (Hants.) 9 SU 2915
Newbridge (I. of W.) 9 SZ 4187
Newbridge (Lothian) 51 NT 1272
Newbridge-on-Usk 16 ST 3894
Newbridge on Wye 23 SO 0158
New Brighton 32 SJ 3093
New Brinsley 33 SK 4550
Newbrough 47 NY 8767
New Buckenham 29 TM 0890
Newburgh (Fife) 56 NO 2318
Newburgh (Grampn.) 62 NJ 9925
Newburgh (Lancs.) 36 SD 4810
Newburn 47 NZ 1765
Newbury 10 SU 4666
Newby (Cumbr.) 41 NY 5921
Newby (N Yorks.) 42 NZ 5012
Newby (N Yorks.) 41 SD 7269
Newby Bridge 40 SD 3686
Newby East 46 NY 4758
New Byth 62 NJ 8254
Newby West 46 NY 3653
Newby Wiske 42 SE 3687
Newcastle (Gwent) 16 SO 4417
Newcastle (Salop) 23 SO 2482
Newcastle Emlyn 14 SN 3040
Newcastleton 46 NY 4887
Newcastle-under-Lyme 33 SJ 8445
Newcastle upon Tyne 47 NZ 2464
Newchapel (Dyfed) 14 SN 2239
Newchapel (Staffs.) 33 SJ 8654
Newchapel (Surrey) 12 TQ 3642
Newchurch (Dyfed) 15 SN 3724
Newchurch (Gwent) 16 ST 4597
Newchurch (I. of W.) 9 SZ 5585
Newchurch (Kent) 13 TR 0531
Newchurch (Powys) 23 SO 2150
Newchurch in Pendle 37 SD 8239
New Clipstone 34 SK 5863
New Costessey 29 TG 1710
Newcott 5 ST 2309
New Cross 22 SN 6376
New Cumnock 50 NS 6113
New Deer 62 NJ 8846
Newdigate 11 TQ 2042
New Duston 26 SP 7162
New Earswick 38 SE 6155
New Edlington 38 SK 5399
New Ellerby 39 TA 1639
Newell Green 11 SU 8771
New Eltham 12 TQ 4573
New End 25 SP 0560
Newenden 12 TQ 8327
Newent 17 SO 7226
New Farnley 37 SE 2431
New Ferry 32 SJ 3385
Newfield (Durham) 42 NZ 2033
Newfield (Highld.) 65 NH 7877
New Fryston 38 SE 4526
Newgale 14 SM 8422
New Galloway 45 NX 6377
Newgate 29 TG 0443
Newgate Street 20 TL 3005
New Gilston 57 NO 4207
New Gord 63 HP 5706
Newgrounds 17 SO 7204
Newhall (Ches.) 32 SJ 6045
Newhall (Derby.) 33 SK 2821
Newham (Gtr London) 20 TQ 4082
Newham (Northum.) 53 NU 1728
Newham Hall 53 NU 1729
New Hartley 47 NZ 3076
Newhaven 12 TQ 4401
New Hedges 14 SN 1302
New Hey 37 SD 9311
New Holland 39 TA 0724
Newholm 43 NZ 8610
New Houghton (Derby.) 33 SK 4965
New Houghton (Norf.) 28 TF 7827
Newhouse 50 NS 7961
New Houses 41 SD 8073
New Hutton 41 SD 5691
New Hythe 12 TQ 7159
Newick 12 TQ 4121
Newington (Kent) 13 TQ 8665
Newington (Kent) 13 TR 1737
Newington (Oxon.) 18 SU 6196
New Inn (Gwent) 16 SO 4800
New Inn (Gwent) 16 ST 3099
New Inn (N Yorks.) 41 SD 8072
New Invention 23 SO 2976
New Kelso 59 NG 9442
New Lanark 50 NS 8742
Newland (Glos.) 16 SO 5509
Newland (Here. and Worc.) 24 SO 7948
Newland (N Yorks.) 38 SE 6824
Newlandrig 51 NT 3662
Newlands (Grampn.) 61 NJ 3051
Newlands (Northum.) 47 NZ 0955
Newlands of Geise 67 ND 0865
New Lane 36 SD 4212
New Leake 35 TF 4057
New Leeds 62 NJ 9954
New Longton 36 SD 5125
New Luce 44 NX 1764
Newlyn 2 SW 4628
Newlyn East 2 SW 8256
Newmachar 62 NJ 8819
Newmains 50 NS 8256
New Mains of Ury 57 NO 8787
Newmarket (Isle of Lewis) 63 NB 4235
Newmarket (Suff.) 20 TL 6463
New Marton 32 SJ 3334
Newmill (Borders) 52 NT 4510
New Mill (Corn.) 2 SW 4534
Newmill (Grampn.) 61 NJ 4352
New Mill (Herts.) 19 SP 9212
New Mill (W Yorks.) 37 SE 1608
Newmill of Inshewan 57 NO 4260
New Mills (Corn.) 2 SW 8952
New Mills (Derby.) 33 SK 0085
New Mills (Gwent) 16 SO 5107
Newmills (Lothian) 51 NT 1667
New Mills (Powys) 23 SJ 0901
Newmiln 56 NO 1230
Newmilns 50 NS 5337
New Milton 9 SZ 2495
New Moat 14 SN 0625
Newnham (Glos.) 17 SO 6911
Newnham (Hants.) 10 SU 7054
Newnham (Herts.) 19 TL 2437
Newnham (Kent) 13 TQ 9557
Newnham (Northants.) 26 SP 5859
Newnham Bridge 24 SO 6469
New Park 9 SU 2904
New Pitsligo 62 NJ 8855
New Polzeath 2 SW 9379
Newport (Devon) 6 SS 5631
Newport (Dyfed) 14 SN 0639
Newport (Essex) 20 TL 5234
Newport (Glos.) 17 ST 7097
Newport (Gwent) 16 ST 3187
Newport (Highld.) 67 ND 1224
Newport (Humbs.) 39 SE 8530
Newport (I. of W.) 9 SZ 4989
Newport (Norf.) 29 TG 5017
Newport (Salop) 32 SJ 7419
Newport-on-Tay 57 NO 4228
Newport Pagnell 27 SP 8743
Newpound Common 11 TQ 0627
New Prestwick 50 NS 3424
Newquay (Corn.) 2 SW 8161
New Quay (Dyfed) 22 SN 3859
New Rackheath 29 TG 2812
New Radnor 23 SO 2161
New Rent 40 NY 4536
New Romney 13 TR 0624
New Rossington 38 SK 6198
New Sauchie 50 NS 8993
New Scone 56 NO 1325
Newseat (Grampn.) 62 NJ 7033
Newseat (Grampn.) 62 NK 0749
Newsham (Northum.) 47 NZ 3079
Newsham (N Yorks.) 42 NZ 1010
Newsholme (Humbs.) 38 SE 7229
Newsholme (Lancs.) 37 SD 8451
New Silksworth 47 NZ 3853
Newstead (Borders) 52 NT 5634
Newstead (Northum.) 53 NU 1526
Newstead (Notts.) 34 SK 5252
New Stevenston 50 NS 7659
Newthorpe 38 SE 4632
Newtimber Place 11 TQ 2613
New Tolsta 63 NB 5348
Newton (Borders) 52 NT 6020
Newton (Cambs.) 35 TF 4314
Newton (Cambs.) 20 TL 4349
Newton (Ches.) 32 SJ 5059
Newton (Ches.) 32 SJ 5274
Newton (Cumbr.) 40 SD 2371
Newton (Dumf. and Galwy.) 45 NY 1194
Newton (Grampn.) 61 NJ 1663
Newton (Hants.) 9 SU 2322
Newton (Here. and Worc.) 23 SO 3433
Newton (Here. and Worc.) 24 SO 5054
Newton (Highld.) 64 NC 2331
Newton (Highld.) 67 ND 3449
Newton (Highld.) 60 NH 7448
Newton (Highld.) 65 NH 7866
Newton (Lancs.) 41 SD 5974
Newton (Lancs.) 36 SD 6950
Newton (Lincs.) 35 TF 0436
Newton (Lothian) 51 NT 0877
Newton (Mid Glam.) 15 SS 8377
Newton (Norf.) 28 TF 8315
Newton (Northants.) 27 SP 8883
Newton (North Uist) 63 NF 8977
Newton (Northum.) 47 NZ 0364
Newton (Notts.) 34 SK 6841
Newton (Staffs.) 33 SK 0325
Newton (Strath.) 55 NS 0498
Newton (Strath.) 50 NS 6560
Newton (Strath.) 51 NS 9331
Newton (Suff.) 21 TL 9140
Newton (Warw.) 26 SP 5378
Newton (W Glam.) 15 SS 6088
Newton (W Yorks.) 38 SE 4427
Newton Abbot 5 SX 8671
Newton Arlosh 46 NY 1955
Newton Aycliffe 42 NZ 2824
Newton Bewley 42 NZ 4626
Newton Blossomville 27 SP 9251
Newton Bromswold 27 SP 9966
Newton Burgoland 33 SK 3609
Newton by Toft 35 TF 0487
Newton Ferrers 4 SX 5447
Newton Flotman 29 TM 2198
Newtongarry Croft 62 NJ 5735
Newtongrange 51 NT 3364
Newton Harcourt 26 SP 6397
Newtonhill 62 NO 9193
Newton Kyme 38 SE 4644
Newton-le-Willows (Mers.) 32 SJ 5894
Newton-le-Willows (N Yorks.) 42 SE 2189
Newton Longville 19 SP 8431
Newton Mearns 50 NS 5456
Newtonmill 57 NO 6064
Newtonmore 60 NN 7199
Newton Mountain 14 SM 9807
Newton of Balcanquhal 56 NO 1510
Newton-on-Ouse 38 SE 5059
Newton-on-Rawcliffe 43 SE 8090
Newton-on-the-Moor 47 NU 1605
Newton on Trent 34 SK 8374
Newton Poppleford 5 SY 0889
Newton Purcell 18 SP 6230
Newton Regis 33 SK 2707
Newton Reigny 40 NY 4731
Newton St. Cyres 6 SX 8797
Newton St. Faith 29 TG 2117
Newton St. Loe 17 ST 7064
Newton St. Petrock 4 SS 4112
Newton Solney 33 SK 2825
Newton Stacey 10 SU 4040
Newton Stewart 44 NX 4165
Newton Toney 10 SU 2140
Newton Tracey 6 SS 5226
Newton under Roseberry 42 NZ 5613
Newton upon Derwent 38 SE 7149
Newton Valence 9 SU 7232
Newtown (Ches.) 32 SJ 6247
Newtown (Ches.) 33 SJ 9784
Newtown (Corn.) 2 SW 7323
Newtown (Cumbr.) 46 NY 5062
Newtown (Dorset) 8 SZ 0393
Newtown (Hants.) 10 SU 2710
Newtown (Hants.) 9 SU 3023
Newtown (Hants.) 10 SU 4763
Newtown (Hants.) 9 SU 6013
Newtown (Here. and Worc.) 24 SO 6145
Newtown (Highld.) 59 NH 3504
Newtown (I. of M.) 43 SC 3273
Newtown (I. of W.) 9 SZ 4290
New Town (Lothian) 52 NT 4470
Newtown (Northum.) 53 NT 9731
Newtown (Northum.) 47 NU 0300
Newtown (Northum.) 53 NU 0425
Newtown (Powys) 23 SO 1091
Newtown (Salop) 32 SJ 4831
Newtown (Staffs.) 33 SJ 9060
Newtown (Wilts.) 8 ST 9128
Newtown Linford 34 SK 5110
Newtown St. Boswells 52 NT 5731
New Tredegar 16 SO 1403
New Tupton 33 SK 3966
Newtyle 57 NO 2941
New Ulva 48 NR 7080
New Walsoken 35 TF 4709
New Waltham 39 TA 2804
New Wimpole 20 TL 3450
New Winton 52 NT 4271
New Yatt 18 SP 3713
New York (Lincs.) 35 TF 2455
New York (Tyne and Wear) 47 NZ 3270
Neyland 14 SM 9605
Nibley 17 ST 6882
Nicholashayne 7 ST 1015
Nicholaston 15 SS 5188
Nidd 42 SE 3060
Nigg (Grampn.) 62 NJ 9402
Nigg (Highld.) 65 NH 8071
Nightcott 6 SS 8925
Nine Ashes 20 TL 5902
Ninebanks 46 NY 7853
Ninfield 12 TQ 7012
Ningwood 9 SZ 3989
Nisbet 52 NT 6725
Niton 9 SZ 5076
Nitshill 50 NS 5160
Noak Hill 20 TQ 5493
Nobottle 26 SP 6763
Nocton 35 TF 0564
Noke 18 SP 5413
Nolton 14 SM 8718
No Man's Heath (Ches.) 32 SJ 5148
No Man's Heath (Warw.) 33 SK 2709
Nomansland (Devon) 6 SS 8313
Nomansland (Wilts.) 9 SU 2517
Noneley 32 SJ 4727
Nonington 13 TR 2552
Nook 46 NY 4679
Noran Water 57 NO 4860
Norbury (Ches.) 32 SJ 5547
Norbury (Derby.) 33 SK 1242
Norbury (Salop) 24 SO 3693
Norbury (Staffs.) 32 SJ 7823
Nordelph 28 TF 5501
Norden (Dorset) 8 SY 9483
Norden (Gtr Mches) 37 SD 8514
Nordley 24 SO 6998
Norham 53 NT 9047
Norley 32 SJ 5672
Norleywood 9 SZ 3597
Normanby (Humbs.) 39 SE 8716
Normanby (Lincs.) 34 SK 9988
Normanby (N Yorks.) 43 SE 7381
Normanby le Wold 39 TF 1294
Norman Cross 27 TL 1691
Normandy 11 SU 9251
Norman's Green 5 ST 0503
Normanton (Derby.) 33 SK 3433
Normanton (Lincs.) 34 SK 9446
Normanton (Notts.) 34 SK 7054
Normanton (W Yorks.) 37 SE 3822
Normanton le Heath 33 SK 3712
Normanton on Soar 34 SK 5123
Normanton on the Wolds 34 SK 6232
Normanton on Trent 34 SK 7868
Normoss 36 SD 3437
Norrington Common 17 ST 8864
Norris Hill 33 SK 3216
Northallerton 42 SE 3793
Northam (Devon.) 6 SS 4429
Northam (Hants.) 9 SU 4312
Northampton 26 SP 7561
North Aston 18 SP 4728
Northaw 19 TL 2802
North Baddesley 9 SU 3920
North Ballachulish 55 NN 0560
North Barrow 7 ST 6029
North Barsham 28 TF 9135
North Benfleet 20 TQ 7590
North Berwick 52 NT 5485
North Boarhunt 9 SU 6010
Northborough 35 TF 1508
Northbourne 13 TR 3352
North Bovey 5 SX 7483
North Bradley 17 ST 8554
North Brentor 4 SX 4781
North Buckland 6 SS 4740
North Burlingham 29 TG 3610
North Cadbury 8 ST 6327
North Cairn 44 NW 9770
North Carlton 34 SK 9477
North Cave 39 SE 8832
North Cerney 17 SP 0208
Northchapel 11 SU 9529
North Charford 8 SU 1919
North Charlton 53 NU 1622
Northchurch 19 SP 9708
North Cliffe 39 SE 8737
North Clifton 34 SK 8272
North Cotes 39 TA 3400
Northcott 4 SX 3392
North Cove 29 TM 4689
North Cowton 42 NZ 2803
North Crawley 27 SP 9244
North Cray 12 TQ 4972
North Creake 28 TF 8538
North Curry 7 ST 3125
North Dalton 39 SE 9352
North Dawn 63 HY 4803
North Deighton 37 SE 3851
North Duffield 38 SE 6837
North Elkington 35 TF 2890
North Elmham 29 TF 9820
North End (Avon) 16 ST 4167
Northend (Avon) 17 ST 7867
North End (Berks.) 10 SU 4063
Northend (Bucks.) 18 SU 7392
North End (Hants.) 9 SU 6502
Northend (Warw.) 26 SP 3852
North End (W Susx) 11 TQ 1209
North Erradale 64 NG 7481
North Fearns 58 NG 5835
North Ferriby 39 SE 9826
Northfield (Borders) 53 NT 9167
Northfield (Grampn.) 62 NJ 9008
Northfield (W Mids.) 25 SP 0179
Northfleet 12 TQ 6274
North Frodingham 39 TA 1053
North Green 29 TM 2288
North Grimston 39 SE 8467
North Haven (Grampn.) 62 NK 1138
North Hayling 9 SU 7203
North Heasley 6 SS 7333
North Heath 11 TQ 0621
North Hill (Corn.) 4 SX 2776
North Hinksey 18 SP 4806
North Holmwood 11 TQ 1646
North Huish 5 SX 7156
North Hykeham 34 SK 9465
Northiam 12 TQ 8324
Northill (Beds.) 27 TL 1446
Northington 10 SU 5637
North Kelsey 39 TA 0401
North Kessock 60 NH 6548
North Kilvington 42 SE 4285
North Kilworth 26 SP 6183
North Kingennie 57 NO 4736
North Kyme 35 TF 1452
North Lancing 11 TQ 1805
Northlands 35 TF 3453
Northleach 17 SP 1114
North Lee (Bucks.) 18 SP 8309
Northleigh (Devon.) 5 SY 1995
North Leigh (Oxon.) 18 SP 3813
North Leverton with Habblesthorpe 34 SK 7882
Northlew 6 SX 5099
North Littleton 25 SP 0847
North Lopham 29 TM 0383
North Luffenham 27 SK 9303
North Marden 9 SU 8015
North Marston 18 SP 7722
North Middleton 51 NT 3559
North Molton 6 SS 7329
Northmoor 18 SP 4202
Northmoor Green or Moorland 7 ST 3332
North Moreton 18 SU 5689
Northmuir 57 NO 3855
North Muskham 34 SK 7958
North Newbald 39 SE 9136
North Newington 18 SP 4139
North Newnton 17 SU 1257
North Newton 7 ST 2931
North Nibley 17 ST 7396
North Oakley 10 SU 5354
North Ockendon 20 TQ 5984
Northolt 19 TQ 1285
Northop 32 SJ 2468
Northop Hall 32 SJ 2767
North Ormsby 39 TF 2893
Northorpe (Lincs.) 39 SK 8996
Northorpe (Lincs.) 35 TF 0917
North Otterington 42 SE 3589
Northover 7 ST 5223
North Owersby 39 TF 0594
Northowram 37 SE 1127
North Perrott 7 ST 4709
North Petherton 7 ST 2832
North Petherwin 4 SX 2889
North Pickenham 28 TF 8606
North Piddle 25 SO 9654
North Poorton 7 SY 5197
North Queensferry 51 NT 1380
Northrepps 29 TG 2439
North Rigton 37 SE 2749
North Rode 33 SJ 8866
North Runcton 28 TF 6416
North Scale 40 SD 1769
North Scarle 34 SK 8466
North Seaton 47 NZ 2986
North Shian 54 NM 9143
North Shields 47 NZ 3468
North Shoebury 21 TQ 9286
North Shore 36 SD 3037
North Side 27 TL 2799
North Somercotes 39 TF 4296
North Stainley 42 SE 2876
North Stainmore 41 NY 8215
North Stifford 20 TQ 6080
North Stoke (Avon) 17 ST 7068
North Stoke (Oxon.) 18 SU 6186
North Stoke (W Susx) 11 TQ 0211
North Street (Berks.) 10 SU 6372
North Street (Hants.) 9 SU 6433
North Sunderland 53 NU 2131
North Tamerton 4 SX 3197

North Tawton Pen-llyn

North Tawton 6 SS 6601
North Thoresby 39 TF 2998
North Tidworth 10 SU 2248
North Tolsta 63 NB 5347
Northton 63 NF 9889
North Tuddenham 29 TG 0413
North Walsham 29 TG 2730
North Waltham 10 SU 5546
North Warnborough 10 SU 7351
North Water Bridge 57 NO 6566
North Watten 67 ND 2458
Northway 25 SO 9234
North Weald Basset 20 TL 4904
North Whilborough 5 SX 8766
Northwich 32 SJ 6573
Northwick (Avon) 16 ST 5586
North Wick (Avon) 17 ST 5865
North Widcombe 17 ST 5758
North Willingham 35 TF 1688
North Wingfield 33 SK 4064
North Witham 34 SK 9221
Northwold 28 TL 7596
Northwood (Gtr London) 19 TQ 1090
Northwood (I. of W.) 9 SZ 4992
Northwood (Salop) 32 SJ 4633
Northwood Green 17 SO 7216
North Wootton (Dorset) 8 ST 6614
North Wootton (Norf.) 28 TF 6424
North Wootton (Somer.) 7 ST 5641
North Wraxall 17 ST 8174
North Wroughton 17 SU 1581
Norton (Ches.) 32 SJ 5581
Norton (Cleve.) 42 NZ 4421
Norton (Glos.) 17 SO 8624
Norton (Here. and Worc.) 25 SO 8750
Norton (Here. and Worc.) 25 SP 0447
Norton (Herts.) 19 TL 2234
Norton (I. of W.) 9 SZ 3489
Norton (Northants.) 26 SP 6063
Norton (Notts.) 34 SK 5772
Norton (N Yorks.) 38 SE 7971
Norton (N Yorks.) 33 SK 3581
Norton (Powys) 23 SO 3067
Norton (Salop) 24 SJ 5609
Norton (Salop) 24 SJ 7200
Norton (Salop) 24 SO 4581
Norton (Suff.) 21 TL 9565
Norton (S Yorks.) 38 SE 5415
Norton (Wilts.) 17 ST 8884
Norton (W Susx) 11 SU 9306
Norton Bavant 8 ST 9043
Norton Canes 25 SK 0108
Norton Canon 24 SO 3847
Norton Disney 34 SK 8859
Norton Ferris 8 ST 7936
Norton Fitzwarren 7 ST 1925
Norton Green 9 SZ 3388
Norton Hawkfield 17 ST 5964
Norton Heath 20 TL 6004
Norton in Hales 32 SJ 7038
Norton in the Moors 33 SJ 8951
Norton-Juxta-Twycross 33 SK 3207
Norton-le-Clay 38 SE 4071
Norton Lindsey 26 SP 2263
Norton Malreward 17 ST 6064
Norton St. Philip 17 ST 7755
Norton Subcourse 29 TM 4098
Norton sub Hamdon 7 ST 4615
Norwell 34 SK 7661
Norwell Woodhouse 34 SK 7462
Norwich 29 TG 2308
Norwick (Unst) 63 HP 6414
Norwood Green 11 TQ 1378
Norwood Hill 11 TQ 2443
Noseley 26 SP 7398
Noss Mayo 4 SX 5447
Nosterfield 42 SE 2780
Nostie 59 NG 8527
Notgrove 17 SP 1020
Nottage 15 SS 8278
Nottingham 34 SK 5741
Notton (Wilts.) 17 ST 9169
Notton (W Yorks.) 37 SE 3413
Nounsbrough 63 HU 2957
Nounsley 20 TL 7910
Noutard's Green 24 SO 7966
Nox 24 SJ 4010
Nuffield 18 SU 6687
Nunburnholme 39 SE 8548
Nuneaton 26 SP 3592
Nuneham Courtenay 18 SU 5599
Nun Monkton 38 SE 5057
Nunney 8 ST 7345
Nunnington 42 SE 6679
Nunnykirk 47 NZ 0892
Nunthorpe 42 NZ 5313
Nunton (Benbecula) 63 NF 7653
Nunton (Wilts.) 8 SU 1525
Nunwick 47 NY 8774
Nursling 9 SU 3615
Nursted 9 SU 7621
Nutbourne 11 TQ 0718
Nutfield 12 TQ 3150
Nuthall 34 SK 5144
Nuthampstead 20 TL 4134
Nuthurst 11 TQ 1926
Nutley 12 TQ 4427
Nutwell 38 SE 6303
Nybster 67 ND 3663
Nyetimber 11 SZ 8998
Nyewood 9 SU 8021
Nymet Rowland 6 SS 7108
Nymet Tracey 6 SS 7200
Nympsfield 17 SO 8000
Nynehead 7 ST 1422
Nyton 11 SU 9305

Oadby 26 SK 6200
Oad Street 13 TQ 8762
Oakamoor 33 SK 0544
Oakbank 51 NT 0866
Oakdale 16 ST 1898
Oake 7 ST 1525
Oaken 25 SJ 8502
Oakenclough 36 SD 5447
Oakengates 24 SJ 7010
Oakenshaw (Durham) 42 NZ 2036
Oakenshaw (W Yorks.) 37 SE 1727
Oakford (Devon.) 6 SS 9021
Oakford (Dyfed) 22 SN 4557
Oakgrove 33 SJ 9169
Oakham 34 SK 8509
Oakhanger 9 SU 7635
Oakhill 8 ST 6347
Oakington 20 TL 4164
Oaklands 31 SH 8158
Oakle Street 17 SO 7517
Oakley (Beds.) 27 TL 0153
Oakley (Bucks.) 18 SP 6412
Oakley (Fife.) 51 NT 0289
Oakley (Hants.) 10 SU 5650
Oakley (Suff.) 29 TM 1678
Oakley Green 11 SU 9376
Oakleypark 23 SN 9886
Oakridge 17 SO 9103
Oaks 24 SJ 4204
Oaksey 17 ST 9893
Oakthorpe 33 SK 3213
Oakwoodhill 11 TQ 1337
Oakworth 37 SE 0238
Oare (Kent) 13 TR 0062
Oare (Somer.) 6 SS 8047
Oare (Wilts.) 17 SU 1563
Oasby 34 TF 0039
Oathlaw 57 NO 4756
Oban 54 NM 8630
Obney 56 NO 0336
Oborne 8 ST 6518
Occlestone Green 32 SJ 6962
Occold 29 TM 1570
Ochertyre 56 NN 8323
Ochiltree 50 NS 5121
Ochtermuthill 56 NN 8216
Ockbrook 33 SK 4235
Ockham 11 TQ 0756
Ockle 54 NM 5570
Ockley 11 TQ 1640
Ocle Pychard 24 SO 5946
Odcombe 7 ST 5015
Oddingley 25 SO 9159
Oddington (Glos.) 18 SP 2225
Oddington (Oxon.) 18 SP 5514
Odell 27 SP 9658
Odiham 10 SU 7350
Odstock 8 SU 1426
Odstone 33 SK 3907
Offchurch 26 SP 3565
Offenham 25 SP 0546
Offham (E Susx) 12 TQ 4012
Offham (Kent) 12 TQ 6557
Offord Cluny 27 TL 2267
Offord Darcy 27 TL 2266
Offton 21 TM 0649
Offwell 5 SY 1999
Ogbourne Maizey 17 SU 1871
Ogbourne St. Andrew 17 SU 1872
Ogbourne St. George 17 SU 2074
Ogil 57 NO 4561
Ogle 47 NZ 1378
Ogmore 15 SS 8877
Ogmore-by-Sea 15 SS 8674
Ogmore Vale 15 SS 9390
Okeford Fitzpaine 8 ST 8010
Okehampton 6 SX 5895
Okehampton Camp 4 SX 5893
Okraquoy 63 HU 4331
Old 26 SP 7873
Old Aberdeen 62 NJ 9408
Old Alresford 9 SU 5834
Oldberrow 25 SP 1165
Old Bewick 53 NU 0621
Old Bolingbroke 35 TF 3564
Oldborough 6 SS 7706
Old Brampton 33 SK 3371
Old Bridge of Urr 45 NX 7767
Old Buckenham 29 TM 0691
Old Burghclere 10 SU 4657
Oldbury (Salop) 24 SO 7092
Oldbury (Warw.) 26 SP 3194
Oldbury (W Mids.) 25 SO 9889
Oldbury-on-Severn 17 ST 6092
Oldbury on the Hill 17 ST 8089
Old Byland 42 SE 5486
Oldcastle 16 SO 3224
Old Cleeve 7 ST 0342
Oldcoates 34 SK 5888
Old Colwyn 31 SH 8678
Old Dailly 44 NX 2299
Old Dalby 34 SK 6723
Old Deer 62 NJ 9747
Old Felixstowe 21 TM 3135
Oldfield 25 SO 8464
Old Fletton 27 TL 1997
Oldford 8 ST 7849
Old Hall (Highld.) 67 ND 2056
Old Hall, The (Humbs.) 39 TA 2717
Oldham 37 SD 9305
Oldhamstocks 53 NT 7470
Old Heath 21 TM 0122
Oldhurst 27 TL 3077
Old Hutton 41 SD 5688
Old Kea 2 SW 8441
Old Kilpatrick 50 NS 4673
Old Knebworth 19 TL 2320
Oldland 17 ST 6771
Old Leake 35 TF 4050
Old Malton 38 SE 7972
Oldmeldrum 62 NJ 8027
Old Milverton 26 SP 2967
Old Monkland 50 NS 7163
Old Newton 21 TM 0662
Oldpark 24 SJ 6909
Old Philpstoun 51 NT 0577
Old Radnor 23 SO 2559
Old Rayne 62 NJ 6728
Old Romney 13 TR 0325
Old Scone 56 NO 1226
Oldshore 66 NC 2059
Old Sodbury 17 ST 7581
Old Somerby 34 SK 9633
Oldstead 42 SE 5280
Old Town 47 NY 8891
Oldtown of Ord 62 NJ 6259
Old Warden 27 TL 1343
Oldways End 6 SS 8624
Old Weston 27 TL 0977
Oldwhat 62 NJ 8551
Old Windsor 11 SU 9874
Old Wives Lees 13 TR 0755
Olgrinmore 67 ND 0955
Oliver 51 NT 0924
Oliver's Battery 9 SU 4527
Ollaberry 63 HU 3680
Ollach 58 NG 5137
Ollerton (Ches.) 32 SJ 7776
Ollerton (Notts.) 34 SK 6567
Ollerton (Salop) 32 SJ 6425
Olney 27 SP 8851
Olton 25 SP 1282
Olveston 17 ST 6087
Ombersley 25 SO 8463
Ompton 34 SK 6865
Onchan 43 SC 4078
Onecote 33 SK 0555
Ongar Hill 28 TF 5724
Ongar Street 24 SO 3967
Onibury 24 SO 4579
Onich 55 NN 0261
Onllwyn 15 SN 8310
Onneley 32 SJ 7542
Onslow Village 11 SU 9849
Opinan (Highld.) 64 NG 7472
Opinan (Highld.) 64 NG 8796
Orby 35 TF 4967
Orchard 8 ST 8216
Orchard Portman 7 ST 2421
Orcheston 8 SU 0545
Orcop 16 SO 4726
Ord 58 NG 6113
Ordhead 62 NJ 6610
Ordiequish 61 NJ 3357
Ore 12 TQ 8311
Oreham Common 11 TQ 2214
Oreton 24 SO 6580
Orford (Ches.) 32 SJ 6090
Orford (Suff.) 21 TM 4250
Orgreave 25 SK 1415
Orlestone 13 TR 0034
Orleton (Here. and Worc.) 24 SO 4967
Orleton (Here. and Worc.) 24 SO 6967
Orlingbury 27 SP 8572
Ormesby 42 NZ 5317
Ormesby St. Margaret 29 TG 4915
Ormesby St. Michael 29 TG 4814
Ormiscaig 64 NG 8590
Ormiston 52 NT 4169
Ormsaigmore 54 NM 4763
Ormskirk 36 SD 4107
Orosay (Isle of Lewis) 63 NB 3612
Orphir 63 HY 3404
Orpington 12 TQ 4665
Orrell 36 SD 5203
Orrin Resr 60 NH 3850
Orrisdale Head 43 SC 3192
Orroland 45 NX 7746
Orsay 48 NR 1651
Orsett 20 TQ 6481
Orslow 24 SJ 8015
Orston 34 SK 7741
Orton (Cumbr.) 41 NY 6208
Orton (Northants.) 26 SP 8079
Orton Longueville 27 TL 1696
Orton-on-the-Hill 26 SK 3004
Orton Waterville 27 TL 1596
Orval 58 NM 3399
Orwell 20 TL 3650
Osbaldeston 36 SD 6431
Osbaston 26 SK 4204
Osborne 9 SZ 5194
Osborne Bay 9 SZ 5395
Osbournby 35 TF 0638
Oscroft 32 SJ 5066
Osdale 58 NG 3241
Osea Island 21 TL 9106
Ose River 58 NG 3442
Osgathorpe 33 SK 4219
Osgodby (Lincs.) 39 TF 0792
Osgodby (N Yorks.) 38 SE 6433
Osgodby (N Yorks.) 43 TA 0585
Oskaig 58 NG 5438
Oskamull 54 NM 4540
Osmaston 33 SK 1944
Osmington 8 SY 7282
Osmington Mills 8 SY 7381
Osmotherley 42 SE 4597
Osnaburgh or Dairsie 57 NO 4117
Ospringe 13 TQ 9960
Ossett 37 SE 2720
Ossington 34 SK 7564
Ostend 21 TQ 9397
Oswaldkirk 42 SE 6279
Oswaldtwistle 36 SD 7327
Oswestry 32 SJ 2829
Otford 12 TQ 5359
Otham 12 TQ 7954
Othery 7 ST 3831
Otley (Suff.) 21 TM 2055
Otley (W Yorks.) 37 SE 2045
Otterbourne 9 SU 4522
Otterburn (Northum.) 47 NY 8893
Otterburn (N Yorks.) 37 SD 8857
Otterburn Camp 47 NY 8995
Otter Ferry 49 NR 9384
Otterham 4 SX 1690
Ottershaw 11 TQ 0264
Otterswick (Yell) 63 HU 5185
Otterton 5 SY 0785
Ottery St. Mary 5 SY 0995
Ottringham 39 TA 2624
Oughtershaw 41 SD 8781
Oughtibridge 37 SK 3093
Oulston 38 SE 5474
Oulton (Cumbr.) 46 NY 2551
Oulton (Norf.) 29 TG 1328
Oulton (Staffs.) 33 SJ 9035
Oulton (Suff.) 29 TM 5194
Oulton (W Yorks.) 37 SE 3627
Oulton Broad 29 TM 5292
Oulton Street 29 TG 1527
Oundle 27 TL 0488
Ousby 41 NY 6134
Ousdale 67 ND 0620
Ousden 20 TL 7359
Ouseburn 38 SE 4461
Ousefleet 39 SE 8223
Ouston 47 NZ 2554
Outertown 63 HY 2310
Outgate 40 SD 3599
Outhgill 41 NY 7801
Outlane 37 SE 0817
Out Newton 39 TA 3822
Out Rawcliffe 36 SD 4041
Outwell 28 TF 5104
Outwood (Surrey) 12 TQ 3246
Outwood (W Yorks.) 37 SE 3223
Oval, The 17 ST 7363
Ovenden 37 SE 0727
Over (Avon) 17 ST 5882
Over (Cambs.) 27 TL 3770
Overbury 25 SO 9537
Over Haddon 33 SK 2066
Over Kellet 40 SD 5169
Over Kiddington 18 SP 4122
Over Norton 18 SP 3128
Overseal 33 SK 2915
Over Silton 42 SE 4593
Overstone 27 SP 8066
Overstrand 29 TG 2440
Overton (Clwyd) 32 SJ 3741
Overton (Dumf. and Galwy.) 45 NX 9864
Overton (Grampn.) 62 NJ 8714
Overton (Hants.) 10 SU 5149
Overton (Lancs.) 36 SD 4357
Overton (Salop) 24 SO 4972
Overton Green 32 SJ 7960
Overtown 50 NS 8052
Over Wallop 10 SU 2838
Over Whitacre 26 SP 2591
Overy Staithe 28 TF 8444
Oving (Bucks.) 18 SP 7821
Oving (W Susx) 11 SU 9005
Ovingdean 12 TQ 3503
Ovingham 47 NZ 0863
Ovington (Durham) 42 NZ 1314
Ovington (Essex) 20 TL 7742
Ovington (Hants.) 9 SU 5631
Ovington (Norf.) 29 TF 9202
Ovington (Northum.) 47 NZ 0663
Ower 9 SU 3216
Owermoigne 8 SY 7685
Owlswick 18 SP 7906
Owmby 34 SK 9987
Owslebury 9 SU 5123
Owston 34 SK 7708
Owston Ferry 39 SE 8000
Owstwick 39 TA 2732
Owthorpe 34 SK 6733
Oxborough 28 TF 7401
Oxenholme 40 SD 5390
Oxenhope 37 SE 0334
Oxen Park 40 SD 3187
Oxenton 25 SO 9531
Oxenwood 10 SU 3059
Oxford 18 SP 5305
Oxhill (Warw.) 26 SP 3145
Oxley 25 SJ 9002
Oxley's Green 12 TQ 6921
Oxnam 52 NT 7018
Oxshott 11 TQ 1460
Oxspring 37 SE 2601
Oxted 12 TQ 3852
Oxton (Borders) 52 NT 4953
Oxton (Notts.) 34 SK 6351
Oxwich 15 SS 4986
Oxwick 28 TF 9125
Oykel Bridge 66 NC 3800
Oyne 62 NJ 6725

Packington 33 SK 3614
Padanaram 57 NO 4251
Padbury 18 SP 7130
Paddington 19 TQ 2482
Paddlesworth 13 TR 1939
Paddockhaugh 61 NJ 2058
Paddock Wood 12 TQ 6645
Paddolgreen 32 SJ 5032
Padeswood 32 SJ 2761
Padiham 37 SD 7933
Padstow 2 SW 9175
Pagham 11 SZ 8897
Paglesham 21 TQ 9292
Paible (W Isles) 63 NF 7367
Paible (W Isles) 63 NG 0299
Paignton 5 SX 8960
Pailton 26 SP 4781
Painscastle 23 SO 1646
Painswick 17 SO 8609
Paisley 50 NS 4864
Pakefield 29 TM 5390
Pakenham 21 TL 9267
Pale 31 SH 9836
Palestine 10 SU 2640
Paley Street 11 SU 8776
Palgowan 44 NX 3783
Palgrave 29 TM 1178
Palmerstown 16 ST 1369
Palnackie 45 NX 8257
Palnure 44 NX 4563
Palterton 33 SK 4768
Pamber End 10 SU 6158
Pamber Green 10 SU 6059
Pamber Heath 10 SU 6262
Pamphill 8 ST 9900
Pampisford 20 TL 4948
Panbride 57 NO 5635
Pancrasweek 4 SS 2905
Pandy (Clwyd) 32 SJ 1935
Pandy (Gwent) 16 SO 3322
Pandy (Powys) 22 SH 9004
Pandy Tudur 31 SH 8564
Panfield 20 TL 7325
Pangbourne 10 SU 6376
Pannal 37 SE 3051
Pant 32 SJ 2722
Pant-glas (Gwyn.) 30 SH 4747
Pant Glas (Powys) 22 SN 7798
Pantgwyn 14 SN 2446
Pant Mawr 22 SN 8482
Panton 35 TF 1778
Pant-pastynog 31 SJ 0461
Pantperthog 22 SH 7504
Pant-y-dwr 23 SN 9875
Pant-y-ffridd 23 SJ 1502
Pantyffynnon 15 SN 6210
Panxworth 29 TG 3413
Papcastle 40 NY 1131
Papple 52 NT 5972
Papplewick 34 SK 5451
Papworth Everard 27 TL 2862
Papworth St. Agnes 27 TL 2664
Par 4 SX 0653
Parbold 36 SD 4911
Parbrook 7 ST 5736
Parc 30 SH 4486
Parcllyn 14 SN 2451
Pardshaw 40 NY 0924
Parham 21 TM 3060
Park (Grampn.) 62 NO 7798
Park (Strath.) 54 NM 9340
Park Corner 18 SU 6988
Parkend (Glos.) 17 SO 6108
Park End (Northum.) 47 NY 8775
Parkeston 21 TM 2332
Parkgate (Ches.) 32 SJ 2778
Parkgate (Ches.) 32 SJ 7874
Parkgate (Dumf. and Galwy.) 45 NY 0288
Park Gate (Hants.) 9 SU 5108
Parkgate (Surrey) 11 TQ 2043
Parkham 4 SS 3821
Parkham Ash 4 SS 3620
Parkhouse 16 SO 5002
Parkhurst 9 SZ 4991
Parkneuk 57 NO 7976
Parkstone 8 SZ 0491
Parley Common 8 SZ 0999
Parley Cross 8 SZ 0898
Parracombe 6 SS 6744
Parrog 14 SN 0439
Parson Drove 35 TF 3708
Partick 50 NS 5567
Partington 32 SJ 7191
Partney 35 TF 4168
Parton (Cumbr.) 40 NX 9720
Parton (Dumf. and Galwy.) 45 NX 6970
Parton (Glos.) 17 SO 8721
Partridge Green 11 TQ 1919
Parwich 33 SK 1854
Passenham 18 SP 7839
Paston 29 TG 3235
Patcham 12 TQ 3009
Patching 11 TQ 0806
Patchole 6 SS 6142
Patchway 17 ST 6082
Pateley Bridge 42 SE 1565
Pathhead (Fife.) 51 NT 2892
Pathhead (Grampn.) 57 NO 7363
Pathhead (Lothian) 51 NT 3964
Pathhead (Strath.) 50 NS 6114
Path of Condie 56 NO 0711
Patmore Heath 20 TL 4526
Patna 50 NS 4110
Patney 17 SU 0758
Patrick 43 SC 2482
Patrick Brompton 42 SE 2290
Patrington 39 TA 3122
Patrixbourne 13 TR 1855
Patterdale 40 NY 3915
Pattingham 25 SO 8299
Pattishall 26 SP 6654
Paul 2 SW 4627
Paulerspury 26 SP 7145
Paull 39 TA 1626
Paulton 17 ST 6456
Pauperhaugh 47 NZ 1099
Pavenham 27 SP 9955
Pawlett 7 ST 2942
Pawston 53 NT 8532
Paxford 25 SP 1837
Paxhill Park 12 TQ 3626
Paxton 53 NT 9352
Payhembury 5 ST 0801
Paythorne 37 SD 8251
Peacehaven 12 TQ 4101
Peachley 24 SO 8057
Peak Dale 33 SK 0976
Peak Forest 33 SK 1179
Peakirk 35 TF 1606
Pearsie 57 NO 3659
Peasedown St. John 17 ST 7057
Peasemore 10 SU 4576
Peasenhall 29 TM 3569
Peaslake 11 TQ 0844
Peasmarsh 13 TQ 8822
Peaston Bank 52 NT 4466
Peathill (Grampn.) 62 NJ 9365
Peat Hill (Tays.) 57 NO 5067
Peat Inn 57 NO 4509
Peatling Magna 26 SP 5992
Peatling Parva 26 SP 5889
Peaton 24 SO 5385
Pebmarsh 20 TL 8533
Pebworth 25 SP 1347
Pecket Well 37 SD 9929
Peckforton 32 SJ 5356
Peckleton 26 SK 4701
Pedmore 25 SO 9182
Pedwell 7 ST 4236
Peebles 51 NT 2540
Peel 43 SC 2484
Pegswood 47 NZ 2287
Pegwell Bay 13 TR 3563
Peinchorran 58 NG 5233
Peinlich 58 NG 4158
Pelaw 47 NZ 2962
Peldon 21 TL 9816
Pelsall 25 SK 0103
Pelton 47 NZ 2553
Pelutho 45 NY 1249
Pelynt 4 SX 2055
Pembrey 15 SN 4201
Pembridge 24 SO 3858
Pembroke 14 SM 9901
Pembroke Dock 14 SM 9603
Pembury 12 TQ 6240
Penallt 16 SO 5210
Penally 14 SS 1199
Penant 22 SN 5163
Penare 4 SW 9940
Penarth 16 ST 1871
Pen-bont Rhydybeddau 22 SN 6783
Penbryn 14 SN 2952
Pencader 15 SN 4436
Pencaitland 52 NT 4468
Pencarreg 15 SN 5345
Pencelli 16 SO 0925
Penclawdd 15 SS 5495
Pencoed (Mid Glam.) 15 SS 9581
Pen Coed (Powys.) 23 SH 9808
Pencombe 24 SO 5952
Pencoyd 16 SO 5126
Pencraig (Here. and Worc.) 17 SO 5621
Pencraig (Powys) 31 SJ 0427
Pendeen 2 SW 3834
Penderyn 15 SN 9408
Pendine 14 SN 2308
Pendlebury 37 SD 7802
Pendleton 37 SD 7539
Pendock 24 SO 7832
Pendoggett 4 SX 0279
Pendoylan 16 ST 0576
Penegoes 22 SH 7701
Pen-ffordd 14 SN 0722
Pengam 16 ST 1797
Penge 12 TQ 3570
Penhalvean 2 SW 7037
Penhow 16 ST 4290
Penhurst 12 TQ 6916
Peniarth 22 SH 6105
Penicuik 51 NT 2359
Penifiler 58 NG 4841
Peninver 48 NR 7524
Pen-isa'r-cwm 31 SJ 0018
Penisar Waun 30 SH 5564
Penistone 37 SE 2402
Penjerrick 2 SW 7730
Penketh 32 SJ 5687
Penkill 44 NX 2398
Penkridge 25 SJ 9214
Penley 32 SJ 4039
Penllergaer 15 SS 6199
Pen-llyn (Gwyn.) 30 SH 3482

Penllyn Pwllmeyric

Penllyn (S Glam.)	15	SS 9776
Penmachno	31	SH 7950
Penmaen	15	SS 5288
Penmaenmawr	30	SH 7176
Penmaenpool	30	SH 6918
Penmark	16	ST 0568
Penmon	30	SH 6381
Penmorfa	30	SH 5440
Penmynydd	30	SH 5174
Penn	19	SU 9193
Pennal	22	SH 6900
Pennan	62	NJ 8465
Pennant	22	SN 8897
Pennant-Melangell	31	SJ 0226
Pennard	15	SS 5688
Pennerley	24	SO 3599
Pennington	40	SD 2577
Penn Street	19	SU 9296
Penny Bridge	40	SD 3082
Pennycross	54	NM 5025
Pennygown	54	NM 6042
Pennymoor	6	SS 8611
Penparc	14	SN 2148
Penparcau	22	SN 5980
Penperlleni	16	SO 3204
Penpillick	4	SX 0756
Penpol	2	SW 8139
Penpoll	4	SX 1454
Penpont (Dumf. and Galwy.)	45	NX 8494
Penpont (Powys)	15	SN 9728
Penrherber	14	SN 2839
Penrhiwceiber	16	ST 0597
Penrhiwllan	15	SN 3742
Penrhiwpal	14	SN 3445
Penrhos (Gwent)	16	SO 4111
Penrhos (Gwyn.)	30	SH 2781
Penrhos (Gwyn.)	30	SH 3433
Penrhos (Powys)	15	SN 8011
Penrhyn Bay	31	SH 8281
Penrhyncoch	22	SN 6484
Penrhyndeudraeth	30	SH 6139
Penrhyn-side	31	SH 8181
Penrice	15	SS 4988
Penrith	40	NY 5130
Penrose	2	SW 8770
Penruddock	40	NY 4227
Penryn	2	SW 7834
Pensarn (Clwyd)	31	SH 9478
Pen-Sarn (Gwyn.)	30	SH 4344
Pen-Sarn (Gwyn.)	30	SH 5728
Pensax	24	SO 7269
Pensby	32	SJ 2683
Penselwood	8	ST 7531
Pensford	17	ST 6163
Penshaw	47	NZ 3253
Penshurst	12	TQ 5243
Pensilva	4	SX 2969
Pentewan	4	SX 0147
Pentir	30	SH 5767
Pentire	2	SW 7961
Pentney	28	TF 7213
Penton Mewsey	10	SU 3247
Pentraeth	30	SH 5278
Pentre (Clwyd)	31	SJ 0862
Pentre (Clwyd)	31	SJ 1334
Pentre (Clwyd)	32	SJ 2840
Pentre (Powys)	23	SO 0686
Pentre (Powys)	23	SO 2466
Pentre (Salop)	24	SJ 3617
Pentrebach (Mid Glam.)	16	SO 0604
Pentre-bach (Powys)	15	SN 9033
Pentrebeirdd	23	SJ 1913
Pentre Berw	30	SH 4772
Pentre-celyn (Clwyd)	31	SJ 1453
Pentre-cwrt	15	SN 3938
Pentre-Dolau-Honddu	15	SN 9943
Pentre-dwfr	32	SJ 1946
Pentre-dwr	15	SS 6996
Pentrefelin	30	SH 5239
Pentrefoelas	31	SH 8751
Pentregat	14	SN 3551
Pentre-Gwenlais	15	SN 6116
Pentre Halkyn	32	SJ 2072
Pentre-poeth	16	ST 2686
Pentre'r-felin	15	SN 9130
Pentre-tafarn-y-fedw	31	SH 8162
Pentre ty gwyn	15	SN 8135
Pentrich	33	SK 3852
Pentridge	8	SU 0317
Pen-twyn	16	SO 5209
Pentyrch	16	ST 1082
Penuwch	22	SN 5962
Penwithick	4	SX 0256
Penybanc	15	SN 6124
Pen-y-bont (Clwyd)	32	SJ 2123
Penybont (Powys)	23	SO 1164
Penybontfawr	31	SJ 0824
Pen-y-bryn	30	SH 6919
Pen-y-bwlch	22	SN 7763
Penycae (Clwyd)	32	SJ 2745
Pen-y-cae (Powys)	15	SN 8413
Pen-y-cae-mawr	16	ST 4195
Pen-y-cefn	31	SJ 1175
Pen-y-clawdd	16	SO 4508
Pen-y-coedcae	16	ST 0587
Penyffordd	32	SJ 3061
Pen-y-garn	15	SN 5731
Penygarnedd	31	SJ 1023
Penygraig	15	SS 9991
Penygroes (Dyfed)	15	SN 5813
Penygroes (Gwyn.)	30	SH 4753
Penysarn	30	SH 4690
Penywaun	15	SN 9704
Penzance	2	SW 4730
Peopleton	25	SO 9350
Peover Heath	32	SJ 7973
Peper Harow	11	SU 9344
Peplow	32	SJ 6324
Percie	62	NO 5991
Percyhorner	62	NJ 9565
Perivale	19	TQ 1682
Perranarworthal	2	SW 7738
Perranporth	2	SW 7554
Perranuthnoe	2	SW 5329
Perranzabuloe	2	SW 7752
Perry	27	TL 1466
Perry Barr	25	SP 0791
Perry Green	20	TL 4317
Pershore	25	SO 9446
Pert	57	NO 6565
Pertenhall	27	TL 0865
Perth	56	NO 1123
Perthy	32	SJ 3633
Perton	25	SO 8598
Peterborough	27	TL 1999
Peterchurch	23	SO 3438
Peterculter	62	NJ 8400
Peterhead	62	NK 1346
Peterlee	42	NZ 4440
Petersfield	9	SU 7423
Peter's Green	19	TL 1419
Peters Marland	6	SS 4713
Peterstone Wentlooge	16	ST 2680
Peterston-super-Ely	16	ST 0876
Peterstow	17	SO 5624
Peter Tavy	4	SX 5177
Petham	13	TR 1251
Petrockstow	6	SS 5109
Pett	13	TQ 8714
Pettaugh	21	TM 1659
Pettinain	51	NS 9542
Pettistree	21	TM 2954
Petton (Devon.)	7	ST 0024
Petton (Salop)	32	SJ 4326
Petty	62	NJ 7636
Pettycur	51	NT 2686
Pettymuk	62	NJ 9024
Petworth	11	SU 9721
Pevensey	12	TQ 6405
Philham	4	SS 2522
Philiphaugh	52	NT 4427
Phillack	2	SW 5539
Philleigh	2	SW 8639
Philpstoun	51	NT 0577
Phoenix Green	10	SU 7655
Pica	40	NY 0222
Piccotts End	19	TL 0509
Pickering	43	SE 7983
Picket Piece	10	SU 3947
Picket Post	8	SU 1905
Pickhill	42	SE 3483
Picklescott	24	SO 4399
Pickmere	32	SJ 6876
Pickwell (Devon.)	6	SS 4540
Pickwell (Leic.)	34	SK 7811
Pickworth (Leic.)	34	SK 9913
Pickworth (Lincs.)	35	TF 0433
Picton (N Yorks.)	42	NZ 4107
Picton Castle (ant.)	14	SN 0113
Piddinghoe	12	TQ 4303
Piddington (Northants.)	26	SP 8054
Piddington (Oxon.)	18	SP 6317
Piddlehinton	8	SY 7197
Piddletrenthide	8	SY 7099
Pidley	27	TL 3377
Piercebridge	42	NZ 2115
Pierowall	63	HY 4348
Pigdon	47	NZ 1588
Pikehall	33	SK 1959
Pilgrims Hatch	20	TQ 5895
Pilham	39	SK 8693
Pill	16	ST 5275
Pillaton	4	SX 3664
Pillerton Hersey	26	SP 2948
Pillerton Priors	26	SP 2947
Pilleth	23	SO 2568
Pilley	37	SE 3300
Pilling	36	SD 4048
Pilling Lane	36	SD 3749
Pilning	16	ST 5585
Pilsbury	33	SK 1163
Pilsdon	7	SY 4199
Pilsley (Derby.)	33	SK 2471
Pilsley (Derby.)	33	SK 4262
Pilton (Leic.)	27	SK 9102
Pilton (Northants.)	27	TL 0284
Pilton (Somer.)	7	ST 5940
Pimperne	8	ST 9009
Pinchbeck	35	TF 2425
Pinchbeck West	35	TF 2024
Pinfold	36	SD 3811
Pinhoe	5	SX 9694
Pinmore	44	NX 2090
Pinner	19	TQ 1289
Pinvin	25	SO 9548
Pinwherry	44	NX 1987
Pinxton	33	SK 4555
Pipe and Lyde	24	SO 5044
Pipe Gate	32	SJ 7340
Piperhill	60	NH 8650
Pipewell	26	SP 8385
Pippacott	6	SS 5237
Pirbright	11	SU 9455
Pirnmill	49	NR 8744
Pirton (Here. and Worc.)	25	SO 8847
Pirton (Herts.)	19	TL 1431
Pishill	18	SU 7289
Pistyll	30	SH 3242
Pitagowan	56	NN 8266
Pitblae	62	NJ 9865
Pitcairngreen	56	NO 0627
Pitcaple	62	NJ 7225
Pitcarity	57	NO 3265
Pitchcombe	17	SO 8408
Pitchcott	18	SP 7720
Pitchford	24	SJ 5303
Pitch Green	18	SP 7703
Pitch Place	11	SU 9752
Pitcombe	8	ST 6732
Pitcox	52	NT 6475
Pitcur	57	NO 2536
Pitfichie	62	NJ 6716
Pitforthie	57	NO 8079
Pitfour Castle	56	NO 1921
Pitgrudy	65	NH 7990
Pitkennedy	57	NO 5454
Pitlessie	57	NO 3309
Pitlochry	56	NN 9458
Pitmedden	62	NJ 8927
Pitminster	7	ST 2119
Pitmuies	57	NO 5649
Pitmunie	62	NJ 6615
Pitney	7	ST 4428
Pitroddie	56	NO 2224
Pitscottie	57	NO 4113
Pitsea	20	TQ 7488
Pitsford	26	SP 7568
Pitstone	19	SP 9415
Pitt Down	9	SU 4128
Pittendreich	61	NJ 1961
Pittentrail	66	NC 7202
Pittenweem	57	NO 5402
Pittington	47	NZ 3245
Pitton	9	SU 2131
Pixey Green	29	TM 2475
Place Newton	39	SE 8872
Plains	50	NS 7966
Plaish	24	SO 5296
Plaistow	11	TQ 0030
Plaitford	9	SU 2719
Plas Gogerddan	22	SN 6283
Plas Gwynant	22	SH 6250
Plashetts	46	NY 6690
Plas Isaf	31	SJ 0442
Plas Llwyd	31	SH 9979
Plas Llwyngwern	22	SH 7504
Plas Llysyn	23	SN 9597
Plas Nantyr	31	SJ 1537
Plastow Green	10	SU 5361
Plas-yn-Cefn	31	SJ 0171
Platt	12	TQ 6257
Plawsworth	47	NZ 2647
Plaxtol	12	TQ 6053
Playden	13	TQ 9121
Playford	21	TM 2148
Play Hatch	10	SU 7376
Playing Place	2	SW 8141
Plealey	24	SJ 4206
Plean	50	NS 8386
Pleasington	36	SD 6425
Pleasley	34	SK 5064
Plenmeller	46	NY 7162
Pleshey	20	TL 6614
Plockton	59	NG 8033
Ploughfield	24	SO 3841
Plowden	24	SO 3888
Ploxgreen	24	SJ 3604
Pluckley	13	TQ 9045
Plumbland	40	NY 1438
Plumley	32	SJ 7275
Plumpton (E Susx)	12	TQ 3613
Plumpton (Lancs.)	36	SD 3732
Plumpton Green	12	TQ 3616
Plumpton Head	40	NY 5035
Plumpton Wall	40	NY 4937
Plumstead	29	TG 1335
Plumtree	34	SK 6133
Plungar	34	SK 7633
Pluscarden	61	NJ 1455
Plush	8	ST 7102
Plwmp	15	SN 3652
Plymouth	4	SX 4755
Plympton	4	SX 5356
Plymstock	4	SX 5152
Plymtree	5	ST 0502
Pockley	42	SE 6385
Pocklington	39	SE 8048
Pode Hole	35	TF 2122
Podimore	7	ST 5424
Podington	27	SP 9462
Podmore	32	SJ 7835
Pointon	35	TF 1131
Pokesdown	8	SZ 1292
Polapit Tamar	4	SX 3389
Polbae	44	NX 2873
Polbain	64	NB 9910
Polbathic	4	SX 3456
Polbeth	51	NT 0364
Polchar	60	NH 8909
Polebrook	27	TL 0687
Polegate	12	TQ 5805
Polesworth	26	SK 2602
Polglass	64	NC 0307
Polgooth	4	SW 9950
Poling	11	TQ 0405
Polkerris	4	SX 0952
Pollachar	63	NF 7414
Pollington	38	SE 6119
Polloch	54	NM 7968
Pollokshaws	50	NS 5560
Pollokshields	50	NS 5663
Polmassick	2	SW 9745
Polnessan	50	NS 4111
Polperro	4	SX 2051
Polruan	4	SX 1250
Polsham	7	ST 5142
Polstead	21	TL 9938
Poltimore	5	SX 9696
Polton	51	NT 2964
Polwarth	53	NT 7450
Polyphant	4	SX 2682
Polzeath	2	SW 9378
Pondersbridge	27	TL 2691
Ponders End	20	TQ 3695
Ponsanooth	2	SW 7336
Ponsworthy	5	SX 7073
Pontamman	15	SN 6312
Pontantwn	15	SN 4412
Pontardawe	15	SN 7204
Pontardulais	15	SN 5903
Pontarsais	15	SN 4428
Pont Cyfyng	30	SH 7357
Pontefract	38	SE 4522
Ponteland	47	NZ 1672
Ponterwyd	22	SN 7481
Pontesbury	24	SJ 3905
Pontfadog	32	SJ 2338
Pontfaen (Dyfed)	14	SN 0234
Pont-faen (Powys)	15	SN 9934
Ponthenry	15	SN 4709
Ponthirwaun	14	SN 2645
Pontllanfraith	16	ST 1895
Pontlliw	15	SN 6101
Pont-Llogel	23	SJ 0315
Pontlottyn	16	SO 1206
Pontlyfni	30	SH 4352
Pont Nedd Fechan	15	SN 9007
Pontnewydd	16	ST 2896
Pont Pen-y-benglog	30	SH 6460
Pontrhydfendigaid	22	SN 7366
Pont Rhyd-y-cyff	15	SS 8788
Pont-rhyd-y-fen	15	SS 7994
Pontrhydygroes	22	SN 7472
Pontrilas	16	SO 3927
Pontrobert	23	SJ 1112
Pont-rug	30	SH 5163
Ponts Green	12	TQ 6717
Pontshaen	15	SN 4346
Pontshill	17	SO 6321
Pontsticill	16	SO 0511
Pontyates	15	SN 4708
Pontyberem	15	SN 4911
Pontybodkin	32	SJ 2759
Pontyclun	16	ST 0381
Pontycymer	15	SS 9091
Pont-y-pant	30	SH 7554
Pontypool	16	SO 2701
Pontypridd	16	ST 0690
Pontywaun	16	ST 2293
Pooksgreen	9	SU 3710
Pool (W Yorks.)	37	SE 2445
Poole (Dorset)	8	SZ 0190
Poole Green	32	SJ 6355
Poole Keynes	17	ST 9995
Poolewe	64	NG 8580
Pooley Bridge	40	NY 4724
Poolhill (Glos.)	17	SO 7329
Pool of Muckhart	56	NO 0001
Pool Quay	23	SJ 2512
Pool Street	20	TL 7637
Popeswood	11	SU 8469
Popham	10	SU 5543
Poplar	20	TQ 3781
Porchfield	9	SZ 4491
Porin	59	NH 3155
Porkellis	2	SW 6933
Porlock	6	SS 8846
Portachoillan	48	NR 7557
Port Ann	49	NR 9086
Port Appin	54	NM 9045
Port Askaig	48	NR 4369
Portavadie	49	NR 9369
Port Bannatyne	49	NS 0867
Portbury	16	ST 4975
Port Carlisle	46	NY 2461
Port Charlotte	48	NR 2558
Portchester	9	SU 6105
Port Corbert	48	NR 6528
Port Cornaa	43	SC 4787
Port Dinorwic	30	SH 5267
Port Doir' a'Chrorain	48	NR 5875
Port Driseach	49	NR 9973
Port Ellen	48	NR 3645
Port Elphinstone	62	NJ 7719
Portencross	49	NS 1748
Port Erin	43	SC 1969
Portesham	7	SY 6085
Port e Vullen	43	SC 4793
Port-Eynon	15	SS 4685
Portfield Gate	14	SM 9115
Portgate	4	SX 4185
Port Gaverne	4	SX 0080
Port Glasgow	50	NS 3274
Portgordon	61	NJ 3964
Portgower	67	ND 0013
Porth	15	ST 0291
Porthallow	2	SW 7923
Porthcawl	15	SS 8176
Porthcurno	2	SW 3822
Port Henderson	64	NG 7573
Porthgain	14	SM 8132
Porthkerry	16	ST 0866
Porthleven	2	SW 6225
Porthmadog	30	SH 5638
Porth Mellin	2	SW 6618
Porthmeor	2	SW 4337
Porth Navas	2	SW 7428
Portholland	2	SW 9541
Porthoustock	2	SW 8021
Porthpean	4	SX 0350
Porthtowan	2	SW 6847
Porthyrhyd (Dyfed)	15	SN 5115
Porthyrhyd (Dyfed)	15	SN 7137
Portincaple	49	NS 2393
Portington	38	SE 7830
Portinnisherrich	55	NM 9711
Port Isaac	4	SW 9980
Portishead	16	ST 4676
Portknockie	61	NJ 4868
Portland Harbour	8	SY 6876
Portlethen	62	NO 9396
Portloe	2	SW 9339
Port Logan	44	NX 0940
Portmahomack	65	NH 9184
Portmeirion	30	SH 5937
Portmore (Hants)	9	SZ 3397
Port Mulgrave	43	NZ 7917
Portnacroish	54	NM 9247
Portnaguiran	63	NB 5537
Portnahaven	48	NR 1652
Portnalong	58	NG 3434
Portnancon	66	NC 4260
Portobello (Dumf. and Galwy.)	44	NW 9666
Portobello (Lothian)	51	NT 3073
Port of Menteith	56	NN 5801
Port of Ness	63	NB 5363
Porton	8	SU 1836
Portpatrick	44	NX 0054
Port Quin	2	SW 9780
Port Ramsay	54	NM 8845
Portreath	2	SW 6545
Portree	58	NG 4843
Portrye	49	NS 1758
Port St. Mary	43	SC 2067
Portscatho	2	SW 8735
Portsea	9	SU 6300
Portskerra	67	NC 8765
Portskewett	16	ST 4988
Portslade	11	TQ 2506
Portslade-by-Sea	11	TQ 2604
Portsmouth	9	SU 6501
Portsmouth City Airport	9	SU 6603
Portsoy	62	NJ 5865
Port Sunlight	32	SJ 3483
Portswood	9	SU 4314
Port Talbot	15	SS 7690
Portuairk	54	NM 4468
Port Vasgo	66	NC 5865
Portvoller	63	NB 5636
Portway (Warw.)	25	SP 0872
Port Wemyss	48	NR 1751
Port William	44	NX 3343
Portwrinkle	4	SX 3553
Poslingford	20	TL 7648
Possingworth Park	12	TQ 5420
Postbridge	5	SX 6579
Postcombe	18	SU 7099
Postling	13	TR 1439
Postwick	29	TG 2907
Potarch	62	NO 6097
Potsgrove	19	SP 9529
Potten End	19	TL 0108
Potterhanworth	35	TF 0566
Potter Heigham	29	TG 4119
Potterne	17	ST 9958
Potterne Wick	17	ST 9957
Potters Bar	19	TL 2501
Potter's Cross	25	SO 8484
Potterspury	26	SP 7543
Potter Street	20	TL 4608
Potto	42	NZ 4703
Potton	27	TL 2249
Potton Island	21	TQ 9591
Pott Row	28	TF 7021
Pott Shrigley	33	SJ 9479
Poughill (Corn.)	4	SS 2207
Poughill (Devon.)	6	SS 8508
Poulshot	17	ST 9659
Poulton	17	SP 1001
Poulton-le-Fylde	36	SD 3439
Pound Bank	24	SO 7373
Pound Hill	11	TQ 2937
Poundon	18	SP 6425
Poundsgate	5	SX 7072
Poundstock	4	SX 2099
Powburn (Northum.)	53	NU 0616
Powderham	5	SX 9784
Powerstock	7	SY 5196
Powfoot	45	NY 1465
Powick	25	SO 8351
Powmill	56	NT 0197
Poxwell	8	SY 7484
Poyle	11	TQ 0376
Poynings	11	TQ 2612
Poyntington	8	ST 6419
Poynton	33	SJ 9283
Poynton Green	32	SJ 5618
Poys Street	29	TM 3570
Poystreet Green	21	TL 9858
Praa Sands	2	SW 5828
Pratt's Bottom	12	TQ 4762
Praze-an-Beeble	2	SW 6336
Predannack Wollas	2	SW 6616
Prees	32	SJ 5533
Preesall	36	SD 3646
Prees Green	32	SJ 5631
Preesgweene	32	SJ 3135
Prees Higher Heath	32	SJ 5636
Prendwick	53	NU 0012
Pren-gwyn	15	SN 4244
Prenteg	30	SH 5841
Prenton	32	SJ 3184
Prescot (Mers.)	32	SJ 4692
Prescott (Salop)	32	SJ 4221
Pressen	53	NT 8335
Prestatyn	31	SJ 0682
Prestbury (Ches.)	33	SJ 8976
Prestbury (Glos.)	17	SO 9724
Presteigne	23	SO 3164
Presthope	24	SO 5897
Prestleigh	8	ST 6340
Preston (Borders)	53	NT 7957
Preston (Devon.)	5	SX 8574
Preston (Dorset)	8	SY 7082
Preston (E Susx)	12	TQ 3107
Preston (Glos.)	24	SO 6734
Preston (Glos.)	17	SP 0400
Preston (Herts.)	19	TL 1724
Preston (Humbs.)	39	TA 1830
Preston (Kent)	13	TR 0060
Preston (Kent)	13	TR 2561
Preston (Lancs.)	36	SD 5329
Preston (Leic.)	27	SK 8602
Preston (Lothian)	52	NT 5977
Preston (Northum.)	53	NU 1825
Preston (Suff.)	21	TL 9450
Preston (Wilts.)	17	SU 0377
Preston Bagot	25	SP 1766
Preston Bissett	18	SP 6530
Preston Brockhurst	32	SJ 5324
Preston Brook	32	SJ 5680
Preston Candover	10	SU 6041
Preston Capes	26	SP 5754
Preston Gubbals	32	SJ 4819
Preston on Stour	25	SP 2049
Preston on Wye	24	SO 3842
Prestonpans	51	NT 3874
Preston-under-Scar	42	SE 0791
Preston upon the Weald Moors	24	SJ 6815
Preston Wynne	24	SO 5646
Prestwich	37	SD 8103
Prestwick (Northum.)	47	NZ 1872
Prestwick (Strath.)	50	NS 3525
Prestwood	19	SP 8700
Price Town	15	SS 9392
Prickwillow	28	TL 5982
Priddy	7	ST 5250
Priest Hutton	40	SD 5273
Priestweston	23	SO 2997
Primethorpe	26	SP 5293
Primrose Green	29	TG 0616
Primrose Hill (Cambs.)	27	TL 3889
Primrosehill (Herts.)	19	TL 0803
Princes Risborough	18	SP 8003
Princethorpe	26	SP 3970
Princetown	4	SX 5873
Prior Muir	57	NO 5213
Priors Hardwick	26	SP 4756
Priors Marston	26	SP 4857
Priory, The	9	SZ 6390
Priory Wood	23	SO 2545
Priston	17	ST 6960
Prittlewell	21	TQ 8787
Privett	9	SU 6726
Probus	2	SW 8947
Prudhoe	47	NZ 0962
Puckeridge	20	TL 3823
Puckington	7	ST 3718
Pucklechurch	17	ST 6976
Puddington (Ches.)	32	SJ 3273
Puddington (Devon)	6	SS 8310
Puddledock	29	TM 0592
Puddletown	8	SY 7594
Pudleston	24	SO 5659
Pudsey	37	SE 2232
Pulborough	11	TQ 0418
Puleston	32	SJ 7322
Pulford	32	SJ 3758
Pulham	8	ST 7008
Pulham Market	29	TM 1986
Pulham St. Mary	29	TM 2185
Pulloxhill	19	TL 0634
Pumpherston	51	NT 0669
Pumsaint	15	SN 6540
Puncheston	14	SN 0029
Puncknowle	7	SY 5388
Punnett's Town	12	TQ 6220
Purbrook	9	SU 6707
Purfleet	12	TQ 5578
Puriton	7	ST 3241
Purleigh	20	TL 8301
Purley (Berks.)	10	SU 6676
Purley (Gtr London)	12	TQ 3161
Purlogue	23	SO 2877
Purls Bridge	27	TL 4787
Purse Caundle	8	ST 6917
Purslow	24	SO 3680
Purston Jaglin	38	SE 4319
Purton (Glos.)	17	SO 6605
Purton (Glos.)	17	SO 6904
Purton (Wilts.)	17	SU 0887
Purton Stoke	17	SU 0890
Pury End	26	SP 7045
Pusey	18	SU 3596
Putley	24	SO 6437
Putney	11	TQ 2274
Puttenham (Herts.)	19	SP 8814
Puttenham (Surrey)	11	SU 9347
Puxton	16	ST 4063
Pwll	15	SN 4801
Pwllcrochan	14	SM 9202
Pwlldefaid	30	SH 1526
Pwllheli	30	SH 3735
Pwllmeyric	16	ST 5192

Pwll-y-glaw Roxwell

Pwll-y-glaw 15 SS 7993
Pyecombe 11 TQ 2912
Pye Corner 16 ST 3485
Pyle (I. of W.) 9 SZ 4879
Pyle (Mid Glam.) 15 SS 8282
Pylle 7 ST 6038
Pymore 28 TL 4986
Pyrford 11 TQ 0458
Pyrton 18 SU 6895
Pytchley 27 SP 8574
Pyworthy 4 SS 3102

Quabbs 23 SO 2080
Quadring 35 TF 2233
Quainton 18 SP 7419
Quanter Ness 63 HY 4114
Quarff 63 HU 4235
Quarley 10 SU 2743
Quarndon 33 SK 3340
Quarrier's Homes 50 NS 3666
Quarrington 35 TF 0544
Quarrington Hill 42 NZ 3337
Quarrybank (Ches.) 32 SJ 5465
Quarry Bank (W Mids.) 25 SO 9386
Quarryhill 65 NH 7281
Quarry, The 17 ST 7399
Quarrywood 61 NJ 1864
Quarter 50 NS 7251
Quatford 24 SO 7390
Quatt 24 SO 7588
Quebec 42 NZ 1743
Quedgeley 17 SO 8114
Queen Adelaide 28 TL 5681
Queenborough 13 TQ 9471
Queenborough in Sheppey 13 TQ 9174
Queen Camel 7 ST 5924
Queen Charlton 17 ST 6366
Queensbury 37 SE 1030
Queensferry (Clwyd) 32 SJ 3168
Queensferry (Lothian) 51 NT 1278
Queenzieburn 50 NS 6977
Quendale 63 HU 3713
Quendon 20 TL 5130
Queniborough 34 SK 6412
Quenington 17 SP 1404
Quernmore 40 SD 5160
Quethiock 4 SX 3164
Quidenham 29 TM 0287
Quidhampton (Hants.) 10 SU 5150
Quidhamptpn (Wilts.) 8 SU 1030
Quilquox 62 NJ 9038
Quindry 63 ND 4392
Quinton 26 SP 7754
Quoditch 4 SX 4097
Quoig 56 NN 8222
Quorndon 34 SK 5616
Quothquan 51 NS 9939
Quoyloo 63 HY 2420
Quoys 63 HP 6112

Raby 32 SJ 3179
Rachub 30 SH 6268
Rackenford 6 SS 8418
Rackham 11 TQ 0514
Rackheath 29 TG 2814
Racks 45 NY 0374
Rackwick (Hoy) 63 ND 1999
Rackwick (Westray) 63 HY 4449
Radcliffe (Gtr Mches) 37 SD 7806
Radcliffe (Northum.) 47 NU 2602
Radcliffe on Trent 34 SK 6439
Radclive 18 SP 6734
Radcot 18 SU 2899
Radernie 57 NO 4609
Radford Semele 26 SP 3464
Radlett 19 TL 1600
Radley 18 SU 5398
Radnage 18 SU 7897
Radstock 17 ST 6854
Radstone 26 SP 5840
Radway 26 SP 3648
Radway Green 32 SJ 7754
Radwell 19 TL 2335
Radwinter 20 TL 6037
Radyr 16 ST 1380
Raerinish 63 NB 4024
Rafford 61 NJ 0656
Ragdale 34 SK 6619
Raglan 16 SO 4107
Ragnall 34 SK 8073
Rahane 49 NS 2386
Rainford 36 SD 4700
Rainham (Gtr London) 20 TQ 5282
Rainham (Kent) 12 TQ 8165
Rainhill 32 SJ 4990
Rainhill Stoops 32 SJ 5090
Rainigadale 63 NB 2201
Rainow 33 SJ 9575
Rainton 42 SE 3775
Rainworth 34 SK 5958
Raisbeck 41 NY 6407
Rait 56 NO 2226
Raithby (Lincs.) 35 TF 3084
Raithby (Lincs.) 35 TF 3767
Rake 9 SU 8027
Ramasaig 58 NG 1644
Rame (Corn.) 2 SW 7233
Rame (Corn.) 4 SX 4249
Ram Lane 13 TQ 9646
Rampisham 7 ST 5502
Rampside 40 SD 2366
Rampton (Cambs.) 20 TL 4268
Rampton (Notts.) 34 SK 7978
Ramsbottom 37 SD 7916
Ramsbury 10 SU 2771
Ramscraigs 67 ND 1427
Ramsdean 9 SU 7021
Ramsdell 10 SU 5957
Ramsden 18 SP 3515
Ramsden Bellhouse 20 TQ 7194
Ramsden Heath 20 TQ 7195
Ramsey (Cambs.) 27 TL 2885
Ramsey (Essex) 21 TM 2130
Ramsey (I. of M.) 43 SC 4594
Ramsey Forty Foot 27 TL 3187
Ramsey Hollow 27 TL 3186
Ramsey Mereside 27 TL 2889
Ramsey St. Mary's 27 TL 2588
Ramsgate 13 TR 3865
Ramsgate Street 29 TG 0933
Ramsgill 42 SE 1170
Ramshorn 33 SK 0845
Ranby 34 SK 6480
Rand 35 TF 1078
Randwick 17 SO 8206
Ranfurly 50 NS 3865
Rangemore 33 SK 1822
Rangeworthy 17 ST 6886
Rankinston 50 NS 4514
Ranskill 34 SK 6587
Ranton 33 SJ 8524
Ranworth 29 TG 3514
Rascarrel 45 NX 7948
Raskelf 38 SE 4971
Rassau 16 SO 1411
Rastrick 37 SE 1321
Ratagan 59 NG 9220
Ratby 26 SK 5105
Ratcliffe Culey 26 SP 3299
Ratcliffe on the Wreake 34 SK 6314
Rathen 62 NK 0060
Rathillet 57 NO 3620
Rathmell 37 SD 8059
Ratho 51 NT 1370
Rathven 61 NJ 4465
Ratley 26 SP 3847
Ratlinghope 24 SO 4096
Rattar 67 ND 2672
Ratten Row 36 SD 4241
Rattery 5 SX 7361
Rattlesden 21 TL 9758
Rattray 56 NO 1745
Rauceby 34 TF 0146
Raughton Head 46 NY 3745
Raunds 27 SP 9972
Ravenfield 38 SK 4895
Ravenglass 40 SD 0896
Raveningham 29 TM 3996
Ravenscar 43 NZ 9801
Ravensdale 43 SC 3592
Ravensden 27 TL 0754
Ravenshead 34 SK 5654
Ravensmoor 32 SJ 6250
Ravensthorpe (Northants.) 26 SP 6670
Ravensthorpe (W Yorks.) 37 SE 2220
Ravenstone (Bucks.) 27 SP 8450
Ravenstone (Leic.) 33 SK 4013
Ravenstonedale 41 NY 7203
Ravenstruther 51 NS 9245
Ravensworth 42 NZ 1407
Raw 43 NZ 9305
Rawcliffe (Humbs.) 38 SE 6822
Rawcliffe (N Yorks.) 38 SE 5855
Rawcliffe Bridge 38 SE 6921
Rawmarsh 38 SK 4396
Rawreth 20 TQ 7793
Rawridge 6 ST 2006
Rawtenstall 37 SD 8122
Raydon 21 TM 0438
Raylees 47 NY 9291
Rayleigh 20 TQ 8090
Rayne 20 TL 7222
Reach 20 TL 5666
Read 37 SD 7634
Reading 10 SU 7272
Reading Street 13 TQ 9230
Reagill 41 NY 6017
Rearquhar 65 NH 7492
Rearsby 34 SK 6514
Rease Heath 32 SJ 6454
Reaster 67 ND 2565
Reawick 63 HU 3244
Reay 67 NC 9664
Reculver 13 TR 2269
Redberth 14 SN 0804
Redbourn 19 TL 1012
Redbourne 39 SK 9699
Redbridge 20 TQ 4389
Redbrook 16 SO 5310
Redbrook Street 13 TQ 9336
Redburn (Highld.) 65 NH 5767
Redburn (Highld.) 60 NH 9447
Redcar 42 NZ 6024
Redcastle (Highld.) 60 NH 5849
Redcastle (Tays.) 57 NO 6850
Redcliff Bay 16 ST 4475
Red Dial 46 NY 2545
Redding 50 NS 9178
Reddingmuirhead 50 NS 9177
Reddish 37 SJ 8993
Redditch 25 SP 0468
Rede 20 TL 8055
Redenhall 29 TM 2684
Redesmouth 47 NY 8681
Redford 57 NO 5644
Redgrave 29 TM 0478
Redheugh 57 NO 4463
Redhill (Avon) 16 ST 4962
Redhill (Grampn.) 62 NJ 6837
Redhill (Grampn.) 62 NJ 7704
Redhill (Surrey) 11 TQ 2850
Redisham 29 TM 4084
Redland (Avon) 17 ST 5875
Redland (Orkney) 63 HY 3724
Redlingfield 29 TM 1871
Redlynch (Somer.) 8 ST 6933
Redlynch (Wilts.) 8 SU 2020
Redmarley D'Abitot 24 SO 7531
Redmarshall 42 NZ 3821
Redmile 34 SK 7935
Redmire 42 SE 0491
Redmoor 4 SX 0761
Rednal 32 SJ 3628
Redpath 52 NT 5835
Redpoint (Highld.) 64 NG 7368
Red Rock 36 SD 5809
Red Roses 14 SN 2012
Red Row 47 NZ 2599
Redruth 2 SW 6941
Red Street 32 SJ 8251
Red Wharf Bay (Gwyn.) 30 SH 5281
Redwick (Avon) 16 ST 5485
Redwick (Gwent) 16 ST 4184
Redworth 42 NZ 2423
Reed 20 TL 3636
Reedham 29 TG 4201
Reedness 38 SE 7922
Reef 63 NB 1134
Reepham (Lincs.) 35 TF 0373
Reepham (Norf.) 29 TG 1023
Reeth 42 SE 0499
Regaby 43 SC 4397
Reiff 64 NB 9614
Reigate 11 TQ 2550
Reighton 39 TA 1275
Reiss 67 ND 3354
Rejerrah 2 SW 8055
Relubbus 2 SW 5632
Relugas 61 NH 9948
Remenham 18 SU 7784
Remenham Hill 18 SU 7883
Rempstone 34 SK 5724
Rendcomb 17 SP 0109
Rendham 21 TM 3564
Renfrew 50 NS 4967
Renhold 27 TL 0953
Renishaw 33 SK 4477
Rennington 53 NU 2118
Renton 50 NS 3878
Renwick 41 NY 5943
Repps 29 TG 4116
Repton 33 SK 3026
Rescobie 57 NO 5152
Resipole 54 NM 7264
Resolis 65 NH 6765
Resolven 15 SN 8202
Reston 53 NT 8861
Reswallie 57 NO 5051
Retew 2 SW 9256
Rettendon 20 TQ 7698
Revesby 35 TF 2961
Rewe 6 SX 9499
Reydon 29 TM 4977
Reymerston 29 TG 0206
Reynalton 14 SN 0909
Reynoldston 15 SS 4890
Rhandirmwyn 15 SN 7843
Rhayader 23 SN 9668
Rhedyn 30 SH 3032
Rheindown 60 NH 5147
Rhemore 54 NM 5750
Rhes-y-cae 32 SJ 1870
Rhewl (Clwyd) 31 SJ 1060
Rhewl (Clwyd) 31 SJ 1744
Rhiconich 66 NC 2552
Rhicullen 65 NH 6971
Rhigos 15 SN 9205
Rhilochan 66 NC 7407
Rhiroy 64 NH 1589
Rhiwbryfdir 30 SH 6946
Rhiwderin 16 ST 2587
Rhiwlas (Clwyd) 32 SJ 1931
Rhiwlas (Gwyn.) 30 SH 5765
Rhiwlas (Gwyn.) 31 SH 9237
Rhodesia 34 SK 5680
Rhodes Minnis 13 TR 1542
Rhondda 15 SS 9696
Rhonehouse or Kelton Hill 45 NX 7459
Rhoose 16 ST 0666
Rhos (Dyfed) 15 SN 3835
Rhos (W Glam.) 15 SN 7303
Rhoscolyn 30 SH 2675
Rhoscrowther 14 SM 9002
Rhosesmor 32 SJ 2168
Rhos-fawr 30 SH 3838
Rhosgadfan 30 SH 5057
Rhosgoch (Gwyn.) 30 SH 4189
Rhosgoch (Powys) 23 SO 1847
Rhoslan 30 SH 4841
Rhoslefain 22 SH 5705
Rhosllanerchrugog 32 SJ 2946
Rhosmeirch 30 SH 4677
Rhosneigr 30 SH 3172
Rhosnesni 32 SJ 3451
Rhos-on-Sea 31 SH 8480
Rhossili 15 SS 4188
Rhosson 14 SM 7225
Rhostryfan 30 SH 4958
Rhostyllen 32 SJ 3148
Rhosybol 30 SH 4288
Rhos-y-gwaliau 31 SH 9434
Rhos-y-llan 30 SH 2337
Rhu (Strath.) 50 NS 2783
Rhuallt 31 SJ 0774
Rhuban 63 NF 7811
Rhuddlan 31 SJ 0277
Rhue 64 NH 0997
Rhulen 23 SO 1350
Rhunahaorine 48 NR 7048
Rhyd (Gwyn.) 30 SH 6341
Rhydargaeau 15 SN 4326
Rhydcymerau 15 SN 5738
Rhydd 25 SO 8345
Rhyd-Ddu 30 SH 5652
Rhydding 15 SS 7498
Rhydlewis 14 SN 3447
Rhydlios 30 SH 1830
Rhyd-lydan 31 SH 8950
Rhydowen 15 SN 4445
Rhydrosser 22 SN 5667
Rhydtalog 32 SJ 2354
Rhyd-y-clafdy 30 SH 3235
Rhydycroesau 32 SJ 2330
Rhydyfelin (Dyfed) 22 SN 5979
Rhydyfelin (Mid Glam.) 16 ST 0988
Rhyd-y-fro 15 SN 7105
Rhydymain 31 SH 7922
Rhyd-y-meirch 16 SO 3107
Rhydymwyn 32 SJ 2066
Rhyd-yr-onnen 22 SH 6102
Rhyl 31 SJ 0181
Rhymney 16 SO 1107
Rhyn 32 SJ 3136
Rhynd 56 NO 1520
Rhynie (Grampn.) 61 NJ 4927
Rhynie (Highld.) 65 NH 8578
Ribbesford 24 SO 7874
Ribblesdale 37 SD 8059
Ribbleton 36 SD 5630
Ribchester 36 SD 6435
Ribigill 66 NC 5854
Riby 39 TA 1807
Riccall 38 SE 6237
Riccarton 50 NS 4235
Richards Castle 24 SO 4969
Richmond 42 NZ 1701
Richmond upon Thames 11 TQ 1874
Rickarton 57 NO 8188
Rickinghall Inferior 29 TM 0475
Rickinghall Superior 29 TM 0475
Rickling 20 TL 4931
Rickmansworth 19 TQ 0594
Riddell 52 NT 5124
Riddings 46 NY 4075
Riddlecombe 5 SS 6013
Riddlesden 37 SE 0742
Ridge (Dorset) 8 SY 9386
Ridge (Herts.) 19 TL 2100
Ridge (Wilts.) 8 ST 9531
Ridgehill (Avon) 16 ST 5362
Ridge Hill (Here. and Worc.) 24 SO 5035
Ridge Lane 26 SP 2994
Ridgeway Cross 24 SO 7147
Ridgewell 20 TL 7340
Ridgewood 12 TQ 4719
Ridgmont 19 SP 9736
Riding Mill 47 NZ 0161
Ridlington (Leic.) 27 SK 8402
Ridlington (Norf.) 29 TG 3430
Ridsdale 47 NY 9084
Riechip 56 NO 0647
Rievaulx 42 SE 5785
Rigg 46 NY 2966
Riggend 50 NS 7670
Righoul 60 NH 8851
Rigside 50 NS 8734
Rileyhill 25 SK 1115
Rilla Mill 4 SX 2973
Rillington 39 SE 8574
Rimington 37 SD 8045
Rimpton 7 ST 6021
Rimswell 39 TA 3128
Rinaston 14 SM 9825
Ringford 45 NX 6857
Ringland 29 TG 1313
Ringmer 12 TQ 4412
Ringmore 5 SX 6545
Ringorm 61 NJ 2644
Ring's End 27 TF 3902
Ringsfield 29 TM 4088
Ringsfield Corner 29 TM 4187
Ringshall (Bucks.) 19 SP 9814
Ringshall (Suff.) 21 TM 0452
Ringshall Stocks 21 TM 0551
Ringstead (Norf.) 28 TF 7040
Ringstead (Northants.) 27 SP 9875
Ringwood 8 SU 1405
Ringwould 13 TR 3648
Rinnigill 63 ND 3193
Rinsey 2 SW 5927
Ripe 12 TQ 5010
Ripley (Derby.) 33 SK 3950
Ripley (Hants.) 8 SZ 1698
Ripley (N Yorks.) 42 SE 2860
Ripley (Surrey) 11 TQ 0556
Riplingham 39 SE 9631
Ripon 42 SE 3171
Rippingale 35 TF 0927
Ripple (Here. and Worc.) 25 SO 8737
Ripple (Kent) 13 TR 3550
Ripponden 37 SE 0319
Rireavach 64 NH 0396
Risabus 48 NR 3143
Risbury 24 SO 5455
Risby (Humbs.) 39 SE 9214
Risby (Suff.) 20 TL 7966
Risca 16 ST 2391
Rise 39 TA 1541
Risegate 35 TF 2029
Riseley (Beds.) 27 TL 0463
Riseley (Berks.) 10 SU 7263
Rishangles 21 TM 1568
Rishton 36 SD 7229
Rishworth 37 SE 0317
Risley 33 SK 4635
Risplith 42 SE 2467
Rispond 66 NC 4565
Rivar 10 SU 3161
Rivenhall End 20 TL 8316
Riverhead 12 TQ 5156
Rivington 36 SD 6214
Roade 26 SP 7551
Roadmeetings 50 NS 8649
Roadside 67 ND 1560
Roadside of Kinneff 57 NO 8476
Roadwater 7 ST 0238
Roag 58 NG 2744
Roa Island 40 SD 2364
Roath 16 ST 1978
Roberton (Borders) 52 NT 4314
Roberton (Strath.) 51 NS 9428
Robertsbridge 12 TQ 7323
Roberttown 37 SE 1922
Robeston Cross 14 SM 8809
Robeston Wathen 14 SN 0815
Robin Hood's Bay 43 NZ 9505
Roborough 6 SS 5717
Roby 32 SJ 4291
Roby Mill 36 SD 5106
Rocester 33 SK 1039
Roch 14 SM 8821
Rochdale 37 SD 8913
Roche 2 SW 9860
Rochester (Kent) 12 TQ 7467
Rochester (Northum.) 47 NY 8397
Rochford (Essex) 21 TQ 8790
Rochford (Here. and Worc.) 24 SO 6268
Rock (Corn.) 2 SW 9475
Rock (Here. and Worc.) 24 SO 7371
Rock (Northum.) 53 NU 2020
Rockbeare 5 SY 0195
Rockbourne 8 SU 1118
Rockcliffe (Cumbr.) 46 NY 3561
Rockcliffe (Dumf. and Galwy.) 45 NX 8553
Rock Ferry 32 SJ 3386
Rockfield (Gwent) 16 SO 4814
Rockfield (Highld.) 65 NH 9282
Rockhampton 17 ST 6593
Rockingham 27 SP 8691
Rockland All Saints 29 TL 9896
Rockland St. Mary 29 TG 3104
Rockland St. Peter 29 TL 9897
Rockley 17 SU 1571
Rockwell End 18 SU 7988
Rodbourne 17 ST 9383
Rodd 23 SO 3162
Roddam 53 NU 0220
Rodden 7 SY 6184
Rode 8 ST 8053
Rode Heath (Ches.) 32 SJ 8056
Rodeheath (Ches.) 33 SJ 8766
Rodel 63 NG 0483
Roden 24 SJ 5716
Rodhuish 7 ST 0139
Rodington 24 SJ 5814
Rodley 17 SO 7411
Rodmarton 17 ST 9397
Rodmersham 13 TQ 9261
Rodney Stoke 7 ST 4849
Rodsley 33 SK 2040
Roecliffe 42 SE 3765
Roehampton 11 TQ 2373
Roesound 63 HU 3365
Roewen 30 SH 7571
Roffey 11 TQ 1931
Rogart 66 NC 7303
Rogate 9 SU 8023
Rogerstone 16 ST 2688
Rogerton 50 NS 6256
Rogiet 16 ST 4587
Roker 47 NZ 4059
Rollesby 29 TG 4415
Rolleston (Leic.) 26 SK 7300
Rolleston (Notts.) 34 SK 7452
Rolleston (Staffs.) 33 SK 2327
Rolston 39 TA 2145
Rolvenden 13 TQ 8431
Rolvenden Layne 13 TQ 8530
Romaldkirk 41 NY 9921
Romanby 42 SE 3693
Romannobridge 51 NT 1547
Romansleigh 6 SS 7220
Romford 20 TQ 5188
Romiley 33 SJ 9390
Romsey 9 SU 3521
Romsley (Here. and Worc.) 25 SO 9679
Romsley (Salop) 24 SO 7883
Ronague 43 SC 2472
Rookhope 41 NY 9342
Rookley 9 SZ 5084
Rooks Bridge 7 ST 3752
Roos 39 TA 2830
Rootpark 51 NS 9554
Ropley 9 SU 6431
Ropley Dean 9 SU 6331
Ropsley 34 SK 9834
Rora 62 NK 0650
Rorrington 23 SJ 3000
Rose 2 SW 7754
Roseacre 36 SD 4336
Rose Ash 6 SS 7821
Rosebank 50 NS 8049
Rosebrough 53 NU 1326
Rosedale 43 SE 7295
Rosedale Abbey 43 SE 7296
Roseden 53 NU 0321
Rosehearty 62 NJ 9367
Rosehill 32 SJ 6630
Roseisle 61 NJ 1367
Rosemarket 14 SM 9508
Rosemarkie 60 NH 7357
Rosemary Lane 7 ST 1514
Rosemount (Strath.) 50 NS 3729
Rosemount (Tays.) 56 NO 2043
Rosewell 51 NT 2862
Roseworthy 2 SW 6139
Rosgill 40 NY 5316
Roshven 54 NM 7078
Roskhill 58 NG 2745
Rosley 46 NY 3245
Roslin 51 NT 2663
Rosliston 33 SK 2416
Rosneath 49 NS 2583
Ross (Dumf. and Galwy.) 45 NX 6444
Ross (Northum.) 53 NU 1336
Ross (Tays.) 56 NN 7621
Rossett 32 SJ 3657
Rossington 38 SK 6298
Rosskeen 65 NH 6869
Rossland 50 NS 4370
Ross-on-Wye 17 SO 6024
Roster 67 ND 2639
Rostherne 32 SJ 7483
Rosthwaite 40 NY 2514
Roston 33 SK 1241
Rosyth 51 NT 1183
Rothbury 47 NU 0601
Rotherby 34 SK 6716
Rotherfield 12 TQ 5529
Rotherfield Greys 10 SU 7282
Rotherfield Peppard 10 SU 7081
Rotherham 38 SK 4492
Rothersthorpe 26 SP 7156
Rotherwick 10 SU 7156
Rothes 61 NJ 2749
Rothesay 49 NS 0864
Rothiebrisbane 62 NJ 7437
Rothiemurchus 60 NH 9206
Rothienorman 62 NJ 7235
Rothiesholm 63 HY 6123
Rothley 34 SK 5812
Rothmaise 62 NJ 6832
Rothwell (Lincs.) 39 TF 1599
Rothwell (Northants.) 26 SP 8181
Rothwell (W Yorks.) 37 SE 3428
Rotsea 39 TA 0651
Rottal 57 NO 3769
Rottingdean 12 TQ 3702
Rottington 40 NX 9613
Roud 9 SZ 5280
Rougham 28 TF 8320
Rougham Green 21 TL 9061
Roughburn 55 NN 3781
Rough Close 33 SJ 9239
Rough Common 13 TR 1359
Roughlee 37 SD 8440
Roughley 25 SP 1399
Roughsike 46 NY 5275
Roughton (Lincs.) 35 TF 2364
Roughton (Norf.) 29 TG 2136
Roughton (Salop) 24 SO 7594
Roundhay 37 SE 3235
Roundstreet Common 11 TQ 0528
Roundway 17 SU 0163
Rounton 42 NZ 4103
Rousdon 7 SY 2990
Rous Lench 25 SP 0153
Routenburn 49 NS 1961
Routh 39 TA 0842
Row (Corn.) 4 SX 0976
Row (Cumbr.) 40 SD 4589
Rowanburn 46 NY 4177
Rowde 17 ST 9762
Rowfoot 46 NY 6860
Rowhedge 21 TM 0221
Rowhook 11 TQ 1234
Rowington 25 SP 2069
Rowland 33 SK 2072
Rowland's Castle 9 SU 7310
Rowland's Gill 47 NZ 1658
Rowledge 10 SU 8243
Rowley (Devon.) 6 SS 7219
Rowley (Humbs.) 39 SE 9732
Rowley (Salop) 23 SJ 3006
Rowley Regis 25 SO 9787
Rowlstone 16 SO 3727
Rowly 11 TQ 0441
Rowney Green 25 SP 0471
Rownhams 9 SU 3816
Rowsham 19 SP 8518
Rowsley 33 SK 2566
Rowston 35 TF 0856
Rowton (Ches.) 32 SJ 4464
Rowton (Salop) 32 SJ 6119
Roxburgh 52 NT 6930
Roxby (Humbs.) 39 SE 9217
Roxby (N Yorks.) 43 NZ 7616
Roxton 27 TL 1554
Roxwell 20 TL 6408

Royal Leamington Spa Seworgan

Royal Leamington Spa 26 SP 3166
Royal Tunbridge Wells 12 TQ 5839
Roybridge 55 NN 2781
Roydon (Essex) 20 TL 4009
Roydon (Norf.) 28 TF 7022
Roydon (Norf.) 29 TM 0980
Royston (Herts.) 20 TL 3541
Royston (S Yorks.) 37 SE 3611
Royton 37 SD 9207
Ruabon 32 SJ 3043
Ruaig 48 NM 0647
Ruan Lanihorne 2 SW 8942
Ruan Minor 2 SW 7115
Ruardean 17 SO 6117
Ruardean Woodside 17 SO 6216
Rubery 25 SO 9777
Ruckcroft 46 NY 5344
Ruckinge 13 TR 0233
Ruckland 35 TF 3378
Ruckley 24 SJ 5300
Ruddington 34 SK 5733
Rudge 8 ST 8252
Rudgeway 17 ST 6286
Rudgwick 11 TQ 0934
Rudhall 17 SO 6225
Rudry 16 ST 1986
Rudston 39 TA 0967
Rudyard 33 SJ 9557
Rufford 36 SD 4515
Rufforth 38 SE 5251
Rugby 26 SP 5075
Rugeley 33 SK 0418
Ruilick 60 NH 5046
Ruishton 7 ST 2624
Ruislip 19 TQ 0987
Ruislip Common 19 TQ 0789
Rumbling Bridge 56 NT 0199
Rumburgh 29 TM 3581
Rumford 2 SW 8970
Rumney 16 ST 2179
Runcorn 32 SJ 5182
Runcton 11 SU 8802
Runcton Holme 28 TF 6109
Runfold 11 SU 8747
Runhall 29 TG 0507
Runham 29 TG 4610
Runnington 7 ST 1121
Runswick 43 NZ 8016
Runtaleave 57 NO 2867
Runwell 20 TQ 7494
Rushall (Here. and Worc.) 24 SO 6434
Rushall (Norf.) 29 TM 1982
Rushall (Wilts.) 17 SU 1255
Rushall (W Mids.) 25 SK 0201
Rushbrooke 21 TL 8961
Rushbury 24 SO 5191
Rushden (Herts.) 20 TL 3031
Rushden (Northants.) 27 SP 9566
Rushford 29 TL 9281
Rush Green 20 TQ 5187
Rushlake Green 12 TQ 6218
Rushmere 29 TM 4987
Rushmere St. Andrew 21 TM 2046
Rushmoor 11 SU 8740
Rushock 25 SO 8871
Rusholme 37 SJ 8494
Rushton (Ches.) 32 SJ 5863
Rushton (Northants.) 27 SP 8483
Rushton (Salop) 24 SJ 6008
Rushton Spencer 33 SJ 9363
Rushwick 25 SO 8353
Rushyford 42 NZ 2828
Ruskie 56 NN 6200
Ruskington 35 TF 0850
Rusland 40 SD 3488
Rusper 11 TQ 2037
Ruspidge 17 SO 6512
Russell's Water 18 SU 7089
Rustington 11 TQ 0502
Ruston Parva 39 TA 0661
Ruswarp 43 NZ 8809
Rutherford 52 NT 6530
Rutherglen 50 NS 6161
Ruthernbridge 4 SX 0166
Ruthin 31 SJ 1257
Ruthrieston 62 NJ 9204
Ruthven (Grampn.) 61 NJ 5046
Ruthven (Highld.) 60 NH 8133
Ruthven (Tays.) 57 NO 2848
Ruthvoes 2 SW 9360
Ruthwell 45 NY 1067
Ruyton-XI-Towns 32 SJ 3922
Ryal 47 NZ 0174
Ryal Fold 36 SD 6621
Ryall 7 SY 4094
Ryarsh 12 TQ 6659
Rydal 40 NY 3606
Ryde 9 SZ 5992
Rye 13 TQ 9220
Rye Foreign 13 TQ 8822
Rye Harbour 13 TQ 9419
Ryhall 35 TF 0311
Ryhill 37 SE 3814
Ryhope 47 NZ 4152
Ryknild Street (Warw.) (ant.) 25 SP 0762
Rylstone 37 SD 9758
Ryme Intrinseca 7 ST 5810
Ryther 38 SE 5539
Ryton (Glos.) 24 SO 7232
Ryton (N Yorks.) 38 SE 7975
Ryton (Salop) 24 SJ 7502
Ryton (Tyne and Wear) 47 NZ 1564
Ryton-on-Dunsmore 26 SP 3874

Sabden 37 SD 7737
Sacombe 20 TL 3419
Sacriston 47 NZ 2447
Sadberge 42 NZ 3416
Saddell 49 NR 7832
Saddington 26 SP 6591
Saddle Bow 28 TF 6015
Saffron Walden 20 TL 5438
Saham Toney 28 TF 9002
Saighton 32 SJ 4462
St. Abbs 53 NT 9167
St. Agnes (Corn.) 2 SW 7150
St. Albans 19 TL 1507
St. Allen 2 SW 8250
St. Andrews 57 NO 5016
St. Andrews Major 16 ST 1471
St. Anne's (Lancs.) 36 SD 3129
St. Ann's (Dumf. and Galwy.) 45 NY 0793
St. Ann's Chapel 4 SX 4170
St. Anthony 2 SW 7725
St. Arvans 16 ST 5196
St. Asaph (Lanelwy) 31 SJ 0374
St. Athan 15 ST 0168
St. Austell 4 SX 0152
St. Bees 40 NX 9611
St. Blazey 4 SX 0654
St. Boswells 52 NT 5930
St. Breock 2 SW 9771
St. Breward 4 SX 0977
St. Briavels 16 SO 5504
St. Brides 14 SM 8010
St. Bride's Major 15 SS 8974
St. Brides Netherwent 16 ST 4289
St. Brides-super-Ely 16 ST 1078
St. Bride's Wentlooge 16 ST 2982
St. Budeaux 4 SX 4558
St. Buryan 2 SW 4025
St. Catherines 55 NN 1207
St. Clears 14 SN 2716
St. Cleer 4 SX 2468
St. Clement 2 SW 8443
St. Clether 4 SX 2084
St. Colmac 49 NS 0467
St. Columb Major 2 SW 9163
St. Columb Minor 2 SW 8362
St. Columb Road 2 SW 9059
St. Combs 62 NK 0563
St. Cross South Elmham 29 TM 2984
St. Cyrus 57 NO 7464
St. David's (Dyfed) 14 SM 7525
St. Davids (Fife.) 51 NT 1582
St. David's (Tays.) 56 NN 9420
St. Day 2 SW 7242
St. Dennis 2 SW 9558
St. Devereux 24 SO 4431
St. Dogmaels 14 SN 1646
St. Dogwells 14 SM 9728
St. Dominick 4 SX 3967
St. Donats 15 SS 9368
St. Edith's Marsh 17 ST 9764
St. Endellion 4 SW 9978
St. Enoder 2 SW 8956
St. Erme 2 SW 8449
St. Erth 2 SW 5435
St. Erth Praze 2 SW 5735
St. Ervan 2 SW 8870
St. Ewe 2 SW 9745
St. Fagans 16 ST 1177
St. Fergus 62 NK 0951
St. Fillans 56 NN 6924
St. Florence 14 SN 0801
St. Gennys 4 SX 1497
St. George (Clwyd) 31 SH 9775
St. George's (S Glam.) 16 ST 0976
St. Germans 4 SX 3557
St. Giles in the Wood 6 SS 5318
St. Giles-on-the-Heath 4 SX 3590
St. Harmon 23 SN 9872
St. Helena 29 TG 1816
St. Helen Auckland 42 NZ 1826
St. Helens (I. of W.) 9 SZ 6288
St. Helens (Mers.) 32 SJ 5095
St. Hilary (Corn.) 2 SW 5531
St. Hilary (S Glam.) 15 ST 0173
St. Illtyd 16 SO 2102
St. Ishmael's 14 SM 8307
St. Issey 2 SW 9271
St. Ive (Corn.) 4 SX 3167
St. Ives (Cambs.) 27 TL 3171
St. Ives (Corn.) 2 SW 5140
St. Ives (Dorset) 8 SU 1203
St. James South Elmham 29 TM 3281
St. John (Corn.) 4 SX 4053
St. Johns (Here. and Worc.) 25 SO 8453
St. John's (I. of M.) 43 SC 2781
St. John's Chapel 41 NY 8837
St. John's Fen End 28 TF 5311
St. John's Highway 28 TF 5314
St. John's Town of Dalry 45 NX 6281
St. Jude's 43 SC 3996
St. Just (Corn.) 2 SW 3631
St. Just (Corn.) 2 SW 8435
St. Katherines 62 NJ 7834
St. Keverne 2 SW 7821
St. Kew 4 SX 0276
St. Kew Highway 4 SX 0375
St. Keyne 4 SX 2460
St. Lawrence (Corn.) 4 SX 0466
St. Lawrence (Essex) 21 TL 9604
St. Lawrence (I. of W.) 9 SZ 5476
St. Leonards (Bucks.) 19 SP 9006
St. Leonards (Dorset) 8 SU 1002
St. Leonards (E Susx) 12 TQ 8009
St. Levan 2 SW 3722
St. Lythans 16 ST 1073
St. Mabyn 4 SX 0373
St. Margarets 24 SO 3534
St. Margaret's at Cliffe 13 TR 3644
St. Margaret's Bay 13 TR 3744
St. Margaret's Hope (Fife.) 51 NT 1181
St. Margaret's Hope (S. Ronaldsay) 63 ND 4493
St. Margaret South Elmham 29 TM 3183
St. Mark's 43 SC 2974
St. Martin (Corn.) 4 SX 2555
St. Martin's (Is. of Sc.) 2 SV 9215
St. Martin's (Salop) 32 SJ 3236
St. Martins (Tays.) 56 NO 1530
St. Martin's Green 2 SW 7324
St. Mary Bourne 10 SU 4250
St. Mary Church 15 ST 0071
St. Mary Cray 12 TQ 4767
St. Mary Hill 15 SS 9678
St. Mary in the Marsh 13 TR 0628
St. Marylebone 19 TQ 2881
St. Mary's (Orkney) 63 HY 4701
St. Mary's Bay 13 TR 0927
St. Mary's Grove 16 ST 4769
St. Mary's Hoo 12 TQ 8076
St. Mary's Isle 45 NX 6749
St. Mawes 2 SW 8433
St. Mawgan 2 SW 8765
St. Mellion 4 SX 3865
St. Mellons 16 ST 2281
St. Merryn 2 SW 8874
St. Mewan 4 SW 9951
St. Michael Caerhays 2 SW 9642
St. Michael Penkevil 2 SW 8542
St. Michaels (Here. and Worc.) 24 SO 5765
St. Michaels (Kent) 13 TQ 8835
St. Michael's Mount 2 SW 5130
St. Michael's on Wyre 36 SD 4640
St. Michael South Elmham 29 TM 3483
St. Minver 4 SW 9677
St. Monance 57 NO 5201
St. Neot (Corn.) 4 SX 1867
St. Neots (Cambs.) 27 TL 1860
St. Nicholas (Dyfed) 14 SM 9035
St. Nicholas (S Glam.) 16 ST 0874
St. Nicholas at Wade 13 TR 2666
St. Ninians 50 NS 7991
St. Osyth 21 TM 1215
St. Owen's Cross 16 SO 5324
St. Pauls Cray 12 TQ 4768
St. Paul's Walden 19 TL 1922
St. Peter's 13 TR 3668
St. Petrox 14 SR 9797
St. Pinnock 4 SX 2063
St. Quivox 50 NS 3723
St. Stephen (Corn.) 2 SW 9453
St. Stephens (Corn.) 4 SX 3285
St. Stephen's (Corn.) 4 SX 4158
St. Teath 4 SX 0680
St. Tudy 4 SX 0676
St. Twynnells 14 SR 9597
St. Vigeans 57 NO 6443
St. Wenn 2 SW 9664
St. Weonards 16 SO 4924
Saintbury 25 SP 1139
Saint Hill 12 TQ 3835
Salcombe 5 SX 7338
Salcombe Regis 5 SY 1488
Salcott 21 TL 9413
Sale 32 SJ 7990
Saleby 35 TF 4578
Sale Green 25 SO 9358
Salehurst 12 TQ 7424
Salem (Dyfed) 15 SN 6226
Salem (Dyfed) 22 SN 6684
Salem (Gwyn.) 30 SH 5456
Salen (Highld.) 54 NM 6864
Salen (Island of Mull) 54 NM 5743
Salesbury 36 SD 6732
Sales Point 21 TM 0209
Salford (Beds.) 27 SP 9339
Salford (Gtr Mches.) 37 SJ 7796
Salford (Oxon.) 18 SP 2828
Salford Priors 25 SP 0751
Salfords 11 TQ 2846
Salhouse 29 TG 3114
Saline 51 NT 0292
Salisbury 8 SU 1429
Sall 29 TG 1024
Sallachy (Highld.) 66 NC 5408
Sallachy (Highld.) 59 NG 9130
Salmonby 35 TF 3273
Salmond's Muir 57 NO 5837
Salperton 17 SP 0720
Salph End 27 TL 0752
Salsburgh 50 NS 8262
Salt 33 SJ 9527
Saltash 4 SX 4259
Saltburn 65 NH 7269
Saltburn-by-the-Sea 42 NZ 6621
Saltby 34 SK 8426
Saltcoats 49 NS 2441
Saltdean 12 TQ 3802
Salter 41 SD 6073
Salterforth 37 SD 8845
Saltergate 43 SE 8594
Salterswall 32 SJ 6267
Saltfleet 39 TF 4593
Saltfleetby All Saints 35 TF 4590
Saltfleetby St. Clements 39 TF 4591
Saltfleetby St. Peter 35 TF 4389
Saltford 17 ST 6867
Salthouse 29 TG 0743
Saltmarshe 38 SE 7824
Saltney 32 SJ 3864
Salton 43 SE 7180
Saltwick 47 NZ 1780
Saltwood 13 TR 1536
Salwarpe 25 SO 8762
Salwayash 7 SY 4596
Samala 63 NF 7962
Sambourne 25 SP 0561
Sambrook 32 SJ 7124
Samlesbury 36 SD 5829
Samlesbury Bottoms 36 SD 6229
Sampford Arundel 7 ST 1018
Sampford Brett 7 ST 0940
Sampford Courtenay 6 SS 6301
Sampford Peverell 7 ST 0214
Sampford Spiney 4 SX 5372
Samuelston 52 NT 4870
Sanaigmore 48 NR 2370
Sancreed 2 SW 4029
Sancton 39 SE 8939
Sand 63 HU 3447
Sandaig 58 NG 7102
Sandbach 32 SJ 7560
Sandbank 49 NS 1580
Sandbanks 8 SZ 0487
Sandend 62 NJ 5566
Sanderstead 12 TQ 3461
Sandford (Avon) 16 ST 4159
Sandford (Cumbr.) 41 NY 7216
Sandford (Devon.) 6 SS 8202
Sandford (Dorset) 8 SY 9289
Sandford (Strath.) 50 NS 7143
Sandfordhill 62 NK 1141
Sandford-on-Thames 18 SP 5301
Sandford Orcas 8 ST 6220
Sandford St. Martin 18 SP 4226
Sandgarth 63 HY 5215
Sandgate 13 TR 2035
Sandgreen 45 NX 5752
Sandhaven 62 NJ 9667
Sandhead 44 NX 0949
Sandhoe 47 NY 9766
Sandholme (Humbs.) 39 SE 8230
Sandholme (Lincs.) 35 TF 3337
Sandhurst (Berks.) 10 SU 8361
Sandhurst (Glos.) 17 SO 8223
Sandhurst (Kent) 12 TQ 8028
Sandhutton (N Yorks.) 42 SE 3881
Sand Hutton (N Yorks.) 38 SE 6958
Sandiacre 33 SK 4736
Sandilands 35 TF 5280
Sandiway 32 SJ 6070
Sandleheath 8 SU 1214
Sandleigh 18 SP 4501
Sandling 12 TQ 7558
Sandness 63 HU 1956
Sandon (Essex) 20 TL 7404
Sandon (Herts.) 20 TL 3234
Sandon (Staffs.) 33 SJ 9429
Sandown 9 SZ 5984
Sandplace 4 SX 2457
Sandridge (Herts.) 19 TL 1710
Sandridge (Wilts.) 17 ST 9465
Sandringham 28 TF 6928
Sandsend 43 NZ 8512
Sand Side 40 SD 2282
Sandsound 63 HU 3548
Sandtoft 38 SE 7408
Sandwich 13 TR 3358
Sandwick (Cumbr.) 40 NY 4219
Sandwick (Isle of Lewis) 63 NB 4432
Sandwick (Shetld.) 63 HU 4323
Sandwick (S. Ronaldsay) 63 ND 4389
Sandy 27 TL 1649
Sandycroft 32 SJ 3366
Sandygate 43 SC 3797
Sandy Lane 17 ST 9668
Sangobeg 66 NC 4266
Sanna 54 NM 4469
Sanquhar 45 NS 7809
Santon Bridge 40 NY 1001
Santon Downham 28 TL 8187
Sapcote 26 SP 4893
Sapey Common 24 SO 7064
Sapiston 28 TL 9175
Sapperton (Glos.) 17 SO 9403
Sapperton (Lincs.) 34 TF 0133
Saracen's Head 35 TF 3427
Sarclet 67 ND 3443
Sarisbury 9 SU 5008
Sarn (Mid Glam.) 15 SS 9083
Sarn (Powys) 23 SO 2090
Sarnau (Dyfed) 14 SN 3151
Sarnau (Dyfed) 14 SN 3318
Sarnau (Gwyn.) 31 SH 9739
Sarnau (Powys) 23 SJ 2315
Sarn-bach 30 SH 3026
Sarnesfield 24 SO 3750
Sarn Meyllteyrn 30 SH 2432
Saron (Dyfed) 15 SN 3738
Saron (Dyfed) 15 SN 6012
Sarratt 19 TQ 0499
Sarre 13 TR 2565
Sarsden 18 SP 2822
Satley 42 NZ 1143
Satterleigh 6 SS 6622
Satterthwaite 40 SD 3392
Sauchen 62 NJ 7010
Saucher 56 NO 1933
Sauchieburn 57 NO 6669
Sauchrie 50 NS 3014
Saughall 32 SJ 3669
Saughtree 46 NY 5696
Saul 17 SO 7409
Saundby 34 SK 7888
Saundersfoot 14 SN 1304
Saunderton 18 SP 7901
Saunton 6 SS 4537
Sausthorpe 35 TF 3869
Savalmore 66 NC 5908
Sawbridgeworth 20 TL 4814
Sawdon 43 SE 9485
Sawley (Derby.) 33 SK 4731
Sawley (Lancs.) 37 SD 7746
Sawley (N Yorks.) 42 SE 2467
Sawrey 40 SD 3695
Sawston 20 TL 4849
Sawtry 27 TL 1683
Saxby (Leic.) 34 SK 8220
Saxby (Lincs.) 34 TF 0086
Saxby All Saints 39 SE 9816
Saxelbye 34 SK 6921
Saxilby 34 SK 8875
Saxlingham 29 TG 0239
Saxlingham Nethergate 29 TM 2397
Saxmundham 21 TM 3863
Saxondale 34 SK 6839
Saxon Street 20 TL 6859
Saxtead 21 TM 2665
Saxtead Green 21 TM 2564
Saxthorpe 29 TG 1130
Saxton 38 SE 4736
Sayers Common 11 TQ 2618
Scackleton 38 SE 6472
Scadabay 63 NG 1792
Scaftworth 38 SK 6691
Scagglethorpe 39 SE 8372
Scalasaig 48 NR 3894
Scalby 43 TA 0090
Scaldwell 26 SP 7672
Scaleby 46 NY 4563
Scalebyhill 46 NY 4363
Scale Houses 46 NY 5845
Scales (Cumbr.) 40 NY 3426
Scales (Cumbr.) 40 SD 2772
Scalford 34 SK 7624
Scaling 43 NZ 7413
Scalloway 63 HU 4039
Scalpay (Harris) 63 NG 2395
Scalpay (Island of Skye) 58 NG 6030
Scamblesby 35 TF 2778
Scamodale 54 NM 8473
Scampston 39 SE 8575
Scampton 34 SK 9479
Scapa 63 HY 4309
Scar 63 HY 6745
Scarastavore 63 NG 0092
Scarborough 43 TA 0388
Scarcliffe 33 SK 4968
Scarcroft 37 SE 3540
Scardroy 59 NH 2151
Scarff 63 HU 2479
Scarfskerry 67 ND 2673
Scargill 42 NZ 0510
Scarinish 48 NM 0444
Scarisbrick 36 SD 3713
Scarning 29 TF 9512
Scarrington 34 SK 7341
Scarth Hill 36 SD 4206
Scartho 39 TA 2606
Scatsta 63 HU 3872
Scaur or Kippford 45 NX 8355
Scawby 39 SE 9605
Scawton 42 SE 5483
Scayne's Hill 12 TQ 3723
Scethrog 16 SO 1025
Scholar Green 32 SJ 8357
Scholes (W Yorks.) 37 SE 1507
Scholes (W Yorks.) 37 SE 3736
Scleddau 14 SM 9434
Scole 29 TM 1579
Scolton 14 SM 9922
Sconser 58 NG 5232
Scoor 54 NM 4119
Scopwick 35 TF 0658
Scoraig 64 NH 0096
Scorborough 39 TA 0145
Scorrier 2 SW 7244
Scorton (Lancs.) 36 SD 5048
Scorton (N Yorks.) 42 NZ 2400
Sco Ruston 29 TG 2821
Scotby 46 NY 4454
Scotforth 36 SD 4759
Scothern 35 TF 0377
Scotland Gate 47 NZ 2584
Scotlandwell 56 NO 1801
Scotney Castle 12 TQ 6835
Scotsburn 65 NH 7275
Scotscraig 57 NO 4428
Scots' Gap 47 NZ 0486
Scotstown 54 NM 8263
Scotter 39 SE 8800
Scotterthorpe 39 SE 8701
Scotton (Lincs.) 39 SK 8899
Scotton (N Yorks.) 42 SE 1895
Scotton (N Yorks.) 37 SE 3259
Scottow 29 TG 2623
Scoughall 52 NT 6183
Scoulton 29 TF 9800
Scourie 66 NC 1544
Scousburgh 63 HU 3717
Scrabster 67 ND 0970
Scrainwood 47 NT 9909
Scrane End 35 TF 3841
Scraptoft 26 SK 6405
Scratby 29 TG 5115
Scrayingham 38 SE 7360
Scredington 35 TF 0940
Scremby 35 TF 4467
Scremerston 53 NU 0049
Screveton 34 SK 7343
Scriven 37 SE 3458
Scrooby 34 SK 6590
Scropton 33 SK 1930
Scrub Hill 35 TF 2355
Scruton 42 SE 2992
Sculthorpe 28 TF 8931
Scunthorpe 39 SE 8910
Seaborough 7 ST 4205
Seacombe 32 SJ 3190
Seacroft 35 TF 5660
Seafield 51 NT 0066
Seaford 12 TV 4899
Seaforth 32 SJ 3297
Seagrave 34 SK 6117
Seaham 47 NZ 4149
Seahouses 53 NU 2132
Seal 12 TQ 5556
Sealand 32 SJ 3268
Seamer (N Yorks.) 42 NZ 4910
Seamer (N Yorks.) 43 TA 0183
Seamill 49 NS 2047
Sea Palling 29 TG 4327
Searby 39 TA 0605
Seasalter 13 TR 0864
Seascale 40 NY 0301
Seathwaite (Cumbr.) 40 NY 2312
Seathwaite (Cumbr.) 40 SD 2296
Seaton (Corn.) 4 SX 3054
Seaton (Cumbr.) 40 NY 0130
Seaton (Devon.) 5 SY 2490
Seaton (Durham) 47 NZ 4049
Seaton (Humbs.) 39 TA 1646
Seaton (Leic.) 27 SP 9098
Seaton (Northum.) 47 NZ 3276
Seaton Carew 42 NZ 5229
Seaton Delaval 47 NZ 3075
Seaton Ross 38 SE 7741
Seaton Sluice 47 NZ 3376
Seave Green 42 NZ 5600
Seaview 9 SZ 6291
Seavington St. Mary 7 ST 3914
Seavington St. Michael 7 ST 4015
Sebergham 40 NY 3541
Seckington 33 SK 2607
Sedbergh 41 SD 6592
Sedbusk 41 SD 8891
Sedgeberrow 25 SP 0238
Sedgebrook 34 SK 8537
Sedgefield 42 NZ 3528
Sedgeford 28 TF 7136
Sedgehill 8 ST 8627
Sedgley 25 SO 9193
Sedgwick 40 SD 5186
Sedlescombe 12 TQ 7818
Seend 17 ST 9460
Seend Cleeve 17 ST 9260
Seer Green 19 SU 9691
Seething 29 TM 3197
Sefton 36 SD 3500
Seghill 47 NZ 2874
Seighford 33 SJ 8725
Seilebost 63 NG 0696
Seisdon 25 SO 8394
Selattyn 32 SJ 2633
Selborne 9 SU 7433
Selby 38 SE 6132
Selham 11 SU 9320
Selkirk 52 NT 4728
Sellack 17 SO 5627
Sellafirth 63 HU 5198
Sellindge 13 TR 0938
Selling 13 TR 0356
Sells Green 17 ST 9462
Selly Oak 25 SP 0482
Selmeston 12 TQ 5007
Selsdon 12 TQ 3562
Selsey 9 SZ 8593
Selsfield Common 12 TQ 3434
Selston 33 SK 4553
Selworthy 6 SS 9146
Semblister 63 HU 3350
Semer 21 TL 9946
Semington 17 ST 8960
Semley 8 ST 8926
Send 11 TQ 0155
Senghenydd 16 ST 1191
Sennen 2 SW 3525
Sennen Cove 2 SW 3425
Sennybridge 15 SN 9228
Sessay 38 SE 4575
Setchey 28 TF 6313
Setley 9 SU 3000
Settascarth 63 HY 3618
Setter (Shetld.) 63 HU 3954
Settle 41 SD 8263
Settrington 39 SE 8370
Sevenhampton (Glos.) 17 SP 0321
Sevenhampton (Wilts.) 17 SU 2090
Seven Kings 20 TQ 4586
Sevenoaks 12 TQ 5355
Sevenoaks Weald 12 TQ 5351
Seven Sisters 15 SN 8108
Severn Beach 16 ST 5384
Severn Stoke 25 SO 8544
Sevington 13 TR 0340
Sewards End 20 TL 5738
Sewerby 39 TA 2068
Seworgan 2 SW 7030

Southwater Sumburgh

Southwater 11 TQ 1526
Southway 7 ST 5142
South Weald 20 TQ 5793
Southwell (Dorset) 8 SY 6870
Southwell (Notts.) 34 SK 7053
South Weston 18 SU 7098
South Wheatley 4 SX 2492
Southwick (Hants.) 9 SU 6208
Southwick (Northants.) 27 TL 0192
Southwick (Tyne and Wear) 47 NZ 3758
Southwick (Wilts.) 17 ST 8354
Southwick (W Susx) 11 TQ 2405
South Widcombe 17 ST 5756
South Wigston 26 SP 5898
South Willingham 35 TF 1983
South Wingfield 33 SK 3755
South Witham 34 SK 9219
Southwold 29 TM 5076
South Wonston 9 SU 4635
Southwood (Norf.) 29 TG 3905
Southwood (Somer.) 7 ST 5533
South Woodham Ferrers 20 TQ 8097
South Wootton 28 TF 6422
South Wraxall 17 ST 8364
South Zeal 5 SX 6593
Soutra Mains 52 NT 4559
Sowerby (N Yorks.) 42 SE 4381
Sowerby (W Yorks.) 37 SE 0423
Sowerby Bridge 37 SE 0523
Sowerby Row 40 NY 3940
Sowton 5 SX 9792
Spa Common 29 TG 2930
Spalding 35 TF 2422
Spaldington 38 SE 7533
Spaldwick 27 TL 1272
Spalford 34 SK 8369
Sparham 29 TG 0619
Spark Bridge 40 SD 3084
Sparkford 7 ST 6026
Sparkwell 4 SX 5757
Sparrowpit 33 SK 0980
Sparsholt (Hants.) 9 SU 4331
Sparsholt (Oxon.) 18 SU 3487
Spaunton 43 SE 7289
Spaxton 7 ST 2236
Spean Bridge 55 NN 2281
Speen (Berks.) 10 SU 4568
Speen (Bucks.) 19 SU 8499
Speeton 39 TA 1574
Speke 32 SJ 4383
Speldhurst 12 TQ 5541
Spellbrook 20 TL 4817
Spelsbury 18 SP 3421
Spencers Wood 10 SU 7166
Spennithorne 42 SE 1489
Spennymoor 42 NZ 2533
Spetchley 25 SO 8953
Spettisbury 8 ST 9002
Spexhall 29 TM 3780
Spey Bay 61 NJ 3866
Spilsby 35 TF 4066
Spindlestone 53 NU 1533
Spinningdale 65 NH 6789
Spirthill 17 ST 9975
Spital 67 ND 1654
Spithurst 12 TQ 4217
Spittal (Dyfed) 14 SM 9723
Spittal (Lothian) 52 NT 4677
Spittal (Northum.) 53 NU 0051
Spittalfield 56 NO 1040
Spittal of Glenmuick 57 NO 3184
Spittal of Glenshee 56 NO 1070
Spixworth 29 TG 2415
Spofforth 37 SE 3650
Spondon 33 SK 3935
Spooner Row 29 TM 0997
Sporle 28 TF 8411
Spott 52 NT 6775
Spratton 26 SP 7170
Spreakley 10 SU 8341
Spreyton 6 SX 6996
Spridlington 34 TF 0084
Springburn 50 NS 5968
Springfield (Fife.) 57 NO 3411
Springfield (Grampn.) 61 NJ 0559
Springfield (W Mids.) 25 SP 1082
Springholm 45 NX 8070
Springside 50 NS 3639
Springthorpe 34 SK 8789
Sproatley 39 TA 1934
Sproston Green 32 SJ 7367
Sprotbrough 38 SE 5302
Sproughton 21 TM 1244
Sprouston 53 NT 7535
Sprowston 29 TG 2412
Sproxton (Leic.) 34 SK 8524
Sproxton (N Yorks.) 42 SE 6181
Spurstow 32 SJ 5556
Stackhouse 41 SD 8165
Stacksteads 37 SD 8421
Staddiscombe 4 SX 5151
Staddlethorpe 39 SE 8428
Stadhampton 18 SU 6098
Staffield 41 NY 5442
Staffin 58 NG 4967
Stafford 33 SJ 9223
Stagsden 27 SP 9849
Stainburn 37 SE 2448
Stainby 34 SK 9022
Staincross 37 SE 3210
Staindrop 42 NZ 1220
Staines 11 TQ 0471
Stainfield (Lincs.) 35 TF 0724
Stainfield (Lincs.) 35 TF 1173
Stainforth (N Yorks.) 41 SD 8267
Stainforth (S Yorks.) 38 SE 6411
Staining 36 SD 3435
Stainland 37 SE 0719
Stainsacre 43 NZ 9108
Stainton (Cleve.) 42 NZ 4714
Stainton (Cumbr.) 40 NY 4827
Stainton (Cumbr.) 40 SD 5285
Stainton (Durham) 42 NZ 0718
Stainton (N Yorks.) 42 SE 1096
Stainton (S Yorks.) 38 SK 5593
Stainton by Langworth 35 TF 0577
Staintondale 43 SE 9898
Stainton le Vale 39 TF 1794
Stainton with Adgarley 40 SD 2472
Stair (Cumbr.) 40 NY 2321
Stair (Strath.) 50 NS 4323
Staithes 43 NZ 7818
Stakeford 47 NZ 2785
Stake Pool 36 SD 4148
Stalbridge 8 ST 7317
Stalbridge Weston 8 ST 7216
Stalham 29 TG 3725
Stalham Green 29 TG 3824
Stalisfield Green 13 TQ 9652
Stallingborough 39 TA 2011
Stalling Busk 41 SD 9185
Stalmine 36 SD 3745
Stalybridge 37 SJ 9698
Stambourne 20 TL 7238
Stamford 34 TF 0207
Stamford Bridge 38 SE 7155
Stamfordham 47 NZ 0772
Stanborough 19 TL 2210
Stanbridge (Beds.) 19 SP 9623
Stanbridge (Dorset) 8 SU 0003
Stand 50 NS 7668
Standburn 51 NS 9274
Standeford 25 SJ 9107
Standen 13 TQ 8539
Standford 9 SU 8134
Standish 36 SD 5609
Standlake 18 SP 3902
Standon (Hants.) 9 SU 4227
Standon (Herts.) 20 TL 3922
Standon (Staffs.) 32 SJ 8134
Stane 50 NS 8859
Stanfield 29 TF 9320
Stanford (Beds.) 27 TL 1641
Stanford (Kent) 13 TR 1238
Stanford Bishop 24 SO 6851
Stanford Bridge 24 SO 7165
Stanford Dingley 10 SU 5771
Stanford in the Vale 18 SU 3493
Stanford le Hope 20 TQ 6882
Stanford on Avon 26 SP 5878
Stanford on Soar 34 SK 5422
Stanford on Teme 24 SO 7065
Stanford Rivers 20 TL 5301
Stanghow 42 NZ 6715
Stanhoe 28 TF 8036
Stanhope 41 NY 9939
Stanion 27 SP 9187
Stanley (Derby.) 33 SK 4140
Stanley (Durham) 47 NZ 1953
Stanley (Staffs.) 33 SJ 9252
Stanley (Tays.) 56 NO 1033
Stanley (W Yorks.) 37 SE 3422
Stanmer 12 TQ 3309
Stanmore (Berks.) 10 SU 4778
Stanmore (Gtr London) 19 TQ 1692
Stannington (Northum.) 47 NZ 2179
Stannington (S Yorks.) 33 SK 2988
Stansbatch 23 SO 3461
Stansfield 20 TL 7852
Stanstead 20 TL 8449
Stanstead Abbots 20 TL 3811
Stansted 12 TQ 6062
Stansted Mountfitchet 20 TL 5124
Stanton (Glos.) 25 SP 0634
Stanton (Northum.) 47 NZ 1390
Stanton (Staffs.) 33 SK 1246
Stanton (Suff.) 29 TL 9673
Stanton by Bridge 33 SK 3627
Stanton by Dale 33 SK 4637
Stanton Drew 17 ST 5963
Stanton Fitzwarren 17 SU 1790
Stanton Harcourt 18 SP 4105
Stanton Hill 33 SK 4860
Stanton in Peak 33 SK 2464
Stanton Lacy 24 SO 4978
Stanton Long 24 SO 5690
Stanton on the Wolds 34 SK 6330
Stanton Prior 17 ST 6762
Stanton St. Bernard 17 SU 0962
Stanton St. John 18 SP 5709
Stanton St. Quintin 17 ST 9079
Stanton Street 21 TL 9566
Stanton under Bardon 33 SK 4610
Stanton upon Hine Heath 32 SJ 5624
Stanton Wick 17 ST 6162
Stanwardine in the Fields 32 SJ 4124
Stanway (Essex) 21 TL 9324
Stanway (Glos.) 25 SP 0532
Stanwell 11 TQ 0574
Stanwell Moor 11 TQ 0474
Stanwick 27 SP 9871
Stanydale 63 HU 2850
Stape 43 SE 7993
Stapehill 8 SU 0500
Stapeley 32 SJ 6749
Staple 13 TR 2756
Staple Cross 12 TQ 7822
Staplefield 11 TQ 2728
Staple Fitzpaine 7 ST 2618
Stapleford (Cambs.) 20 TL 4751
Stapleford (Herts.) 20 TL 3117
Stapleford (Leic.) 34 SK 8018
Stapleford (Lincs.) 34 SK 8757
Stapleford (Notts.) 33 SK 4837
Stapleford (Wilts.) 8 SU 0637
Stapleford Abbots 20 TQ 5096
Stapleford Tawney 20 TQ 5098
Staplegrove 7 ST 2126
Staple Hill 7 ST 2416
Staplehurst 12 TQ 7843
Staplers 9 SZ 5189
Stapleton (Avon) 17 ST 6175
Stapleton (Cumbr.) 46 NY 5071
Stapleton (Here. and Worc.) 23 SO 3265
Stapleton (Leic.) 26 SP 4398
Stapleton (N Yorks.) 42 NZ 2612
Stapleton (Salop) 24 SJ 4604
Stapleton (Somer.) 7 ST 4621
Stapley 7 ST 1813
Staploe 27 TL 1460
Star (Dyfed) 14 SN 2435
Star (Fife.) 57 NO 3103
Star (Somer.) 16 ST 4358
Starbotton 41 SD 9574
Starcross 5 SX 9781
Starston 29 TM 2384
Startforth 42 NZ 0416
Startley 17 ST 9482
Stathe 7 ST 3728
Stathern 34 SK 7731
Station Town 42 NZ 4036
Staughton Highway 27 TL 1364
Staunton (Glos.) 16 SO 5412
Staunton (Glos.) 17 SO 7929
Staunton on Arrow 24 SO 3660
Staunton on Wye 24 SO 3645
Staveley (Cumbr.) 40 SD 3786
Staveley (Cumbr.) 40 SD 4698
Staveley (Derby.) 33 SK 4374
Staveley (N Yorks.) 42 SE 3662
Staverton (Devon.) 5 SX 7964
Staverton (Glos.) 17 SO 8923
Staverton (Northants.) 26 SP 5461
Staverton (Wilts.) 17 ST 8560
Stawell 7 ST 3638
Staxigoe 67 ND 3852
Staxton 43 TA 0179
Staylittle 22 SN 8892
Staythorpe 34 SK 7554
Stean 42 SE 0873
Stearsby 38 SE 6171
Steart 7 ST 2745
Stebbing 20 TL 6624
Stedham 9 SU 8622
Steele Road 46 NY 5292
Steen's Bridge 24 SO 5457
Steep 9 SU 7525
Steeple (Dorset) 8 SY 9080
Steeple (Essex) 21 TL 9303
Steeple Ashton 17 ST 9056
Steeple Aston 18 SP 4725
Steeple Barton 18 SP 4424
Steeple Bumpstead 20 TL 6741
Steeple Claydon 18 SP 7027
Steeple Gidding 27 TL 1381
Steeple Langford 8 SU 0337
Steeple Morden 27 TL 2842
Steeton 37 SE 0344
Steinmanhill 62 NJ 7642
Stelling Minnis 13 TR 1446
Stemster 67 ND 1862
Stenalees 4 SX 0157
Stenhousemuir 50 NS 8682
Stenness 63 HU 2176
Stenton 52 NT 6274
Steppingley 19 TL 0135
Stepps 50 NS 6668
Sternfield 21 TM 3861
Stert 17 SU 0259
Stetchworth 20 TL 6458
Stevenage 19 TL 2325
Stevenston 50 NS 2642
Steventon (Hants.) 10 SU 5547
Steventon (Oxon.) 18 SU 4691
Stevington 27 SP 9853
Stewartby 27 TL 0242
Stewarton 50 NS 4246
Stewkley 19 SP 8525
Stewton 35 TF 3687
Steyning 11 TQ 1711
Steynton 14 SM 9108
Stibb 4 SS 2210
Stibbard 29 TF 9828
Stibb Cross 4 SS 4314
Stibb Green 10 SU 2262
Stibbington 27 TL 0898
Stichill 52 NT 7138
Sticker 2 SW 9750
Stickford 35 TF 3560
Sticklepath 6 SX 6394
Stickney 35 TF 3456
Stiffkey 29 TF 9743
Stifford's Bridge 24 SO 7348
Stilligarry 63 NF 7638
Stillingfleet 38 SE 5940
Stillington (Cleve. Durham) 42 NZ 3723
Stillington (N Yorks.) 38 SE 5867
Stilton 27 TL 1689
Stinchcombe 17 ST 7298
Stinsford 8 SY 7191
St Ippollitts 19 TL 1927
Stirchley 24 SJ 6906
Stirling 50 NS 7993
Stisted 20 TL 8024
Stithians 2 SW 7336
Stivichall 26 SP 3376
Stixwould 35 TF 1765
Stoak 32 SJ 4273
Stobieside 50 NS 6239
Stobo 51 NT 1837
Stoborough 8 SY 9286
Stoborough Green 8 SY 9184
Stock 20 TQ 6998
Stockbridge 9 SU 3535
Stockbriggs 50 NS 7936
Stockbury 13 TQ 8461
Stockcross 10 SU 4368
Stockdalewath 46 NY 3845
Stockerston 26 SP 8397
Stock Green 25 SO 9859
Stockingford 26 SP 3391
Stocking Pelham 20 TL 4529
Stockinish 63 NG 1391
Stockland 5 ST 2404
Stockland Bristol 7 ST 2443
Stockleigh English 6 SS 8406
Stockleigh Pomeroy 6 SS 8703
Stockley 17 SU 0067
Stockport 33 SJ 8989
Stocksbridge 37 SK 2798
Stocksfield 47 NZ 0561
Stockton (Here. and Worc.) 24 SO 5161
Stockton (Norf.) 29 TM 3894
Stockton (Salop) 24 SO 7299
Stockton (Warw.) 26 SP 4363
Stockton (Wilts.) 8 ST 9738
Stockton Heath 32 SJ 6185
Stockton-on-Tees 42 NZ 4419
Stockton on Teme 24 SO 7167
Stockton on the Forest 38 SE 6556
Stockwith 38 SK 7994
Stock Wood 25 SP 0058
Stodmarsh 13 TR 2160
Stody 29 TG 0535
Stoer 64 NC 0428
Stoford (Somer.) 7 ST 5613
Stoford (Wilts.) 8 SU 0835
Stogumber 7 ST 0937
Stogursey 7 ST 2042
Stoke (Devon.) 4 SS 2324
Stoke (Hants.) 10 SU 4051
Stoke (Hants.) 9 SU 7202
Stoke (Kent) 12 TQ 8275
Stoke Abbott 7 ST 4500
Stoke Albany 26 SP 8088
Stoke Ash 29 TM 1170
Stoke Bardolph 34 SK 6441
Stoke Bliss 24 SO 6562
Stoke Bruerne 26 SP 7450
Stoke by Clare 20 TL 7443
Stoke-by-Nayland 21 TL 9836
Stoke Canon 6 SX 9397
Stoke Charity 10 SU 4839
Stoke Climsland 4 SX 3574
Stoke D'Abernon 11 TQ 1259
Stoke Doyle 27 TL 0286
Stoke Dry 27 SP 8597
Stoke Ferry 28 TF 7000
Stoke Fleming 5 SX 8648
Stokeford 8 SY 8787
Stoke Gabriel 5 SX 8457
Stoke Gifford 17 ST 6280
Stoke Golding 26 SP 3997
Stoke Goldington 26 SP 8348
Stokeham 34 SK 7876
Stoke Hammond 19 SP 8829
Stoke Holy Cross 29 TG 2301
Stokeinteignhead 5 SX 9170
Stoke Lacy 24 SO 6149
Stoke Lyne 18 SP 5628
Stoke Mandeville 18 SP 8310
Stokenchurch 18 SU 7596
Stoke Newington 20 TQ 3286
Stokenham 5 SX 8042
Stoke-on-Trent 33 SJ 8745
Stoke Orchard 17 SO 9128
Stoke Poges 19 SU 9884
Stoke Prior (Here. and Worc.) 24 SO 5256
Stoke Prior (Here. and Worc.) 25 SO 9467
Stoke Rivers 6 SS 6335
Stoke Rochford 34 SK 9127
Stoke Row 18 SU 6883
Stoke St. Gregory 7 ST 3426
Stoke St. Mary 7 ST 2622
Stoke St. Michael 8 ST 6646
Stoke St. Milborough 24 SO 5682
Stokesay 24 SO 4381
Stokes Bay 9 SZ 5897
Stokesby 29 TG 4310
Stokesley 42 NZ 5208
Stoke sub Hamdon 7 ST 4717
Stoke Talmage 18 SU 6799
Stoke Trister 8 ST 7328
Stoke upon Tern 32 SJ 6327
Stolford 7 ST 2245
Stondon Massey 20 TL 5800
Stone (Bucks.) 18 SP 7812
Stone (Glos.) 17 ST 6895
Stone (Here. and Worc.) 25 SO 8675
Stone (Kent) 12 TQ 5774
Stone (Kent) 13 TQ 9427
Stone (Staffs.) 33 SJ 9034
Stone Allerton 7 ST 3950
Ston Easton 8 ST 6253
Stonebroom 33 SK 4159
Stone Cross 12 TQ 6104
Stonefield 50 NS 6957
Stonegate 12 TQ 6628
Stonegate Crofts 62 NK 0339
Stonegrave 42 SE 6577
Stonehaugh 46 NY 7976
Stonehaven 57 NO 8685
Stone House (Cumbr.) 41 SD 7785
Stonehouse (Glos.) 17 SO 8005
Stonehouse (Northum.) 46 NY 6958
Stonehouse (Strath.) 50 NS 7546
Stoneleigh 26 SP 3272
Stonely 27 TL 1067
Stonesby 34 SK 8224
Stonesfield 18 SP 3917
Stones Green 21 TM 1626
Stoneybridge 63 NF 7433
Stoneyburn 51 NS 9762
Stoney Cross 9 SU 2511
Stoneygate 26 SK 6102
Stoneyhills 21 TQ 9497
Stoneykirk 44 NX 0853
Stoney Middleton 33 SK 2275
Stoney Stanton 26 SP 4894
Stoney Stratton 8 ST 6539
Stoney Stretton 24 SJ 3809
Stoneywood 62 NJ 8910
Stonganess 63 HP 5402
Stonham Aspal 21 TM 1359
Stonnall 25 SK 0603
Stonor 18 SU 7388
Stonton Wyville 26 SP 7395
Stonybreck HZ 2071
Stony Stratford 26 SP 7840
Stoodleigh 6 SS 9218
Stopham 11 TQ 0219
Stopsley 19 TL 1023
Storeton 32 SJ 3084
Stornoway 63 NB 4333
Storridge 24 SO 7448
Storrington 11 TQ 0814
Storth 40 SD 4780
Stotfold 19 TL 2136
Stottesdon 24 SO 6782
Stoughton (Leic.) 26 SK 6402
Stoughton (Surrey) 11 SU 9851
Stoughton (W Susx) 9 SU 8011
Stoul 58 NM 7594
Stoulton 25 SO 9049
Stourbridge 25 SO 8984
Stourhead 8 ST 7734
Stourpaine 8 ST 8509
Stourport-on-Severn 25 SO 8171
Stour Provost 8 ST 7921
Stour Row 8 ST 8220
Stourton (Here. and Worc.) 25 SO 8585
Stourton (Warw.) 18 SP 2936
Stourton (Wilts.) 8 ST 7733
Stourton Caundle 8 ST 7114
Stove 63 HY 6036
Stoven 29 TM 4481
Stow (Borders) 52 NT 4644
Stow (Lincs.) 34 SK 8781
Stow Bardolph 28 TF 6205
Stow Bedon 29 TL 9596
Stowbridge 28 TF 6007
Stow cum Quy 20 TL 5260
Stowe (Salop) 23 SO 3173
Stowe (Staffs.) 33 SK 0027
Stowell 8 ST 6822
Stowford 4 SX 4386
Stowlangtoft 21 TL 9568
Stow Longa 27 TL 1171
Stow Maries 20 TQ 8399
Stowmarket 21 TM 0458
Stow-on-the-Wold 17 SP 1925
Stowting 13 TR 1241
Stowupland 21 TM 0659
Straad 49 NS 0462
Strachan 62 NO 6792
Strachur 55 NN 0901
Stradbroke 29 TM 2373
Stradishall 20 TL 7452
Stradsett 28 TF 6605
Stragglethorpe 34 SK 9152
Straiton (Lothian) 51 NT 2766
Straiton (Strath.) 44 NS 3804
Straloch (Grampn.) 62 NJ 8621
Straloch (Tays.) 56 NO 0463
Stramshall 33 SK 0735
Strands 40 NY 1204
Stranraer 44 NX 0660
Strata Florida 22 SN 7465
Stratfield Mortimer 10 SU 6764
Stratfield Saye 10 SU 6961
Stratfield Turgis 10 SU 6959
Stratford St. Andrew 21 TM 3560
Stratford St. Mary 21 TM 0434
Stratford Tony 8 SU 0926
Stratford-upon-Avon 25 SP 2055
Strathan (Highld.) 64 NC 0821
Strathan (Highld.) 59 NM 9891
Strathaven 50 NS 7044
Strathblane (Central) 50 NS 5679
Strathcarron (Highld.) 59 NG 9442
Strathconon 60 NH 4055
Strathdon 61 NJ 3513
Strath Fleet 66 NC 6702
Strath Gairloch 64 NG 7977
Strathkanaird (Highld.) 64 NC 1501
Strathkinness 57 NO 4516
Strathmiglo 56 NO 2109
Strathpeffer 60 NH 4858
Strathwhillan 49 NS 0235
Strathy 67 NC 8465
Strathyre 55 NN 5617
Stratton (Corn.) 4 SS 2306
Stratton (Dorset) 8 SY 6593
Stratton (Glos.) 17 SP 0103
Stratton Audley 18 SP 6026
Stratton-on-the-Fosse 8 ST 6550
Stratton St. Margaret 17 SU 1787
Stratton St. Michael 29 TM 2093
Stratton Strawless 29 TG 2220
Stravithie 57 NO 5311
Streat 12 TQ 3515
Streatham 11 TQ 2972
Streatley (Beds.) 19 TL 0728
Streatley (Berks.) 10 SU 5980
Street (Lancs.) 36 SD 5252
Street (N Yorks.) 43 NZ 7304
Street (Somer.) 7 ST 4836
Street End 9 SZ 8599
Streethay 25 SK 1410
Streetly 25 SP 0898
Strefford 24 SO 4485
Strensall 38 SE 6360
Strensham 25 SO 9040
Stretcholt 7 ST 2943
Strete 5 SX 8447
Stretford 37 SJ 7894
Stretford Court 24 SO 4455
Strethall 20 TL 4939
Stretham 28 TL 5174
Strettington 11 SU 8807
Stretton (Ches.) 32 SJ 4452
Stretton (Ches.) 32 SJ 6182
Stretton (Derby.) 33 SK 3961
Stretton (Leic.) 34 SK 9415
Stretton (Staffs.) 25 SJ 8811
Stretton (Staffs.) 33 SK 2526
Stretton en le Field 33 SK 3012
Stretton Grandison 24 SO 6344
Stretton Heath 24 SJ 3610
Stretton-on-Dunsmore 26 SP 4072
Stretton on Fosse 18 SP 2238
Stretton under Fosse 26 SP 4581
Stretton Westwood 24 SO 5998
Strichen 62 NJ 9455
Stringston 7 ST 1742
Strixton 27 SP 9061
Stroat 17 ST 5798
Stromeferry 59 NG 8634
Stromemore 59 NG 8635
Stromness (Orkney) 63 HY 2509
Stronachlachar 55 NN 4010
Strond 63 NG 0384
Strone (Highld.) 60 NH 5228
Strone (Strath.) 49 NS 1880
Stronenaba 55 NN 2084
Stronmilchan 55 NN 1528
Strontian 54 NM 8161
Strood 12 TQ 7369
Stroud (Glos.) 17 SO 8504
Stroud (Hants.) 9 SU 7223
Struan 58 NG 3438
Struan Station 56 NN 8065
Strubby 35 TF 4582
Strumpshaw 29 TG 3507
Strutherhill 50 NS 7650
Struy 60 NH 4039
Stuartfield 62 NJ 9745
Stubbington 9 SU 5503
Stubbins 37 SD 7918
Stubhampton 8 ST 9113
Stubton 34 SK 8748
Stuckgowan 55 NN 3202
Stuckton 8 SU 1613
Studham 19 TL 0215
Studland 8 SZ 0382
Studley (Oxon.) 18 SP 5912
Studley (Warw.) 25 SP 0763
Studley (Wilts.) 17 ST 9671
Studley Roger 42 SE 2970
Stump Cross 20 TL 5044
Stuntney 28 TL 5578
Sturbridge 32 SJ 8330
Sturmer 20 TL 6944
Sturminster Common 8 ST 7812
Sturminster Marshall 8 SY 9499
Sturminster Newton 8 ST 7813
Sturry 13 TR 1760
Sturton by Stow 34 SK 8980
Sturton le Steeple 34 SK 7884
Stuston 29 TM 1378
Stutton (N Yorks.) 38 SE 4741
Stutton (Suff.) 21 TM 1434
Styal 32 SJ 8383
Suckley 24 SO 7151
Sudborough 27 SP 9682
Sudbourne 21 TM 4153
Sudbrook 16 ST 5087
Sudbrooke 34 TF 0276
Sudbury (Derby.) 33 SK 1631
Sudbury (Suff.) 21 TL 8741
Suddie 60 NH 6654
Sudgrove 17 SO 9307
Suffield 29 TG 2332
Sugnall 32 SJ 7930
Sulby 43 SC 3994
Sulgrave 26 SP 5545
Sulham 10 SU 6474
Sulhamstead 10 SU 6368
Sullington 11 TQ 0913
Sullom 63 HU 3573
Sully 16 ST 1568
Sumburgh 63 HU 4009

Upper Seagry West Halton

Upper Seagry 17 ST 9580
Upper Shelton 27 SP 9943
Upper Sheringham 29 TG 1441
Upper Skelmorlie 49 NS 1968
Upper Slaughter 17 SP 1523
Upper Soudley 17 SO 6610
Upper Stondon 19 TL 1535
Upper Stowe 26 SP 6456
Upper Street (Hants.) 8 SU 1418
Upper Street (Norf.) 29 TG 3516
Upper Sundon 19 TL 0527
Upper Swell 17 SP 1726
Upper Tasburgh 29 TM 2095
Upper Tean 33 SK 0139
Upperthong 37 SE 1208
Upper Tillyrie 56 NO 1006
Upperton 11 SU 9522
Upper Tooting 11 TQ 2772
Upper Town (Avon) 16 ST 5265
Uppertown (Island of Stroma) 67 ND 3576
Upper Tysoe 26 SP 3343
Upper Upham 10 SU 2277
Upper Wardington 26 SP 4946
Upper Weald 18 SP 8037
Upper Weedon 26 SP 6258
Upper Wield 10 SU 6238
Upper Winchendon 18 SP 7414
Upper Woodford 8 SU 1237
Uppingham 27 SP 8699
Uppington 24 SJ 5909
Upsall 42 SE 4587
Upshire 20 TL 4100
Up Somborne 9 SU 3932
Upstreet 13 TR 2262
Up Sydling 8 ST 6201
Upton (Berks.) 11 SU 9879
Upton (Bucks.) 18 SP 7711
Upton (Cambs.) 27 TL 1778
Upton (Ches.) 32 SJ 4069
Upton (Dorset) 8 SY 9893
Upton (Hants.) 10 SU 3555
Upton (Hants.) 9 SU 3716
Upton (Lincs.) 34 SK 8686
Upton (Mers.) 32 SJ 2687
Upton (Norf.) 29 TG 3912
Upton (Northants.) 26 SP 7160
Upton (Northants.) 27 TF 1000
Upton (Notts.) 34 SK 7354
Upton (Notts.) 34 SK 7476
Upton (Oxon.) 18 SU 5186
Upton (Somer.) 7 SS 9928
Upton (W Yorks.) 38 SE 4713
Upton Bishop 17 SO 6427
Upton Cheyney 17 ST 6969
Upton Cressett 24 SO 6592
Upton Cross 4 SX 2872
Upton Grey 10 SU 6948
Upton Hellions 6 SS 8303
Upton Lovell 8 ST 9440
Upton Magna 24 SJ 5512
Upton Noble 8 ST 7139
Upton Pyne 6 SX 9197
Upton St. Leonards 17 SO 8615
Upton Scudamore 8 ST 8647
Upton Snodsbury 25 SO 9454
Upton upon Severn 25 SO 8540
Upton Warren 25 SO 9267
Upwaltham 11 SU 9413
Upware 28 TL 5370
Upwell 28 TF 5002
Upwey 8 SY 6684
Upwood 27 TL 2582
Uradale 63 HU 4137
Urafirth (Shetld.) 63 HU 3078
Urchal 60 NH 7544
Urchany 60 NH 8849
Urchfont 17 SU 0356
Urdimarsh 24 SO 5249
Ure 63 HU 2180
Urgha 63 NG 1799
Urishay Common 23 SO 3137
Urlay Nook 42 NZ 4014
Urmston 37 SJ 7695
Urquhart 61 NJ 2863
Urra 42 NZ 5702
Urray 60 NH 5053
Urswick 40 SD 2674
Ushaw Moor 42 NZ 2342
Usk 16 SO 3701
Usselby 39 TF 0993
Utley 37 SE 0542
Uton 6 SX 8298
Utterby 39 TF 3093
Uttoxeter 33 SK 0933
Uwchmynydd (Gwyn.) 30 SH 1425
Uwch-mynydd (Gwyn) 30 SH 6419
Uxbridge 19 TQ 0583
Uyeasound (Unst) 63 HP 5901
Uzmaston 14 SM 9714

Valley 30 SH 2979
Valleyfield 51 NT 0086
Valsgarth 63 HP 6413
Valtos (Island of Skye) 58 NG 5163
Valtos (Isle of Lewis) 63 NB 0936
Vange 20 TQ 7287
Vardre 15 SN 6902
Varteg 16 SO 2506
Vatten 58 NG 2843
Vaul 48 NM 0448
Vauld, The 24 SO 5349
Vaynol Hall 30 SH 5369
Vaynor 16 SO 0410
Veensgarth 63 HU 4244
Velindre (Dyfed) 14 SN 1039
Velindre (Dyfed) 14 SN 3538
Velindre (Powys) 23 SO 1836
Veness (Eday) 63 HY 5729
Vennington 23 SJ 3309
Venn Ottery 5 SY 0791
Ventnor 9 SZ 5677
Vernham Dean 10 SU 3356
Vernham Street 10 SU 3457
Vernolds Common 24 SO 4780
Verwig 14 SN 1849
Verwood 8 SU 0908
Veryan 2 SW 9139
Vicarage 5 SY 2088
Vickerstown 40 SD 1868
Victoria 4 SW 9961
Vidlin 63 HU 4765
Viewpark 50 NS 7161
Villavin 6 SS 5816
Vinehall Street 12 TQ 7520
Vine's Cross 12 TQ 5917
Virginia Water 11 SU 9967
Virginstow 4 SX 3792
Vobster 8 ST 7048
Voe (Shetld.) 63 HU 4062
Vowchurch 24 SO 3636
Voxter 63 HU 3769
Voy 63 HY 2515

Wackerfield 42 NZ 1522
Wacton 29 TM 1891
Wadborough 25 SO 8947
Waddesdon 18 SP 7416
Waddingham 39 SK 9896
Waddington (Lancs.) 36 SD 7243
Waddington (Lincs.) 34 SK 9764
Wadebridge 4 SW 9972
Wadeford 7 ST 3110
Wadenhoe 27 TL 0083
Wadesmill 20 TL 3517
Wadhurst 12 TQ 6431
Wadshelf 33 SK 3171
Wadworth 38 SK 5697
Waen Fach 23 SJ 2017
Wainfleet All Saints 35 TF 4959
Wainfleet Bank 35 TF 4759
Wainhouse Corner 4 SX 1895
Wainscott 12 TQ 7471
Wainstalls 37 SE 0428
Waitby 41 NY 7507
Wakefield 37 SE 3320
Wakerley 27 SP 9599
Wakes Colne 21 TL 8928
Walberswick 29 TM 4974
Walberton 11 SU 9705
Walcot (Lincs.) 35 TF 0535
Walcot (Lincs.) 35 TF 1256
Walcot (Salop) 24 SJ 5912
Walcot (Salop) 23 SO 3485
Walcot (Warw.) 25 SP 1258
Walcote 26 SP 5683
Walcott (Norf.) 29 TG 3632
Walden 41 SE 0082
Walden Head 41 SD 9880
Walden Stubbs 38 SE 5516
Walderslade 12 TQ 7563
Walderton 9 SU 7910
Walditch 7 SY 4892
Waldridge 47 NZ 2549
Waldringfield 21 TM 2744
Waldron 12 TQ 5419
Wales 33 SK 4782
Walesby (Lincs.) 39 TF 1392
Walesby (Notts.) 34 SK 6870
Walford (Here. and Worc.) 24 SO 3872
Walford (Here. and Worc.) 17 SO 5820
Walford (Salop) 32 SJ 4320
Walgherton 32 SJ 6948
Walgrave 26 SP 8071
Walkden 36 SD 7303
Walker 47 NZ 2864
Walkerburn 51 NT 3637
Walker Fold 36 SD 6742
Walkeringham 38 SK 7692
Walkerith 38 SK 7892
Walkern 19 TL 2926
Walker's Green 24 SO 5248
Walkerton 56 NO 2301
Walkhampton 4 SX 5369
Walkington 39 SE 9936
Walk Mill 37 SD 8629
Wall (Northum.) 47 NY 9168
Wall (Staffs.) 25 SK 0906
Wallacetown 50 NS 3422
Wallasey 32 SJ 2992
Wall Bank 24 SO 5092
Wallend 13 TQ 8775
Walling Fen 39 SE 8829
Wallingford 18 SU 6089
Wallington (Gtr London) 11 TQ 2863
Wallington (Hants.) 9 SU 5806
Wallington (Herts.) 19 TL 2933
Wallis 14 SN 0125
Walliswood 11 TQ 1138
Walls 63 HU 2449
Wallsend 47 NZ 2766
Wallyford 51 NT 3671
Walmer 13 TR 3750
Walmer Bridge 36 SD 4724
Walmersley 37 SD 8013
Walmley 25 SP 1393
Walpole 29 TM 3674
Walpole Highway 28 TF 5113
Walpole St. Andrew 28 TF 5017
Walpole St. Peter 28 TF 5016
Walsall 25 SP 0198
Walsall Wood 25 SK 0403
Walsden 37 SD 9322
Walsgrave on Sowe 26 SP 3781
Walsham le Willows 29 TM 0071
Walsoken 35 TF 4710
Walston 51 NT 0545
Walterstone 16 SO 3425
Waltham (Humbs.) 39 TA 2503
Waltham (Kent) 13 TR 1148
Waltham Abbey 20 TL 3800
Waltham Chase 9 SU 5614
Waltham on the Wolds 34 SK 8025
Waltham St. Lawrence 10 SU 8276
Walthamstow 20 TQ 3788
Walton (Bucks.) 27 SP 8936
Walton (Cumbr.) 46 NY 5264
Walton (Derby.) 33 SK 3569
Walton (Leic.) 26 SP 5987
Walton (Powys) 23 SO 2559
Walton (Salop) 32 SJ 5818
Walton (Somer.) 7 ST 4636
Walton (Suff.) 21 TM 2935
Walton (Warw.) 26 SP 2853
Walton (W Yorks.) 38 SE 3516
Walton (W Yorks.) 38 SE 4447
Walton Cardiff 25 SO 9032
Walton East 14 SN 0123
Walton-in-Gordano 16 ST 4273
Walton-le-Dale 36 SD 5627
Walton-on-Thames 11 TQ 1066
Walton-on-the-Hill (Staffs.) 33 SJ 9520
Walton on the Hill (Surrey) 11 TQ 2255
Walton on the Naze 21 TM 2521
Walton on the Wolds 34 SK 5919
Walton-on-Trent 33 SK 2118
Walton West 14 SM 8713
Walworth 42 NZ 2218
Walwyn's Castle 14 SM 8711
Wambrook 7 ST 2907
Wanborough 17 SU 2082
Wandsworth 11 TQ 2673
Wangford 29 TM 4679
Wanlip 34 SK 5910
Wanlockhead 50 NS 8712
Wansford (Cambs.) 27 TL 0799
Wansford (Humbs.) 39 TA 0656
Wanstead 20 TQ 4087
Wanstrow 8 ST 7141
Wanswell 17 SO 6801
Wantage 18 SU 4087
Wapley 17 ST 7179
Wappenbury 26 SP 3769
Wappenham 26 SP 6245
Warbleton 12 TQ 6018
Warborough 18 SU 6093
Warboys 27 TL 3080
Warbstow 4 SX 2090
Warburton 32 SJ 7089
Warcop 41 NY 7415
Warden 13 TR 0271
Ward Green 21 TM 0564
Wardington 26 SP 4946
Wardlaw Hill 50 NS 6822
Wardle (Ches.) 32 SJ 6057
Wardle (Gtr Mches.) 37 SD 9116
Wardley 26 SK 8300
Wardlow 33 SK 1874
Wardy Hill 27 TL 4782
Ware 20 TL 3614
Wareham 8 SY 9287
Warehorne 13 TQ 9832
Warenford 53 NU 1328
Waren Mill 53 NU 1534
Warenton 53 NU 1030
Wareside 20 TL 3915
Waresley 27 TL 2454
Warfield 11 SU 8872
Wargrave 10 SU 7878
Warham All Saints 29 TF 9441
Warham St. Mary 29 TF 9441
Wark (Northum.) 53 NT 8238
Wark (Northum.) 47 NY 8576
Warkleigh 6 SS 6422
Warkton 27 SP 8980
Warkworth 47 NU 2406
Warlaby 42 SE 3591
Warland 37 SD 9419
Warleggan 4 SX 1569
Warley 25 SP 0086
Warlingham 12 TQ 3658
Warmfield 37 SE 3720
Warmingham 32 SJ 7161
Warmington (Northants.) 27 TL 0791
Warmington (Warw.) 26 SP 4147
Warminster 8 ST 8644
Warmsworth 38 SE 5400
Warmwell 8 SY 7585
Warndon 25 SO 8856
Warnford 9 SU 6223
Warnham 11 TQ 1633
Warninglid 11 TQ 2526
Warren (Ches.) 33 SJ 8870
Warren (Dyfed) 14 SR 9397
Warren Row 10 SU 8180
Warren Street 13 TQ 9253
Warrington (Bucks.) 27 SP 8954
Warrington (Ches.) 32 SJ 6088
Warsash 9 SU 4905
Warslow 33 SK 0858
Warsop 34 SK 5667
Warter 39 SE 8750
Warthill 38 SE 6755
Wartling 12 TQ 6509
Wartnaby 34 SK 7123
Warton (Lancs.) 36 SD 4028
Warton (Lancs.) 40 SD 4972
Warton (Northum.) 47 NU 0002
Warton (Warw.) 26 SK 2803
Warwick (Cumbr.) 46 NY 4656
Warwick (Warw.) 26 SP 2865
Warwick Bridge 46 NY 4756
Wasbister 63 HY 3932
Washaway 4 SX 0369
Washbourne 5 SX 7954
Washfield 6 SS 9315
Washfold 42 NZ 0502
Washford 7 ST 0441
Washford Pyne 6 SS 8111
Washingborough 34 TF 0170
Washington (Tyne and Wear) 47 NZ 3356
Washington (W Susx) 11 TQ 1212
Wasing 10 SU 5764
Waskerley 47 NZ 0545
Wasperton 26 SP 2659
Wass 42 SE 5579
Watchet 7 ST 0743
Watchfield (Oxon.) 18 SU 2490
Watchfield (Somer.) 7 ST 3446
Watchgate 40 SD 5399
Water 37 SD 8425
Waterbeach 20 TL 4965
Waterbeck 46 NY 2477
Waterden 28 TF 8835
Water End (Herts.) 19 TL 0310
Water End (Herts.) 19 TL 2304
Waterfall 33 SK 0851
Waterfoot (Lancs.) 37 SD 8321
Waterfoot (Strath.) 50 NS 5654
Waterford 20 TL 3114
Waterhead (Cumbr.) 40 NY 3703
Waterhead (Strath.) 50 NS 5411
Waterheads 51 NT 2451
Waterhouses (Durham) 42 NZ 1841
Waterhouses (Staffs.) 33 SK 0850
Wateringbury 12 TQ 6853
Wateringhouse 63 ND 3090
Waterloo (Dorset) 8 SZ 0194
Waterloo (Mers.) 32 SJ 3297
Waterloo (Norf.) 29 TG 2219
Waterloo (Strath.) 50 NS 8153
Waterloo (Tays.) 56 NO 0636
Waterlooville 9 SU 6809
Water Meetings 51 NS 9513
Watermillock 40 NY 4322
Water Newton 27 TL 1097
Water Orton 25 SP 1791
Waterperry 18 SP 6206
Waterrow 7 ST 0525
Watersfield 11 TQ 0115
Waterside (Strath.) 44 NS 4308
Waterside (Strath.) 50 NS 4843
Waterside (Strath.) 50 NS 5160
Waterside (Strath.) 50 NS 6773
Waterstock 18 SP 6305
Waterston 14 SM 9306
Water Stratford 18 SP 6534
Waters Upton 32 SJ 6319
Water Yeat 40 SD 2889
Watford (Herts.) 19 TQ 1196
Watford (Northants.) 26 SP 6069
Wath (N Yorks.) 42 SE 1467
Wath (N Yorks.) 42 SE 3277
Wath Upon Dearne 38 SE 4300
Watlington (Norf.) 28 TF 6211
Watlington (Oxon.) 18 SU 6994
Watnall Chaworth 33 SK 4946
Watten 67 ND 2454
Wattisfield 29 TM 0174
Wattisham 21 TM 0151
Watton (Humbs.) 39 TA 0150
Watton (Norf.) 28 TF 9100
Watton-at-Stone 20 TL 3019
Wattston 50 NS 7770
Wattstown 15 ST 0194
Waunarlwydd 15 SS 6095
Waunfawr 30 SH 5259
Wavendon 19 SP 9137
Waverton (Ches.) 32 SJ 4663
Waverton (Cumbr.) 46 NY 2247
Wawne 39 TA 0836
Waxham 29 TG 4326
Waxholme 39 TA 3229
Wayford 7 ST 4006
Way Village 6 SS 8810
Wealdstone 19 TQ 1689
Weare 7 ST 4152
Weare Giffard 6 SS 4721
Weasenham All Saints 28 TF 8421
Weasenham St. Peter 28 TF 8522
Weaverham 32 SJ 6173
Weaverthorpe 39 SE 9670
Webheath 25 SP 0266
Weddington 26 SP 3693
Wedhampton 17 SU 0557
Wedmore 7 ST 4347
Wednesbury 25 SP 0095
Wednesfield 25 SJ 9400
Weedon 18 SP 8118
Weedon Bec 26 SP 6259
Weedon Lois 26 SP 6047
Weeford 25 SK 1404
Week 6 SS 7316
Weekley 27 SP 8880
Week St. Mary 4 SX 2397
Weeley 21 TM 1422
Weeley Heath 21 TM 1520
Weem 56 NN 8449
Weeping Cross 33 SJ 9421
Weeting 28 TL 7788
Weeton (Lancs.) 36 SD 3834
Weeton (W Yorks.) 37 SE 2846
Weir 37 SD 8724
Welbeck Colliery Village 34 SK 5869
Welborne 29 TG 0610
Welbourn 34 SK 9654
Welburn 38 SE 7168
Welbury 42 NZ 3902
Welby 34 SK 9738
Welches Dam 27 TL 4786
Welcombe 4 SS 2218
Weldon 27 SP 9289
Welford (Berks.) 10 SU 4073
Welford (Northants.) 26 SP 6480
Welford-on-Avon 25 SP 1552
Welham 26 SP 7692
Welham Green 19 TL 2305
Well (Hants.) 10 SU 7646
Well (Lincs.) 35 TF 4473
Well (N Yorks.) 42 SE 2682
Welland 24 SO 7940
Wellesbourne Hastings 26 SP 2755
Wellesbourne Mountford 26 SP 2755
Well Hill (Kent) 12 TQ 4963
Welling 12 TQ 4575
Wellingborough 27 SP 8968
Wellingham 28 TF 8722
Wellingore 34 SK 9856
Wellington (Here. and Worc.) 24 SO 4948
Wellington (Salop) 24 SJ 6411
Wellington (Somer.) 7 ST 1320
Wellington Heath 24 SO 7140
Wellow (Avon) 17 ST 7358
Wellow (I. of W.) 9 SZ 3887
Wellow (Notts.) 34 SK 6666
Wells 7 ST 5445
Wellsborough 26 SK 3602
Wells-Next-The-Sea 28 TF 9143
Wells of Ythan 62 NJ 6338
Wellwood 51 NT 0888
Welney 28 TL 5294
Welshampton 32 SJ 4334
Welsh Bicknor 17 SO 5917
Welsh End 32 SJ 5035
Welsh Frankton 32 SJ 3633
Welsh Hook 14 SM 9327
Welsh Newton 16 SO 4918
Welshpool (Trallwng) 23 SJ 2207
Welsh St. Donats 15 ST 0276
Welton (Cumbr.) 46 NY 3544
Welton (Humbs.) 39 SE 9527
Welton (Lincs.) 34 TF 0079
Welton (Northants.) 26 SP 5865
Welton le Marsh 35 TF 4768
Welton le Wold 35 TF 2787
Welwick 39 TA 3421
Welwyn 19 TL 2316
Welwyn Garden City 19 TL 2412
Wem 32 SJ 5129
Wembdon 7 ST 2837
Wembley 19 TQ 1985
Wembury 4 SX 5148
Wembworthy 6 SS 6609
Wemyss Bay 49 NS 1869
Wenallt 31 SH 9842
Wendens Ambo 20 TL 5136
Wendlebury 18 SP 5519
Wendling 29 TF 9213
Wendover 19 SP 8708
Wendron 2 SW 6731
Wendy 20 TL 3247
Wenhaston 29 TM 4275
Wennington (Cambs.) 27 TL 2379
Wennington (Essex) 20 TQ 5381
Wennington (Lancs.) 41 SD 6169
Wensley (Derby.) 33 SK 2661
Wensley (N Yorks.) 42 SE 0989
Wentbridge 38 SE 4817
Wentnor 24 SO 3892
Wentworth (Cambs.) 27 TL 4878
Wentworth (S Yorks.) 37 SK 3898
Wenvoe 16 ST 1272
Weobley 24 SO 4051
Weobley Marsh 24 SO 4151
Wereham 28 TF 6801
Wergs 25 SJ 8601
Wernrheolydd 16 SO 3913
Werrington (Devon.) 4 SX 3287
Werrington (Northants.) 27 TF 1703
Werrington (Staffs.) 33 SJ 9647
Wervin 32 SJ 4171
Wesham 36 SD 4132
Wessington 33 SK 3757
West Acre 28 TF 7715
West Allerdean 53 NT 9646
West Alvington 5 SX 7243
West Anstey 6 SS 8527
West Ashby 35 TF 2672
West Ashling 9 SU 8007
West Ashton 17 ST 8755
West Auckland 42 NZ 1826
West Bagborough 7 ST 1633
West Barns 52 NT 6578
West Barsham 28 TF 9033
West Bay (Dorset) 7 SY 4690
West Beckham 29 TG 1339
Westbere 13 TR 1961
West Bergholt 21 TL 9527
West Bexington 7 SY 5386
West Bilney 28 TF 7115
West Blatchington 11 TQ 2706
Westbourne (Dorset) 8 SZ 0690
Westbourne (W Susx) 9 SU 7507
West Bradenham 29 TF 9209
West Bradford 36 SD 7444
West Bradley 7 ST 5536
West Bretton 37 SE 2813
West Bridgford 34 SK 5837
West Bromwich 25 SP 0091
West Buckland (Devon.) 6 SS 6510
West Buckland (Somer.) 7 ST 1720
West Burrafirth 63 HU 2557
West Burton (N Yorks.) 41 SE 0186
West Burton (W Susx) 11 TQ 0014
Westbury (Bucks.) 18 SP 6235
Westbury (Salop) 24 SJ 3509
Westbury (Wilts.) 8 ST 8751
Westbury Leigh 8 ST 8649
Westbury-on-Severn 17 SO 7114
Westbury-sub-Mendip 7 ST 5049
Westby 36 SD 3731
West Caister 29 TG 5011
West Calder 51 NT 0163
West Camel 7 ST 5724
West Challow 18 SU 3688
West Charleton 5 SX 7542
West Chelborough 7 ST 5405
West Chevington 47 NZ 2297
West Chiltington 11 TQ 0918
West Clandon 11 TQ 0452
West Cliffe 13 TR 3445
Westcliff-on-Sea 20 TQ 8685
West Coker 7 ST 5113
Westcombe 8 ST 6739
West Compton (Dorset) 7 SY 5694
West Compton (Somer.) 7 ST 5942
Westcote 17 SP 2120
Westcott (Bucks.) 18 SP 7117
Westcott (Devon) 5 ST 0104
Westcott (Surrey) 11 TQ 1348
Westcott Barton 18 SP 4224
West Cross 15 SS 6189
West Curry 4 SX 2893
West Curthwaite 46 NY 3248
Westdean (E Susx) 12 TV 5299
West Dean (Wilts.) 9 SU 2526
West Dean (W Susx) 9 SU 8512
West Deeping 35 TF 1009
West Derby 32 SJ 3993
West Dereham 28 TF 6500
West Ditchburn 53 NU 1320
West Down (Devon.) 6 SS 5142
West Down (Wilts.) 8 SU 0548
West Drayton (Gtr London) 11 TQ 0679
West Drayton (Notts.) 34 SK 7074
West End (Avon) 16 ST 4469
West End (Beds.) 27 SP 9853
West End (Hants.) 9 SU 4614
West End (Herts.) 20 TL 3306
West End (Norf.) 29 TG 4911
West End (N Yorks.) 37 SE 1457
West End (Oxon.) 18 SP 4204
West End (Surrey) 11 SU 9461
West End Green 10 SU 6661
Wester Clynekirton 67 NC 8906
Wester Culbeuchly Crofts 62 NJ 6562
Westerdale (Highld.) 67 ND 1251
Westerdale (N Yorks.) 42 NZ 6605
Westerdale Moor 42 NZ 6502
Wester Denoon 57 NO 3543
Westerfield (Shetld.) 63 HU 3551
Westerfield (Suff.) 21 TM 1747
Wester Fintray 62 NJ 8116
Westergate 11 SU 9305
Wester Gruinards 65 NH 5292
Westerham 12 TQ 4454
Westerleigh 17 ST 6979
Wester Lonvine 65 NH 7172
Wester Skeld 63 HU 2943
Wester Teaninich 65 NH 6267
Westerton 57 NO 6654
Wester Wick 63 HU 2842
West Farleigh 12 TQ 7152
West Felton 32 SJ 3425
Westfield (Caithness) 67 ND 0564
Westfield (E Susx) 12 TQ 8115
Westfield (Lothian) 51 NS 9372
Westfield (Norf.) 29 TF 9909
West Firle 12 TQ 4707
Westgate (Durham) 41 NY 9038
Westgate (Humbs.) 38 SE 7707
Westgate (Norf.) 29 TF 9740
Westgate on Sea 13 TR 3270
West Geirinish 63 NF 7741
West Ginge 18 SU 4386
West Grafton 10 SU 2460
West Green 10 SU 7456
West Grimstead 8 SU 2026
West Grinstead 11 TQ 1721
West Haddlesey 38 SE 5526
West Haddon 26 SP 6371
West Hagbourne 18 SU 5187
Westhall (Cumbr.) 46 NY 5667
Westhall (Suff.) 29 TM 4280
West Hallam 33 SK 4341
West Halton 39 SE 9020

Westham Witham

Westham (E Susx) 12 TQ 6404
West Ham (Gtr London) 20 TQ 4081
Westham (Somer.) 7 ST 4046
Westhampnett 11 SU 8706
West Handley 33 SK 3977
West Hanney 18 SU 4092
West Hanningfield 20 TQ 7399
West Hardwick 38 SE 4118
West Harnham 8 SU 1229
West Harptree 16 ST 5556
West Hatch 7 ST 2820
Westhay 7 ST 4342
Westhead 36 SD 4407
West Heath 11 SU 8556
West Helmsdale 67 ND 0114
West Hendred 18 SU 4488
West Heslerton 39 SE 9175
Westhide 24 SO 5844
West Hill 5 SY 0694
West Hoathly 12 TQ 3632
West Holme 8 SY 8885
Westhope (Here. and Worc.) 24 SO 4651
Westhope (Salop) 24 SO 4786
West Horndon 20 TQ 6288
Westhorpe (Lincs.) 35 TF 2131
Westhorpe (Suff.) 29 TM 0469
West Horrington 7 ST 5747
West Horsley 11 TQ 0753
West Hougham 13 TR 2640
Westhoughton 36 SD 6505
Westhouse 41 SD 6673
Westhouses 33 SK 4257
West Humble 11 TQ 1652
West Hyde 19 TQ 0391
West Ilsley 10 SU 4682
Westing 63 HP 5705
West Itchenor 9 SU 7900
West Kennet 17 SU 1167
West Kilbride 49 NS 2048
West Kingsdown 12 TQ 5762
West Kington 17 ST 8077
West Kirby 32 SJ 2186
West Knighton 8 SY 7387
West Knoyle 8 ST 8532
Westlake 5 SX 6253
West Langdon 13 TR 3247
West Langwell 66 NC 6909
West Lavington (Wilts.) 8 SU 0052
West Lavington (W Susx) 11 SU 8920
West Layton 42 NZ 1409
West Leake 34 SK 5226
Westleigh (Devon) 6 SS 4628
Westleigh (Devon) 7 ST 0517
Westleton 29 TM 4469
West Lexham 28 TF 8417
Westley (Salop) 24 SJ 3507
Westley (Suff.) 20 TL 8264
Westley Waterless 20 TL 6256
West Lilling 38 SE 6465
Westlington 18 SP 7610
West Linton (Borders) 51 NT 1551
Westlinton (Cumbr.) 46 NY 3964
West Littleton 17 ST 7575
West Looe 4 SX 2553
West Lulworth 8 SY 8280
West Lutton 39 SE 9269
West Lynn 28 TF 6120
West Mains 51 NS 9550
West Malling 12 TQ 6857
West Malvern 24 SO 7646
West Marden 9 SU 7613
West Markham 34 SK 7272
Westmarsh 13 TR 2761
West Marton 37 SD 8850
West Meon 9 SU 6424
West Mersea 21 TM 0112
Westmeston 12 TQ 3313
Westmill 20 TL 3627
West Milton 7 SY 5096
West Monkton 7 ST 2528
West Moors 8 SU 0802
Westmuir (Tays.) 57 NO 3652
West Muir (Tays.) 57 NO 5661
Westness (Rousay) 63 HY 3829
Westnewton (Cumbr.) 45 NY 1344
West Newton (Norf.) 28 TF 6927
West Norwood 12 TQ 3171
West Ogwell 5 SX 8170
Weston (Avon) 17 ST 7266
Weston (Berks.) 10 SU 3973
Weston (Ches.) 32 SJ 5080
Weston (Ches.) 32 SJ 7252
Weston (Dorset) 8 SY 6870
Weston (Hants.) 9 SU 7221
Weston (Herts.) 19 TL 2630
Weston (Lincs.) 35 TF 2925
Weston (Northants.) 26 SP 5847
Weston (Notts.) 34 SK 7767
Weston (Salop) 32 SJ 5628
Weston (Salop) 24 SO 5993
Weston (Staffs.) 33 SJ 9727
Weston (W Yorks.) 37 SE 1747
Weston Beggard 24 SO 5841
Weston by Welland 26 SP 7791
Weston Colville 20 TL 6153
Weston Favell 26 SP 7862
Weston Green 20 TL 6252
Weston Heath 24 SJ 7813
Weston Hills 35 TF 2821
Westoning 19 TL 0332
Weston-in-Gordano 16 ST 4474
Weston Jones 32 SJ 7524
Weston Longville 29 TG 1116
Weston Lullingfields 32 SJ 4224
Weston-on-the-Green 18 SP 5318
Weston-on-Trent 33 SK 4027
Weston Patrick 10 SU 6946
Weston Rhyn 32 SJ 2835
Weston Subedge 25 SP 1240
Weston-super-Mare 16 ST 3261
Weston Turville 19 SP 8511
Weston-under-Lizard 24 SJ 8010
Weston under Penyard 17 SO 6323
Weston under Wetherley 26 SP 3569
Weston Underwood (Bucks.) 27 SP 8650
Weston Underwood (Derby.) 33 SK 2942
Westonzoyland 7 ST 3534
West Overton 17 SU 1367
Westow 38 SE 7565
West Parley 8 SZ 0997
West Peaston 52 NT 4265
West Peckham 12 TQ 6452
West Pennard 7 ST 5438
West Pentire 2 SW 7760
Westport 7 ST 3819
West Putford 4 SS 3515
West Quantoxhead 7 ST 1141
West Rainton 47 NZ 3246
West Rasen 35 TF 0589
West Raynham 28 TF 8725
Westrigg 50 NS 9067
West Row 28 TL 6775
West Rudham 28 TF 8127
West Runton 29 TG 1842
Westruther 52 NT 6349
Westry 27 TL 3998
West Saltoun 52 NT 4667
West Sandwick 63 HU 4488
West Scrafton 42 SE 0783
West Stafford 8 SY 7289
West Stoke 9 SU 8208
West Stonesdale 41 NY 8802
West Stoughton 7 ST 4149
West Stour 8 ST 7822
West Stourmouth 13 TR 2562
West Stow 28 TL 8170
West Stowell 17 SU 1362
West Street 13 TQ 9054
West Tanfield 42 SE 2778
West Tarbert 49 NR 8467
West Thorney 9 SU 7602
West Thurrock 12 TQ 5877
West Tilbury 12 TQ 6677
West Tisted 9 SU 6429
West Tofts 56 NO 1134
West Torrington 35 TF 1381
West Town 16 ST 4767
West Tytherley 9 SU 2730
West Tytherton 17 ST 9474
West Walton 35 TF 4713
West Walton Highway 28 TF 4912
Westward 46 NY 2744
Westward Ho! 6 SS 4329
Westwell (Kent) 13 TQ 9947
Westwell (Oxon.) 18 SP 2210
Westwell Leacon 13 TQ 9647
West Wellow 9 SU 2818
West Wemyss 51 NT 3294
West Wick (Avon) 16 ST 3661
Westwick (Cambs.) 20 TL 4265
Westwick (Norf.) 29 TG 2727
West Wickham (Cambs.) 20 TL 6149
West Wickham (Gtr London) 12 TQ 3866
West Winch 28 TF 6316
West Wittering 9 SZ 7999
West Witton 42 SE 0688
Westwood (Devon) 5 SY 0199
Westwood (Wilts.) 17 ST 8158
West Woodburn 47 NY 8986
West Woodhay 10 SU 3962
West Woodlands 8 ST 7743
Westwoodside 38 SK 7499
West Worldham 9 SU 7436
West Wratting 20 TL 6052
West Wycombe 18 SU 8394
West Yell 63 HU 4582
Wetheral 46 NY 4654
Wetherby 38 SE 4048
Wetherden 21 TM 0062
Wetheringsett 21 TM 1266
Wethersfield 20 TL 7131
Wethersta 63 HU 3565
Wetherup Street 21 TM 1464
Wetley Rocks 33 SJ 9649
Wettenhall 32 SJ 6261
Wetton 33 SK 1055
Wetwang 39 SE 9359
Wetwood 32 SJ 7733
Wexcombe 10 SU 2758
Weybourne 29 TG 1143
Weybread 29 TM 2480
Weybridge 11 TQ 0764
Weydale 67 ND 1464
Weyhill 10 SU 3146
Weymouth 8 SY 6778
Whaddon (Bucks.) 18 SP 8034
Whaddon (Cambs.) 20 TL 3546
Whaddon (Glos.) 17 SO 8313
Whaddon (Wilts.) 8 SU 1926
Whale 40 NY 5221
Whaley 34 SK 5171
Whaley Bridge 33 SK 0181
Whaligoe 67 ND 3240
Whalley 36 SD 7335
Whalton 47 NZ 1281
Wham 41 SD 7762
Whaplode 35 TF 3224
Whaplode Drove 35 TF 3113
Whaplode Fen 35 TF 3220
Wharfe 41 SD 7869
Wharles 36 SD 4435
Wharncliffe Side 37 SK 2994
Wharram le Street 39 SE 8666
Wharton (Ches.) 32 SJ 6666
Wharton (Here. and Worc.) 24 SO 5055
Whashton 42 NZ 1406
Whatcombe 8 ST 8301
Whatcote 26 SP 2944
Whatfield 21 TM 0246
Whatley 8 ST 7347
Whatlington 12 TQ 7618
Whatstandwell 33 SK 3354
Whatton 34 SK 7439
Whauphill 44 NX 4049
Whaw 41 NY 9804
Wheatacre 29 TM 4594
Wheathampstead 19 TL 1713
Wheatley (Hants.) 10 SU 7840
Wheatley (Notts.) 34 SK 7685
Wheatley (Oxon.) 18 SP 5905
Wheatley Hill 42 NZ 3839
Wheatley Lane 37 SD 8337
Wheaton Aston 25 SJ 8412
Wheatsheaf 32 SJ 3253
Wheddon Cross 6 SS 9238
Wheedlemont 61 NJ 4726
Wheelerstreet 11 SU 9440
Wheelock 32 SJ 7458
Wheelton 36 SD 6021
Wheldrake 38 SE 6744
Whelford 17 SU 1698
Whelpley Hill 19 TL 0004
Whenby 38 SE 6369
Whepstead 20 TL 8358
Wherstead 21 TM 1540
Wherwell 10 SU 3840
Wheston 33 SK 1376
Whetsted 12 TQ 6546
Whetstone 26 SP 5597
Whicham 40 SD 1382
Whichford 18 SP 3134
Whickham 47 NZ 2061
Whiddon Down 5 SX 6992
Whigstreet 57 NO 4844
Whilton 26 SP 6364
Whim 51 NT 2153
Whimple 5 SY 0497
Whimpwell Green 29 TG 3829
Whinburgh 29 TG 0009
Whinnyfold 62 NK 0733
Whippingham 9 SZ 5193
Whipsnade 19 TL 0117
Whipton 5 SX 9493
Whissendine 34 SK 8214
Whissonsett 28 TF 9123
Whistley Green 10 SU 7974
Whiston (Mers.) 32 SJ 4791
Whiston (Northants.) 27 SP 8560
Whiston (Staffs.) 25 SJ 8914
Whiston (Staffs.) 33 SK 0347
Whiston (S Yorks.) 33 SK 4489
Whitbeck 40 SD 1184
Whitbourne 24 SO 7156
Whitburn (Lothian) 51 NS 9464
Whitburn (Tyne and Wear) 47 NZ 4061
Whitby (Ches.) 32 SJ 4075
Whitby (N Yorks.) 43 NZ 8911
Whitchurch (Avon) 17 ST 6167
Whitchurch (Bucks.) 18 SP 8020
Whitchurch (Devon) 4 SX 4972
Whitchurch (Dyfed) 14 SM 8025
Whitchurch (Hants.) 10 SU 4648
Whitchurch (Here. and Worc.) 16 SO 5417
Whitchurch (Oxon.) 10 SU 6377
Whitchurch (Salop) 32 SJ 5441
Whitchurch (S Glam.) 16 ST 1680
Whitchurch Canonicorum 7 SY 3995
Whitcott Keysett 23 SO 2782
Whitebrook 16 SO 5306
Whitecairns 62 NJ 9218
White Chapel 36 SD 5542
Whitechurch 14 SN 1436
White Coppice 36 SD 6119
White Court 20 TL 7421
Whitecraig (Lothian) 51 NT 3570
Whitecroft 17 SO 6106
Whitecross 51 NS 9676
Whiteface 65 NH 7189
Whitefield (Gtr Mches.) 37 SD 8005
Whitefield (Tays.) 56 NO 1734
Whiteford 62 NJ 7126
Whitehall 63 HY 6528
Whitehaven 40 NX 9718
Whitehill (Hants.) 10 SU 7934
Whitehills 62 NJ 6565
Whitehouse (Grampn.) 62 NJ 6214
Whitehouse (Strath.) 49 NR 8161
Whitekirk 52 NT 5981
White Lackington 8 SY 7198
White Ladies Aston 25 SO 9252
Whiteley Village 11 TQ 0962
Whitemans Green 12 TQ 3025
Whitemire 60 NH 9854
Whitemoor 2 SW 9757
White Notley 20 TL 7818
Whiteparish 9 SU 2423
Whiterashes 62 NJ 8523
White Roding 20 TL 5613
Whiterow 67 ND 3548
Whiteshill 17 SO 8307
Whiteside (Lothian) 51 NS 9667
Whitesmith 12 TQ 5214
Whitestaunton 7 ST 2810
Whitestone 6 SX 8694
White Waltham 11 SU 8577
Whiteway 17 SO 9110
Whitewell 36 SD 6546
Whitewreath 61 NJ 2356
Whitfield (Glos.) 17 ST 6791
Whitfield (Kent) 13 TR 3146
Whitfield (Northants.) 26 SP 6039
Whitfield (Northum.) 46 NY 7758
Whitford 31 SJ 1477
Whitgift 39 SE 8022
Whitgreave 33 SJ 8928
Whithorn 44 NX 4440
Whiting Bay (Island of Arran) 49 NS 0425
Whitington 28 TL 7199
Whitland 14 SN 1916
Whitletts 50 NS 3622
Whitley (Berks.) 10 SU 7170
Whitley (Ches.) 32 SJ 6178
Whitley (N Yorks.) 38 SE 5521
Whitley Bay 47 NZ 3572
Whitley Chapel 47 NY 9257
Whitley Row 12 TQ 5052
Whitlock's End 25 SP 1076
Whitminster 17 SO 7708
Whitmore 32 SJ 8041
Whitnage 7 ST 0215
Whitnash 26 SP 3263
Whitney 23 SO 2647
Whitrigg (Cumbr.) 40 NY 2038
Whitrigg (Cumbr.) 46 NY 2257
Whitsbury 8 SU 1218
Whitsome 53 NT 8650
Whitson 16 ST 3783
Whitstable 13 TR 1166
Whitstone 4 SX 2698
Whittingham 53 NU 0611
Whittingslow 24 SO 4288
Whittington (Derby.) 33 SK 3975
Whittington (Glos.) 17 SP 0120
Whittington (Here. and Worc.) 25 SO 8582
Whittington (Here. and Worc.) 25 SO 8752
Whittington (Lancs.) 41 SD 5976
Whittington (Salop) 32 SJ 3230
Whittington (Staffs.) 25 SK 1508
Whittlebury 26 SP 6943
Whittle-le-Woods 36 SD 5822
Whittlesey 27 TL 2797
Whittlesford 20 TL 4748
Whitton (Cleve.) 42 NZ 3822
Whitton (Humbs.) 39 SE 9024
Whitton (Northum.) 47 NU 0501
Whitton (Powys) 23 SO 2667
Whitton (Salop) 24 SO 5772
Whitton (Suff.) 21 TM 1447
Whittonditch 10 SU 2872
Whittonstall 47 NZ 0757
Whitwell (Derby.) 34 SK 5276
Whitwell (Herts.) 19 TL 1821
Whitwell (I of W.) 9 SZ 5277
Whitwell (Leic.) 34 SK 9208
Whitwell (N Yorks.) 42 SE 2899
Whitwell-on-the-Hill 38 SE 7265
Whitwick 33 SK 4316
Whitwood 38 SE 4124
Whitworth 37 SD 8818
Whixall 32 SJ 5034
Whixley 38 SE 4457
Whorlton (Durham) 42 NZ 1014
Whorlton (N Yorks.) 42 NZ 4802
Whygate 46 NY 7675
Whyle 24 SO 5560
Whyteleafe 12 TQ 3358
Wibdon 17 ST 5797
Wibtoft 26 SP 4787
Wichenford 24 SO 7860
Wichling 13 TQ 9256
Wick (Avon) 17 ST 6972
Wick (Dorset) 8 SZ 1591
Wick (Here. and Worc.) 25 SO 9645
Wick (Highld.) 67 ND 3650
Wick (S Glam.) 15 SS 9272
Wick (Shetld.) 63 HU 4439
Wick (Wilts.) 8 SU 1621
Wick (W Susx) 11 TQ 0203
Wicken (Cambs.) 28 TL 5770
Wicken (Northants.) 26 SP 7439
Wicken Bonhunt 20 TL 5033
Wickenby 35 TF 0882
Wickersley 38 SK 4891
Wickford 20 TQ 7593
Wickham (Berks.) 10 SU 3971
Wickham (Hants.) 9 SU 5711
Wickham Bishops 20 TL 8412
Wickhambreaux 13 TR 2158
Wickhambrook 20 TL 7454
Wickhamford 25 SP 0642
Wickham Market 21 TM 3056
Wickhampton 29 TG 4205
Wickham St. Paul 20 TL 8336
Wickham Skeith 29 TM 0969
Wickham Street (Suff.) 20 TL 7554
Wickham Street (Suff.) 29 TM 0869
Wicklewood 29 TG 0702
Wickmere 29 TG 1633
Wick Rissington 17 SP 1821
Wick St. Lawrence 16 ST 3665
Wickwar 17 ST 7288
Widdington 20 TL 5331
Widdrington 47 NZ 2595
Widecombe In the Moor 5 SX 7176
Wide Open 47 NZ 2472
Widewall 63 ND 4391
Widford (Essex) 20 TL 6905
Widford (Herts.) 20 TL 4115
Widmerpool 34 SK 6327
Widnes 32 SJ 5185
Wigan 36 SD 5805
Wiggaton 5 SY 1093
Wiggenhall St. Germans 28 TF 5914
Wiggenhall St. Mary Magdalen 28 TF 5911
Wiggenhall St. Mary the Virgin 28 TF 5814
Wigginton (Herts.) 19 SP 9410
Wigginton (N Yorks) 38 SE 5958
Wigginton (Oxon.) 18 SP 3833
Wigginton (Staffs.) 25 SK 2106
Wigglesworth 37 SD 8056
Wiggonby 46 NY 2953
Wiggonholt 11 TQ 0616
Wighill 38 SE 4746
Wighton 29 TF 9339
Wigmore (Here. and Worc.) 24 SO 4169
Wigmore (Kent) 12 TQ 8063
Wigsley 34 SK 8570
Wigsthorpe 27 TL 0482
Wigston 26 SP 6099
Wigtoft 35 TF 2636
Wigton 46 NY 2548
Wigtown 44 NX 4355
Wilbarston 26 SP 8188
Wilberfoss 38 SE 7350
Wilburton 27 TL 4875
Wilby (Norf.) 29 TM 0389
Wilby (Northants.) 27 SP 8666
Wilby (Suff.) 29 TM 2472
Wilcot 17 SU 1461
Wildboarclough 33 SJ 9868
Wilden 27 TL 0955
Wildhern 10 SU 3550
Wildsworth 39 SK 8097
Wilford 34 SK 5637
Wilkesley 32 SJ 6241
Wilkhaven 65 NH 9486
Wilkieston 51 NT 1168
Willand 5 ST 0310
Willaston (Ches.) 32 SJ 3277
Willaston (Ches.) 32 SJ 6752
Willen 27 SP 8741
Willenhall (W Mids.) 25 SO 9698
Willenhall (W Mids.) 26 SP 3676
Willerby (Humbs.) 39 TA 0230
Willerby (N Yorks.) 43 TA 0079
Willersey 25 SP 1039
Willersley 23 SO 3147
Willesborough 13 TR 0441
Willesden 19 TQ 2284
Willett 7 ST 1033
Willey (Salop) 24 SO 6799
Willey (Warw.) 26 SP 4984
Williamscot 26 SP 4745
Willian 19 TL 2230
Willimontswick 46 NY 7763
Willingale 20 TL 5907
Willingdon 12 TQ 5902
Willingham (Cambs.) 27 TL 4070
Willingham (Lincs.) 34 SK 8784
Willington (Beds.) 27 TL 1150
Willington (Derby.) 33 SK 2928
Willington (Durham) 42 NZ 1935
Willington (Tyne and Wear) 47 NZ 3167
Willington (Warw.) 18 SP 2638
Willington Corner 32 SJ 5367
Willitoft 38 SE 7434
Williton 7 ST 0740
Willoughby (Lincs.) 35 TF 4772
Willoughby (Warw.) 26 SP 5167
Willoughby-on-the-Wolds 34 SK 6325
Willoughby Waterleys 26 SP 5792
Willoughton 39 SK 9293
Wilmcote 25 SP 1658
Wilmington (Devon.) 5 SY 2199
Wilmington (E Susx) 12 TQ 5404
Wilmington (Kent) 12 TQ 5372
Wilmslow 33 SJ 8480
Wilnecote 26 SK 2201
Wilpshire 36 SD 6832
Wilsden 37 SE 0935
Wilsford (Lincs.) 34 TF 0043
Wilsford (Wilts.) 17 SU 1057
Wilsford (Wilts.) 8 SU 1339
Wilshamstead 27 TL 0643
Wilsill 42 SE 1864
Wilson 33 SK 4024
Wilsthorpe 35 TF 0913
Wilstone 19 SP 9014
Wilton (Borders) 52 NT 4914
Wilton (Cleve.) 42 NZ 5819
Wilton (N Yorks.) 43 SE 8582
Wilton (Wilts.) 8 SU 0931
Wilton (Wilts.) 10 SU 2661
Wimbish 20 TL 5936
Wimbish Green 20 TL 6035
Wimbledon 11 TQ 2470
Wimbledon Park 11 TQ 2472
Wimblington 27 TL 4192
Wimborne Minster 8 SZ 0199
Wimborne St. Giles 8 SU 0212
Wimbotsham 28 TF 6205
Wimpstone 25 SP 2148
Wincanton 8 ST 7128
Wincham 32 SJ 6675
Winchburgh 51 NT 0874
Winchcombe 17 SP 0228
Winchelsea 13 TQ 9017
Winchelsea Beach 13 TQ 9115
Winchester 9 SU 4829
Winchfield 10 SU 7654
Winchmore Hill (Bucks.) 19 SU 9394
Winchmore Hill (Gtr London) 20 TQ 3195
Wincle 33 SJ 9565
Windermere (Cumbr.) 40 SD 4198
Winderton 26 SP 3240
Windlesham 11 SU 9363
Windley 33 SK 3045
Windmill Hill (E Susx) 12 TQ 6412
Windmill Hill (Somer.) 7 ST 3116
Windrush 17 SP 1913
Windsor 11 SU 9676
Windygates 57 NO 3400
Wineham 11 TQ 2320
Winestead 39 TA 2924
Winfarthing 29 TM 1085
Winford 16 ST 5364
Winforton 23 SO 2947
Winfrith Newburgh 8 SY 8084
Wing (Bucks.) 19 SP 8822
Wing (Leic.) 27 SK 8903
Wingate (Durham) 42 NZ 4036
Wingates (Gtr Mches.) 36 SD 6507
Wingates (Northum.) 47 NZ 0995
Wingerworth 33 SK 3867
Wingfield (Beds.) 19 SP 9926
Wingfield (Suff.) 29 TM 2276
Wingfield (Wilts.) 17 ST 8256
Wingham 13 TR 2457
Wingrave 19 SP 8719
Winkburn 34 SK 7158
Winkfield 11 SU 9072
Winkfield Row 11 SU 9071
Winkhill 33 SK 0651
Winkleigh 6 SS 6308
Winksley 42 SE 2471
Winless 67 ND 3054
Winmarleigh 36 SD 4748
Winnersh 11 SU 7870
Winscales 40 NY 0226
Winscombe 16 ST 4157
Winsford (Ches.) 32 SJ 6566
Winsford (Somer.) 6 SS 9034
Winsham 7 ST 3706
Winshill 33 SK 2623
Winskill 41 NY 5835
Winslade 10 SU 6547
Winsley 17 ST 7960
Winslow 18 SP 7627
Winson 17 SP 0908
Winster (Cumbr.) 40 SD 4193
Winster (Derby.) 33 SK 2460
Winston (Durham) 42 NZ 1416
Winston (Suff.) 21 TM 1861
Winstone 17 SO 9609
Winswell 6 SS 4913
Winterborne Clenston 8 ST 8302
Winterborne Herringston 8 SY 6887
Winterborne Houghton 8 ST 8104
Winterborne Kingston 8 SY 8697
Winterborne Monkton (Dorset) 8 SY 6787
Winterborne Stickland 8 ST 8304
Winterborne Whitechurch 8 SY 8399
Winterborne Zelston 8 SY 8997
Winterbourne 17 ST 6480
Winterbourne Abbas 7 SY 6190
Winterbourne Bassett 17 SU 1074
Winterbourne Dauntsey 8 SU 1734
Winterbourne Earls 8 SU 1633
Winterbourne Gunner 8 SU 1735
Winterbourne Monkton (Wilts.) 17 SU 0972
Winterbourne Steepleton 8 SY 6289
Winterbourne Stoke 8 SU 0740
Winterburn 37 SD 9358
Winteringham 39 SE 9222
Winterley 32 SJ 7457
Wintersett 37 SE 3815
Winterslow 9 SU 2232
Winterton 39 SE 9218
Winterton-on-Sea 29 TG 4919
Winthorpe (Lincs.) 35 TF 5665
Winthorpe (Notts.) 34 SK 8156
Winton (Cumbr.) 41 NY 7810
Winton (Dorset) 8 SZ 0894
Wintringham 39 SE 8873
Winwick (Cambs.) 27 TL 1080
Winwick (Ches.) 32 SJ 6092
Winwick (Northants.) 26 SP 6273
Wirksworth 33 SK 2854
Wirswall 32 SJ 5444
Wisbech 35 TF 4609
Wisbech St. Mary 35 TF 4208
Wisborough Green 11 TQ 0526
Wiseton 34 SK 7189
Wishaw (Strath.) 50 NS 7954
Wishaw (Warw.) 25 SP 1794
Wispington 35 TF 2071
Wissett 29 TM 3679
Wistanstow 24 SO 4385
Wistanswick 32 SJ 6629
Wistaston 32 SJ 6853
Wiston (Dyfed) 14 SN 0218
Wiston (Strath.) 51 NS 9531
Wiston (W Susx) 11 TQ 1512
Wistow (Cambs.) 27 TL 2781
Wistow (N Yorks.) 38 SE 5835
Wiswell 36 SD 7437
Witcham 27 TL 4680
Witchampton 8 ST 9806
Witchford 28 TL 5078
Witham 20 TL 8114

Witham Friary Zennor

Witham Friary 8 ST 7440
Witham on the Hill 35 TF 0516
Witherenden Hill 12 TQ 6426
Witheridge 6 SS 8014
Witherley 26 SP 3297
Withern 35 TF 4382
Withernsea 39 TA 3328
Withernwick 39 TA 1940
Withersdale Street 29 TM 2781
Withersfield 20 TL 6547
Witherslack 40 SD 4384
Withiel 4 SW 9965
Withiel Florey 7 SS 9832
Withington (Ches.) 32 SJ 8170
Withington (Glos.) 17 SP 0315
Withington (Gtr Mches.) 37 SJ 8392
Withington (Here. and Worc.) 24 SO 5643
Withington (Salop) 24 SJ 5713
Withleigh 6 SS 9012
Withnell 36 SD 6322
Withybrook 26 SP 4384
Withycombe 7 ST 0141
Withyham 12 TQ 4935
Withypool 6 SS 8435
Witley 11 SU 9439
Witnesham 21 TM 1850
Witney 18 SP 3509
Wittering 27 TF 0502
Wittersham 13 TQ 8927
Witton 29 TG 3331
Witton Gilbert 47 NZ 2345
Witton le Wear 42 NZ 1431
Witton Park 42 NZ 1730
Wiveliscombe 7 ST 0827
Wivelsfield 12 TQ 3420
Wivelsfield Green 12 TQ 3519
Wivenhoe 21 TM 0321
Wivenhoe Cross 21 TM 0423
Wiveton 29 TG 0343
Wix 21 TM 1628
Wixford 25 SP 0854
Wixoe 20 TL 7142
Woburn 19 SP 9433
Woburn Sands 19 SP 9235
Wokefield Park 10 SU 6765
Woking 11 TQ 0058
Wokingham 10 SU 8068
Woldingham 12 TQ 3755
Wold Newton (Humbs.) 39 TA 0473
Wold Newton (Humbs.) 39 TF 2496
Wolferlow 24 SO 6661
Wolferton 28 TF 6528
Wolfhill 56 NO 1533
Wolf's Castle 14 SM 9627
Wolfsdale 14 SM 9321
Woll 52 NT 4622
Wollaston (Northants.) 27 SP 9062
Wollaston (Salop) 23 SJ 3212
Wollerton 32 SJ 6229
Wolsingham 42 NZ 0737
Wolston 26 SP 4175
Wolvercote 18 SP 4809
Wolverhampton 25 SO 9198
Wolverley (Here. and Worc.) 25 SO 8279
Wolverley (Salop) 32 SJ 4631
Wolverton (Bucks.) 26 SP 8141
Wolverton (Hants.) 10 SU 5557
Wolverton (Warw.) 25 SP 2062
Wolvey 26 SP 4387
Wolviston 42 NZ 4525
Wombleton 42 SE 6683
Wombourne 25 SO 8793
Wombwell 37 SE 3902
Womenswold 13 TR 2250
Womersley 38 SE 5319
Wonastow 16 SO 4811
Wonersh 11 TQ 0145
Wonston 10 SU 4739
Wooburn 19 SU 9187
Wooburn Green 19 SU 9188
Woodale 42 SE 0279
Woodbastwick 29 TG 3315
Woodbeck 34 SK 7777
Woodborough (Notts.) 34 SK 6347
Woodborough (Wilts.) 17 SU 1059
Woodbridge 21 TM 2749
Woodbury 5 SY 0087
Woodbury Salterton 5 SY 0189
Woodchester 17 SO 8302
Woodchurch 13 TQ 9434
Woodcote (Oxon.) 10 SU 6481
Woodcote (Salop) 24 SJ 7715
Woodcroft 16 ST 5495
Wood Dalling 29 TG 0927
Woodditton 20 TL 6559
Woodeaton 18 SP 5311
Woodend (Cumbr.) 40 SD 1696
Wood End (Herts.) 20 TL 3225
Woodend (Northants.) 26 SP 6149
Wood End (Warw.) 25 SP 1071
Wood End (Warw.) 26 SP 2498
Woodend (W Susx) 9 SU 8108
Wood Enderby 35 TF 2764
Woodfalls 8 SU 1920
Woodford (Corn.) 4 SS 2113
Woodford (Gtr Mches.) 33 SJ 8982
Woodford (Northants.) 27 SP 9676
Woodford (Wilts.) 8 SU 1136
Woodford Bridge 20 TQ 4291
Woodford Green 20 TQ 4192
Woodford Halse 26 SP 5452
Woodgate (Here. and Worc.) 25 SO 9666
Woodgate (Norf.) 29 TG 0215
Woodgate (W Mids.) 25 SO 9982
Woodgate (W Susx) 11 SU 9304
Wood Green (Gtr London) 20 TQ 3191
Woodgreen (Hants.) 8 SU 1717
Woodhall 41 SD 9790
Woodhall Spa 35 TF 1963
Woodham 11 TQ 0261
Woodham Ferrers 20 TQ 7999
Woodham Mortimer 20 TL 8205
Woodham Walter 20 TL 8006
Woodhaven 57 NO 4127
Wood Hayes 25 SJ 9501
Woodhead (Grampn.) 62 NJ 7938
Woodhead (Grampn.) 62 NJ 9061
Woodhill 24 SO 7384
Woodhorn 47 NZ 2988
Woodhouse (Leic.) 34 SK 5315
Woodhouse (S Yorks.) 33 SK 4184
Woodhouse Eaves 34 SK 5214
Woodhouselee 51 NT 2364
Woodhurst 27 TL 3176
Woodingdean 12 TQ 3605
Woodland (Devon) 5 SX 7968
Woodland (Durham) 42 NZ 0726
Woodlands (Dorset) 8 SU 0508
Woodlands (Grampn.) 62 NO 7895
Woodlands (Hants.) 9 SU 3111
Woodlands Park 11 SU 8578
Woodleigh 5 SX 7348
Woodlesford 37 SE 3629
Woodley 10 SU 7973
Woodmancote (Glos.) 17 SP 0008
Woodmancote (W Susx) 9 SU 7707
Woodmancott 10 SU 5642
Woodmansey 39 TA 0537
Woodmansterne 11 TQ 2760
Woodminton 8 SU 0122
Woodnesborough 13 TR 3156
Woodnewton 27 TL 0394
Wood Norton 29 TG 0128
Woodplumpton 36 SD 4934
Woodrising 29 TF 9803
Woodseaves (Salop) 32 SJ 6830
Woodseaves (Staffs.) 32 SJ 7925
Woodsend 10 SU 2275
Woodsetts 34 SK 5483
Woodsford 8 SY 7690
Woodside (Berks.) 11 SU 9371
Woodside (Herts.) 19 TL 2506
Woodside (Tays.) 56 NO 2037
Woodstock 18 SP 4416
Wood Street 11 SU 9551
Woodthorpe (Derby.) 33 SK 4574
Woodthorpe (Leic.) 34 SK 5417
Woodton 29 TM 2894
Woodtown 6 SS 4926
Woodville 33 SK 3119
Wood Walton 27 TL 2180
Wood Wick 63 HY 3923
Woodyates 8 SU 0219
Woofferton 24 SO 5168
Wookey 7 ST 5145
Wookey Hole 7 ST 5347
Wool 8 SY 8486
Woolacombe 6 SS 4543
Woolaston 17 ST 5999
Woolavington 7 ST 3441
Woolbeding 11 SU 8722
Wooler 53 NT 9928
Woolfardisworthy (Devon) 4 SS 3321
Woolfardisworthy (Devon) 6 SS 8208
Woolfords Cottages 51 NT 0057
Woolhampton 10 SU 5766
Woolhope 24 SO 6135
Woollage Green 13 TR 2449
Woolland 8 ST 7706
Woolley (Cambs.) 27 TL 1474
Woolley (W Yorks.) 37 SE 3113
Woolmer Green 19 TL 2518
Woolpit 21 TL 9762
Woolscott 26 SP 4968
Woolstaston 24 SO 4498
Woolsthorpe 34 SK 8334
Woolston (Ches.) 32 SJ 6589
Woolston (Hants.) 9 SU 4410
Woolston (Salop) 32 SJ 3224
Woolston (Salop) 24 SO 4287
Woolstone (Bucks.) 19 SP 8738
Woolstone (Oxon.) 18 SU 2987
Woolton 32 SJ 4286
Woolton Hill 10 SU 4261
Woolverstone 21 TM 1838
Woolverton 8 ST 7853
Woolwich 12 TQ 4478
Wooperton 53 NU 0420
Woore 32 SJ 7242
Wootton (Beds.) 27 TL 0045
Wootton (Hants.) 9 SZ 2498
Wootton (Humbs.) 39 TA 0815
Wootton (Kent) 13 TR 2246
Wootton (Northants.) 26 SP 7656
Wootton (Oxon.) 18 SP 4319
Wootton (Oxon.) 18 SP 4701
Wootton (Staffs.) 32 SJ 8227
Wootton (Staffs.) 33 SK 1045
Wootton Bassett 17 SU 0682
Wootton Bridge 9 SZ 5491
Wootton Common 9 SZ 5390
Wootton Courtenay 6 SS 9343
Wootton Fitzpaine 7 SY 3695
Wootton Rivers 17 SU 1962
Wootton St. Lawrence 10 SU 5953
Wootton Wawen 25 SP 1563
Worcester 25 SO 8555
Worcester Park 11 TQ 2266
Wordsley 25 SO 8887
Worfield 24 SO 7595
Workington 40 NX 9928
Worksop 34 SK 5879
Worlaby 39 TA 0113
World's End (Berks.) 10 SU 4876
World's End (Clwyd) 32 SJ 2347
Worle 16 ST 3562
Worleston 32 SJ 6856
Worlingham 29 TM 4489
Worlington (Devon.) 6 SS 7713
Worlington (Suff.) 28 TL 6973
Worlingworth 21 TM 2368
Wormbridge 24 SO 4230
Wormegay 28 TF 6611
Wormelow Tump 24 SO 4930
Wormhill 33 SK 1274
Wormiehills 57 NO 6239
Wormingford 21 TL 9332
Worminghall 18 SP 6408
Wormington 25 SP 0336
Worminster 7 ST 5742
Wormit 57 NO 3925
Wormleighton 26 SP 4453
Wormley 20 TL 3605
Wormshill 13 TQ 8857
Wormsley 24 SO 4248
Worplesdon 11 SU 9753
Worrall 37 SK 3092
Worsbrough 37 SE 3503
Worsley 36 SD 7400
Worstead 29 TG 3026
Worsthorne 37 SD 8732
Worston 37 SD 7642
Worth (Kent) 13 TR 3356
Worth (W Susx) 12 TQ 3036
Worth Abbey 12 TQ 3134
Wortham 29 TM 0777
Worthen 23 SJ 3204
Worthenbury 32 SJ 4146
Worthing (Norf.) 29 TF 9919
Worthing (W Susx) 11 TQ 1402
Worthington 33 SK 4020
Worth Matravers 8 SY 9777
Wortley 37 SK 3099
Worton 17 ST 9757
Wortwell 29 TM 2784
Wotherton 23 SJ 2800
Wotton 11 TQ 1348
Wotton Under Edge 17 ST 7593
Wotton Underwood 18 SP 6815
Woughton on the Green 19 SP 8737
Wouldham 12 TQ 7164
Wrabness 21 TM 1731
Wragby 35 TF 1378
Wramplingham 29 TG 1106
Wrangham 62 NJ 6331
Wrangle 35 TF 4250
Wrangway 7 ST 1217
Wrantage 7 ST 3022
Wrawby 39 TA 0108
Wraxall (Avon) 16 ST 4872
Wraxall (Somer.) 7 ST 5936
Wray 41 SD 6067
Wraysbury 11 TQ 0173
Wrea Green 36 SD 3931
Wreay (Cumbr.) 46 NY 4349
Wreay (Cumbr.) 40 NY 4423
Wrekenton 47 NZ 2758
Wrelton 43 SE 7686
Wrenbury 32 SJ 5947
Wreningham 29 TM 1699
Wrentham 29 TM 4982
Wressle 38 SE 7031
Wrestlingworth 27 TL 2547
Wretton 28 TF 6800
Wrexham 32 SJ 3349
Wribbenhall 24 SO 7975
Wrightington Bar 36 SD 5313
Wrinehill 32 SJ 7546
Wrington 16 ST 4662
Writtle 20 TL 6606
Wrockwardine 24 SJ 6212
Wroot 38 SE 7102
Wrotham 12 TQ 6159
Wrotham Heath 12 TQ 6258
Wroughton 17 SU 1480
Wroxall (I. of W.) 9 SZ 5579
Wroxall (Warw.) 26 SP 2271
Wroxeter 24 SJ 5608
Wroxham 29 TG 3017
Wroxton 26 SP 4141
Wyaston 33 SK 1842
Wyberton 35 TF 3240
Wyboston 27 TL 1656
Wybunbury 32 SJ 6949
Wychbold 25 SO 9166
Wych Cross 12 TQ 4231
Wyche 24 SO 7643
Wyck 10 SU 7539
Wycombe Marsh 19 SU 8992
Wyddial 20 TL 3731
Wye 13 TR 0546
Wyke (Dorset.) 8 ST 7926
Wyke (Salop) 24 SJ 6402
Wyke (W Yorks.) 37 SE 1526
Wykeham (N Yorks.) 39 SE 8175
Wykeham (N Yorks.) 43 SE 9683
Wyke Regis 8 SY 6677
Wyke, The (Salop) 24 SJ 7306
Wykey 32 SJ 3925
Wylam 47 NZ 1164
Wylde Green 25 SP 1293
Wylye 8 SU 0037
Wymering 9 SU 6405
Wymeswold 34 SK 6023
Wymington 27 SP 9564
Wymondham (Leic.) 34 SK 8518
Wymondham (Norf.) 29 TG 1101
Wymondley 19 TL 2128
Wyndburgh Hill 46 NT 5504
Wyndham 15 SS 9391
Wynford Eagle 7 SY 5895
Wyre Piddle 25 SO 9647
Wysall 34 SK 6027
Wythall 25 SP 0775
Wytham 18 SP 4708
Wyverstone 21 TM 0468
Wyverstone Street 21 TM 0367

Yaddlethorpe 39 SE 8806
Yafford 9 SZ 4581
Yafforth 42 SE 3494
Yalding 12 TQ 7050
Yanworth 17 SP 0713
Yapham 38 SE 7851
Yapton 11 SU 9703
Yarburgh 39 TF 3493
Yarcombe 5 ST 2408
Yardley 25 SP 1385
Yardley Gobion 26 SP 7644
Yardley Hastings 27 SP 8656
Yardro 23 SO 2258
Yarkhill 24 SO 6042
Yarlet 33 SJ 9129
Yarlington 8 ST 6529
Yarm 42 NZ 4111
Yarmouth 9 SZ 3589
Yarnfield 33 SJ 8632
Yarnscombe 6 SS 5523
Yarnton 18 SP 4711
Yarpole 24 SO 4665
Yarrow 51 NT 3527
Yarrow Feus 51 NT 3325
Yarsop 24 SO 4047
Yarwell 27 TL 0697
Yate 17 ST 7082
Yateley 10 SU 8160
Yatesbury 17 SU 0671
Yattendon 10 SU 5474
Yatton (Avon) 16 ST 4265
Yatton (Here. and Worc.) 24 SO 4367
Yatton (Here. and Worc.) 24 SO 6330
Yatton Keynell 17 ST 8676
Yaverland 9 SZ 6185
Yaxham 29 TG 0010
Yaxley (Cambs.) 27 TL 1892
Yaxley (Suff.) 29 TM 1173
Yazor 24 SO 4046
Yeading 19 TQ 1182
Yeadon 37 SE 2040
Yealand Conyers 40 SD 5074
Yealand Redmayne 40 SD 5075
Yealmpton 4 SX 5751
Yearsley 38 SE 5874
Yeaton 32 SJ 4319
Yeaveley 33 SK 1840
Yedingham 43 SE 8979
Yelford 18 SP 3504
Yelling 27 TL 2562
Yelvertoft 26 SP 5975
Yelverton (Devon) 4 SX 5267
Yelverton (Norf.) 29 TG 2901
Yenston 8 ST 7120
Yeoford 6 SX 7898
Yeolmbridge 4 SX 3187
Yeovil 7 ST 5515
Yeovil Marsh 7 ST 5418
Yeovilton 7 ST 5422
Yerbeston 14 SN 0609
Yesnaby 63 HY 2215
Yetlington 47 NU 0209
Yetminster 7 ST 5910
Yettington 5 SY 0585
Yetts o'Muckhart 56 NO 0001
Y Fan 23 SN 9487
Yielden 27 TL 0167
Yieldshields 50 NS 8750
Yiewsley 19 TQ 0680
Ynysboeth 16 ST 0696
Ynysddu 16 ST 1892
Ynyshir 15 ST 0292
Ynyslas 22 SN 6092
Ynysybwl 16 ST 0594
Yockenthwaite 41 SD 9079
Yockleton 24 SJ 3910
Yokefleet 39 SE 8124
Yoker 50 NS 5168
Yonder Bognie 62 NJ 5946
York 38 SE 6052
Yorkletts 13 TR 0963
Yorkley 17 SO 6306
Yorton 32 SJ 4923
Youlgreave 33 SK 2164
Youlstone 4 SS 2715
Youlthorpe 38 SE 7655
Youlton 38 SE 4863
Young's End 20 TL 7319
Yoxall 33 SK 1419
Yoxford 21 TM 3968
Y Rhiw 30 SH 2228
Ysbyty Ifan 31 SH 8448
Ysbyty Ystwyth 22 SN 7371
Ysceifiog 31 SJ 1571
Ysgubor-y-coed 22 SN 6895
Ystalyfera 15 SN 7608
Ystrad 15 SS 9796
Ystrad Aeron 22 SN 5256
Ystradfellte 15 SN 9313
Ystradffin 15 SN 7846
Ystradgynlais 15 SN 7910
Ystrad Meurig 22 SN 7067
Ystrad-Mynach 16 ST 1493
Ystradowen (Dyfed) 15 SN 7512
Ystradowen (S Glam.) 15 ST 0177
Ythanbank 62 NJ 9034
Ythsie 62 NJ 8830

Zeal Monachorum 6 SS 7103
Zeals 8 ST 7731
Zelah 2 SW 8051
Zennor 2 SW 4538

British Tourist Authority
239 Old Marylebone Road   London   NW1 5QT   England

BTA OVERSEAS OFFICES

Enquiries from prospective overseas visitors to Britain will be welcome at the offices of the British Tourist Authority in the following countries:

ARGENTINA
Av Cordoba 645 (piso 2)
1054 Buenos Aires
☎ 392–9955

AUSTRALIA
171 Clarence Street
Sydney NSW 2000
☎ 29–8627

BELGIUM
23 Place Rogierplein 23
1000 Brussels
☎ 02/218 67 70

BRAZIL
Avenida Ipiranga 318–A
12° Andar conj 1201
01046 Sao Paulo–SP
☎ 257–1834

CANADA
151 Bloor Street West,
Suite 460
Toronto
Ontario M5S IT3
☎ (416) 925–6326

DENMARK
PO Box 46
DK-1002 Copenhagen K
☎ (01) 12 07 93

FRANCE
6 Place Vendôme
75001 Paris
☎ 296 47 60

GERMANY
Neue Mainzer str 22
6000 Frankfurt a M
☎ (0611) 23 64 28

HOLLAND
Leidseplein 5
Amsterdam
☎ (020) 23 46 67

ITALY
Via S Eufemia 5
00187 Rome
☎ 678. 5548

JAPAN
Tokyo Club Building
3-2-6
Kasumigaseki
Chiyoda-ku Tokyo 100
☎ (03) 581-3603

MEXICO
Tiber 103 6–piso
Mexico 5D F
☎ 511 39 27

NEW ZEALAND
Box 3655
Wellington

NORWAY
For visitors : Haakon VII's gt 5, Oslo
For mail : Postboks 1781 vika, Oslo I
☎ (02) 41 18 49

SOUTH AFRICA
Union Castle Building
36 Loveday Street
Box 6256   Johannesburg
☎ 838 1881

SPAIN
Torre de Madrid 6/4
Plaza de Espana
Madrid 13
☎ 241 13 96

SWEDEN
For visitors :
Malmskillnadsgatan 42 (1st floor)
For mail : Box 7293
S–103 90 Stockholm
☎ 08–21 24 44

SWITZERLAND
Limmatquai 78
8001 Zurich
☎ 01/47 42 77

USA
680 Fifth Avenue
New York NY 10019
☎ (212) 581–4700

612 South Flower Street
Los Angeles CA 90017
☎ (213) 623–8196

John Hancock Center (suite 2450)
875 North Mitchigan Avenue
Chicago IL 60611
☎ (312) 787–0490

INFORMATION FOR VISITORS TO BRITAIN

The following tourist organisations will be able to give advice and directions on how best to enjoy your holiday in Britain:

British Tourist Authority
'Welcome to Britain' Tourist Information Centre
64 St James's Street
London SW1A 1NF
☎ 01-499 9325

*English Tourist Board
4 Grosvenor Gardens
London SW1W 0DU

Northern Ireland Tourist Board
River House
48 High Street
Belfast BT1 2DS
☎ Belfast 31221/46609

*Scottish Tourist Board
23 Ravelston Terrace
Edinburgh EH4 3EU

*Wales Tourist Board
3 Castle Street
Cardiff CF1 2RE

London Tourist Board
26 Grosvenor Gardens
London SW1W 0DU
☎ 01–730 0791

* written enquiries only

BREAKDOWN SERVICE TELEPHONE NUMBERS

The Breakdown Service Centres are listed below together with hours in which they are open for service. Members needing breakdown service should normally ring the nearest centre shown to be available at the time. In case of difficulty, however, ring any 24hr centre.

England and Wales

Abergele Clwyd
08.00-23.00
Abergele 824649
Aberystwyth Dyfed
09.00-17.30
Aberystwyth 4801
Barnstaple Devon
24-hour service
Barnstaple 5691
Barrow-in-Furness Cumbria
09.00-17.30
Barrow 20665
Barton Mills Suffolk
09.00-17.30
Mildenhall 712928
Basingstoke Hants
24-hour service
Basingstoke 56565
Bath Avon
24-hour service
Bath 24731
Bedford Beds
09.00-17.30
Bedford 45825
Bexhill E. Sussex
09.00-17.30
Bexhill 214014
Birkenhead Merseyside
09.00-17.30
051-647 7252
Birmingham W Midlands
24-hour service
021-550 4858
Blackburn Lancs
09.00-17.30
Blackburn 51369
Blackpool Lancs
24-hour service
Blackpool 44947
Bolton Gt Manchester
09.00-17.30
Bolton 33815
Boston Lincs
09.00-17.30
Boston 63905
Bournemouth Dorset
24-hour service
Bournemouth 25751
Bradford W Yorks
24-hour service
Bradford 24703
Brecon Powys
09.00-17.30
Brecon 2015
Brighton E Sussex
24-hour service
Brighton 24933
Bristol Avon
24-hour service
Bristol 298531
Caernarfon Gwynedd
09.00-17.30
Caernarfon 3935
Cambridge Cambs
24-hour service
Cambridge 63101
Cardiff S Glam
24-hour service
Cardiff 394111
Carlisle Cumbria
24-hour service
Carlisle 24274
Carnforth Lancs
09.00-17.30
Carnforth 2036
Chelmsford Essex
24-hour service
Chelmsford 61711
Chester Cheshire
07.00-17.30
Chester 20438
Chichester W Sussex
09.00-17.30
Chichester 83111
Copdock (Ipswich) Suffolk
09.00-17.30
Copdock 353
Coventry W Midlands
24-hour service
021-550 4858 *

Crawley W Sussex
24-hour service
Crawley 25685
Derby Derbys
24-hour service
Derby 41496
Dewsbury W Yorks
09.00-17.30
Dewsbury 468216
Doncaster S Yorks
09.00-17.30
Doncaster 60733
Dorchester Dorset
08.00-23.00
Dorchester 2330
Dunstable Beds
09.00-17.30
Dunstable 607218
Durham Co Durham
09.00-17.30
Durham 62894
Eastbourne E Sussex
09.00-17.30
Polegate 3312
Epping Essex
09.00-17.30
Theydon Bois 4121
Esher Surrey
09.00-17.30
01-398 5374
Exeter Devon
24-hour service
Exeter 32121
Faversham Kent
09.00-17.30
Faversham 2536
Feering Essex
09.00-17.30
Kelvedon 70229
Gailey Staffs
09.00-17.30
Standeford 790211
Gallows Corner Gt London
09.00-17.30
Ingrebourne 42310
Gatwick W Sussex
09.00-17.30
Crawley 26842
Gloucester Glos
24-hour service
Gloucester 23278
Gravesend Kent
09.00-17.30
Gravesend 52814
Great Yarmouth Norfolk
09.00-17.30
Great Yarmouth 58939
Grimsby Humberside
09.00-17.30
Grimsby 41393
Guildford Surrey
24-hour service
Guildford 72841
Halifax W Yorks
09.00-17.30
Halifax 57810
Harrogate N Yorks
09.00-17.30
Harrogate 69545
Hartlepool Cleveland
09.00-17.30
Hartlepool 62786
Hatfield Herts
24-hour service
Hatfield 62852
Heathrow Airport Gt London
09.00-17.30
01-897 8842
Hounslow Gt London
09.00-17.30
01-759 0107
Howdon Tyne & Wear
09.00-17.30
North Shields 76302
Huddersfield W Yorks
09.00-17.30
Huddersfield 20039
Hull Humberside
24-hour service
Hull 28580

Keswick Cumbria
24-hour service
Keswick 73458
Kilgetty (Tenby) Dyfed
09.00-17.30
Saundersfoot 812896
King's Lynn Norfolk
09.00-17.30
King's Lynn 3731
Lamberhurst Kent
09.00-17.30
Lamberhurst 248
Leamington Spa Warwicks
09.00-17.30
Leamington Spa 21952
Leatherhead Surrey
09.00-17.30
Leatherhead 72085
Leeds W Yorks
24-hour service
Leeds 38161
Leicester Leics
24-hour service
Leicester 20491
Lincoln Lincs
09.00-17.30
Lincoln 22873
Liskeard Cornwall
09.00-17.30
Dobwalls 484
Liverpool Merseyside
24-hour service
051-709 7252
Llandudno Gwynedd
09.00-17.30
Llandudno 79453
London
24-hour service
01-954 7373
Maidstone Kent
24-hour service
Maidstone 55353
Manchester Gt Manchester
24-hour service
061-485 6299
Middlesbrough Cleveland
24-hour service
Middlesbrough 246832
Monkton (Honiton) Devon
09.00-17.30
Upottery 215
Newcastle upon Tyne
Tyne & Wear
24-hour service
Newcastle upon Tyne 610111
Newport Gwent
24-hour service
Newport 62559
Newport Isle of Wight
24-hour service
Newport 522653
Newtown Powys
09.00-17.30
Newtown 26103
Northampton Northants
24-hour service
Northampton 61389
Northolt Gt London
09.00-17.30
01-845 6281
Norwich Norfolk
24-hour service
Norwich 29401
Nottingham Notts
24-hour service
Nottingham 77751
Oldham Gt Manchester
09.00-17.30
061-652 0859
Ollerton Notts
09.00-17.30
Mansfield 822339
Oxford Oxon
24-hour service
Oxford 40286
Pampisford Cambs
09.00-17.30
Cambridge 832879
Peterborough Cambs
09.00-17.30
Peterborough 63797

Plymouth Devon
24-hour service
Plymouth 69989
Portsmouth Hants
09.00-17.30
Portsmouth 67012
Purfleet Essex
09.00-17.30
Purfleet 6495
Reading Berks
24-hour service
Reading 581122
Rotherham S Yorks
09.00-17.30
Rotherham 71353
St Helens Merseyside
09.00-17.30
St Helens 34189
St Nicholas at Wade
(Margate) Kent
24-hour service
Thanet 81226
Salisbury Wilts
08.00-23.00
Salisbury 22246
Scarborough N Yorks
09.00-17.30
Scarborough 60344
Sheffield S Yorks
24-hour service
Sheffield 28861
Shrewsbury Salop
09.00-17.30
Shrewsbury 53003
Sidcup Gt London
09.00-17.30
01-300 6681
Skipton N Yorks
09.00-17.30
Skipton 3354
Southampton Hants
24-hour service
Southampton 36811
Southport Merseyside
09.00-17.30
Southport 36431
South Shields Tyne & Wear
09.00-17.30
South Sheilds 67804
South Woodford Gt London
09.00-17.30
01-989 6567
Stockport Gt Manchester
09.00-17.30
061-477 3673
Stockton-on-Tees Cleveland
09.00-17.30
Stockton 67215
Stoke-on-Trent Staffs
24-hour service
Stoke-on-Trent 25881
Sutton Scotney Hants
09.00-17.30
Sutton Scotney 630
Swansea W Glam
24-hour service
Swansea 463163
Swindon Wilts
24-hour service
Swindon 21446
Taunton Somerset
09.00-17.30
Taunton 3363
Torquay Devon
24-hour service
Torquay 25903
Truro Cornwall
24-hour service
Truro 76455
Wakefield W Yorks
24-hour service
Wakefield 77957
Wolverhampton W Midlands
24-hour service
021-550 4858 *
Worcester Heref & Worcs
09.00-17.30
Worcester 51070
Wrotham Kent
09.00-17.30
Borough Green 882103

Yeovil Somerset
24-hour service
Yeovil 27744
York N Yorks
24-hour service
York 27698

Channel Islands

Guernsey
09.00-19.00
Guernsey 22984
Jersey
09.00-19.00
Jersey Central 23344

Scotland

Aberdeen Grampian
07.00-23.00
Aberdeen 51231
Aviemore Highland
09.00-17.30
Aviemore 810300
Dalkeith Lothian
09.00-17.30
031-663 0624
Douglas Strathclyde
09.00-17.30
Douglas 223
Dundee Tayside
24-hour service
Dundee 25585
Edinburgh Lothian
24-hour service
031-225 8464
Falkirk Central
09.00-17.30
Falkirk 25454
Fort William Highland
09.00-17.30
Fort William 2099
Galashiels Borders
09.00-17.30
Galashiels 55615
Glasgow Strathclyde
24-hour service
041-812 0101
Gretna Dum & Gall
09.00-17.30
Gretna 242
Inverness Highland
09.00-17.30
Inverness 33213
Kilmarnock Strathclyde
09.00-17.30
Kilmarnock 25240
Kinross Tayside
09.00-17.30
Kinross 63156
Kirkcaldy Fife
09.00-17.30
Kirkcaldy 62371
Motherwell Strathclyde
09.00-17.30
Motherwell 69752
Oban Strathclyde
09.00-17.30
Oban 2854
Perth Tayside
09.00-17.30
Perth 23551
Prestwick Strathclyde
09.00-17.30
Prestwick 77789
Stranraer Dum & Gall
09.00-17.30
Stranraer 2659

*Calls are queued and answered in turn, if ringing tone obtained DO NOT RING OFF

THOUSAND MILLIONS